To Jim,
A Steelers' fan
forever, even
for away in
Kentucky. Your
Mom and Dad miss
you and thought you'd
like this.
                Best wishes,
                Jim O'Brien
                11-16-2003

THEY PLAYED AND STAYED IN PITTSBURGH

STEELERS FOREVER

Jim O'Brien

> *"I know now that we were*
> *the greatest football team*
> *that ever played and it has become a*
> *lifelong experience. It never ends."*
> — John Banaszak

Books By Jim O'Brien

COMPLETE HANDBOOK OF PRO BASKETBALL 1970-1971

COMPLETE HANDBOOK OF PRO BASKETBALL 1971-1972

ABA ALL-STARS

PITTSBURGH: THE STORY OF THE CITY OF CHAMPIONS

HAIL TO PITT: A SPORTS HISTORY OF
THE UNIVERSITY OF PITTSBURGH

DOING IT RIGHT

WHATEVER IT TAKES

MAZ AND THE '60 BUCS

REMEMBER ROBERTO

PENGUIN PROFILES

DARE TO DREAM

KEEP THE FAITH

WE HAD 'EM ALL THE WAY

HOMETOWN HEROES

GLORY YEARS

THE CHIEF

STEELERS FOREVER

To order copies of these titles directly from the publisher, send $26.95 for hardcover edition. Please send $3.50 to cover shipping and handling costs per book. Pennsylvania residents add 6% sales tax to price of book only. Allegheny County residents add an additional 1% sales tax for a total of 7% sales tax. Copies will be signed by author at your request. Discounts available for large orders. Contact publisher regarding availability and prices of all books in Pittsburgh Proud series, or to request an order form. Some books are sold out and no longer available. You can still order the following: Doing It Right, MAZ And The '60 Bucs, Remember Roberto, Keep The Faith, We Had 'Em All The Way, Hometown Heroes, Glory Years, The Chief and Steelers Forever. E-mail address: jpobrien@stargate.net.

Bill Amatucci

Some familiar faces from Steelers past help open Heinz Field in All-Pro manner. Joining Coach Chuck Noll, from left to right, are Franco Harris, Lynn Swann, Louis Lipps, Dermonti Dawson, Mel Blount and Mike Wagner.

This book is dedicated to the memory of my father-in-law, Harvey M. Churchman Jr.

Cover photo by Mike Fabus/Pittsburgh Steelers

James P. O'Brien — Publishing
P.O. Box 12580
Pittsburgh PA 15241
Phone: (412) 221-3580
E-mail: jpobrien@stargate.net

First printing: August, 2002

Manufactured in the United States of America

Printed by Geyer Printing Company, Inc.
3700 Bigelow Boulevard
Pittsburgh PA 15213

Typography by Cold-Comp
810 Penn Avenue
Pittsburgh PA 15222

ISBN 1-886348-07-3

Contents

*"We did not win the Super Bowl.
We did not win the championship.
So we have a lot of room for improvement."*
—Bill Cowher,
July 22, 2002

Acknowledgments

History is everywhere. It seeps into
the soil, the subsoil. Like rain,
or hail, or snow, or blood.
— Edna O'Brien
House of Splendid Isolation

Everyone needs help to get anything worthwhile accomplished. I have been privileged to have a great support team in my efforts to write and publish my "Pittsburgh Proud" sports book series. It would not be possible to do this without the broad-based support I have enjoyed the past 20 years.

Special thanks to patrons who contributed to the building of Heinz Field, the new football stadium on the North Side: Jack Mascaro of Mascaro Construction Co., Fred Sargent and Ed Prebor of Sargent Electric Co., Miles Bryan of Bryan Mechanical Inc. and David L. Casiani of Sauer, Inc.

Other loyal patrons include Anthony W. Accamando, Jr. of Adelphia Cable Communications; Louis Astorino and Dennis Astorino of LD Astorino Associates, Ltd.; Pat McDonnell of Atria's Restaurant & Tavern; Ronald B. Livingston Sr. of Babb, Inc.; Bill Baierl of Baierl Automotive Group; Rich Barcelona of Bailey Engineers, Inc.; Andrew F. Komer of Bowne of Pittsburgh; Boys & Girls Club of Western Pennsylvania; the National Baseball Hall of Fame and Museum, Ralph Papa of Citizens Bank; Howard "Hoddy" Hanna of Hanna Real Estate Services.

Don Carlucci of Carlucci Construction Co.; Kenneth F. Codeluppi of Wall-Firma. Inc.; Tom Sweeney and Joe Reljac of Compucom, Inc.; Tom Snyder of Continental Design & Management Group; James T. Davis of Davis & Davis Law Offices, Armand Dellovade of A.C. Dellovade, Inc.; Don DeBlasio of DeBlasio's Restaurant; Jim and Suzy Broadhurst of Eat'n Park Restaurants; Everett Burns of E-Z Overhead Door & Window Co., James S. Hamilton of Federated Securities Corporation; David J. Malone of Gateway Financial; and Dennis White of GlaxoSmithKline.

John E. McGinley Jr. and John R. McGinley of Wilson-McGinley Co.; Steve Fedell of Ikon Office Solutions; Doug Roe of Giant Eagle, Inc.; Hartley King of King's Family Restaurants; Lou Grippo of the Original Oyster House; Frank Gustine Jr. and George P. Jordan of Armstrong Gustine Development, Inc.; George "Mike" Kelly of Kelly Chevrolet-Cadillac-Oldsmobile Inc.; Fred Kienast of Limbach Company; Don Lehr of Linc Corporation; Ed Lewis of Oxford Development Co.; Patty and Al Moriarty of Moriarty Enterprises; Paul Walsh III of Pittsburgh Athletic Association; Jeffrey Berger of

Heinz, U.S.A.; Mike Hagan of Iron & Glass Bank; William V. Campbell of Intuit; Larry Werner of Ketchum Public Relations; Joseph A. Massaro, Jr. of The Massaro Company.

F. James McCarl, Robert Santillo and Danny Rains of McCarl's, Inc.; David B. Jancisin of Merrill Lynch; Jack B. Piatt of Millcraft Industries, Inc.; Thomas W. Golonski, John C. Williams Jr., Anthony J. Molinero, Angela Longo, and William S. Eiler of National City Bank of Pennsylvania; George Steinbrenner of the New York Yankees; Jack Perkins of Mr. P's in Greensburg; Dan R. Lackner of Paper Products Company, Inc.; A. Robert Scott of *Point*; Joe Browne Sr. of National Football League; Joseph Piccirilli and Tony Ferraro of Pittsburgh Brewing Company; Bill Steiner, Northwest Pa. Regional Planning & Development Commission.

Lloyd Gibson and John Schultz of NorthSide Bank; Pat and John Rooney of Palm Beach Kennel Club; Patrick J. Santelli of Pfizer Labs; Thomas H. O'Brien, James E. Rohr, Sy Holzer and George R. Whitmer of PNC Bank Corp.; Joseph Costanzo, Jr. of The Primadonna Restaurant; John Tedesco of Giant Eagle; Pennsylvania Sports Hall of Fame; Pro Football Hall of Fame.

Jim Roddey and Michael J. Fetchko of SportsWave, Inc. (International Sports Marketing); Robert B. Czerniewski of Stevens Painton Corporation; Daniel A. Goetz of Stylette, Inc.; Charles H. Becker Jr. of Marsh USA Inc.; Dick Swanson of Swanson Group Ltd.; Robert J. Taylor of Taylor & Hladio Law Offices; Jim, Barbara and Ted Frantz of TEDCO Construction Corp.; W. Harrison Vail of Three Rivers Bank; Art Modell of Baltimore Ravens.

John Paul of University of Pittsburgh Medical Center; John Lucey and Alex J. Pociask of USFilter; Thomas J. Usher of USX Corporation; Clark Nicklas of Vista Resources, Inc.; Stephen Previs of Waddell & Reed Financial Services; John Seretti Chevrolet Inc.; Ray Conaway of Zimmer Kunz; Tom Volovich of Interstate Baking Co.; Gordon R. Oliver of Steeltech, Inc.; Bill Shields of McCann Shields Paint Company, Bob Randall of Traco, Inc..

Friends who have been boosters include Aldo Bartolotta, Mel Bassi of Charleroi Federal Savings Bank, Andy Beamon, Dick Bestwick, Jon C. Botula, Judge John G. Brosky, John Bruno, Michael C. Cassidy of Aon Risk Services, Ann and Art Cipriani, Beano Cook, Bob Friend of Babb, Inc., Ralph Cindrich of Cindrich & Company in Carnegie, Jim Godwin of J. Allan Steel, Joe Goldstein, Ed Harmon, Dave R. Hart, Darrell Hess, Harvey Hess, Mrs. Elsie Hillman, Zeb Jansante, Dr. Dan Kanell, Tommy Kehoe, Zundy Kramer, Gregory L. Manesiotis, John Marous, Paul Martha, Ron Maser of Maser Galleries, Robert F. McClurg, George Morris, Mark Nordenberg, Andy Ondrey, Rev. Robert Reardon, Jim Rimmel, Dave Roderick, Art Rooney Jr., Sean Rooney of Aramark, Capt. Thomas J. Rooney, Len Stidle, Dr. Edward Sweeney, George Schoeppner, Steven A. Stepanian II, State Senator Jack Wagner, Dorothy Weldon, Gene Zappa, Rudy Zupancic of Giant Eagle.

Friends who have offered special encouragement and prayer and those who have opened up doors include Bill Priatko, Rudy Celigoi, Ron Temple, Herb Douglas, Bob Shearer, Jim Kriek, Dennis Meteny, Foge Fazio, Stan Goldmann, Pete Mervosh, Thomas J. Bigley, Mike Ference, Mario Tiberi, Bob Lovett and Art Stroyd of Reed Smith Shaw & McClay, Patrick T. Lanigan of Lanigan's Funeral Home, Tom O'Malley Jr. of the Bob Purkey Insurance Agency, Sally O'Leary of the Pirates' Black & Gold Alumni Newsletter, Chuck Klausing, Nellie Briles of Pittsburgh Pirates, John Longo of WCNS Radio in Latrobe, Rob Pratte of KDKA Radio and Jack Bogut of WJAS Radio, J.D. Fogarty. My heartfelt thanks to Mavis Trasp, my "Christmas angel" and her daughter, Sherry Kisic, and their friends at Century III Mall.

Another of my angels, Gerry Hamilton of Oakmont, handled the proof-reading for this book, and provided kind assistance at many of my booksignings. She deserves a special star on her forehead.

I do all my work with Pittsburgh firms. All of my books have been produced at Geyer Printing. Bruce McGough, Tom Samuels, Charlie Stage and Keith Maiden are great to work with each year. Denise Maiden, Cathy Pawlowski and Rebecca Hula Fatalsky of Cold-Comp Typographers did their usual outstanding job.

The *Almanac* newspaper in the South Hills, for which I have been writing a man-about-town column for the past 15 years, has promoted my book-signing appearances through the years, as has *The Valley Mirror* in Homestead-Munhall.

Special thanks to the Pittsburgh Steelers' organization, Dan Rooney, Art Rooney II, Ron Wahl, Dave Lockett, Lynne Molineaux and all the coaches and players past and present who cooperated with us.

I have always appreciated the efforts of Pittsburgh photographers David Arrigo, Michael F. Fabus, Bill Amatucci, George Gojkovich and Ted Thompson.

My support team begins with my wife of 35 years, Kathleen Churchman O'Brien, and our daughters, Dr. Sarah O'Brien-Zirwas, Rebecca O'Brien and Rebecca's dog, Bailey O'Brien. We can't forget our son-in-law, Dr. Matthew Zirwas. They make it all worthwhile.
— *Jim O'Brien*

Sign of times at Steelers' summer training camp at St. Vincent's College.

Bill Cowher
Committed to winning

"I'll let my record speak for itself."

The Steelers and Bill Cowher made quite a comeback during the 2001 season. The Steelers had two sub-par seasons in 1998 and 1999 and failed to make the playoffs again in 2000. Before the start of the 2001 season, not many fans or critics — and we were among them — expected them to do much better in 2001.

Cowher and his Steelers surprised everyone. They didn't look good when they lost their season opener at Jacksonville, bowing by 21-3. The tragic events of September 11, coupled with an NFL-scheduled bye week, gave the Steelers an unusual three-week period to lick their wounds and get whole again.

The Steelers came back to win 13 of their last 15 football games and made it all the way to the AFC Championship game. When they gained the home-field advantage late in the schedule, their fans felt they had a good chance of going all the way, certainly making it to the Super Bowl. But they blew it, and got knocked off by the New England Patriots, 24-17. The Patriots stopped the Steelers' running game cold, and took advantage of two special teams touchdowns to deliver the knockout punches. Everybody in Pittsburgh was upset.

No one was more upset than Bill Cowher was. He was determined to get back to work and make sure the Steelers didn't come up short again. He had won his 100th coaching victory during the season, and he recognized it had been a good one. He also knew he was on solid footing with his bosses, Dan Rooney and his son, Art Rooney II. Cowher is just 44 years old, and the Rooneys kept their previous coach for 23 years. Chuck Noll was 60 when he retired from coaching. The Steelers like stability, something they never had until Noll came along.

Before the 2001 season, the Rooneys had extended Cowher's contract, to the chagrin of some, the confusion of others. After all, Cowher was coming off a string of sub-par seasons and he still had two years remaining on his contract. The Steelers hadn't been in the playoffs for three years. Why not wait another year?

"We wanted to show Bill what we thought of him," declared Dan Rooney. "He's one of us. He's a Pittsburgh Steeler."

Cowher has coached the Steelers for ten years, coming into the 2002 season, and he has the longest tenure of any current NFL coach with one team. He and his wife Kaye, whom he met during their respective days at North Carolina State University, have a home near Wexford. They have three beautiful daughters: Meagan Lyn, 16, Lauren Marie, 14, and Lindsay Morgan, 11. Cowher shows up at a lot of their school activities, and that always sets off a buzz in the crowd. Everybody in Pittsburgh recognizes Bill Cowher.

9

He came out of Crafton. His parents, Laird and Dorothy, still live in the same three-story yellow brick home on Hawthorne Avenue. I have visited them there and their pride in their son, as well as his brothers Doug and Dale, is quite evident. They sit in the family's box at Heinz Field and go through torment and joy at every home game. To them, he'll always be "Billy," and they love it when he comes home, gets a beer out of the refrigerator, and sits down and talks to them.

Bill Cowher covered a lot of ground at a press conference he conducted on January 29, 2002, and interviews since then.

Bill Cowher:

I knew what I was doing. I had a plan. Am I demanding? Sure, I'm demanding. Sometimes you have to show tough love. But I also like to think I'm very fair and compassionate. And I also like to think I demand more of myself than anyone else does. When something goes wrong, I look at me first, "Did I cover that? Did I make the point clear?"

I like to believe one of my strengths is my ability to delegate. I give Mike Mularkey and Tim Lewis a lot of responsibility and let them do their thing (as offensive and defensive coordinators, respectively). Now, that doesn't mean I won't veto something from time to time. But you need good people around you, and you have to trust them. We've got good people here.

Every person I've hired hasn't been the right fit. Sometimes you don't know about people until you actually start working with them. Through these tough times I've gone through in recent years, I've learned a lot about people. I've learned who my friends really are and who will stick by you in difficult times. You learn a lot about people in tough times.

I don't hold grudges, but I don't forget either.

I still love what I'm doing and I love where I'm doing it. A big motivation for me is to have my kids grow up here and not have to move. That's so rare in this business. But we've got a chance. My youngest, Lindsay, is in fifth grade. That means I've got at least seven more years to sustain this.

In looking at the season as a whole, I think in many ways a very solid foundation has been set. From my perspective personally, it may be the healthiest atmosphere that I have ever experienced on a football team. The organization, the coaching staff, the players, the openness, the unselfishness, the consistency that we played at this year, the way this organization worked as one — like I have said, in many respects is the healthiest that I have ever been involved with since I entered the league in 1980.

"I want them to know the expectations are great."
—Bill Cowher

Bill Amatuce

I think while we set a solid foundation, there is still going to be an emptiness with how this season ended. But, as I looked at this team, I made an analogy and reference to 1994 where we won a playoff game for the first time in many years. Having lost in the playoffs the first two years upon coming here in 1992 and 1993, and then in 1994 we beat the Cleveland Browns in the playoffs and then we played against San Diego in the AFC title game. We were the favored team, much like we were against New England this year, and we fell short.

We have the same feeling we felt then and we want to use it to fuel us the next time out. The year after we lost to San Diego we beat the Indianapolis Colts in the AFC championship game and we got to the Super Bowl. We didn't win there, but we got there. We still have to take that last step.

Time will tell, but there is a very solid nucleus here and that is how we are going to approach the coming year.

"The resolve is greater."

It is about us finding a way to win a championship. If you think Sunday's disappointment did anything to this guy, the resolve is greater. I am going to be someone's worst nightmare and keep coming back. If that is how you want to view it, so be it. We are not stopping until we win a championship. That is genuinely how I feel.

I talked to every player and there is not a player that does not understand and does not feel — to a degree — the resolve that I am referring to. When you get that far, is the hurt greater? Yes, it hurts because we threw a lot more into it. We reached emotional highs that some people have never reached before.

Some of the risk involved in doing that is that you end up reaching emotional lows that you have never reached before because the farther you go the more it hurts.

But, that same hurt has to be the same fuel that brings you back next year to say that you are going to the next step.

You look at 22 out of 24 starters coming back and that's a pretty solid foundation from a team that played pretty consistently throughout the season. We'll start soon. We would like to keep this thing intact. This has been a special group of guys; it really has. Not just the free agents, but I look at the group that we brought in last year. Draft choices and free agents. Those are solid, solid people. Jeff Hartings and Mike Logan — they're solid people now. That's strong, strong fiber.

> "We left the (2001) season very much with unfinished business. Your last game is a very lasting game."
> — Bill Cowher at opening of training camp, July 22, 2002

Coach Bill Cowher greets Jerome Bettis (36) and the troops as they leave field following voluntary practice on June 5, 2002 at UPMC Sports Performance Complex on South Side as they prepared for Steelers' 70th season.

Photos by Jim O'Brien

Andy Russell's Celebrity Classic on May 17, 2002 drew, left to right, John Paul, executive vice president of sponsor UPMC, and Steelers coaches Chuck Noll and Bill Cowher to The Club at Nevillewood.

Casey Hampton, Kendrell Bell, Rodney Bailey — that's strong.

It's important to keep what you have, and what you do bring in, they have to fit the makeup of the team and it's a team that knows how to work. They've grown tremendously through this year together. In some respects, they can't wait until next year starts.

This is not a bad place to come to and I think people understand that. That in itself will never get things done, but it certainly will help.

Kordell will come back strong. This game meant a lot to him. He wanted an opportunity to go back home (to New Orleans) where he grew up. He had a solid year now. This guy, he was our leader. After talking to the other players through the course of two days, you could see how well he is respected on this football team. He is eager to get back, too. He's not looking back now.

"I think these two guys will get better."

I think Plaxico Burress had a great year. Where is he from where he was? It's light years. I think that he finished up on a high. If you watched us throw the ball against Buffalo and someone would have said that after that game that we were going to have two 1,000-yard receivers I would have said, "What?"

Where we were at the end of the season; the confidence we had throwing the ball; the emergence of Hines Ward and Plaxico, and some of the other guys like Troy Edwards. That's something. I think Plax has a tremendous upside. I think he has a lot going for him as I do Hines Ward. I think these two guys will get nothing but better because I think they're still young receivers. I think as an offensive football team, when you sit there and say that you're not losing one player (they ended up not signing guard Rich Tylski), it's a pretty good nucleus to begin next year after a year in this system. (Defensively, the Steelers did not sign starter Earl Holmes.)

Hines Ward is self-made. He's worked so hard to get where he's at today. He's a football player. Some guys you say are so talented, they have this and they have that. Hines Ward, to me, is one of those guys that may not be fast enough, may not be big enough and may not be quick enough but he's a football player. He makes plays. He does all the little things. He studies the game. On gameday is when he thrives. He's a player. He's one of those guys that when you watched him at Georgia — they didn't even know where to put him because he was one of those guys that do everything well but nothing really great. This guy, we found a place for him at receiver and he's got a chance to be pretty special.

> *"You can make history. You don't have to be defined by history."*
> — Bill Cowher

When you get to the championship and you realize that you're one of four teams and you watch the teams play and you know how you are — you talk about a championship the next year and there's a realistic feeling going in. After finishing strong the year before and not making the playoffs, when you talked about a championship at the beginning of this season I'm sure some people said, "Oh, yeah." But I'm not sure they really felt that way.

When you go and play the way that we were able to play and develop the kind of belief that we developed, you take that into next year. That's not a guarantee that anything is going to happen. You're not just going to get to January by just showing up. You're going to go through minicamps, you're going to go through an off-season program, you're going to have to go through the same commitment, the same approach, the same tough dog days of training camp, the same unfolding of the preseason and probably a different makeup of a squad. The season will take on its own personality again, but there's going to be that belief in knowing that when you just stick together and take that same approach and you have to believe that anything is possible. That's what we have to do.

I don't want anybody here that doesn't want to be here. If you don't want to be here then there's the door. There are plenty of other people that want to come in here; there are a lot of good coaches. I like the guys that we have and I don't think any of them don't want to be here.

My feelings are irrelevant. My results speak for themselves and I'll live with that. You guys all have your opinions on me and I'm respectful of that and I understand that you guys have jobs to do. All I can tell you is that the resolve has never been greater and time heals all wounds.

George Gojkovich

Steelers quarterback Kordell Stewart (10) seems pleased to draw praise from Coach Bill Cowher in sideline exchange.

Mel Blount
A cowboy at heart

O f all the Steelers from the past, the one who continues to stick out the most in a crowd is Mel Blount. He remains, at age 53, such a physically impressive specimen. Everyone who sees Blount, 6-4, 215 pounds, says the same thing: "He looks like he could still play." Today's Steelers see Blount in person and they can't believe — at his size — that he was a cornerback in the NFL. To them, by today's standards, he looks more like a linebacker or defensive end.

Blount remains quite visible in the Pittsburgh scene, attending many charity balls and social functions for good causes. He remains in demand. He always makes a spectacular appearance. No one looks better in formal attire. He always speaks from the heart and makes a positive impression. I caught him at the Coaches Corner luncheon, shortly after the terrorist attacks on America on September 11, 2001 and he was especially impressive. He's had his share of ups and downs in the country but he remains a most spirited patriot. He is proud to be an American, proud to represent the Pittsburgh Steelers and the National Football League. Blount does his best to pay back for all the good things that have happened to him.

Before retiring from the Steelers in 1983, Blount decided to found the Mel Blount Youth Home in his hometown of Vidalia, Georgia. Then, in 1989, he established another Mel Blount Youth Home in Taylorstown, out in Washington County. He has met with some resistance from the folks in that neck of the woods. Early on, there were racist remarks scratched into the wooden fence that surrounds his ranch. More recently, his home was shut down for awhile because of complaints lodged about its operation.

It was reopened in the summer of 2002, but with some restrictions. He could not have more than 20 kids on the premises, and certain kinds of juvenile offenders would not be welcome. The community didn't want any kids there who'd committed serious crimes. At the same time, there were people in Taylorstown who rallied round Blount to show their support of his project, believing it was a well-run facility and that Blount's intentions were worthy of their support. They thought he was a good neighbor.

Blount joined the Steelers in 1970. He and first-round pick Terry Bradshaw were the prize recruits from that class, and joined Joe Greene and L.C. Greenwood from the previous year's class to form the foundation for the glory days of the '70s. Blount was a third-round pick. He had gained All-America attention as a defensive back at Southern University in Louisiana.

> *"Mommas, don't let your sons grow up to be Cowboys . . . or Oilers."*
> — Chuck Noll's version of
> Waylon Jennings' song

George Gojkovich

Blount led the NFL in interceptions with 11 in 1975. During his 14-year career with the Steelers, he played in five Pro Bowls and was an all-conference choice as a defensive back three consecutive years, from 1975 through 1977. Blount had 57 career interceptions and returned them for 736 yards, a 12.9-yard average and scored three touchdowns. He also returned 36 kickoffs for 911 yards, a 25.3-yard average.

Blount was inducted along with Bradshaw into the Pro Football Hall of Fame in 1989. On April 18, 2002, he was among the NFL Alumni inducted into the organization's Order of the Leather Helmet along with Jim Otto and referee Jim Tunney.

"On and off the field, these honorees have exhibited their total commitment to excellence," said NFL Alumni president and CEO Frank Krauser. "Each of them serves as an exemplary role model for today's youth."

Blount was the youngest of 11 children to grow up on a farm in Vidalia, Georgia. He often returns there to visit with his mother. He loves to go horseback riding on his ranch, he likes to play basketball and he says he spends a lot of time chasing after his kids.

I recall sitting next to Blount on a charter bus that was taking the Steelers to an exhibition game at the start of the 1982 season. The Steelers were playing the New England Patriots in Knoxville at the University of Tennessee. As we were riding through downtown Knoxville, we passed a restored historic house that had a fence around it and a large plaque on display in the front yard. It identified the place as The Blount House.

"Lookit that," cried out Blount. "That home was probably owned by the same people who gave me their name. They probably had my family as slaves." Blount was smiling as he shouted out. The Steelers won that game, 24-20.

He was in attendance in January, 2002 when the Steelers played the Patriots once again, 20 years later, this time for the AFC title at Heinz Field. He took part in halftime ceremonies and he sat in a box hosted by the Rooneys.

Mel Blount:

I was on the field as an honorary captain for the AFC title game against the Patriots at Heinz Field. I was standing next to Franco Harris. The Steelers had no snap. They looked like they were in stage shock. Franco and I had a hard time understanding what was going on. They — and that includes the coaches — have to prove that they not only can get to the big one, but that they can win the big one.

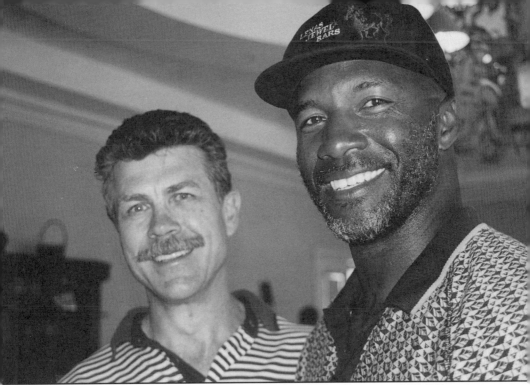

Former stalwarts in "Steel Curtain" secondary Mike Wagner and Mel Blount enjoy reunion at the Mellon Mario Lemieux Celebrity Invitational at The Club at Nevillewood.

Photos by Jim O'Brien

Traci and Mark Malone of ESPN and TiAnda and Mel Blount meet at dinner at The Club at Nevillewood on the eve of the 2002 Andy Russell Celebrity Classic to raise money for several local children's programs.

I was in one of the Rooney's box suites for most of the game, sitting next to Chuck Noll. With about three minutes left in the game, I said to him, "Chuck, this only makes me appreciate even more what we were able to accomplish."

When I raised a question about the Steelers' performance, Chuck said, "New England had a lot to do with it."

Tom Ridge and Jim Roddey and Mayor Murphy all spent time in that suite that same day. That hit me, being with all those big shots. It's a long way from our little farm down in Vidalia, Georgia.

When the Steelers were playing so well this year, I know that some people started comparing them to the Steelers of the '70s. That was a little premature, I think. It's like the year before when the Baltimore Ravens won the Super Bowl and had such great defensive statistics. All of a sudden they were the greatest defense in history. Hey, let's see what they do in the next few years. I was glad to see John Stallworth follow Lynn Swann into the Hall of Fame. But L.C. Greenwood and Donnie Shell and some others belong in there, too. I think we had an awful lot of Hall of Famers on those teams.

"I just had raw talent."

When I came to the Steelers, it was a blessing from the Lord. When I went to the Steelers, I knew nothing about football. I had no football knowledge. I couldn't recognize offensive formations. At Southern University, I just had to go out and cover somebody.

I was fortunate to have Chuck Noll and the Rooneys and the assistant coaches to bring me along. Charley Sumner was my first defensive backfield coach. He'd ask me to identify formations at team meetings, and I couldn't do it. I was lost. I nearly got cut a couple of times my rookie year. I just had raw talent. Then Bud Carson came in, and he really brought me along, taught me what I needed to know.

It took me longer, just like it took Bradshaw time to become comfortable, and to know what we were supposed to be doing. I was just a young country kid from an all-black high school and an all-black college. I was thrown into a world dealing with white people. I worked for my daddy on the farm. That was my background, the only world I knew.

I didn't want to be second to anyone. I wanted to set standards for my position.

I feel the same way about my farm as I did about coming to the Steelers. I'm convinced God brought me to this place.

The kids love all these animals. That's probably one of the biggest therapeutic aspects of the program here. There's something about kids and animals that just click. Animals can sense love and these kids are so innocent. It's a good therapy for the kids. They love these horses. They're always after me to let them ride them.

Everything out here is designed for the kids. This can be a life-long experience for them, something they can take with them when they leave. They're here for a half-year to a year, and they can build on it for the rest of their lives.

Pittsburgh Steelers

Andy Russell (34) and Mel Blount (47) parade after Blount picked off pass against Denver Broncos at Three Rivers Stadium.

Franco Harris

Still doesn't like getting hit

"I dream of long runs."

'Twas the week before Christmas, late in the 1982 season, my last as the Steelers' beat writer for *The Pittsburgh Press*. The Steelers were preparing for a game with the Browns at Cleveland Stadium.

Dick Hoak was telling the other Steeler assistant coaches about a National Football League film he had seen the night before on cable TV. It was a feature about great running backs.

This was during a lunch break at Three Rivers Stadium. Hoak talked about Jim Brown, who had played nine seasons as a running back for the Browns. "He was the best I ever saw," said the Steelers' offensive backfield coach. "What I didn't realize until I watched the film, though, was that he never missed a game in nine seasons. He never even lay on the field once with an injury. He always got up slow, but he always got up."

Hoak mentioned the highlights he saw of Gale Sayers, O.J. Simpson and Earl Campbell.

Asked if Franco Harris had been in the film, Hoak flinched. He cocked his head the way a jeweler does when he's about to inspect a diamond. Or maybe when a jeweler sees a flaw in a diamond.

"Doing what? Catching a pass?" asked Hoak in a sarcastic comeback, showing a side of himself even darker than the omnipresent stubble on his chin. "Throwing a block?"

So Hoak wasn't happy about how Harris was being used, or not used, in the Steelers' new-fangled offense. This was his subtle, or not-so-subtle way, of blowing off some steam.

Hoak was never one to make waves, but he wasn't pleased that his favorite running back wasn't carrying the ball more often. Harris had averaged just over 13 carries a game in the previous six games. Hoak believed that Harris had to carry the ball at least 20 times just to work out the kinks. "He has to do that to be effective," said Hoak. "He has to get a feel for the game.

"Even when he was younger, he might not get more than three yards on his first 15 carries, then he'd break one for 10, 15 yards, and then maybe all the way. That's the way he's always been."

Hoak was sitting in the dimly lit screening room, moments before his charges were to come back from lunch and study film of the Browns' defense against the San Diego Chargers. What offensive backs could learn from watching the pass-happy Chargers offense against anyone was hard to grasp.

Harris was hopping around in the hallway, like a boxer jumping imaginary rope, when he stuck his handsome head into the room and,

22

sensing the subject of the conversation, said in a stage whisper, "Be careful, Hoakie."

He need not have cautioned his coach. Hoak has always been cautious about what he says. He's honest, often brutally honest, but he is not a troublemaker. He says his strongest stuff off the record. He was a hard-working running back for 10 seasons with the Steelers, and was now in his 11th season as an assistant coach on Chuck Noll's staff. He would go on to be a member of Bill Cowher's staff as well, and would be there more than 30 years as a valuable aide.

Hoak told Noll how he felt at team meetings, but he didn't make waves about the issue. That was not his style. Hoak was always a team man.

So was Harris. He knew there'd be bad weather in Cleveland, just as there had been in Buffalo the week before. Both cities were on Lake Erie. "I don't care about the weather," said Harris. "What I care about is how we execute. What kind of enthusiasm do we have? What kind of will to win?"

Franco Harris didn't like to talk much in those days, and he doesn't like to talk much these days. But when he spoke he said meaningful things. Harris spoke from his head and his heart.

Harris was careful when he spoke, and when he looked for daylight to run. He spoke the same way he looked for openings to dance through. He preferred to be positive, to look ahead, to see what others often didn't see.

"I dream of long runs — the extinct species," he said. "No negative stuff. Most of the time I think about the team we're playing that week, and I'm running plays through my head. If they do certain things, I think about what I want to do in response.

"Sometimes I think about those things when I'm sleeping, too. It's nice dreaming about them, anyway."

There are times when Franco Harris seems to be sleepwalking. He has always moved to the beat of his own drummer. He was born March 7, 1950, so he was 52 at the start of the 2002 football season. He was born at Fort Dix, New Jersey. His father, Cad, was a career soldier and had met Franco's mother, Gina Parenti, during a tour in Italy during World War II. She was what was called a war bride.

"My mother went through the war in Italy," said Franco. "They had to flee to the mountains for their lives and two of her brothers were brutalized and cut to bits by the Nazis. Her village was destroyed by the Nazis. Then she married a black soldier from America and came here. She has quite a story."

It reminded me of stories Bruno Sammartino had told me about his boyhood experience in Italy. Sammartino remembers eating snow in those mountains to stay alive while fleeing from the Nazis. He was a 90-pound weakling as a schoolboy at Schenley High School after his family came to America. He built himself up at the nearby YMHA and became the wrestling champion of the world. These are Horatio Alger rags-to-riches stories with an Italian accent.

Franco is the owner and president of Super Bakery, Inc., with an office in Pittsburgh's North Hills. The company turns out nutritional donuts, fortified with vitamins and minerals, that go to schools for subsidized breakfast programs for disadvantaged youth, to make sure kids get some good nutrition to start their day. He has been involved in several ventures. He and former Penn State teammate Lydell Mitchell were unsuccessful in their attempt to revive a sausage-making company in Baltimore — Park Sausage. They were bolstered by state and federal funding, but they couldn't pull it off.

Franco and his wife, Dana Dokmanovich, reside in Sewickley. They are so proud of their son, Dok, 23, a graduate of Princeton University. When Dok was a student at Sewickley Academy, he scored a perfect 1600 on his SAT exams for college admittance, and was accepted for admission to Princeton, MIT and Stanford. Dok was doing an internship in financial analysis in the Washington, D.C. area, and planned to go to graduate school.

Sometimes, when I am signing books at Waldenbooks at Ross Park Mall, Franco will appear, almost magically, and say hello. He stays close to the wall and says hello in a stage whisper. He does not like to call attention to himself. He winks and does a little dip and he's gone. Just like in the old days. There's some gray these days in that once-so-dark hair, but he still has a classically handsome Roman face punctuated by a closely-cropped black beard and mustache. There's still a special warmth as well as mystery about this theatrically hand-some man.

The way he says hello at Ross Park reminds me of a scene I witnessed when the Steelers were at an airport before the holidays during his playing days. Franco approached just about everybody who was on the plane that day and shook everybody's hand, and said, "Merry Christmas to you."

Once, when I was trying to line up Steelers for a sports night at The Press Club, Franco surprised me by sneaking up behind me when I was in the Steelers' offices and whispering to me, "Say, about that Sports Night, I'll come for an hour. I won't be having dinner. I'll come after dinner and I'll sign autographs for an hour. Then I'm outta there. One hour!"

It was the best hour of the evening for everyone who attended.

His name is secure in the Steelers' record book. He led the team in rushing all 12 seasons (1972-1983) he played for the team. He put in a half season with the Seattle Seahawks before he was released. He should have stayed in Pittsburgh to complete his career. He and the ballclub and his agent are to blame for that bad move. But he didn't make many in those days. He was inducted into the Pro Football Hall of Fame along with teammate Jack Lambert in 1990. I was in Canton for the ceremonies and it was a memorable afternoon for anyone who rooted or cared about the Steelers. Here's what Harris had to say that day, as he stood on the steps of the Pro Football Hall of Fame, follow-ing his introduction by Lynn Swann.

"It all started with the coming of Joe Greene," said Harris. "He was a great leader, and a man who anchored a great defensive line.

"Joe was joined by Jack Ham. What can you say about Jack Ham?

"But that he was the greatest linebacker. Then Mel Blount and Terry Bradshaw were inducted into the Hall of Fame. Mel was the cornerstone of our defensive secondary."

He took time to call attention to J.T. Thomas, who was in the audience, and also played in that same defensive secondary. It was a nice gesture, so typical of Harris.

"Bradshaw had a will that was second to none. And, on the other side, Jack Lambert wouldn't let anybody play anything less than their best. Truly, the best guys were on that team. With Lammie, my teammate, getting in today, it's something. Thanks, Lammie, for setting the tone for our defense.

"Thanks, Lammie, for teaching us to run out of bounds by always chasing me in practice [he allowed time for laughs on that line]. What makes your talent come through? What makes you work? God, I was with the right teammates. They were great. They brought out the best in me. They made me a better ballplayer."

Then he smiled in the direction of Rocky Bleier, his running mate for so many seasons with the Steelers.

"The next guy, I can't say enough about. Thanks, Rocky. Thanks for leading the way here. Thanks for being unselfish. This guy shows you what playing from the heart is all about. Lynn Swann and John Stallworth were the best. Thanks guys, you made it easy to run. We were the best."

Harris was the highest-scoring non-kicker in club history, with 600 points to his credit, third overall behind only Gary Anderson and Roy Gerela. His 100 touchdowns were first, with John Stallworth (64), Lynn Swann (53) and Louis Lipps (46) next in line.

Harris leads everyone in rushing with 11,950 yards, and it's unlikely Jerome Bettis will be able to catch him. Franco is first with 47 100-yard rushing games and 41 rushing attempts in a game — against the Cincinnati Bengals on October 17, 1976 — most rushing touchdowns with 91, the best rushing average in a season (5.6 yards per carry as a rookie in 1972).

I have interviewed Franco Harris on many occasions, for *The Pittsburgh Press*, for *SPORT* magazine, for *The Washington Post* and *The Sporting News*.

"In order to win, and to be successful, we will do whatever it takes."
— Chuck Noll

"There's nobody else like him."

Chuck Noll is eager to talk about Franco Harris these days. "What makes life interesting is that everyone is different," he began. "Franco is Franco. He's unique. There's nobody else like him.

"He was very much, for the most part, into his job. He got himself ready in a businesslike manner. And the bigger the challenge the readier Franco was. He was there.

"Sometimes in short-yardage situations, you'd have liked to see him fight for the extra half-yard. But he did that when it had to be done. He always did.

"Everybody is different. Everyone wants to put people in niches — like the fullback should be a line-bucker type — but Franco was a fullback, and he didn't fit that mold.

"Franco had quickness and great vision. Those were some of the things that made him an exceptional runner. It was one of the things that startled us when he came here as a rookie. We were practicing one day at camp, and he took a pitch and got, almost instantaneously, to the outside. It amazed the coaches; we just looked at each other and smiled.

"You didn't have to say a thing. It was evident we had something special.

"The parts of his body didn't go all over the place like Walter Payton's did when he ran, but he had the same kind of quickness as Tony Dorsett, and the strength of Billy Sims. Franco didn't have Dorsett's speed, but Franco had competitive speed. I've seen a lot of 4.5s who didn't catch him when he was in the clear.

"He did it with his actions, not words. His actions spoke very loudly. A lot of people like to talk a lot, but they don't get it done. Franco was a doer."

Jack Ham went to Penn State with Franco and remains a close friend of Franco. "He's gone down in history, but he hasn't changed much from his freshman year in college," offered Ham. "He's still a low-key guy. With him, getting to the Super Bowl was the only thing that mattered.

"We both agreed that individual goals were secondary to the success of the team. In my sophomore and junior seasons at Penn State, we went undefeated both years and finished No. 2 in the country both times. But we'd had successful seasons and we knew that. What the team accomplished mattered the most."

Rocky Bleier said, "Someday I'll be boasting to my children and grandchildren that I played next to Franco Harris. In a steady, quiet way he accomplished what he accomplished. He could have cared less about the criticism of his running style. He could not give a damn. And look at what he accomplished. He was special, but he never asked for special treatment around here. That was not his style."

"Franco has a charisma with people," said Joe Gordon, the former Steelers' publicist. "He's always there for them. He seems to always be surrounded by kids. He's especially good with kids."

27

Ron Rossi, the vice-president of sales and marketing for Super Bakery, is based in Tipton, Pennsylvania, between Altoona and Tyrone. He and Franco became friends the second week of their freshman year at Penn State. Lydell Mitchell, from that same class, is the national sales manager. "You couldn't write a script like this," relates Rossi, a super exuberant type who must eat a lot of the 70 million "super" donuts the company produces and distributes annually from bakeries around the country.

"We have a niche," related Rossi. "We're not in the retail business like Dunkin' Donuts or Krispy Kremes. We're in food service, mainly for schools. We offer donuts and buns. We had the first donut approved by the USDA. It's a fortified product aimed at being good for the kids.

"Franco is really focused on this. He brings the same intensity to our staff meetings that he did to the Super Bowl. I've seen him at dinners with some of his former teammates like Lynn Swann and Mike Wagner, and it's like they've never been apart. They're like that book, *Band of Brothers*, by Stephen Ambrose, except they don't carry guns like soldiers. But they have that same bonding. It's something to see.

"I was in Pittsburgh during Franco's rookie season. I was living in East Liberty, and working as an intern in the sports department at KDKA-TV. Bill Currie was there at the time, and Marie Torre, Bill Burns and Patti Burns. They're all gone now. But I was there for The Immaculate Reception. I was in Canton when he was enshrined into the Pro Football Hall of Fame. It's been fun."

Franco Harris:

I always thought I was an all-right guy. But there was talk when I was still at Penn State that I might be blackballed from the NFL. I wanted to find out where that was coming from. Joe Paterno was on vacation, out on a boat somewhere. I tracked him down and called him, and asked him if he was saying anything negative about me. He assured me he wasn't.

But it was going around that I might have been a problem. I remember wanting to send the Steelers a telegram not to draft me, because I didn't want to go where the fans threw snowballs at the players. But the guy who was my agent then told me not to send the telegram because I probably had a bad rap now, and it would just make it worse. I got a call that the Steelers had drafted me, and I was in shock.

I think the Steelers thought I might be lazy, and that image persisted after my first week in training camp. I'm still trying to figure that out. After the first exhibition game, the coaches came up saying, "Good game," like they didn't expect it from me. It was hard to believe they were disappointed in me the first week of practice. Maybe it was because I didn't allow people to beat on me.

I always feel that the easiest thing you can do is run into somebody. If it's a matter of winding up in the same place, I'd rather not get hit than get hit; chicken as that may sound.

I will always watch runners run. We're studying films, supposed to be watching defenses, and I find myself running along with the runner, putting myself in his shoes. Lots of running backs are faster than I am on a straight-ahead run, but not in the first 10 or 15 yards, dodging people and being quick about it. I'm watching where other backs' feet are, how they move their hips. I see a certain move I like, and I run it over and over in my mind, and I'll try it.

Every play is different. I can run 19-Straight 10 times, and every time get a different read. The hole is never where it's supposed to be. So I adjust to what I see.

I still consider O.J. the best running back. I'd like to look at myself in the same light. He, to me, has so much natural ability. I know there's no way that I can touch him.

In some ways, though, I've been luckier than he has. Being on a team that wins the Super Bowl, not just once but four times. I've had the good fortune to be with a winner, and not have anything bad — injury-wise — happen to me.

"I'm just never done."

You either win or else. I don't like to be a loser. I always like to come away with something. I always feel we should win and I go out and try to make that happen. In the playoffs, if you don't win you go home.

I just keep passing certain milestones. As long as I keep on playing, there is no finish line. I'm just never done. When I leave, I'd like to be known as being on one of the best teams ever. More than anything else, I'd like that. I'll still feel like our team was the best when it's over and I feel very proud to be a part of it.

If you do what you're supposed to do, and just work hard at it, those other things will come. It's not the most important thing on my mind right now. If they come as a result of doing other things, fine. Now is not the time to sit back and pat myself on the back.

I'm not that interested in individual goals. I've never won the rushing title and that's all right. I just want to continue to contribute my part — and that's what it is, a part, as best I can. I want to help us win another championship.

I think the game is won in the pits. I like big plays — I think that's just great — but I think you live and die on what goes on in the pits.

I'm one of the only players to be known better by his first name than his last. I've never understood why. When we were making the jerseys for the shop, they put a number and a name on the back. They put everybody's last name but mine. They held up the jersey and asked the guys making them what's wrong with this jersey. No one could see it. I guess it's OK, but I can't figure it out.

I've been in the league 10 years and been a lot of places and seen a lot of people and in those 10 years I've only seen drugs used once. But, then again, those that use drugs tend to hang around with guys who use them and guys who don't use drugs hang around with guys who don't use drugs. I don't. Really, cocaine is fashionable and guys who want to be fashionable use it.

"I won't undercut them and play big star."

I like to visit Children's Hospital when it's possible, and I've done this in different cities. I always try to see the kids and go to the hospital. It depends on what town I'm in. Sometimes, if I'm in a town with an NFL team, I don't do it. I feel it's their responsibility to see the kids in their own town, and I won't infringe on players who live in that city. I won't undercut them and play big star, but it's a nice thing to do. To make a kid feel happy makes you feel pretty good. It's important to see the kids. I have a boy of my own and, when you have children, you realize it's important to look after them.

I liked being able to do nice things for my parents. Football afforded me that opportunity. As a child, we never went to a restaurant. I mean never. We never went on a vacation. I was the third oldest of nine children. We always had what we needed, and we were never without essentials, but there were no extras. It felt good to give them something back.

Coming from a situation where my father didn't have much of a formal education — really couldn't read or write — and my mother had only an eighth grade education. Well, when it came to school, they were very strict about it. We had to show them our report card. If we got anything less than a "C" it was whipping time. I remember one time my sister did it, and how he tore her up. Man, my dad didn't play.

He was always there, though. He worked two jobs to make ends meet. He worked hard. He had his certain way. When you have nine kids, I guess you've got to have rules. It's funny, but with all those kids he still controlled the total situation in the home. He controlled everything. He only said something once and you better do it.

I'd have to say it was because of him and the way he controlled the house that none of us ever went astray in any way. There could have been opportunities when I was young, of being on that thin line when I could have done something bad, and I thought of my dad and the consequences, and I didn't do it.

I really had a happy childhood, relating to other people, other kids. My father was great with people. He didn't care about color. He knew all kinds of people. When I was three or four, we moved into this project area of Mt. Holly. I guess we were like the second black family to move into that area. Soon the street was full of families with mixed marriages, blacks with European wives, Italian and German. There was quite a bit of that.

At the funeral for my dad, I saw a lot of them. I hadn't seen some of them since between the time I was five and ten. A lot of the old Italian ladies who came over with my mom were there. They were all shipped over together, and they had stayed together.

I think it helped, coming from a family like I did. I really do. My mom, she thought European. She was strict and conservative. The children always came first. They would do without certain things for us.

One thing they had a dream of doing. They wanted to get out of that project area. When I was nine, my mother went out, by herself, bought a piece of land. She had to go by herself. My dad couldn't go; they wouldn't have sold it to him. It was seven years later before they had the money to build a home on that piece of land. They did it and we moved into the new house. They had accomplished that dream. Maybe that's where I got my patience.

George Gojkovich

Russ Grimm
Happy to be back in Pittsburgh

"We could play with anybody."

Russ Grimm was getting all sorts of hugs and firm handshakes and smiles. Joe Moore, his former line coach at the University of Pittsburgh, and nearly a dozen former teammates or Panther alumni, were all in attendance at a picnic on the grounds of the palatial home of Team Pittsburgh stalwart Armand Dellovade on June 7, 2001. They were happy to see Grimm, and Grimm — whose name hardly captures his personality — has a perpetual glad-to-see-everyone glow about him. Grimm is always great company and guys like Jimbo Covert and Emil Boures, who all went from Moore's mentoring at Pitt to the pro ranks, were squeezing and teasing him at the same time on Dellouade's patio in Lawrence, Pennsylvania.

His name ought to be Russ Grin. He's a funny guy, a natural comic. He had joined Bill Cowher's coaching staff on the Pittsburgh Steelers five months earlier, and had come away from a mini-camp to the party. He has to be the best after-dinner speaker on the staff, judging from a performance two years earlier at a testimonial dinner in Munhall for Joe Bugel, who had been his line coach during their glory days with the Washington Redskins. Grimm loves his line coaches now, though they put his nose into mud more than a few times during his playing days. Grimm brought another local product on the Steelers' staff along with him for Dellovade's "Italian Day" celebration in Washington County, one with the proper heritage to rate such an invitation. That was Tommy Clements, who came out of McKees Rocks and Canevin High School to star at Notre Dame and then the Canadian Football League and the National Football League. Clements went from coaching with Mike Ditka and then Jim Haslett at New Orleans to returning home to work. Clements must have felt a little out of it as the Pitt alumni roughhoused with each other physically and verbally.

Moore would not let Grimm come up for air before he told another embarrassing tale about their days together at Pitt. Moore drove them all mad during their days at practice on the Pitt campus and different summer training venues, but they have all grown to appreciate his gruffness and that he only wanted to get the best out of them.

"He was just the coach back then," offered Bill Fralic, when talking about Moore on a separate occasion. "It took quite awhile, till we got older, that he became our friend."

Grimm goes along with that thinking. "It took awhile to appreciate what he'd been doing," he said. "You have to know Joe Moore for ten to fifteen years before you get to hug him."

Russ Grimm got comfortable in a hurry in his new surroundings at the Steelers' training facilities at the UPMC Sports Performance Complex on South Side. He and Tom Clements were valuable additions to Bill Cowher's coaching staff and shared in the credit for the fine 2001 season.

Grimm, at age 42, had signed up with the Steelers on January 10, after spending the previous 19 years as a player and coach with the Washington Redskins. "He's doing a great job," said Bill Cowher, "and we're happy to have him on our side."

Moore was cracking up his audience with a tale about what he did to get under Grimm's chin in the Gator Bowl that capped off the 1980 season. Pitt beat the Gamecocks, who were led by Heisman Trophy winner George Rodgers, 39-7, so the story had a happy ending. Moore removed Grimm from the game early on, calling down from a booth high above the stadium in Jacksonville. He replaced him in the lineup with Jim Sweeney.

Grimm got angry and he grabbed the telephone away from Curt Ferrence, a graduate assistant coach. "Why are you taking me out of the game?" Grimm growled at Moore. "Because I think you're gonna get drafted pretty high by the pros, and I don't want to spoil that for you," came back Moore. "This guy's eating you alive! I don't want you to look bad. I'm looking out for you." Grimm shouted something Moore might've recognized from his own colorful vocabulary. "I'm going back in!" shouted Grimm, and he did at the next opportunity. Needless to say, Grimm's game picked up considerably after that.

"Coach Moore was a great motivator, no doubt about that," said Grimm. "I remember this one time we were getting ready for a game, and all week long he kept referring to me as 'the center.' He mentioned May by name, and he mentioned Boures and Fada, but me, I was just 'the center.' He did that every day, for a week. He was trying to get under my skin, and he succeeded."

Today, Moore regards Grimm as the smartest lineman he coached during his Pitt tenure. "He had a great understanding for the game. Boures was like that, too, maybe a half-step behind. Grimm was a quarterback in high school. That might have helped," said Moore.

Grimm grew up in Scottdale, and he played quarterback and linebacker on the Southmoreland High School team. He played linebacker when he first reported to Pitt. "I weighed between 205 and 210 when I came out of high school," said Grimm. "I just got bigger and bigger." At the start of his junior season, he was switched to center by Jackie Sherrill, who was looking for someone who could play the position the way Tom Brzoza had when he was named All-America in 1977.

Grimm was not too happy about the plan, and told Sherrill he didn't want to make the switch when he was called into his office. "It's not open for debate," said Sherrill sternly. "It's not an option. If you're going to play for us, you're going to play center."

Shortly thereafter, Grimm got on the telephone and called Joe Pendry, an assistant coach at West Virginia University who had recruited him in high school. "I told him I wanted to transfer to West Virginia, and he told me he'd have to check out whether they would want to do that or not. I had played linebacker my first two years at Pitt, and I had never taken a three-point stance in my life.

"The next thing I know, I see Pendry at Pitt Stadium one day, just before we were to start our winter workouts. I said, 'What are you doing here?' He said, 'I'm going to be coaching on Sherrill's staff, and you're staying at Pitt.' I'm glad I stayed."

Grimm was part of the Sherrill success story at Pitt. The Panthers posted 11-1 records in Grimm's junior and senior seasons, and the year after he was gone. He played on teams with Hugh Green, Rickey Jackson, Dan Marino, Jimbo Covert, Mark May, Bill Neill, Jerry Boyarsky, Randy McMillan, Tim Lewis, Carlton Williamson, Emil Boures, Sal Sunseri, Tommy Flynn and Bill Maas. He missed out on Bill Fralic, who was a freshman on a team that went 11-1 the following year.

"That was the best football team ever assembled, talent-wise," Sherrill would later say of those three 11-1 teams.

"To me," said Grimm, "even though we didn't win a national championship, we could play with anybody. We had so many guys drafted into the pros. We had a great coaching staff, too. Guys like Jimmy Johnson, Pat Jones and Dave Wannstedt went on to be real successes themselves. Tony Wise was there, and he's with Wannstedt now in Miami. Joe Pendry is with the Redskins now, on Marty Schottenheimer's staff. Foge Fazio was on our Pitt staff, too, back then. I always liked him."

Grimm wasn't an All-American at Pitt, as it says in the Steelers' 2001 media guide, but he came that close, and got some All-American mention. Marty Schottenheimer has been similarly acknowledged as an All-American in NFL press guides, but All-East was his top collegiate honor. Grimm did get to play in the East-West All-Star Game. In short, he was pretty good.

Teammate Mark May, who won the Outland Trophy as the nation's outstanding offensive lineman, was the first round draft pick of the Washington Redskins in 1981, and Grimm was grabbed by the same team in the third round. They became members of the famous "Hogs" offensive line in D.C. May's No. 73 was retired this September at Pitt. Grimm started 11 seasons at guard for the Redskins (1981-1991) and helped lead the team to four Super Bowl appearances under Joe Gibbs. The Redskins won three of those games. He was voted to four consecutive Pro Bowls (1983-1986) and was a first-team selection to the 1980s all-decade team.

His younger brother, Donn, was a starting linebacker on Notre Dame's 1988 national championship team.

In August, 2001, I had an opportunity to drive through their hometown of Scottdale, about 55 miles east of Pittsburgh, and neighboring Mount Pleasant. Russ Grimm spent a lot of time in both places. They are rural communities with modest but mostly attractive white frame homes, about half of them with swings and flower boxes on the front porches. There is a Doughboy statue at a war memorial in the center of town in Mount Pleasant. Grimm wasn't the only tough guy to come out of that quiet, laidback neighborhood.

I caught up with Grimm on a Friday afternoon in late August, following the Steelers' first practice session on the grass at Heinz Field, the new football stadium on the North Side. He had just returned to the UPMC Sports Performance Complex on the South Side. The Panthers and Steelers share these new facilities on the city's riverfronts.

"We had state-of-the-art facilities with the Redskins," said Grimm, "but this is even better. Not too many pro or college teams can boast of facilities like this. I'll always be a Pitt man, so I am happy so see what's happening there. Walt Harris seems to have the program headed in the right direction.

"I have no problem with the team practicing here on the South Side. Some think it's bad that the players have to be bussed here, but we had to walk up the hill to practice. What's the difference? I think he's doing a good job, and I like him. I've talked to him a couple of times, briefly, and he's a likeable guy."

Asked to explain why Sherrill was so successful at Pitt, Grimm said, "He knew how to assess talent, he was a great recruiter, and he had a great coaching staff. He let the offensive coaches handle the offense, and the defensive coaches handle the defense. He handled the coaches and set the tone for a winning program. He was a players' coach. He gave us credit for being able to handle ourselves, and he made sure we were properly prepared for games. We were always ready."

Well, almost every game. Under Sherrill, Pitt lost the second game of the 1979 season, a 17-7 setback at North Carolina, and the fifth game of the 1980 season, a 36-22 setback at Florida State. "We started out high in the rankings, dropped down some when we lost, and never could get back to the top again," said Grimm.

"To me, it was a major disappointment that we didn't win it all in my junior or senior seasons. We had the best team. We just couldn't get back to No. 1.

"I felt I was taught by some of the best coaches during my college and pro years," he continued. "Joe Moore was a great motivator. With Washington, I had Joe Bugel and then Jim Hanifan. Bugel was a great teacher and Hanifan was probably as good as there was about technique.

"I think I'm a mix of all three of them. I learned a lot from each of them. Some guys you have to pat them on the ass, and some guys you have to grab them by the collar. I like to associate with guys with pride. You don't have to say much to them. There are three main factors that motivate guys in this game. Money is a motivator, for sure. Pride is another. And fear is the third. Guys are afraid to fail. They don't want to look bad on Saturday or Sunday.

"The biggest adjustment from the college to the pros is being strong enough mentally. That's where Joe really helped us. He toughened us up. In the late '70s, when the offensive linemen were permitted to use their hands, Joe immediately got hold of Dan

Radakovich, a friend of his who was the line coach for the Steelers. He had Mike Webster and Jon Kolb from the Steelers come and work with us, teaching us how to use our hands.

"We were prepared. That's what made us better. We had a collection of guys who had a certain mentality that was developed under Joe Moore. We knew how the game was supposed to be played. If they didn't go along with Joe's program they wouldn't play for Joe. Joe had one way to play the game. If you didn't respond, you didn't play. It was that simple.

"You didn't want to be near Joe Moore on game day. You stayed away from him on game day. I laugh about it now, but I was afraid of him then. He's in me now, I'm sure, somewhere. I love coaching. Football's been my life. I've only been in two places most of my life. I spent the first half of my life here, and then I spent the next half in northern Virginia.

"I missed some things here, being away like that. I like to go to high school games. My younger brother (Donn) was ten years behind me, and I never got to see him play in high school or live when he was with Lou Holtz at Notre Dame. So I'm glad to be back."

He was living in an apartment at Allegheny Center on the North Side, not far from PNC Park and Heinz Field.

"I feel comfortable with the Steelers," he said. "I know the landscape. There are familiar places and familiar faces. I played with (defensive coordinator) Timmy Lewis at Pitt. (Special teams coach) Jay Hayes and (quarterback coach) Tom Clements were both with Joe Moore at Notre Dame. So we can compare Joe Moore stories. It's a great time to be in Pittsburgh. The facilities are great, and I'm looking forward to seeing the Steelers and Pitt play in the new stadium."

Jim O'Brien

Steelers offensive line coach Russ Grimm credits Joe Moore for getting him off to a great start at University of Pittsburgh. Grimm went on to a highly-successful career as a member of the "Hogs" offensive line for Joe Gibbs and the Washington Redskins, and later as a coach with the D.C. team.

L.C. Greenwood
Canton is more than a hometown

"I wasn't playing to get in the Hall of Fame."

L.C. Greenwood was tugging at his neatly trimmed beard, now salt and pepper in color, as he considered a question. He has always been a thoughtful interview, given to deep reflection, and it was no different this time. He still looked so noble. He still had a presence about him that was arresting. His bass voice was pleasant to the ear, his laughter, more of a chortle, was contagious. It was a Barry White kind of voice that was being used at the time to sell jewelry on local radio commercials. L.C. Greenwood was a spokesman for LS Jewelers in the Robinson Town Centre. "Go for the gold," he said in his sultry style. L.C. Greenwood was still a popular Pittsburgh Steeler and he was still quite the salesman. People enjoyed being in his company.

At times during our visit, he clasped his hands behind his head, his elbows extended the width of his broad shoulders, as he drew on and sorted out his memories. Holding his head must have helped.

He was leaning back in his leather swivel chair behind his desk in a large office at L.C. Greenwood Enterprises and Greenwood-McDonald Supply Company on East Main Street in Carnegie. It is an old railroad and coal mining community, just 20 to 25 minutes south of downtown Pittsburgh, that is famous as the hometown of Honus Wagner, the Hall of Fame shortstop for the Pittsburgh Pirates in the early 1900s. There's a road sign, not far from Greenwood's office, acknowledging Wagner's ties with Carnegie.

It's also the birthplace of Mike Ditka, the Hall of Fame football player for the Chicago Bears, Philadelphia Eagles and Dallas Cowboys. There's a room at the local library dedicated in Ditka's name. He grew up and attended school in Aliquippa, though, and that city is more often referred to as his hometown. He was an All-American as a senior at Pitt in 1960.

L.C. Greenwood Enterprises markets coal that is mined in West Virginia, and Greenwood-McDonald Supply is an electrical supply company. Greenwood has gotten into other ventures through the years and is always on the lookout for business opportunities.

This was on Thursday, January 31, and football was on his mind.

He was 55 and would turn 56 on September 8, and the clock was ticking. This was two days before the Pro Football Hall of Fame voters would meet in New Orleans, the site of Super Bowl XXXVI, to vote on the Class of 2002. Greenwood had been under consideration for 12 years, and was running out of time. Greenwood was feeling good about his chances of getting elected this time. He had been assured that he had a good chance by callers in the media, who pointed up some of his

Jim O'Brien

credentials that supported his candidacy for inclusion in the Canton shrine to pro football. I talked to Greenwood as well over the telephone the following day, on the eve of the election, and he remained most optimistic about his chances. I was hoping he'd get in, especially since I was speaking to him so close to the announcement date. Once he got in, it would be difficult to get in touch with him, I thought, because so many media people would be seeking his attention and thoughts about his honor.

Sitting on a couch, directly across from Greenwood's desk, one might have thought Greenwood was a professional golfer rather than a former football star. There were golf balls and golf clubs and golf photos everywhere in the room. The wall to my left was completely covered with a photographic mural of a golf hole at the Williams Country Club in Weirton, West Virginia, where Greenwood is a member and where he often plays.

Out in the long hallway that leads from the door at the street past several offices, there are more photos and plaques showing Greenwood with former teammates and other celebrities at charity-related golf events around the country. There are photos showing him in his days with the Steelers, sitting on the bench next to Jack Lambert, posing with Joe Greene, Ernie Holmes and Dwight White. They formed the most famous foursome on the front line of "The Steel Curtain" defensive unit that gained fame in the '70s when the Steelers won four Super Bowls in six years. Greenwood showed me some photos and clippings he had recently come across, including one showing him in a Steelers' uniform when he was featured on the cover of *Sports Illustrated*. He had his best seasons in the Super Bowl years of 1974 and 1975 when he was considered the National Football League's top defensive end and was recognized accordingly by being named to more All-Pro teams than any other player at his position.

He had combined with Joe Greene and Jack Ham to give the Steelers an almost impregnable left side. He had tremendous quickness and — at 6-6$\frac{1}{2}$ — was one of the most intimidating pass rushers in the league. His quickness also gave him tremendous range on running plays, and his long arms were an asset in wrapping up runners. He became a starter in 1971 and led the team in sacks with a career-high 11 and topped the NFL in opponents' fumbles recovered with five, tying a team record.

He had two of the best games of his career and was the outstanding defensive lineman in both of the Steelers' first two Super Bowl triumphs. In Super Bowl IX, also played in New Orleans, he batted down three of Fran Tarkenton's passes and received considerable support for game MVP. He sacked Roger Staubach three times in Super Bowl X at Miami. His sack total of 73$\frac{1}{2}$ in regular season games is still a Steelers' record.

He played in six Pro Bowls and recovered a fumble that led to a touchdown and an AFC victory in the 1977 game. He was always a big-game player. He had chronically bad ankles and often skipped practices because of that problem, and perhaps because of a lack of enthusiasm for the tedium. But he was always ready on Sunday. Greenwood makes his home in the Point Breeze section of Pittsburgh. He was married to Jane Greenwood for ten years, but had been divorced just as long. Their daughter, L.C. Greenwood — for Lason Chelsea — is a 19-year-old sophomore at Fisk University in Nashville. She certainly has a catchy name.

It was quiet in his office complex. He had come to the front door and unlocked it himself when I showed up at the appointed hour, and pressed the doorbell. No one else was there when we talked. The place was eerily empty.

L.C. Greenwood:

As a kid growing up in Canton, Mississippi, I never even heard of Canton, Ohio. I guess it's about a thousand miles from where I grew up. It might as well have been at the other end of the world for me, growing up in a rural area like I did, in the backwoods of Mississippi. I know it's about a thousand miles from Canton, Mississippi to Pittsburgh when I've driven that distance and I guess Canton, Ohio is about a hundred miles southwest of Pittsburgh. Sometimes, for me anyhow, it seems a lot farther away.

I've been there about two or three times, to see others get inducted into the Hall of Fame. I was there when Joe Greene got in. I've never actually been inside the Hall of Fame, or seen the exhibits there. It wasn't something I thought about when I was young. Football was just something we did for fun. We went out and played football wherever there was some grass. We played without pads or helmets. We just hit each other, and no one ever got really hurt. Sometimes we'd go out in a parking lot and just throw a football around. Canton, Ohio was something I didn't know about.

It was really hot out there when Joe Greene got into the Hall of Fame. I remember that. I guess it was late July. I was kinda impressed with the ceremonies, and seeing all those great players up there on the front steps of the Hall of Fame. I never anticipated having the opportunity to be sitting up there in one of those gold blazers. But now people in the know are telling me about my accomplishments and telling me I belong in the Hall of Fame. I had all the stuff as good as anyone, and better than some of the guys who are in there.

I always thought the Hall of Fame was for football players who were drafted high, not someone like me who was taken in the tenth round. I always thought it was something for No. 1 draft choices.

41

But you're telling me that Dick "Night Train" Lane was a free agent when he came into the league. I didn't know that. He just died, I know. I used to see him play. He was such a terror out there as a defensive back. He really hit people. I had a chance to meet him at the many charity golf outings I attend around the country. He wanted to meet me. I didn't recognize him or know who he was until he shook my hand and introduced himself. I always loved his name. It's one of the great nicknames in sports. I'd see him, after that, about three or four times a year. I was just thinking about calling him. I usually call him about every three or four months just to stay in touch.

It would be great to be honored and join people like Dick "Night Train" Lane in the Hall of Fame. I kind of have mixed thoughts about my chances. I have positive thoughts this time, though. I kind of feel like this is the year that I should get in.

I wasn't playing to get in the Hall of Fame. I wasn't interested in all that. I was just trying to get a job done. But I've been reminded that I was All-Pro six times, and I played in seven Pro Bowls during the '70s. I was regarded as the best defensive end in the NFL during that decade. So maybe I do belong in the Hall of Fame. Now it kinda looks like I am supposed to be there. I have all the things you need to get in, I'm told.

Look who's up for consideration this year. There's John Stallworth and Donnie Shell and myself. We all went to small black colleges in the South. Art Rooney Jr. and Bill Nunn Jr. were among the first NFL scouts I ever saw. I know they had a hand in getting us. Because of Nunn, the Steelers knew more about the guys at the black schools before most of the other NFL teams. That was a big factor in our success in the '70s. Those guys were important in our success. They were down there at those black schools looking at those prospects some teams overlooked.

They were not only great players they were great guys. Sam Davis was another player from a small black school they signed as a free agent. They were not just athletes who came in and played the game. They were a credit to the team and to the game itself.

"When we had a chance to win, we usually did."

I thought this year's team was good enough to go all the way. A lot of good things happened to them as the season went along. I don't think they played great offensively or defensively, but they hung in there and they won. I thought the quarterback coach and the offensive line coach they brought in made a big difference. The new receiver coach deserves credit, too, and the offensive coordinator must have done a good job. Things improved in all those areas. I thought they had good offensive linemen the year before, but they didn't play well together for some reason. This year they gave Stewart time to pass. This year Bettis ran well before he got hurt. Stewart was doing things he was capable of doing. I always thought he was a good football player. In the end (of the AFC title game with the New England Patriots), he wanted so much to win, he was kinda taking chances. He had to throw the football. Maybe he was rushing it. He threw two balls he'd love to have back. He was trying to beat them deep, and I think he should've taken what they were giving him, and thrown some short ones. There was time. He doesn't usually throw deep, and the Patriots were taking that away from him in the late going. We had the capability of beating New England, I know that. But New England's coaches and players came prepared, too, and they deserved to win.

We had a lot of great players on our team in the '70s, and they all had their own egos. But we played together. When we had a chance to win, we usually did. There are days when you just don't play up to your potential.

Offensively, I've always been impressed with Zereoue. He should have carried the ball more in that title game. I thought he could add another dimension. Bettis wasn't at his best, but there weren't many holes opened up for any of the backs. New England was stacking the line with nine men. It's tough to run against that.

I think the kid who grew up a lot this year was Burress, but he's got a ways to go. He doesn't have the right attitude. Maybe he didn't grow up with the best support system. I've seen him make some great catches, but I've seen him drop some routine throws he should have had. He has to be more consistent. He has to work at it. He needs to change his approach and how he handles some things. It's not just about him. I thought Stewart grew up a lot, so Burress might do that, too.

I think Stewart should have said that he didn't play well after that last game. You have to be accountable. I don't think Flowers should have singled out the special teams for criticism. Hey, those guys are your teammates. You don't blame them. I heard that Bettis wasn't happy about that, and that he said "we win as a team and we lose as a team." That's the right attitude.

Seeing that final game, it didn't look to me like they were really into it. That's when you've got to let it all hang out. You've got to get down there and make that tackle.

43

I was disappointed to see Jay Hayes get let go as special teams' coach. They had problems on special teams, for sure, but the head coach determines who's available to play on those teams. The head coach determines how much practice time is devoted to special teams. I hear they spent only ten minutes at each practice on that. That's not enough. Some of our starters played on special teams and they took great pride in it. Lee Flowers could have been on some of those special teams, but I hear he didn't want to be.

They have the former players come in when the rookies report after the draft. They have us talk to them. They don't always want to hear it. Dwight and I were talking to some new defensive linemen. Dwight was talking and I was watching. One of the guys rolled his eyes, and he said, "That was then and this is now." You've got that kind of thinking. That's what I don't understand. Ben McGee and Chuck Hinton took me under their wing. I was hanging out with those guys when I first joined the team. Hinton would tell me, "Rook, you gotta do it like this." And I'd do it the way he showed me. Voss helped me, too. Eventually, I found my own way. That's what I don't understand about these young players today. They don't want to get wisdom. I wanted to know what was going on.

I got along well with those guys. You can't lose if you do the right thing, if you treat people right. If I go to a golf tournament, I treat the people who are paying their way the same way I'd want to be treated. My father taught me that. I hate it when kids disappoint me. Kids are a product of their environment. I've had kids give me a hard time when I'm giving them an autograph. Some of them are asking me for autographs and they don't even know who I am. I'm big, so in their minds, I must be a football player. Maybe they think I'm a basketball player.

The players today are different. They're always looking up into the stands to see people. I never knew what was going on up there. They're looking for family and friends. They pay a lot of attention to what's up in the stands. I see guys staring up there while the game's going on. I never looked up in the stands. When I came on the field I was into the game. Now I can hear voices in the stands. When I was playing, I didn't hear voices in the stands.

I like Jason Gildon. He and Earl Holmes and Kendrell Bell look like good athletes. I'm not impressed with their defensive secondary. The two kids they paid $5 million (Chad Scott and Dewayne Washington) aren't that good. The times I see them I see receivers running past them. Rod Woodson was considered a great back, but I think he just played on his ability. I saw him get beat a lot of times. Rod got beat on quick outs.

44

L.C. Greenwood

I hate some of the stuff I see, all that celebrating on average plays. It just gets under my skin. A player gets paid to make a tackle — a lot more than I ever got paid — and he celebrates every tackle. A running back runs down the field and does all kinds of gyrations when he gets up. A running back gains two yards and he's up and celebrating. I don't understand that. What's the big deal?

I wasn't into trash talking, but I did a little taunting. Dwight talked a lot. Ernie talked a lot. Glen Edwards never shut up. He walked on the field talking. It takes different kinds to play this game. If you're doing the job, and you want to do a little celebrating I can live with that. That wasn't my personality, unless I was getting held. Then I'd have a little conversation. That would get my attention. I'd holler, "That's not the way to play football! You better stop that!" Otherwise, the only thing I might say when I lined up at the start of the game was "I hope you brought your lunch. Today you got to work."

You couldn't get me off the field. Today they do so much situational substitution. I wouldn't have liked that. Today these guys decide they're tired and they come off the field. They thought I was better as a pass rusher than I was against the run, but I never bought into that. If you're a football player you want to play. The pride in me wanted to be in the football game. I didn't come off the field. I never came off because I was tired.

We had a lot of good young guys in my early years with the team. The guy who deserves credit for putting it all together is Chuck Noll. He knew where to put people. After he got Bennie Cunningham, for instance, he moved Larry Brown from tight end to tackle. Gerry Mullins could play up and down the line. He found a place for Jon Kolb and Sam Davis. They were undersized, but they were good athletes.

We had good assistant coaches and Noll knew how to use them. Dan Radakovich, Bob Fry, Rollie Dotsch, George Perles and Woody Widenhofer fit in fine with Noll. Bud Carson really knew football. George Perles was more of a rah-rah guy. I didn't learn a whole lot from George. What I learned I learned from Bad Rad — Dan Radakovich. But it was pretty tough to keep him in a system. He's like a renegade. He's very confident and outspoken. He ruffles feathers. But he sticks up for his guys. Some of them were just baby-sitters; they learned on the job. Noll taught them how he wanted things handled. What could Dick Walker tell Mel Blount and Mike Wagner about playing in the defensive secondary? Some of those guys were just cheerleaders and baby-sitters.

Dick Hoak has become a good coach. He was a player, and a good player, when I first came to the team. He's a good man, a good organization man, pretty much. He just fit in.

46

Chuck Noll had the ability to do what he wanted to do. He had his hand in the scouting, every part of the program. He coached every aspect of the team. He kept the players he wanted. He didn't blame everybody when things went wrong. He didn't use other people as scapegoats. They didn't realize that at the time. Not only did he coach the coaches, but also he coached the players on the field. He worked both sides of the ball. He went in the huddles.

I worked for Chuck. That was our relationship. I wasn't looking for a father or a friend. I was working for him, that's all. I didn't expect anything from him. He gave me a job. I tried to do the best I could do to keep the job. I wasn't going to lie down on him. I did what they paid for.

There were certain guys he went to after games and said something to them and patted them on the head or the shoulders. Steve Furness was in the locker next to mine. He'd get on me because Chuck never came over to see me. He'd say, "What's wrong, L.C.? You had a great game. He doesn't ever come over to you!" I'd just laugh. I didn't need Noll patting me on the back.

This team they have now has to do what their leader wants. He has to get them with the right mindset. They did go beyond what was expected of them at the start of the season. But they could have done a lot more. Once they got to the championship part of the schedule they should have put it away. They have to learn how to close the game.

Bill Cowher is a person I can respect. I don't know what he does during the week. One thing I don't like is his antics on the field. He could be a bit more poised. He sets the example. Players are like their coach. They take their lead from the coach. He's the example of what the players are looking at. If he's cursing and screaming it's how they'll behave. I never liked anybody getting into my face.

These guys are making a lot of money these days. They don't have respect for other people the way they ought to. They don't always treat people the way they ought to be treated. Some of them didn't have that good upbringing.

We had that religious background to give us good values. We had a Tuesday afternoon meeting at Bradshaw's house. We had a Bible study there. Tony Dungy and Donnie Shell and John Stallworth were all buddies, and Jon Kolb was good at doing a program for us. We used to go to chapel in the morning on the road. We learned the right lessons. That helped. And it was a bond for all of us.

"Just do what you do best."
— Red Auerbach

"We all respected each other."

When I was playing, I wanted to know the defensive call as quickly as possible so I could get lined up properly and be ready. I was always in the game. I knew formations and the possibilities. I knew all that. I wanted to get back to the line of scrimmage so I'd be ready.

There was so much turmoil in our defensive huddles. Mike Wagner and I used to stand back and laugh. Eighty-five per cent of the time, Ham never knew the coverage when we broke the huddle. There were so many distractions; it was hard to know what was going on. I'm down in my stance and Ham is hollering at me, "Holly, what's the coverage?" Remember that my nickname then was "Hollywood Bags." To "Hammer," I was just "Holly" back then. J.T. tells me "Hammer" would be holding up his fingers, to get the right number from him. Whatever he was doing, "Hammer" would always be in the right place at the right time. He knew what he was doing, even if he didn't always know what we were doing.

Ernie and Dwight were always crying about something. They were mad at the opposition, they were mad at the officials, they were mad at us. Lambert was in the middle, cussing at someone, trying to get the play from the sideline, cussing at the coaches if they were late getting the call in to us. Woody (Widenhofer) is not getting the call in quick enough and Lambert is exploding. Wagner and I were the only ones not shouting something. We were always on the outside of the huddle. You didn't want to be in the middle.

Even so, we got the job done. Our front four and our linebackers were the best in the business. I have no doubt in my mind about that. Also the secondary was first rate. We were really the only guys in the NFL who played together as well as we did.

I see comparisons between current teams and us and I don't think it's fair. The game has changed; the rules have changed. We had great athletes on defense. We were able to put a lot of pressure on the quarterback and there were only four of us up front. We didn't blitz like they do now. Joe, Ernie, Dwight and I were putting more pressure on quarterbacks than they do with the blitz.

I think the offensive linemen are different now. Now these kids are just big and strong. A lot of them are not athletes. They don't have body tone. They're not fast. Our guys were smaller than most team's offensive linemen but they were all good athletes. They looked like athletes. Now they're feeding themselves constantly and growing up with no body definition. They spend so much time weightlifting. They don't

48

Pro Bowl lineup in 1980 game in Hawaii includes, left to right front row, Donnie Shell, Mike Webster and John Stallworth and, in rear, Franco Harris, Joe Greene, Jack Lambert, Mel Blount and L.C. Greenwood. Terry Bradshaw and Jack Ham are missing from photo. Steelers had ten entries in the post-season contest.

Famed "Steel Curtain" defense of '70s began with fearsome foursome of, left to right, Dwight White, Ernie Holmes, Joe Greene and L.C. Greenwood.

do much running. If they have to run more than ten yards they have to go to the sideline. They're breathing hard. To me, they're big and lazy. They're not athletes. They let them eat everything they want to eat. They eat like pigs, and they look like pigs.

When I was in high school, I played football and basketball and baseball. I ran on the track and field team. I was an athlete and I was proud of that. I had good grades and I was proud of that, too.

I like to say that was a special time in my life. Football was something I did because I enjoyed it. I wanted to get out of my hometown. I wanted to go to college. When I was in college, I had to maintain my scholarship. It was an academic scholarship, not an athletic scholarship. So I had to maintain my grades. Things just kept evolving for me. I was built like a basketball player — which was a sport I loved to play — and I had no aspirations of playing pro ball. I could run faster than most people. I wasn't trying to get to the NFL. I wanted to have a degree. I wanted to get a good job. I didn't want to do the kind of work stuff I did as a kid.

I came to Pittsburgh and I had no idea what I was getting into. I came in Chuck Noll's first year. Joe Greene was coming in, too. He was their No. 1 draft choice. They already had Chuck Hinton, Ben McGee and Lloyd Voss playing defensive end when I arrived. I'm the smallest guy in the group. At practice at St. Vincent's, none of them could run as fast as I could or last as long.

Clarence Washington came in with me that year from Arkansas AM&N. He was an 11th round draft choice, right after me. He was also a defensive lineman. We were roommates at St. Vincent's in the beginning. One day, after practice, he said he thought we didn't have a shot.

I said, "Man, I'm not going home. They paid to bring me here, and nobody is talking me into going home." And I made the Steelers' team. It was not out of my reach. The more I saw of what was going on, and caught on to what was going on, the more I thought I could play with these guys. I played about a quarter of the game, behind Lloyd Voss and Ben McGee, in the early years.

Before my third camp, Chuck Noll told me I had gotten off to a good start. He said to me, "Maybe we can get you more playing time next year." I said, "No, Coach, I'm going to start next year!" And I did. Dan Radakovich came in that same year and took over coaching the defensive line. He liked my speed and range. My drive wasn't just a football thing. I've had good drive for as long as I can remember. Even as a little kid, doing menial jobs, I wanted to do the best I could.

When I came here, I was not making enough money to be able to go back and forth to my home in Mississippi. I couldn't go home and live off my parents. I wanted to find something to do. I was looking to go to school and come away with a degree in something. I ended up teaching school in the off-season in my early years with the Steelers.

When we were working out at camp, Radakovich told me, "You have a good shot at starting." That's how I ended up starting. I think they waited awhile because they didn't want to start two rookies on the same side of the line. Joe Greene got to play right away. Rad didn't care whether we had rookies or not. He put Dwight White at the other end in 1971 when he was just a rookie. We improved our speed with Dwight and me in there.

When I was ten or eleven years old, my dad had me doing so many chores every day it drove me crazy. There were nine of us children and I was the oldest. There were always people dying in town and my parents would give me cards to deliver to the funeral homes expressing their condolences. I hated doing that. I'd stop halfway and there'd be four or five guys playing basketball and I'd join in. Then I'd run all the way to and from the funeral home so I wouldn't be late getting home. I was always running around town. But I had to get me a game in somehow. You could see the basket on a pole from my home. I knew when there was a game to be had. So I ran a lot.

During the summer, they'd have buses and trucks come into town to pick up kids to help pick cotton. It was a chance to make some extra money. It would be 105 degrees in the shade. I'd have a big bag over my shoulder. We'd get paid $2.50 for 100 pounds of cotton. You'd try to make at least $5 and on a good day you could make $7.50 or even $10. Picking cotton was hard on the hands and even harder on the back. I can still feel pain in my back, just thinking about it.

When I was at St. Vincent's camp, on those days when you couldn't see the surrounding mountains because of the haze, when it was so hot and humid, I was reminded of those days when I was out in the fields picking cotton as a kid. I'd pick 250 pounds some days, starting out when the sun first came up and working till 6:30 or 7 o'clock at night. So I knew what it was like to be out in the fields when it was hotter than hell.

I've always worked hard at staying out of people's way. I minded my own business.

I don't know if I was one of Chuck's favorite players. I was fortunate to fit into his scheme of things. I've never been a popular player, even in college. Because of my size, they were always trying to replace me. They could never replace me. When the ball was snapped, I was always the starter. They had some good players like Lloyd Voss, Ben McGee and Chuck

51

Hinton when I first came here, but I did some things in camp that caught their eye. Some of the things I did, well, they had to take a chance on me. He didn't want to start Joe Greene and I together and have two rookies in there. But there was no one who came in who could play that position better than I could. He didn't know I had my head in the game.

Joe was something special. When I first saw him he was very impressive. When he put his pads on he was like a god. I was there three or four weeks before he came in to camp. He stayed out because he wanted a better contract. So he held out. When he finally came in, all the veterans were talking about him. They didn't give him any respect; that's just the way they were with rookies. His first day, in the first drill, Joe hit one of our guys and about knocked him out. And then another guy. The offensive linemen didn't want any part of him. He beat every offensive lineman. He would just kick their butt. In the first practice, Joe kicked the hell out of every offensive lineman. They didn't want to go against him; they all started hanging back, not wanting to take their turn. He was nasty and tough, but we always got along. I got along with everybody.

Lambert was like that, too, but we got along. We all respected each other. We did what we had to do to win.

"It was time to let it go."

I was there for the final game at Three Rivers Stadium and I enjoyed seeing all the guys again. I wasn't sad when I saw it going down. To me, it was a building. I have a lot of great memories about the place. You have to keep moving on. It was time. It was time to let it go.

It's like my alma mater. I went to Arkansas AM&N. Now it's called the University of Arkansas at Pine Bluff. So my school no longer exists. That's kinda the way I felt about Three Rivers. What I got out of Three Rivers they can't take away from me. I know what I got out of there.

I'm real satisfied with myself now. I have a lot of peace. When I'm not at the office, I love to play golf. I work out. I go to church. I should have said I go to church first. I spend a lot of time now at church-related functions. I have a church family now. I'm happy with my life.

I have some physical problems. My back bothers me. I've had some back surgery. I need more surgery. My back is all screwed up. But I'm not as bad off as I could be. Sure, I feel aches and pains when I get out of bed in the morning. It's part of getting old. I dealt out my share of hits and absorbed my share of hits. I can almost feel the hits sometimes.

That's why I'm a golfer.

I used to be a basketball junkie. It was my dad's fault that I didn't become a basketball player. He told me one day I had to decide and pick between football and basketball. That I couldn't play both when I was in high school. There was work to be done at home. I liked football because you could be aggressive. I played intramural basketball. When I was playing football for the Pittsburgh Steelers I played for our basketball team in the winter. I have played in recent years at the YMCA Downtown. But I had to give up basketball. I taught myself how to play golf in the beginning, and then I went to golf school and really got serious about it.

As long as I was here, I found things I could do around here. It helped me pay my rent. I just liked the area. Pittsburgh lets me be a person and not a celebrity. I cause more of a fuss when I'm traveling through airports out of town than I do when I'm in Pittsburgh. Here, I'm just one of the people.

But I guess I'm still a celebrity. I get invited to play in golf tournaments by Michael Jordan, Don Shula, Mario Lemieux and Dan Marino, people like that. I'm still having more than my share of fun.

L.C. Greenwood relaxes at his desk in Carnegie offices.

Tunch Ilkin
A glad Turk

"I know how to get there."

His full name is Tunch Ali Ilkin. He was born in Istanbul, Turkey on September 23, 1957. According to the Steelers' 1987 press guide, his name was pronounced Toonch Ill-kin. Nowadays, it's pronounced Tunch, as in Punch. For one thing, he offers clinics on Power Punch blocking techniques. For another, it plays better on all the commercials he does on radio and TV. And Myron Cope can pronounce it better and in less time that way.

No matter how you say it, Tunch Ilkin is one former Steelers' player who is doing quite well, thank you. He proves that it pays to be a nice guy. Everybody who loves Raymond also loves Tunch. He was always a media favorite and he made the switch to the other side quite nicely. He managed to remain friendly with all the fellows in the locker room as well.

He was a nice guy to begin with, when he first showed up in Pittsburgh in 1980 as a 6th-round draft choice from Indiana State. His wife Sharon was a cheerleader at Indiana State. She once appeared on the cover of *Sports Illustrated* with one of the Sycamores' basketball players, a blond fellow from French Lick, Indiana named Larry Bird.

Ilkin's kids have since asked their dad why he never made the cover of *SI* since Mom did. The best Ilkin could do was to have his shoe or helmet show up in the corner of an *SI* cover. At least, he claims it was his shoe or helmet.

Even that represented a comeback for Ilkin. He was cut by Chuck Noll late in training camp his rookie year. He went back to Chicago where he had grown up and worked at a health club, cleaning up in the locker rooms, among other chores, and stayed in shape. When injuries piled up early in the season on the Steelers' offensive line, Ilkin got a call to come back to Pittsburgh. He was a 6-3, 265 pound tackle and he played tight end in short-yardage situations.

He played in 26 games his first two seasons, but didn't start until the final game of his third season, 1982, when he opened against the Cleveland Browns in the season finale. He managed to play 13 seasons with the Steelers, and one more bonus season with the Green Bay Packers for big bucks. There are only seven Steelers who've seen more service time with the Black & Gold and five of them are in the Pro Football Hall of Fame and one of them is in the waiting room.

There were a lot of nice guys in that Steelers' draft class of 1980, back when I was covering the club for *The Pittsburgh Press*. So I can vouch for their outstanding virtues. The class included Mark Malone, Bob Kohrs, Bill Hurley, Craig Wolfley, Frank Pollard and Tyrone McGriff.

Tunch Ilkin with best friend Craig Wolfley and, below, with Bill Hurley and Mark Malone. They were all in the Steelers' 1980 draft class and thought they'd help Steelers win "one for the thumb."

In review, Ilkin turned out to be the most productive player from that class, with Wolfley a close second. Ilkin is the only one who ever played in the Pro Bowl, and he did it twice, in 1989 and 1990. McGriff died in 2001, which was a blow to everybody in the class. He had been the last player taken in the entire draft that year and he made the team. The Steelers were selecting last, of course, because they had won the Super Bowl that year, their fourth in six years. Ilkin and his buddies were so happy to be joining such a strong Steelers' team. They figured they, too, would be playing in Super Bowls. But it never happened.

Ilkin is on nearly as many TV stations and radio stations as Stan Savran these days. He's doing commercials. He's involved in some business ventures. The kid from Turkey is doing just fine. His mother, who was Miss Turkey in 1950, is so proud of him. She lives on Mt. Washington and sees Tunch and his family often.

He was so impressed and influenced by some of the Steelers he met at St. Vincent's, and their strong religious acumen, that he converted from being a Muslim to a Christian. He was so fearful of what his father would say that he never told him. His dad learned of his decision about two years later, and didn't make a big deal about it. Soon after, both his father and his mother became Christians as well.

Ilkin and Wolfley — they're like Dean Martin and Jerry Lewis, or Bud Abbott and Lou Costello — do a lot of Christian inspirational talks to church groups in western Pennsylvania. Ilkin is chairman of the board for the Light of Life Mission that serves the needs of homeless men and women on the North Side of Pittsburgh.

His best gig these days is as an analyst in the broadcast booth with Bill Hillgrove and Myron Cope for the WDVE Radio coverage of Steelers' football. He actually graduated from Indiana State with a degree in radio broadcasting, so he knew what he wanted to be when he grew up. Ilkin and I were playing phone tag to try to set up an interview in early February, 2002. Then on Wednesday, February 6, I received a telephone call from Ilkin. He said he was driving around Upper St. Clair and wanted to know if I was free to do the interview. "I'll come to your house," he said. "I know you live near Wolfley, so I know how to get there." Within ten minutes, Ilkin was filling my front door. He came into the family room and sat down, and we discussed his days with the Steelers.

In late June, he went with his two sons, and Ted Petersen and his two sons, and two former Penn State and NFL players, Lee and Steve Wisniewski, and their sons, to a Fellowship of Christian Athletes camp in Montana. Tunch and Leo are partners in Athletic Training Network, which develops athletic training tapes and clinics around the country. They were going to extend their stay from three to six days to do some fishing, rafting, and hiking in Glacier National Park.

Tunch Ilkin:

I'm having fun with all this. I'm thankful. I live in a wonderful community and I've got lots of wonderful friends. I've had great opportunities for employment. It's great. Pittsburgh is home. I really love the city and the community.

Being a part of the Steelers' radio team, working with Bill Hillgrove and Myron Cope, is a blast. I'm still around the Steelers, I get to travel with the team, and I enjoy the life. Bill Cowher offered me a chance to coach the offensive line a year ago, and I turned it down. That doesn't mean I don't get the desire or the urge to coach. There are times when I'd like to be coaching, but it's so time-consuming. It's more important for me to be a part of my family's life and activities.

This way I get the best of both worlds.

My wife, Sharon, and our three children like it here. My parents moved here in March of 1994. My father passed in March of 1999. My mother is still living up on Mt. Washington, and she's involved in our church. It's great having her here, and getting to see her.

Am I a Steeler forever? I feel like I am. At the end of my NFL career, I played one year in Green Bay. It's almost like that year doesn't figure in, though. I made some good friends in Green Bay, but I don't watch Green Bay on TV and say, "Geez, I hope Green Bay wins!" I don't have ties to their organization, like I do the Steelers' organization

And to think it almost didn't happen, yeah. I was cut late in my first training camp with the Steelers. Then they invited me back midway through the season and I stayed 13 years (1980-1992). That's the grace of God. But I never thought of "What if?" I always felt I would play pro football.

I was fortunate to come here and be surrounded by the kind of people I was surrounded by. My conversion (from being a Muslim to being a Christian) happened here. In giving my life to Christ — I can remember it so vividly — I changed my life. So many of the Pittsburgh Steelers had such strong faith.

Someone like Jon Kolb had such an impact on my life. My roomie, Craig Wolfley, impressed me so much the way he dealt with his father's illness and death while we were at camp. He had such inner strength, a sense of acceptance. I wanted to know more about how he was able to be that way. We've had a great friendship for 22 years. There's a chemistry there, and that's why we work so well together when we're teamed on TV or the radio.

Jon Kolb, in particular, pointed the way for me, sharing the gospel message. I looked at him and I said, "This is what a man of God looks like." He led Bible study classes at his home. He was so humble. First, his home was in Peters Township, and then he moved to the North Hills and then to Grove City. But he remained a powerful influence for all of us.

Hollis Haff, who's now a pastor at the New Community Church in Wexford, was the Steelers' chaplain when I was playing, and he really challenged me to grow in my faith. He, too, helped me a lot. John Stallworth and Donnie Shell were two guys I looked up to. "These are what men of God look like," I said at the time. They were both humble men. It makes you do a double take. Like John Stallworth, so soft-spoken. So bright. He runs an aeronautics company. He was the Alabama Businessman of the Year. But the most important thing in his life was not the Pittsburgh Steelers or the Super Bowls, but Jesus Christ. Donnie Shell . . . he was like a human torpedo. He'd just blast guys when he played strong safety or on special teams. Yet he was such a great guy. So intense. So was his passion for God. They were never guys who said, "Boy, am I great!" They were more inclined to say, "Boy, do I serve a great God!"

The Steelers had so many guys who were in tune with mentorship. They welcomed you to the team and embraced you. When you got here you didn't feel like you weren't part of it. The guys were eager to share with you. People like John Stallworth, Donnie Shell, Mike Webster, Jon Kolb, Sam Davis and Larry Brown talked to and told you how they did things and what worked for them. They taught you what helped them.

"Even on the other side of the line, they helped. I remember Dwight White told me one day, "You're really improving, Homes." Another time, Joe Greene told me, "You're really good with your hands." Coming from those guys, it meant a great deal to me. I remember thinking, "Wow, that's good." I knew I was making progress.

"I wish I had played in one Super Bowl."

I came here in 1980, right after the Steelers had won their fourth Super Bowl in six years. Most of the guys from those great teams were still here when I showed up at St. Vincent. We thought it would continue, but it didn't. I wish I had played in one Super Bowl, just one year earlier. I benefited from that team in so many ways, though. I learned so much from them. They were champions in so many ways.

I still count the experience as something very rich.

You always think there will be another chance to do it, but it doesn't always work that way. When we lost in the AFC championship game in 1984, I figured we'd make it back and win it all the next year. But it didn't happen. The game is so different today. You can't keep those teams together any more because of free agency and the salary cap. They were all great guys.

Some of them are gone now, and that hurt a lot. Ray Mansfield died. I didn't play with him, but he was here in Pittsburgh and living in Upper St. Clair where I lived. I met him at a lot of alumni get-togethers and golf outings and dinners. He was such a great guy. Having Steve Furness die; that hurt. Then Dan Turk and Tyrone McGriff, two guys I had played with, guys I had friendships with. Tyrone came to the Steelers the same summer I did. I had a real love for Tyrone. About three years ago I saw Tyrone at a conference where I was a speaker, and we had lunch with him. I had my daughter Natalie with me, and she got to meet him. Two years later, he has a massive heart attack and dies. I didn't know Joe Gilliam, but I got to meet him at the last game at Three Rivers Stadium when they brought back all the old ballplayers. He died a week or so later. What it all showed me was the brevity of life. The Bible says life is like a puff of smoke. So you'd better spend your time on earth in the best possible way. It strengthens you to know that there is eternal life in heaven and that it's even a better place.

Today's Steelers aren't as close-knit as we were. The environment is different now. There's such a turnover in personnel every year. Players move to other teams when they get better offers through free agency. Because of the high salaries and the money involved the guys don't have to spend the off-season in town.

When I was here I had to get a job in the off-season. I couldn't afford to have a home here and a home somewhere else, not in the early days anyhow. So you started laying down roots. You got an off-season job, and tried to prepare for life after football.

You played for the Steelers' basketball team in the winter. We stayed in town. You hung out together and did social things together. I remember going on a cruise with several of the guys, stuff like that. Sharon and I, Joy and Dwayne Woodruff, Linda and Robin Cole and Mary Ellen and Mark Malone. We used to go down to the Florida Keys where Gary Dunn had a place and go fishing together.

Tom Beasley had a farm in Ruff Creek, near Waynesburg, and we'd go deer hunting there, and we'd ride our dirt bikes there. Some of us even got baptized in a pond at Ruff Creek.

Me, Jon Kolb, Ted Petersen, Rick Woods and Tom Beasley had never been baptized, so we were baptized there in the pond. You'll never forget that experience.

"The guys now go their own separate ways."

I'm not on the team now so I don't know what it's like for them. I'm close to some of the guys, but I'm not one of them anymore. About three years ago, a bunch of us old guys where invited out to a turkey-hunting tournament with some of the guys who were on the team. Jon Kolb, Tom Beasley, Steve Courson were there, and Tom Myslinski and Mark Bruener who were on the team were there.

We were sitting around the bunkhouse, telling old war stories. We weren't talking about games, but rather experiences we had shared. Like on our day off, we used to go trapshooting at the Millvale Sportsmen's Club in Wexford. That's one of the many things we used to do. As we were swapping stories, Mark Bruener piped up and said, "Am I jealous? You guys used to do so many things together. That'd be great."

Was it better? I don't know. The guys now go their own separate way. I'm very thankful for my time and the experiences I had.

I still like to do some of those things. My son Tanner and I are going down to fish in the Florida Keys pretty soon. I see Steve Courson at his place up in the mountains near Uniontown. I have a cabin not far from him on Youghiogheny Lake. I live near Edmund Nelson and we get to see each other.

This year's team had a bunch of very good guys. I especially was impressed with guys like Hines Ward. I really admire him, the way he plays the game. I think the world of Mark Bruener. He's just a good guy, and so involved in the community.

I was really happy for Kordell Stewart. He was able to weather the storm and come back with a Pro Bowl season. Jerome Bettis is special. I've never seen him turn down an interview. He's so accessible.

Kimo von Oelhoffen is a great guy. The whole offensive line is a bunch of good guys.

When you're coaching, you must be thinking about football all the time. I'm sure you take it home with you. Doing what I do, I don't bring it home. When I walk in the door, I turn off my cell phone. I'm with my kids; I'm with my family.

If I come to the end of my life and I've never coached in the NFL I'll have no regrets about that. If I missed the development of my children I'd regret that.

"Bill was more like a regular guy."

I'm often asked to compare Bill Cowher with Chuck Noll. Going from one coach to the other was strange for me. Bill comes in and he's my age — here's a guy I had played against — and he's the head coach. He called me into his office and he starts asking me questions about the team. He's asking my opinion. That was so different from my previous experience.

I think the world of Chuck Noll. I enjoyed playing for him. I don't think I would have become the player I became if it hadn't been for Chuck Noll. But Bill was more like a regular guy. Chuck used to intimidate everybody, except maybe Mel Blount.

J.T. Thomas used to say that Chuck was the king of non-verbal communication. Now my coach is a young guy and he wants my read on things. That was different. I enjoyed playing for Bill, too. I was with him for one year, in 1992. I was 35 that year.

I was a free agent the first year there was free agency. The Steelers didn't need me anymore. They felt they had a young player in Leon Searcy who was ready to take over the position. Bill was up front with me, and he told me he wanted me to stay around as insurance. Green Bay signed me as a starter for starter's money and it was more than I'd made to play for the Steelers. Mike Holmgren was looking for some veterans to show the way in Green Bay, and they came after me. It was a no-brainer.

Then I came back to Pittsburgh a year later. I hadn't moved. This was going to be my home. And I have had one opportunity after another here. I was lucky that Mark Malone left WPXI to go to ESPN. They had an opening, and they invited me to take his place. I learned a lot from the way Mark approached it. He had really worked at learning the TV business. He did everything behind the scenes as well as on camera. He was a good role model.

It's been great to work with Bill Hillgrove and Myron Cope. We have a great time doing the games. It's been a lot of fun. I've heard so many of Myron's old stories. We poke fun at each other during the game. We'll agree to disagree. We debate things, but it's always with a smile on our faces. Bill is a solid pro. He sets the table and gets us back on track when we wander.

I thought the Steelers were going to the Super Bowl. I thought they would beat New England. What I saw on tape, I thought they were going to win. The Patriots played at their best and they did it again against the St. Louis Rams in the Super Bowl.

I think there's a uniqueness about the Steelers, the organization and the team and the city. I feel the embrace of the community for the players and for former players. You feel a connection. The Steelers have such a rich history. You're proud to say, "I was a Pittsburgh Steeler.' I think it's more important than playing for the Tampa Bay Buccaneers or the Philadelphia Eagles.

There's a legacy that's been handed down, as far as what's expected on the field and off the field. There's a strong community involvement. I think the Steelers took their cue from Art Rooney, who was so generous and cared about this city and its people. When I came in and saw that Jon Kolb was doing, and what Mike Webster was doing, and what Robin Cole and Franco were doing. You just think that's what you're supposed to do. Those guys are still involved in the community. They still care about one another.

John Stallworth was in town for the AFC title game and Franco made an effort to get some of us together. Franco is so genuine. Stallworth, Lynn Swann, Larry Brown and John Banaszak and their wives all went to Morton's Chicago Steak House for dinner after the game. Me and Wolf came from work and we came stag. So did J.T. Thomas. We always enjoy each other's company.

I just thank God for all he's given me and my family. I've had my lovely wife Sharon (Senefeld) for 20 years this April. I have come a long way since I came to this country from Turkey when I was 2½ years old. I was probably shy in school in the beginning because I was an immigrant and I had a strange name. I used to tell people my name was Tom when I was in high school, but I had a girlfriend named Carol who convinced me that Tunch was really a special name, so I went back to being Tunch Ilkin. I've been comfortable being Tunch Ilkin ever since.

Jim O'Brien

Bill Hillgrove and Tunch Ilkin cover NFL draft at Steelers' offices.

Dan Radakovich
They call him Bad Rad

"Radakovich is an unsung hero..."
— Howard Cosell

D an Radakovich's resumé requires several pages, and it still doesn't tell his complete coaching history. But it is honest and would not get him into any trouble, even if he were applying for a job at Notre Dame. Born and bred in Duquesne, Pennsylvania, he played and served as an assistant at Penn State University to Rip Engle and Joe Paterno in the '50s and '60s.

He was an assistant on two different occasions with Chuck Noll's staff for the Steelers in the '70s. He has three Super Bowl rings, two for the Steelers in their first two NFL championship efforts, and one from the Los Angeles Rams when they lost to the Steelers in the Super Bowl in 1980. Radakovich has gotten around. He has traveled more than Marco Polo for coaching positions in college and the pro ranks, even to Europe.

"When I was with the Rams, I thought we were going to beat the Steelers in the Super Bowl (XIV)," Radakovich recalled. "We were leading for three quarters. If Nolan Cramwell had intercepted that pass, but he dropped it. They ran a hook-and-go for a touchdown with Stallworth. Then Lambert intercepted the ball, and Stallworth gets another touchdown. That was the ballgame. Ham and Wagner were hurt and didn't play in that game, and that was another reason we thought we'd win. But they managed to make up for that."

John Stallworth would soon be inducted into the Pro Football Hall of Fame, the ninth player from the Steelers of the '70s to be so honored, and Radakovich recalls them all fondly. He smiles broadly at the mere mention of their names. He has a story or two about all of them.

Going into his eighth year as an assistant to Joe Walton at Robert Morris University in suburban Pittsburgh in 2002, Radakovich claimed 24 years of coaching experience in the college ranks and 18 in the pro ranks. His hair is pure white and wispy and blows upward as he walks across a hill on the Coraopolis campus on a brisk day in mid-February. There is a pink to his cheeks, like he had just come in out of the cold.

This was familiar territory for me. I had taught a class at Robert Morris in public relations for sports management majors for three years in the mid-80s. I still bump into young men and women who were in my class, and it is always gratifying to find out what they are doing, or to be introduced to their families. There were some new buildings and it looked better than ever. There was not a football team at Robert Morris when I was there. There has been great growth and development at the school during the reign of President Edward Nicholson. He and his wife, Kathy, are neighbors of mine.

The football offices are in John Jay Center, where the school's varsity basketball team once played its home games back when Gus Krop was the coach. A beautiful student center, completed just a few years earlier, dominates the horizon on the rolling hills that make up the school's suburban campus. It was part of an $18 million building and renewal plan. The school used to be Robert Morris Junior College in the city, between the old jail and Duquesne University, and still has a classroom and administrative complex there. It became Robert Morris College, or RMC, and, at the start of 2002, its name was changed to Robert Morris University, or RMU.

Radakovich is an emotional man. His face flushes red in a hurry. His nickname is Bad Rad. He's probably been called Mad Rad behind his broad back and a few other things in his time. He is respected in the business as a guy who knows what he's talking about and what he's doing. During his stints with the Steelers, he was credited with developing some creative practice drills and blocking techniques. Noll still speaks of him in glowing terms.

When I was interviewing former Steelers for this book, several of them offered unsolicited praise for Radakovich as a coach who had made a difference in their pro lives. L.C. Greenwood, a defensive lineman, and Randy Grossman, a tight end, and Ted Petersen, an offensive lineman, all volunteered rave reviews for Radakovich, giving him high marks for teaching them proper techniques early in their careers, and for bringing innovative drills and ideas to the organization.

Radakovich is not reluctant to sound his own praises, or to support such boasts. He played a tape for us at his RMU offices in which the late Howard Cosell refers to Radakovich as an "unsung hero" in the Steelers' success in the '70s for what he did in forming "The Steel Curtain" defense. Cosell devoted one of his commentaries to the former Steelers' assistant. Radakovich smiled with pride as he played that tape. Radakovich is easy to talk to. We had lunch at the Ground Round Restaurant across Narrows Run Road from the main entrance at Robert Morris University. Radakovich is outspoken and eager to tell stories, not as guarded as his old boss, Chaz Noll. His old boss remains cautious in interviews, allowing a thin smile to suffice if he doesn't want to respond to a particular question.

Radakovich can't wait to tell you inside stuff. That, along with his celebrated temper, may account somewhat for his itinerant history. He began his coaching career after graduation from Penn State, serving as a graduate-student assistant there from 1953-1956, then as a full-fledged assistant coach from 1957 to 1969.

He was an assistant at Cincinnati for one season in 1970, and accepted the head coaching position there briefly in the off-season before departing for a position as a defensive line coach with the Steelers in 1971. He left Pittsburgh to go to the University of Colorado

Dan Radakovich discusses offensive line play with Larry Brown (87) and Moon Mullins (72) during Steelers game at Three Rivers Stadium, and enjoys light moment as assistant to head coach Joe Walton at Robert Morris University.

from 1972-73 and returned to the Steelers as their offensive line coach from 1974 to 1977. It was rare that Noll allowed anyone back in the fold once they said goodbye. Radakovich was the only assistant coach ever to return during Noll's 23-year run as head coach of the Steelers.

Radakovich spent the 1978 season with the San Francisco 49ers, and was with the Los Angeles Rams from 1979 to 1981. He was at North Carolina State University in 1982, the Denver Broncos in 1983, and the Minnesota Vikings in 1984. He joined Joe Walton with the New York Jets from 1985 to 1988, and was with the Cleveland Browns from 1989-1990. He hooked up again as the first hire of Walton when Walton became the first football coach at Robert Morris in 1993. Radakovich left Robert Morris for the 1995 season when he returned to the NFL for a one-year stint as a line coach with the St. Louis Rams. Walton had served as offensive coordinator for Noll's Steelers during the 1990 and 1991 seasons, but it didn't work out that well.

Walton had followed his father Frank to play football at Pitt, and was an All-American end for the Panthers, and later starred with the New York Giants and Washington Redskins. He and his wife Ginger live in his hometown of Beaver Falls, just north of the RMU campus, and he hosts a celebrity golf tournament there each year. In 1994, after 35 years in the NFL, he took 64 freshmen at a school that never had football in its 73 years of existence and posted a 7-1-1 record. Radakovich was his first hire at Robert Morris. Radakovich and his wife, Nancy, live in Green Tree. They have been married 46 years and they have four adult children, Daniel, Lisa, Leslie and Lori.

Radakovich shared stories that shed light on Noll, the draft selection of Franco Harris, the departure of Joe Gilliam in his playing days, Radakovich's role as a mentor for Joe Moore. Moore became known as one of the best offensive line coaches in the country while serving at Pitt, Temple and Notre Dame. Radakovich reminds me of Chuck Klausing the way he claims credit for revolutionizing the game in so many respects. They are fun to talk to just the same, and I admire and respect them both.

Dan Radakovich:

Chuck Noll was a good football coach and a good man. He was stable, persistent and willing to do different things. He welcomed input from his players and assistant coaches. He didn't panic. He was 1-13 in his first season (1969) as coach of the Steelers and I've heard the story where Mr. Rooney told his sons, "You guys finally got a coach. He may have lost a lot of games, but he never lost the team."

Patience was one of his strongest virtues. For me, he was easy to work for. If you knew what you were doing he left you alone. I must have done something right. He brought me back

and he never did that with any other assistant. I think he liked my methods and attention to detail. Noll was a big believer in teaching proper techniques and skills, more like a college or high school coach.

I was the defensive line coach that first year. He let me make some moves personnel-wise that I believe formed the basis for the team's success. It helped move us to a new level. I put L.C. Greenwood into the starting lineup right away as the left end, and I put Dwight White in as a starter at the other end as a rookie. So our line was very young. I took Lloyd Voss and Ben McGee, who had been our starting defensive ends and were both very good players, and put them at right tackle with Chuck Hinton. The three of them had to compete for a starting position. They thought I was destroying the defensive unit. Ernie Holmes came in the next year, after I was gone, and he eventually grabbed that job. He and Joe Greene were great inside and they were there when I came back in 1974. That was the first year Ernie started.

L.C. and White could both run the 40 in 4.6 seconds on grass. The Steelers didn't have "fast" times, either. They were accurate times. Those two were a full second faster in the 40 than McGee and Voss. That speed made our defensive line better in the pass rush and in their range against the run.

L.C. used to lap players in the 12-minute run, including Andy Russell and people like that. He and White were undersized, but they made up for it with their speed and aggressive styles. Our pursuit speed jumped up considerably. That's the year they got the "Steel Curtain" nickname.

When we ran the 12-minute run in 1971, L.C. lapped the whole team, every player. Whoever was second ran more than one lap behind him. I said to him, "You tell everybody you don't work out. But you must be out here in the middle of the night to run like you do." He'd say, "Rad, you must be crazy to think that." Those were great guys. I heard Joe Greene was upset that I was leaving. I know that Joe Greene mentioned me in his Hall of Fame acceptance speech. That meant a lot to me.

I'm not sure how Dwight White felt about me leaving. One time, in the last pre-season game in 1971, like our fifth game, I grabbed White as he was coming off the field after he'd played a great game. He was getting all this press. I hollered at him, "You're getting a lot of publicity, and I hope you're not getting a big head about it. You're the first guy I coached here. I've got you doing 18 good things today. But you had 19 loafs. That's right, 19 times when you didn't go full speed. So you grade out at a minus one."

He was upset. He went to Lionel Taylor, one of our other assistant coaches, and accused me of being prejudiced. Lionel told me that he told White, "Dwight, how many rookies are starting on the defensive line? So he's not prejudiced. He moved two veteran ends to make room for you and L.C. One of them was black and one of them was white. You're telling me he's prejudiced! Get the hell outta here!"

When I came back, White and I got along just fine. I remember one time, in 1977, we were playing the last game of the season at San Diego. Loren Toews was in the game at linebacker. Dwight came running off the field, and he said, "Hey, Rad, get Toews out of the game! I can't believe what he just said!" He said Toews couldn't understand what White had said to him at one point, and that Toews said, "I beg your pardon." That kind of polite talk during a football game got Dwight nervous.

White was an under-rated member of that defensive line. He started as a rookie. Joe Greene was outstanding right from the start. So they both made an immediate impact. Ernie is one of the guys who came along. He had a lot to learn about footwork and technique. He was just strong and mean as hell when he first came in.

Holmes signed with the Steelers in 1972, but he didn't come into his own until 1974. In 1974, 1975 and 1976, Ernie was as good as anyone. He was as good as Joe during that spell. Who's to say who was better? Leroy Selman might have been as good as anybody who ever played in the defensive line and they were playing the wrong scheme for him when he joined the Tampa Bay Buccaneers, and they were one of the worst teams in the league. Maybe he was as good as anyone.

Joe Greene was an inconsistent player, but in the three games in the playoffs in 1974 he was awesome. No one else ever played better than he did in those three playoff games. He wanted that ring so badly. In that stretch, he was as good as anyone who ever played the game. In 1975, he had the neck injury and was not himself.

I know that Dwight White and Joe Greene had a love-hate relationship, but I know Dwight truly loves Joe. They used to get into arguments when I was there. I remember one time Dwight jumped out of a car in a rage — "I'm outta here!" he hollered — and Joe was just going to drive off without him. I told Joe to hold up, and Dwight got back in the car. They were both their own man. They'd go at it now and then, on the field, and in the locker room and at practice. The bottom line is they were two of the reasons the Steelers were so outstanding.

Ernie ate himself out of the league in 1976 and 1977. They called him "Fats" but he wasn't fat when he was playing so great. His body was like concrete then. But he couldn't keep his weight under control, and Noll would not tolerate that. To Noll, that meant he wasn't committed to doing what needed to be done to be at his best. He traded him to Tampa Bay.

"He sounds like a deadhead to me."
—Chuck Noll on Franco

I left after that year to become the defensive coordinator at Colorado. I wasn't impressed with professional football; that's all. Chuck had offered me the defensive coordinator's post. We didn't have one at the time. Chuck was the linebacker coach and the head coach in 1971. He was usually with the offense, though. The defense was coached by Charley Sumner and me, just two guys.

I had already accepted the job and was preparing to leave for Colorado when Chuck asked me not to leave until after the draft. I'd gone to the all-star games and gone over the film of prospects, plus I was the only one on the staff who knew Franco Harris. I was a coach at Penn State when Franco was there. He used to come over to our house with some other players and my wife, Nancy, baked cookies for them. So I agreed to stay, even though Colorado was pressing me to report there so they could make the announcement.

Art Rooney Jr., who headed up the personnel department at the time, and his staff were pushing for the Steelers to draft Franco. Art had done a lot of work on him. To support his position, Art brought a tape to the office in which all the Blesto scouts gave their personal recommendations regarding Franco. Art Jr. had called them all and asked them to give their reports on Franco. Art Jr. played it for the staff, including Chuck. He was the only one who wasn't sure that Franco should be our first pick. Chuck was hedging a bit. He was leaning toward Robert Newhouse, who ended up with the Dallas Cowboys and was a productive running back. But Franco was a future Hall of Famer, as it turned out. I think the Steelers selected the right man.

I'm standing in the doorway in the room where all the coaches and scouts are gathered on draft day at Three Rivers Stadium. I'm already halfway gone to Colorado. Our turn comes up. We have 15 minutes to make our pick. Chuck looks over at me, and says, "Well?"

I said, "Take him! We all decided we were going to take Franco Harris!"

So Chuck makes the choice. Then he leaves the room so he can talk to Franco on the telephone and welcome him to the Steelers. He comes back in the room, and comes over to me. Almost in a whisper, he says, "He sounds like a deadhead to me." I said, "He'll be fine, you'll see. Chuck, he's a smart kid. He's just shy."

It wasn't my deal to draft Franco, though. It was Art Rooney Jr.'s deal. Max Coley was the backfield coach (1969-71) that season and he was leaving for a job with the Denver Broncos. Chuck asked him to stay for the draft, too. The Steelers were like family. You didn't leave there with a bad feeling.

"To Mr. Rooney, I was still a Steeler."

On the second day of the draft, I told Chuck I'd really like to be on my way to Colorado. He said, "Fine. I don't need you anymore. Before you go, make sure you stop at the office and drop off your keys."

So I went down to the other end of the hall to see one of their business guys. His name was Dennis (Thimons) and he was about 25 years old. He was the assistant business manager. I gave him my keys. He said, "Here's an envelope Mr. Rooney told me to give you." I said, "What's this?" He said, "It's for the rest of your contract."

I opened the envelope and there was a check for $7,000 or maybe a little more. "This isn't mine," I said. "This is a mistake. I started in June. I wasn't here for the full year." He said, "Take it; it's yours."

So I went back down the hall and went to Mr. Rooney's office, which was midway between the business office and the coaches' offices. Mr. Rooney was sitting behind his desk.

I came in and waved the check in front of him, and I said, "Mr. Rooney, this is a mistake!"

He said, "No, that's yours."

I said, "I started here in June and now it's January. I got my Christmas bonus of $5,000, and I'm grateful."

Mr. Rooney got up out of his chair and came over and put his hand on my shoulder to calm me down. He said, "Dan, just take it. You did a great job. Come back and coach again for us sometime."

I bought a new station wagon to go to Colorado. We called it the Rooney Wagon. And I came back to coach for the Steelers two years later.

I've got another Art Rooney story for you. About 15 years later, in 1986, I'm coaching with the New York Jets and my mother, Bridget Radakovich, dies. I fly home for the funeral. The viewing the first night is at 7 o'clock. I figure I'm going to be the first one at the Shaughnessy Funeral Home on Second Avenue in Duquesne. I go in and there's Art Rooney and Ed Kiely waiting for me. I couldn't believe it. They stayed for about a half hour, and Mr. Rooney had a word for everyone in our family. To Mr. Rooney, I was still a Steeler. Once a Steelers coach, always a Steelers' coach. I thought that was amazing.

"You have to give the scouting department a lot of credit."

There was criticism when we let Bruce Van Dyke go in 1974. He wasn't going to make the team, so we dealt him. The move met with some resistance in the personnel department. He was a good football player. Van Dyke was our best offensive lineman in 1971. But it had gotten to the point where Ham was beating Van Dyke and "scoring" on him routinely in our practice scrimmages. Van Dyke got a full bonus from the Super Bowl that year. He just didn't make the team.

I had quite a line to work with. We had Jon Kolb at left tackle, Sam Davis or Jim Clack at left guard, Ray Mansfield or Mike Webster at center, Clack or Moon Mullins at right guard, and Gordon Gravelle or Mullins at right tackle. Rick Druschel was the backup guard and Dave Reavis was the backup tackle. I played seven of them. Some people thought we did that because they weren't that good, but we had seven solid offensive linemen who jelled. We had the best of everything. You could make a case for us having the best football team of all time. We built the team through the draft and free agents, the old-fashioned free agents, not the kind you have today. We did a super job as far as free agents were concerned. We picked up guys like Sam Davis, John Banaszak, Glen Edwards, Donnie Shell and Randy Grossman.

We had a better team than anybody else, so you have to give the scouting department a lot of credit. It was a team effort. We were well organized. Chuck got everybody involved in scouting and the draft. He had everybody listen to scouting reports. Even Ralph Berlin, our trainer, went out and saw some players. He was the only one to see Steve Furness, and he was a fine addition.

What part did luck play? It was big, but you have to be good enough for luck to help you. Some guys get overlooked from those teams. John Rowser was the best secondary player we had in 1971. He wasn't fast, but he was a good player. He helped some of our other guys, like Wagner, Blount, Thomas and Edwards learn how to play back there. Some of those guys came from programs where they didn't get a lot of coaching in the fine points.

"I'll tell you what I think they ought to do with drug dealers. I'd have them taken off to the public square and hung by the neck till the wind whistled through their bones."
— Jack Lambert

"Why is Joe Greene sitting on the bench?"

I can tell you stories about Joe Greene and Joe Gilliam. I remember we lost three of four games midway through the 1971 season. We lost at Baltimore (34-21), and Joe Greene was so disappointed. We go out to practice a few days later and Joe loafs on me. I get on his case. We go out the next day and he loafs on me again. That was in the days when if you didn't want to stay somewhere you'd just loaf in practice. So I got on Joe again. He snapped at me, "Hey, if you don't like it, just trade me!"

I told him I wanted him to come and see me after practice. I told him, "I know you're down about the season. You do what you want, but you're not going to get traded no matter what you do. You're going to sit on the bench. This is a steel town and those fans are going to be asking, 'Why is Joe Greene sitting on the bench?' They'll get down on you if the word gets out that you're loafing in practice. I can tell you this: the Rooneys are not going to trade you. You'd better make up your mind about helping make the Steelers a better team. They're not going to trade you." Greene said, "I didn't know they felt that way." After that, he was fine.

Terry Bradshaw and Joe Gilliam could throw the ball better than anybody else in practice. In 1974, it was a joy to watch the seven-on-seven drills. You had to be able to catch it to play receiver for the Steelers then. Those guys fired that ball hard more often than not. They were firing that ball all over the field. It was a show.

Bradshaw loved practice. Frenchy Fuqua loved practice. He may not have been a model citizen off the field, but he was first-class and so competitive on the field. Bradshaw and Fuqua loved practice more than anybody in the game. You had to keep them off the field. Bradshaw would play receiver. He would be punting the ball, just for the helluva it.

Later on, Bradshaw was a high-low guy. He was inconsistent. Noll let his quarterbacks have more leeway than most teams. Bradshaw audibled 90 per cent of the running plays. He'd make the calls at the line of scrimmage. He was good that way. He was truly a team player. He got as much a kick from the running game as he got from the passing game.

There was a strike at summer training camp in 1974. Gilliam came back earlier. Bradshaw was behind him when he came back. Gilliam was the starter at the beginning of the season. Gilliam was outstanding. He had a quick release and a strong arm. He could learn plays quickly. He was quick-footed, he could do it all. He was a talented young man. So was Bradshaw. We had two great quarterbacks.

72

We beat Baltimore pretty badly in the first game of the season. We should have won the second game at Denver, but Joe couldn't protect a 35-28 lead. Joe wouldn't stop throwing the ball. He threw six straight passes with a lead, and they took one of them back and tied the game. Joe could have taken a knee and we'd have won the game. Joe used to love to say, "Passing is my game." I was one of the people who pushed to replace Gilliam in favor of Bradshaw.

A lot of people thought Bradshaw deserved a chance. I stayed late three nights in a row and talked to Chuck about it. I was trying to convince him to give Bradshaw a shot at starting. The argument then was that he was afraid to throw over the middle, but he started throwing more post patterns. Before long, he became known for doing that.

Gilliam was told on Friday by Chuck that he wasn't going to start the next game. I'm walking down the hall at Three Rivers following practice, and Gilliam hollers out to me, "Hey, Rad, you weren't part of that lynch mob, were you?"

I replied, "Joe, I'm sorry to tell you but I was not only a part of it, I led it." I told him to wait for me, that I wanted to talk to him about it. I had to drop off something. When I came back, he was gone. There were other times when Chuck was upset with Bradshaw and he'd go with Hanratty. Joe got some other chances; there were times he was awesome. The next year Joe was awful. We were 12-1 going into the final game at Los Angeles and Joe stunk up the joint. He was awful. He was on drugs and we didn't know it. Joe had been late or slept through about 30 quarterback meetings, and Noll was the quarterback coach the following season. The word got out that Gilliam's days were growing short with the Steelers. Ham and Wagner came in to see me and they were appealing on Gilliam's behalf. They said, "You gotta keep Gilliam." They thought he could help them win another Super Bowl. I went to Chuck and told him what they had said. I said, "I just met with two of the best attitude guys on the team, and they want to give Gilliam another chance. Chuck said, "No, he's gone. I can't keep him." He said the black players had told him that Gilliam was an embarrassment to them. The black players knew that Gilliam was on drugs.

"I looked like Frankenstein."

When I became the offensive line coach, the defensive linemen were able to grab hold of their jerseys and pull them aside. I gave one of the jerseys — it was one that had belonged to Bruce Van Dyke — to our equipment guy Tony Parisi and he

73

had his mother-in-law cut it and tailor-made it to fit snugly. Some other teams in the league had some guys who wore smaller-sized jerseys so they'd fit snugly.

Tony took the jerseys of all the offensive linemen to his mother-in-law and had them cut down till they were skintight. A guy like Joe Greene could still grab their jerseys, so I asked my wife what we might be able to do to make them fit even tighter.

She went out and got some carpet tape. That was two-way tape. We put it on the shoulder pads. Then I put on one of the cut-down jerseys to see what it was like. I was walking around the house and I looked like Frankenstein, with my arms sticking straight out. I couldn't get my arms down. It didn't look like that was going to work. Then we pulled the jerseys down tight and it was great. We also got some gauze pads and filled in a hole just under the shoulder pads and that made the surface even smoother and harder to grab.

I told the coaches what we were doing. One of them — I won't say who — was skeptical. He said we were giving the players crutches, and excuses. I showed the jerseys to the players, and how we'd use the tape. They loved it. Guys like Ray Mansfield and Mike Webster were cheering. So we were the first offensive line to wear tailor-made jerseys in the NFL.

"He always had a Bad Rad Day."

Joe Moore was regarded as the best offensive line coach in the country when he was at Pitt, Temple and Notre Dame. But I think Joe will tell you that he learned much of what he coached from me.

When Joe came out of Schenley High School, he was one of the most sought-after athletes in western Pennsylvania. He went to Tennessee, which had one of the best football teams in the country. He transferred to Penn State, and had to sit out a season. Then he went into the military service, so it was a while before he could play at Penn State. He came back around 1955 and we were teammates for a year. He hurt his back and he couldn't play anymore. He went out for the baseball team and became a starter there. He was quite the ballplayer.

We coached together at Penn State. I was the freshman line coach under Earl Bruce, and Joe coached the backs in the fall of 1958. I moved up to coach the varsity linebackers from there. I told Joe about an opening for a high school job in Ridgefield Springs, New York, up near Cooperstown.

He was there for two years and he had me come up and talk to his players and coaches. He had a Bad Rad Day. Wherever he went from there, Upper St. Clair High School and Pitt, he kept that up. He always had a Bad Rad Day. When I was with the Steelers, I used to bring Mike Webster and Jon Kolb out to Pitt Stadium to show their kids how to do things properly.

Joe and I are very close. He is the godfather for my oldest daughter. His wife, Fran, and he are good friends of my wife, and we go out together. Him and Fran are a lot of fun. Everywhere he coached, he called on me. If we came up with anything new, he knew about it before anyone else.

Joe enjoyed a great rapport with his players. He got their attention and he taught them how to play the line as well as anyone in the game. I learned a lot from Joe, too. He was a good football coach in his own right. If I helped in any way, I'm proud of that. Now I get him to come out and talk to our kids. It's gone full cycle.

"Bad Rad" in action on sideline for Robert Morris University.

Moon Mullins
He blocked for O.J. and Franco

*"My dream was to someday play
for the high school football team."*

Gerry "Moon" Mullins was a starting guard on the Steelers' four Super Bowl champion teams of the '70s. He was on the small side for that position, even then, at 6-3, 230 pounds, about 15 pounds less than he was listed in the game programs and press guides. But he was quick and nimble of foot, and his heart was bigger than most. He knew how to play Chuck Noll's intricate game, executing trap blocks, pulling out of the line and leading the running backs on end sweeps. He had been a tight end who was mostly a blocker at the University of Southern California where John McKay's offense was labeled "Student body right and student body left." It was a modernized version of the old single-wing offense.

It was the kind of power football made famous by Vince Lombardi in Green Bay with his Packers.

Mullins was a handsome, fun-loving individual, especially in his early days with the Steelers when he wore his hair fashionably long. He had that California beach boy coolness and laid-back approach about him. He sported a beard now and then. He was called "a free spirit," the team's most "eligible bachelor" and a few other things.

He was born in a hospital in Fullerton, California on August 24, 1949 and grew up to be a football star on the highly successful football teams at nearby Anaheim High School. His home was just a block away from the school.

"My dream was to some day play for the high school football team," he says now. "I never thought about playing college ball and I didn't know much about pro ball. I didn't really follow it that much. My world never revolved around football."

It still doesn't. He disclosed that he had not been to Heinz Field in its first season as the home of the Steelers. "I'm still waiting for my maiden voyage there," he said. Frankly, he didn't pay that much attention to the Steelers since he was cut from the squad prior to the 1980 season, the year after the Steelers had won their fourth Super Bowl in six seasons. He was the first player who performed for those four championship teams to be cut loose by Chuck Noll. Mullins had performed valiantly and with distinction for the Steelers for ten years (1970-79). There were so many great players on those teams, though, and he never got to play in a Pro Bowl even when the Steelers sent eleven players to the post-season all-star game in 1976.

Few of the Steelers' offensive linemen were so honored, yet Chuck Noll has often said they were vastly under-rated and were at the core of his club's success, the force that made the rushing and passing attacks work so well.

At office in South Fayette

With wife Joan

Moon Mullins

Photos by Jim O'Brien

Gerry "Moon" Mullins enjoys seeing former teammates Dwight White and Steve Furness at United Way function at Doubletree Hotel, now the Westin Convention Center Hotel in 1999.

That was then and this is now. Moon Mullins, at age 52, was sitting at his desk on a sunny but cool Thursday afternoon on February 7, 2002 at Industrial Metals and Minerals Company in South Fayette, less than a mile from the Bridgeville exit off I-79. He was alone in a nondescript one-story building. He said his secretary had the afternoon off. She was the only other worker in the building Mullins referred to as "a ghost town now."

I had last visited him there ten years earlier, in January of 1992. There had been eight employees in residence at that time. He was in a different office then. At that time, he was the company's vice-president, the right-hand man for company owner Bob Keaney, working with him for 11 years, being groomed to take over the company some day. Mullins bought the company from Keaney in 1995. He admitted that business had declined. "I'm still making a living at it," he said. "I'm still hanging in there. It still pays the bills. This business had started to decline even before I took over."

Moon Mullins explained his good fortune in getting into his "life's work," as Noll always referred to it, when his playing days with the Steelers were over. Keaney was a next door neighbor of sports broadcasting legend Bob Prince in the Deerfield Manor section of Upper St. Clair. Keaney was looking for someone to bring into his business, someone he could groom to take over for him someday down the road.

Keaney was a Steelers' fan. He had heard that some of the smartest guys on the team were the offensive linemen, and he liked the fact that Mullins could play so many positions, that he was versatile. Prince had met Mullins at Three Rivers Stadium and spoken to him a few times. Keaney asked Prince if he could introduce him to Mullins.

They hit it off, and a wonderful business opportunity was presented to Mullins.

The company he presides over sells ores and minerals and industrial-related materials around the country. It has represented companies like Kennecott Copper and Dresser Industries. Glass is one of its businesses — thus the collection of antique glass bottles on a shelf behind Mullins' desk — but he said the glass business had fallen on hard times, too. Such companies had been impacted greatly by the events of September 11. The American economy took a big hit from the terrorist attack on our country.

Mullins didn't look much different from the way he appeared ten years earlier, though he confessed that he now weighed about 250 pounds, up from his playing weight. I knew I looked older, but he looked much the same. There might have been a little more salt in his salt-and-pepper hair, but he looked fine. He was wearing a ski sweater, as he had during my previous visit. This ski sweater was blue, black and white, over a light blue open-collared shirt. He still had a pinch of chewing tobacco under his lower lip, bulging out a bit. He asked me if I wanted him to remove that tobacco plug when he posed for some pictures.

He showed me a photo of a beautiful home he had built on a 5-acre plot near a pond up north near Butler and Saxonburg. He had remarried in 1995 — the same year he took over the company — and his second wife, Joan, and her children had lived in that area and wanted to remain there. They moved into their new home in March of 1999. "So I've got an hour's commute every day," Mullins mentioned with a bit of a sigh.

Mullins had come to the Steelers with one of their strongest and certainly deepest draft class in the team's history. The Steelers' 1971 draft class included 1: wide receiver Frank Lewis of Grambling; 2: linebacker Jack Ham of Penn State; 3: running back Steve Davis of Delaware State; 4: guard/tackle Gerry Mullins of Southern California; 5: tight end/tackle Larry Brown of Kansas; 6: guard Craig Hanneman of Oregon State; 8: defensive lineman Ernie Holmes of Texas Southern; 11: defensive back Mike Wagner of Western Illinois; 13: wide receiver Al Young of South Carolina State. As many as nine starters came out of that draft. Ham is in the Pro Football Hall of Fame. That same year the Steelers also signed a free agent defensive back, Glen "Pine" Edwards of Florida A&M, who would play seven seasons and twice played in the Super Bowl and the Pro Bowl.

Mullins reflected on his stay with the Steelers and what's happened to him since then in an hour-and-a-half interview:

Gerry "Moon" Mullins:

I don't think we realized what a remarkable group of players we had in the Class of 1971 when we first arrived at training camp. I buddied with Jack Ham and Mike Wagner initially. Our top priority was making the football team. That class turned out to be the one that made the Steelers able to contend for the title. When we arrived at St. Vincent's, though, our concentration focused on one thought: "Are we going to be around after the final cut day?"

I had played defensive end as a sophomore at Southern Cal, and tight end as a junior and senior. But I caught only 15 passes in college. We just ran the ball right over you for the most part. We ran the ball 90 per cent of the time. So I was primarily a lead blocker. When the Steelers drafted me, they called me on the telephone and I spoke with Dan Rooney and Chuck Noll. I guess it was Noll who told me they had drafted me as a guard. I guess that was his way of saying you better bulk up between now and training camp.

Yes, I was at USC at the same time as O.J. Simpson. When I was a freshman and sophomore he was a junior and senior. Freshmen weren't eligible to play varsity football in those days. O.J. led the team to a national championship in my first year in school.

Clarence Davis was the tailback in my last two years at USC and Sam Cunningham was the fullback. Those were the big-name guys when I was starting. They both went on to play pro ball.

When O.J. was on trial for murdering his wife a few years back, everybody was asking me questions about what he was like. Hey, he was always a good guy to me. He was a superstar in college, but he treated me like one of his buddies. I went to his apartment a few times. He was always available to everybody. The media loved him.

I think he had some Hollywood connections even then, and I think he got some guidance about how to handle his situation. I remember Bill Cosby and Rock Hudson coming into our clubhouse to see him.

We went to the Rose Bowl all four years I was there. Each of us players received 16 tickets to the Rose Bowl and we all sold most of them. It was a way — I know it wasn't permitted by the NCAA rules — to pick up some extra spending money. It was sort of a subsidy. Most of us sold our tickets for $100 apiece. We heard Charlton Heston bought O.J.'s tickets and that he paid $1,000 apiece for them. That was a nice chunk of change. That's what I heard, anyhow. I guess actors are frustrated jocks and they liked being around us.

I don't know what happened to O.J. or how he could have gotten involved in some of the things he apparently got involved in. I liked the guy; he was always good with me. You wonder what changed.

It's like that with Mike Webster. He was the most solid guy on our team. He was a family man, really into religion. He was such a dedicated football player. No one worked harder than he did to strengthen himself or to be in shape. He was reliable, a real rock in our dressing room.

Now I don't even know Mike Webster. I don't know what happened to him. His marriage broke up; he was estranged from his family. You hear all kinds of stories. He lost all his money. They say he was sleeping in cars, moving around. I heard he's getting a disability pension from the NFL, but that he was petitioning for a disability pension on a higher level.

I was invited to a get-together to see him a few years back. It was out at Steve Courson's place in the woods near Nemacolin, down around Uniontown. I drove about three hours to get there. I was eager to see him, to see how he was doing. We were told to be there around one o'clock. Steve Furness was there. Ted Petersen was there. Courson's wife was there, I remember. She has since committed suicide. And Furness has died. So everything about the Steelers isn't Shangri-La. Well, Webster still hadn't showed up when it was around five o'clock. I was ready to leave because I had a long drive home. They asked me to stay. They said Webster had called on his cell phone and said he was held up, but was on his way. I heard he had been a no-show for autograph signings the Steelers had set up for him to help him make some money, and that he'd become totally unreliable. But I stayed. When he got out of his car, I walked up to him and he walked right past me. One of the guys called out, "Hey, Webby, that's Moon!" He turned back and shook my hand. It looked like Webster's body, but it didn't seem like the Mike Webster I knew and admired. It was like he was having some kind of outer-body experience. He just didn't make much sense. He didn't look right; his color was bad. He had lost a lot of weight. It was disappointing. It was strange. I haven't seen him since then.

I don't socialize with any of the Steelers, really. I see Randy Grossman more than most, Ted Petersen now and then. I always look forward to any of the dinners or fund-raisers or golf outings where I get to see the guys. They had a reunion of the team from the '70s a few years back at the Convention Center. It was great to see everyone. It didn't take long before we were talking about the old days, reminiscing about what we had experienced, and telling old war stories.

We got away with a lot of stuff in our day. We weren't under the microscope that these guys are under today, with the constant surveillance, the drug testing, the media scrutiny. We were wild and crazy at times. It seems like the media today is always looking for some shocking story or controversy.

"How do I fit in?"

I was a big-time high school player for a very successful program. I played for a high school legend. My coach was Clair Van Horbeck, and he had been at Anaheim High School some 40 years, and his team was almost always in the playoffs. We went to the Southern California championship; it was like the state title game here in Pennsylvania. Jimmy Fassel, the coach of the New York Giants, was on my high school championship team. He and Mike Holmgren, the coach and general manager of the Seattle Seahawks, were both players at USC when I was there.

I remember when I first made a visit to USC. They had a running back named Danny Scott show me around the campus. He was about 5-9 or 5-10, so I felt OK walking with him. Then he introduced me to two seniors who were tight ends. They were Bob Klein and Bob Miller, and they were both 6-5, 240 pounds. I started thinking I had made a mistake in wanting to go to USC. If these guys are tight ends, I thought, how do I fit in?

I was about six or seven years old, growing up in Anaheim, when they built and opened Disney Land there. So I know what it was like before and after. There used to be orange groves there and only about 30,000 people living in the community. They've had pro sports teams there, but it's never been a real sports town.

"It's worked out great."

It was a real shot in the dark. I was the first four-time Super Bowl guy to get cut, and it captured a lot of media attention. I actually had offers from a half-dozen different companies. I came here in 1980, and I've been here ever since. It's worked out great.

Bob Keaney was like a father to me. I got to be real close to him. He taught me the ropes of the business. He wanted to sell his business, too, and that idea appealed to me.

I'm envious of the kind of money they're making today. They can really retire after they're finished with football and never work again, if they don't want to. But few of them have the experiences we had or accomplished as much as athletes. What we accomplished is unbelievable. And a lot of our guys have been successful since they left football.

I remember the stir it caused when Joe Namath signed with the New York Jets of the AFL for a $400,000 multi-year contract. That's not even rookie minimum now in the NFL. They've all benefited from the guys who came before them, as we did.

We'll take those times to our graves. They can't take that away from you. We have those rings. We may not wear them, but we have them. It's not the rings so much as what we did to get them. You were thought of as the best of the best.

From Day One at my first training camp, I was adopted by two of the team's veteran linemen, Ray Mansfield and Bruce Van Dyke. They took me under their wing. I could digest all the stuff in the playbook pretty easily. I knew what to do. It wasn't taxing to me. A lot of it came naturally to me. I never had to overdo it in the classroom. I'm not saying I was smarter than the next guy, but those things just came naturally to me.

So when those veterans went out at night to the local bars and restaurants I went with them. I tagged along with them early on. They showed me some fine points of what I needed to know to make the team, to make the grade. The veteran players had more to offer that way. You might be having drinks, but they were moving salt and pepper shakers and sugar containers around the table to explain some schemes and maneuvers.

These were the glory days when Steelers return to Pittsburgh with victory in hand. All smiles, left to right, are Franco Harris, Terry Bradshaw and Moon Mullins. Mullins says he and Bradshaw were buddies, but he never hears from him anymore.

Moon Mullins observes from doorway as legendary figures Billy Conn and Art Rooney have some fun with Sam Davis. Mullins and Davis were the offensive guards on the best Steelers' teams. Conn and Rooney have since died, and Davis is in an assisted care facility in McKeesport. Mullins counts his blessings.

I think the Steelers are one of the best teams in the league right now. I believe they have a good offensive line, possibly the best group in the league, from what I hear. They've obviously been successful. Being a former offensive lineman, I know that how well they play dictates how well the offense does. I've had several conversations with Chuck Noll, and he always tells me our offensive line was very under-rated. He said it was one of the main strengths of the team. We had athletes on the line, and we did a lot of things they don't do much anymore, pulling and trapping. It's different today. You can't compare apples and oranges.

They're looking for big bodies, who can do straight-ahead blocking and pass-blocking. They have good backs who look for the hole and run. The game has changed. I remember a few years back when some of us former players were called in to meet the rookies. I remember meeting their No. 1 draft choice. His name was Jamain Stephens and he was 6-5 and 300 and some pounds. To look at that guy was unbelievable. Andy Russell was there, too, and he had been an undersized player, too. We started talking about how they wouldn't even draft guys like us anymore.

I hear the analysts today saying that guys like Jack Lambert and Jack Ham couldn't play now. That's nonsense. Those guys were so smart. They knew how to play the game. And they'd be bigger now. They would meet the expectations of today. There are football players who know what the hell they're doing. The great players have brains.

A guy like Jimmy Brown was bigger than most backs in his day. But he'd be a great player today, too. He was so far ahead of his time.

Another thing that has shaken me in recent years is to see guys dying that I played with. To see Ray Mansfield and Steve Furness and Tyrone McGriff go...that hurts. I saw Joe Gilliam at the last game at Three Rivers Stadium when they brought back all the old ballplayers. He seemed to have gotten his act together. He had a new wife; he looked great. Then he's dead a week or so later. That was the biggest shock.

I still feel like I did when I was 20, or so I think anyhow. You want to keep that youthful outlook. I saw Andy Russell and Mike Wagner on PCNC-TV last week. They look older. It's hard to believe that Andy is 60, but I'm not that far behind, either. I'm not that much younger.

When guys you played with are dying, well, mortality strikes home. Who's next? Is it going to be me?

> *"Chuck Noll is a good football coach. He and I don't talk much; we don't have to. I think we respect each other but we don't go around patting each other on the back about it. It's not his style, and it certainly isn't mine."*
> — Jack Lambert

"Chuck Noll was like the field general."

I think Chuck Noll was a great coach. He put together all that talent and kept it together. He managed all those egos and kept them under control. In retrospect, Chuck is really a good guy. At the time we were playing, though, he stayed aloof. Chuck Noll was like the field general. He didn't let you become buddies. He had to make tough personnel decisions. Looking back, he had some deep feelings about the guys. But he got rid of some talented players in the beginning because he didn't think they were going to fit into his team concept. In the '70s, when I came here, there were some good football players who didn't fit into his mold. He didn't feel their interests and the team interests were the same. He was obviously a good judge of talent, and he always had that team concept in mind.

There were outbreaks of egos during that 10-year period, but no real problems. There were a lot of great players. Look how many are in the Hall of Fame now. But no one let their ego be detrimental to the team. I remember Joe Greene and how if people got out of line Joe would get their attention in a hurry, and remind them how to behave. Chuck was always forthright with me. He let you know how he wanted things done. I never had any problems with him.

In retrospect, a lot of times you didn't agree. Some of the things didn't jibe with what you had in mind. As I got older, as I matured, I began to see the light in regard to some of his actions. I've had a chance to sit down with him at breakfasts at these golf outings, or situations like that, and talk to him. He's a lot more outgoing now than he was then. Back then, he was the authority figure, and you watched your Ps and Qs when you were around him. You didn't ask too many questions.

It's pretty impressive the way he kept things so cohesive for such a period of time. He was dealing with 40 to 45 idiots. He had a lot of egos to deal with; you know the guys we had.

There were no racial problems; it was never an issue. Chuck had something to do with that, too. Those guys were like brothers to me. I didn't give a damn about what color anybody was. We all went out together. I went to the Hall of Fame when Lynn Swann was inducted and I went when Jack Ham was inducted. I stayed the whole time when Swann went in — Ron Yary of USC was inducted that day, too — and it was pretty moving, seeing some of the old guys up there on the steps of the Hall of Fame. I didn't know Jack Youngblood personally, but I knew some of those guys from the Rams because I lived out there.

I didn't know the Rams players that well when I was growing up in Anaheim. My big goal in life was to be a high school football player. That's as far as I was looking. I lived a block away from the high school and I'd see the buses, with the football players on them, and the bands, going by my house to the football field. People would park in front of our house. There was so much excitement. I went to a lot of the games with my father. I loved the atmosphere, but football was never going to be my big interest in life. I didn't think about pro football until my junior year at USC when some pro scouts started coming around and talking to me.

John McKay was our head coach and I didn't think too highly of him, but he was one of the most successful coaches in the country. My offensive line coach at USC was Joe Gibbs. He went on to coach the Washington Redskins to Super Bowl titles. Now he's in the Hall of Fame. I was fortunate in my football career. I always had good coaches and I was always in good programs, from high school through college and in the pros. My high school team won championships, USC was right up there with Notre Dame as one of the nation's top college programs, and we know what the Steelers of the '70s accomplished.

I was very disappointed that the Steelers didn't get to the Super Bowl this year. They had a glaring weakness with their special teams. Their special teams coach (Jay Hayes) paid the ultimate price. He got his ass fired. In Chuck's era, he paid a lot of attention to special teams. That was one of his babies. I played on special teams throughout my whole career with the Steelers. A lot of guys who were starters played on special teams. That was a big deal to Chuck Noll. You took great pride in being a part of one of the special teams.

That was one of the things the veterans told me. They said you had to show your value right out of the blocks, and the best way to do it was to show your stuff on special teams. In Chuck's mind, it was a most important part of the team and the game preparation. Donnie Shell was the captain of the special teams even after he became a starter at strong safety in, I think, his fourth season with the team. Early on, he was a star special teams player. That's probably how he stuck as a free agent in the first place. That was true for Randy Grossman, another free agent that same year (1974).

Another coach who helped me a great deal was Dan Radakovich. He pushed all of us. He developed some interesting drills. He had us tape down our jerseys. He had us wear heavy bag boxing gloves to protect our hands. He never wanted any of us to get hurt in practice. That was a big thing with him. We all fought tooth and nail to maintain our positions. Now they can use their hands more; they can just latch on to guys and hold on. Rad, he stood out from a coaching standpoint. He's the guy who pushed me the hardest.

Whether you liked the guy or not didn't matter. He made me stand out.

I've been out a few times to see him since he started coaching at Robert Morris. There was a time when I didn't like him that well, but now he's become a good friend of mine. He's like the strict teacher you didn't like in grade school but you came to admire and appreciate when you got older. We were fortunate to have good assistant coaches, too, when I played for the Steelers.

From ownership all the way down we had a great organization. Art Rooney . . . he was the greatest. And Dan knew what he was doing in running the business and holding everything together. It was really amazing to me how Art Rooney treated us, and how much he liked to be with us. A guy in that position riding in the back of the plane or the bus with the guys on road trips. I think he really took a sincere interest. You're willing to play hard for a guy like that. The whole Rooney family was great to me.

I just don't think the players today could put themselves in the position to know what we had.

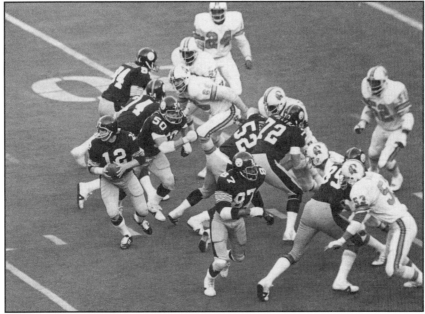

George Gojkovich

Steelers took great pride in executing intricate blocking schemes. Terry Bradshaw gets set to hand off ball behind blocking of, left to right, Randy Grossman (84), Ray Pinney (74), Jim Clack (50), Mike Webster (52), Moon Mullins (72), Larry Brown (87) and Bennie Cunningham (89).

J.T. Thomas
The Reverend

"Life is a dash or a blank."

From his spacious corner office on the third floor of the Edgewood Towne Centre Building, which used to be the Union Switch & Signal corporate headquarters, on South Braddock Avenue in Swissvale, J. T. Thomas can see the Mt. Royal Towers. That is an apartment complex in Squirrel Hill where he lived when he first joined the Pittsburgh Steelers in the fall of 1973.

That is where he first got to know Larry Brown, one of the other Steelers who stayed there. Now Thomas and Brown are partners who own and operate 13 Applebee's Neighborhood Grill and Restaurants in the western half of Pennsylvania under the umbrella of B.T. Woodlipp, Inc. For information, you can check their website at www.steelapple.com. As you see, they still pride themselves on their Steeler connection.

Brown was busy at his desk in the adjoining office when I visited on Monday, February 11, 2002. One of their restaurants was nearby in the Edgewood Towne Centre, on the border of Edgewood and Swissvale, just off the Parkway East. Thomas had gotten into the restaurant business in 1987.

Thomas, a defensive back, was the first round draft choice of the Steelers in 1973. He was the first black to play football at Florida State University in Tallahassee. He was among the first black children to integrate the public schools in his hometown of Macon, Georgia. Thomas liked being first in a lot of ways. He was a member of three Super Bowl championship teams, missing the 1979 title game because of an illness that sidelined him the entire season. He was stricken with a life-threatening viral illness called Boeck's Sarcoidosis. He recovered to rejoin the team the following season when they repeated as Super Bowl champions.

He has taught Sunday school and he directs the choir at the Ebenezer Baptist Church in the Hill District. He had recently undergone arthroscopic surgery on his left hip. Dr. Marc Philippon of UPMC Sports Medicine Center told him, "I'm taking your thoroughbred card away, and giving you a Clydesdale card. Don't bitch; you could be a mule."

He also turned the big 50 on April 22, 2001. He had been married since 1973 to Deborah Thomas, a librarian/reading specialist teacher in the Gateway Area School District. They had two children of their own, Kimberly, 26, and James Terrell, 22. They also adopted two children of his sister Frashia when she died in 1989. His teenage nieces are Ava, 17, and Amanda, 15. He also has a sister, Adriane, 41, and a brother, Victor, 39.

Jim O'Brien

Thomas doesn't get as much attention as some Steelers Alumni, but he is definitely one of the most successful in his post-playing career.

J.T. Thomas:

I know a lot about praying and about celebrating, but I am puzzled and disappointed by what I see going on during NFL games these days. I have a deep knowledge of religion. I went to a Catholic grade school in Macon even though we were Baptists. I went to mass on Sunday morning with my class, and then I was at a Baptist church the rest of the day. With the Baptists in the South, Sunday was an all-day deal at church. You even ate there.

My religion is Baptist, but my faith is Christianity. My faith means a lot to me. It's been the backbone of my life. At the same time, I believe that God doesn't really give a damn about football games. I never prayed at pre-game prayer when I was playing for the Steelers. I thought it was dumb. There were 28 NFL teams praying to God that day, asking him to help them do well, to stay well, and to help them win the game. I thought they were all putting God on the spot. He couldn't answer everyone's prayers.

I used to pray to God at mid-week. So I was already in by Sunday. I never asked him to help my team win, or me to do super things. I just prayed for his blessing. Now I see these guys making the sign of the cross in the end zone after they score a touchdown. Or, I see them gathering at mid-field, from both teams, to say a prayer after the game. I don't understand it. To me, there's a proper time and place to do one's praying. It should be more of a private thing. It shouldn't be for show.

I love to go to church. It's just something that's in me. I play the piano and the organ, and I have been involved with church choirs since I was a kid.

I don't understand the constant celebrations on the field. They celebrate like they were surprised they just did what they did. It's like a little kid trying to impress his father. Chuck Noll used to say. "Look like you've been there before." He didn't want us showing anyone up, or carrying on after we made a tackle or scored a touchdown or intercepted a pass. These guys are celebrating on every play anymore: a routine tackle or a routine catch, a five-yard-run. It's crazy.

They run down the field 20 or 30 yards after they've done something, and they're losing the game! It's a waste of time in many ways. You have to invest some time into choreographing some of those dances and celebrations. A football game is like a chess game. You've got to keep your head about you. You should be in the huddle, getting the call for the next play. You can't get fouled up psychologically. You lose focus if you're more concerned about how you're going to celebrate the next play. My talking was done in the huddle.

Hey, we were crazy in our own way when I was playing left cornerback for the Steelers when we had those great teams in the '70s. Our first Super Bowl teams had some real personalities on both sides of the ball, but especially on our defensive side.

On our defensive line, left to right, we had L.C. Greenwood, Joe Greene, Ernie Holmes and Dwight White. Behind them, we had Jack Ham, Jack Lambert and Andy Russell. Then we had Mel Blount and me at the corners, and Mike Wagner and Pine Edwards at the safeties.

That was some group; that was a great group. But what went on in those defensive huddles was so funny people don't believe me when I tell them about it. I still have to laugh when I reflect on what went on in the huddle.

Greene was getting on them. He was so nasty in those days. He really was Mean Joe Greene in the beginning. He mellowed out when he got that Coke commercial, tossing his towel to that kid in the hallway when he was coming off the field. He started living up to his new TV image. Before that, believe me, he was Mean Joe Greene. Then you had Lambert; he was nasty, too. If you're going down a dark alley at night you want to have Greene and Lambert with you.

Ernie wouldn't even come into the huddle half the time. He'd be up there standing over the ball, like he wasn't going to let them touch it, telling his man what he was going to do to him on the next snap. Lambert would be hollering at him, "Fats, get your ass in the huddle!" And Ernie, or Fats, whatever he was going by that day, didn't pay him no mind. Ernie didn't get the play half the time. He didn't give a damn what the play was anyhow. He did what he wanted to do. That upset Dwight. He said you couldn't trust Ernie to do what he was supposed to be doing. He'd leave you out there on an island sometimes.

White and I were roommates for a long time. He'd say, "Home, I can't trust Fats. No matter what we call, he might change his mind." Fats had a psychological reason for why he changed his mind when he'd get called on it. He never did anything wrong.

Edwards was from the old school. He and Fats always wanted to take out people, cold-cock them and leave them for dead. Glen was always saying he was going to knock somebody out. He raised a whole lot of hell if somebody let a running back get through the line and he had to make the tackle. He was always praising the line when they did well. "Hey, you make me look good!" he'd holler. He would say something on every play.

White was always hollering in the huddle about how he was being held, and how he was getting cut at the knees. He was going to get back at his guy. He was always talking. He'd tell the guy across from him, "Do your Momma know you're out here?" Those guys were always talking about somebody's momma. White was always talking non-stop. You tell White I knew what was going on in the trenches, no matter what he says, because I watched them, and I knew things weren't right when they let some 250-pound back slip past them and I'd have to take him on head-on. So I do know.

Andy Russell always seemed out of place on that right side of the field. He was more sophisticated than the rest of the guys. He was quieter and more reserved. He was caught in the middle. Sandwiched between some mad characters. Sometimes, Andy was the mediator out there.

Mike Wagner and L.C. Greenwood — they were both great guys — but they were on the quiet side, too. So they stayed on the outside of the huddle, talking to each other, and laughing at the scene.

Mel felt he could go bump and run on any receiver in the league, and that's what he wanted to do, no matter what coverage was called. We had a lot of calls and checks, but sometimes we did our own thing within the concept of a call.

We weren't always on the same page, and Chuck Noll knew it. Bud Carson, our defensive backfield coach, really knew his stuff. But sometimes we didn't like his call, and we'd do something else and say we were confused if he called us over and asked us what the hell we were doing. Carson would go crazy at times when we'd make our own adjustments. We knew what we could do because we knew each other's strengths and habits.

The other team knew what Mel was going to do. He didn't care. I'm trying to disguise our defensive set-up so the other team isn't sure. Mel didn't care what they thought. He was going to bump and run. They knew exactly where he was going to be when the ball was snapped. By the way, and I know they didn't keep track of these things, but Mel got beat for more TDs than I did. I've got to stay ahead of him some way.

When they'd hand out the playbook at training camp, Mel would stick it in his car trunk, next to the spare tire, so he could find it. Because they fined you $500 if you lost the playbook. Mel would tell the coaches, "I don't have to read the playbook. What are you passing those books out for? I wrote the playbook!"

We had more check-offs and audibles. We had good athletes and we were versatile. We didn't like zone. We wanted to go man-to-man. The rules were different then than they are now. We could jam those receivers and stay in their face. Mel liked to hit them in the face before they even got off the line.

Ham is in the middle of all that, and he didn't know the set we were in half the time. He'd be hollering to L.C. or me, asking what the call was. "What are we in?" he'd be hollering. "What's the check?"

I told him my name should be on his plaque at the Pro Football Hall of Fame as his sponsor or something. He'd be waving his fingers at me, trying to get the number we were in. He was such a good athlete, and had a nose for the ball, and had L.C. and Joe doing the dirty work in front of him. So Jack did the right thing more often than not. At the snap of the ball, Ham knew where to go. How he got it, or how he learned what to do, was a mystery sometime. He would make the play. He had such great instincts. He could size up what he was seeing in a hurry and know how to respond.

That whole defense was like that. We did some things instinctively. After years of playing with each other, we knew what the other guy was going to do in a certain situation. Carson was a genius. He knew how to coach us. We had a lot of improvisation, and he learned to live with it.

Bud Carson had you thinking that guy doesn't belong on the field with you. He wanted you to bump them into the ground.

One time in a game at Denver, Haven Moses caught a touchdown pass on me; he went up high and pulled it in, jumping above me and catching it one-handed in the end zone. They were at the five-yard line and we were jammed pretty tight. Greene got upset, and came back and got in my face. He screamed in my face, "What the hell's wrong with you? You can't defend against a pass like that?" Dwight came in and defended me. He hollered at Greene, "If they hadn't been trapping your ass one play after another, they wouldn't have been on the five yard line in the first place." Dwight and Greene are going at it in the huddle. It was unreal.

Chuck picked up on it and at halftime he comes to me and asks, "T., what is going on out there? Are they pointing fingers out there?" I told him that was exactly what was going on.

There were other times that Dwight and Fats were going at it. You wouldn't believe the stuff they were saying. Fats gets mad. Next thing you know, Fats is mad at Greene, too. Fats is saying he's going to bring his piece (gun) to practice that week, that he ain't taking shit from anybody. There's no doubt that Fats was the most intimidating person on the defensive line.

He automatically hurt people. He was probably the strongest of the linemen, and he went at it the same way in practice. Dan Radakovich never wanted his offensive linemen to get hurt in practice, and they had to pull Ernie out of practice a lot because he didn't know how to go half-speed. He was even nastier than Joe Greene. Joe was more of a finesse guy.

Chuck would say to Ernie, "Save something for the game!" But Ernie didn't know the difference. He had intensity and stamina. If he had taken his personal conditioning seriously, he would have been one of the all-time greats. But he ate himself out of the league, and he had some personal behavioral problems.

There was a commitment to excellence. Conditioning was important to Chuck. If you weren't in good shape, he didn't want you around. Even the defensive backs had to trim down after we got to camp. If you had a 33" or 34" waistline when you came to camp, you were down to 31" by the time you broke camp.

Chuck had a sense of his team. I think Chuck's greatest asset was a communicator. Verbally and non-verbally. He could play with your mind. He could motivate you with a few words, or with a look. He could look at you with a certain look in his eyes and you knew what he wanted.

Look at the characters he had to deal with. Yet he could communicate with them. I liked him. The guys who didn't, well, I don't think they understood him. From my rookie year in camp, he knew what buttons to push. I was the L3 guy on the kickoff team. I was supposed to go down and break the blocking wedge. I'd be working my way down field, dodging this guy and that one, trying to make my way to the ballcarrier. I'm picking and choosing my way. He'd look at me and holler, "Where is that 4.4 speed?" He knew I was a church person, and he'd add, "T., you know what they say about how the meek shall inherit the earth...." He just stabbed me. He knew I knew the Bible. He knew how to get to me.

I was on the punt return and speed team when I was starting at the corner. Chuck took a personal interest in the special teams — he was the special teams' coach, really — and made sure the best people were out there.

I was talking to Mel and Franco after the AFC title game this year. They were on the sideline for that game. Franco couldn't believe the way they were communicating with each other on the sideline during the game. Franco was appalled by their attitude. They were getting on each other. He and Mel thought the Steelers had a better team than New England, but that New England was more into the game. We had a breakdown with our special teams that afternoon, the way we

Steelers celebrate interception by Donnie Shell. Defenders, from left to right, are Jack Ham (59), Shell (31), Dwayne Woodruff and J.T. Thomas (24). Below, Thomas breaks up pass at Three Rivers Stadium.

Photos by George Gojkovich

saw it. On our team, guys took pride in being on the special teams. Donnie Shell was the captain of the special teams even after he became a starter at strong safety, after he replaced Glen Edwards in our lineup.

New England put eleven men up on the line defensively. You're saying, "OK, now beat me." That's what we used to do. Every third-down situation, we'd get up in their face. We did the same thing in the Super Bowl.

They pointed at the special teams after the game as the reason they lost. To us, we were all in it together. If our offense was struggling, Chuck would say, "C'mon, defense, you gotta score! We're struggling, we need some help!"

I think, mentally, there's a level you go to in the playoffs and Super Bowl. It starts at the top. There's an old saying that where a snake's head goes so goes his body. There's a certain mind-set you have to have. That comes from the top. It's not emotions; it's not rah rah.

I know where that zone is. Chuck had us thinking we already won the game. We were gonna win, no mistake about that. We didn't take the game for granted, but we were going to win. We never thought about losing.

I remember Super Bowl X, when we were playing the Dallas Cowboys in Miami. Both teams were in the tunnels, waiting to be introduced. We could see some of the Cowboys from where we were standing. Our defense was going to be introduced, and their offense was going to be introduced. We could see Roger Staubach and Drew Pearson. Dwight White starts hollering. He said their eyes were glazed. "Lookit, their eyes!" White is screaming. "We got their ass!" He was right, they looked petrified. They looked like the Children of the Damned. Pine Edwards was on them, too, before we even took the field! We beat them better than the final score (21-17) would indicate.

I think the current Steelers have a lot of ability. Talent-wise, they're fine. But I see an immaturity. They don't know what their role is. Maybe they'll grow in that respect. Kordell Stewart's maturity was a big difference in the team this year. He really came a long way. He handled the interviews better, too. Before, he was saying, "Get off my back and leave me alone." Now he is more mature. He had always been a great athlete. He had to go through certain adversities, and he came through that. I admired that.

It reminded me of Joe Gilliam. His biggest problem was not being able to manage the time he was in, the era. He came out of a middle-class, protected environment, where he had gone to a little black school at Tennessee State University. He was immune to the world of politics. I was the first African-American at Florida State University, and I had gone through the integration days in the Deep South schools, so I was a little better prepared for the pro environment. Gilly got involved in drugs and it shortened his pro career and, in the end, killed him.

It hurt when Joe Gilliam died. I saw Gilly at that last game at Three Rivers Stadium. I talked to him about where he was in life. He looked good. He appeared to be OK. He had a new perspective, he had become spiritual and said he had Christ in his life. I thought he had his life in order. You can tell when a guy is leveling with you. He couldn't bullshit us. But drugs are powerful; I guess you never get over it, really. Maybe coming back and seeing how everyone was doing had a negative affect on his psyche. Who knows? He might have asked himself, "Where am I in my life?" Maybe he heard the guys talking about their different ventures. Maybe he never had a good support system.

Athletes are very insecure. They're always comparing themselves with the other guy. "Am I as good as you?" There's a lot of "if I coulda, woulda, shoulda . . ." When their athletic careers are over it's like a death. A lot of them can't handle it. They're constantly trying to regain the spotlight. That's all they know.

"I was scared for my life."

They used to call me "Rev" because I always carried my Bible on the airplane. When there was some air turbulence they wanted to come and sit with me. Most of the guys grew up in church-oriented families, and some of them got away from it for awhile. The Catholic nuns scared me so much about hell when they taught me in grade school, and then I was at Baptist services all day Sunday, so I was scared for my life.

I was superstitious, too. So I always sat in the last seat on the left hand side of the airplane. When I was in college, I used to see pictures of airplane wrecks and the tail of the plane was always visible. So I figured that was a good place to be. I always sat by the window and Lynn Swann sat in the aisle seat and we kept one seat open between us so we'd have more room. When anyone asked if the seat was open we made up the name of somebody who was going to be sitting there. The only exception was Art Rooney. We let The Chief sit there when he came back looking for a place to sit. I liked The Chief.

He knew I went to a parochial school. I went back to my old school, St. Peter Claver School, after we won our first Super Bowl. They ran a picture of that in a national Catholic newspaper, and The Chief saw that. He thought I was a Catholic. He and Tom Foerster went around on Tuesday

97

nights and visited Catholic schools, and they had me come with them and speak. I learned a lot from The Chief as a person. For two years, he always called me "T.J." Finally, I said to him, "Mr. Rooney, my name is not T.J." He said, "I called you that because I had a friend named T.J. Tell me, what's the name on your paycheck?" I said it was J.T. He said, "OK, then you don't have a problem." I will say this. After I brought it up, he never called me "T.J." after that.

I think Mr. Rooney was important to the success of our team. He set the tone for treating people the right way. You'd see him at practices standing in the middle of the ground crew, talking to them. He took them on road trips, even to the Super Bowl. He had time for everybody. He treated everyone the same. I learned a lot from him.

We've tried to create a culture in our restaurant business that will enable us to be successful. We stress teamwork. I'm in the people business. Everyone has to concern themselves with profit-and-loss statements, but I manage homo sapiens. I don't want to manage people; I want to lead people. I can manage you with a .38 or a whip. I want to be a mentor. I want to inspire people to give their best effort, to extend themselves to be at their best, and to give the customers the best meal and the best experience possible. I want our restaurants to be a place of comfort for our customers in every respect. We're into casual dining and we want to do it better than the next guy.

Otis Redding Jr., James Brown and Tarzan

When I got sick between the 1978 and 1979 seasons, they said it was a blood disorder at first. It wasn't cancer or leukemia, as was first feared. It was a rare disease called Boeck's Sarcoidosis. It first showed up in chest x-rays. I went in for a check-up because I had no speed or stamina. I know the value of good health now. Life has no meaning if you're not healthy. That was a big wake-up call.

When you go to a cemetery, you realize that life is a dash or a blank. They have your birth date and your death date and there's a dash or blank in between. That's what your life is. How you fill that dash or blank is what it's all about. You come into life with a beginning date and you wind up with an end date. I value life.

What's the purpose of life? It's not about J.T. It's very little about me. One time I didn't think that way. You have to help others. It's more residual. Initially, everything was centered around me.

I came out of a poor background in Macon, Georgia. I had the opportunity to go to a parochial school, and was taught by the Sisters of Blessed Sacrament. They provided me with tutelage and guidance. We wore uniforms and there was a lot of structure in our school. I was with all my friends, mostly black students. When it was time to go to junior high school, Mother Josepha, I remember her name, told my mother I should go to one of the white schools when they were integrated. So I was thrown right into the heat of integration at the age of 13.

I was escorted to school by state troopers and dogs. They used the same dogs they had used earlier to control us during demonstrations. Now those dogs were protecting us. That's a bit of an irony. There were 17 other African-American students. One of them was my friend Ken Nixon, who was the brother of Norm Nixon, who played here at Duquesne University and later with the Los Angeles Lakers.

Hey, if I wanted to get something at our Burger King, I had to go to the back door to pick it up. I remember when I couldn't sit in the front of the bus, and I remember when we were allowed, and a lot of blacks still didn't do it. I did. I wanted to sit up front. If you did, you got looked at. I sat right behind the bus driver. And that wasn't so long ago. I shined shoes at a stand at the Burger King. That's how I made some extra money. I could spit shine shoes with the best of them. My shoes always looked good.

I was a piano player, and I played at several churches. Otis Redding Sr. has his own Baptist church. His son sang there at times when he came to town. I used to go to a talent show at our local movie theater and Otis Redding and James Brown would be performing. That was before the "Tarzan" movie.

That was the Douglas Theater. It's still there. It's a national landmark. It was a black theatre. I went to watch Tarzan beat up on all the black natives. I'd be wearing my PF Flyers tennis shoes, white T-shirt and black pants. I was dressed up. I was 13 years old and thinking I was real liberal in my thinking. And there I was rooting for Tarzan. I was definitely a work in progress.

I was fighting for liberation. I didn't realize the whole psychology of what I was watching. Tarzan could talk to all the elephants, lions and apes and get them to do things, and the Africans, who'd been there all along, are afraid of the animals. Tarzan can talk those animals into helping him kick the asses of the natives. What was I thinking?

> *"Great artists are people who find themselves in their art."*
> — Margot Fonteyn

"We were playing to belong."

There were efforts made at one time in this country to get blacks not to trust one another. There was some real brainwashing. It was different with the guys who were on those great Steelers teams. Most of the guys had come from backgrounds where they were principled and value-based. The African-Americans had come out of situations where they'd seen the transition from segregation to integration. We were playing for our manhood and dignity. We were playing to belong. We were saying, "Hey, we are equal." A lot of our players came from the South, and they had a spiritual background, even the white players like Terry Bradshaw from Louisiana and Jon Kolb from Oklahoma, had been raised in Christian homes. Those two often hosted and led Bible study sessions for the rest of us at their apartments and homes.

That helped bring our team together. Another thing that helped us that doesn't get a lot of attention is something I think really brought the team together. In the early '60s, Dr. Vaughn Nixon had parties for the team, and he invited everyone. The guys brought their families. There was not a lot of integrating of the players otherwise, but we all came. Dr. Nixon's parties had as much to do with our coming together as anything. That's where we got to know each other. The bonding began there.

"His attitude sets him apart."

Looking at the current team, I think Chad Scott, from an ability standpoint, has the greatest talent of the cornerbacks.

I don't think they've got a defensive back who plays as physical as Ty Law (of the New England Patriots). His attitude sets him apart. I think Scott has the same skills as Ty Law. He may have more skills in the raw. Law is a smart cornerback, too.

I look at the Steelers' secondary as probably the most vulnerable part of their defense. If I had to rate them one to ten, I'd give them a five. Up front, they're very good.

Part of the Steelers' and the Rams' problem was they weren't used to being contested. They weren't used to teams getting in their face and challenging them to get off the line, making it tough to run their patterns.

I thought Rod Woodson was a first-rate defensive back. I never would have played him at cornerback. I think he could have been the greatest free safety in history. The way he played, I don't think he was a great one-on-one guy. He could be beaten. If he had played safety, his speed and intelligence would have served him better. He'd have had a hundred interceptions and he could come up and stick people.

We had a good and under-rated safety in Mike Wagner. Mike had good speed. Mike had a heart and he was very, very intelligent. His heart was bigger or just as big as anybody on our team then. He was mean, too, though people didn't think of him that way. He looked like a college teacher or a Sunday school teacher, but we thought he was dirty, too.

He was really the quarterback of our secondary. Mel and I got locked into the man-to-man thing, and Mike was like a coordinator out there on the field. Mike was the first guy to see how the other team was lining up. He called the audibles. Most of our adjustments were made by Lambert and Wagner. But Mike had an even better view of things. He was the first guy who could recognize what the other team was doing. He's in the middle of the field; he has the best view. You see everything.

The play is so different, the way they play today. The margin for error or the risk is not as great. My second year in the league, I got beat once for a touchdown. Bud Carson (the defensive coordinator) came up to me and said, "You've got two more of those!" The meaning was that if you gave up three touchdowns you were going to lose your starting job. I remember another time when Ken Burroughs of Houston beat me for a touchdown. As I came to the sideline, Chuck Noll came up to me and said, "T., is that one or two?" That got your attention. You knew the standards. They were strict.

Today, you can get beat five or six times and still be out there. It's not a stat that the league keeps, but it's one that the players and coaches kept.

Former Steeler teammates and friends Larry Brown, left, and J.T. Thomas have forged successful business careers as partners in 13 Applebee's Neighborhood Grill & Bar establishments in western end of Pennsylvania.

Larry Brown
He had high expectations

"I knew what I wanted to be."

Larry Brown was an offensive lineman for the Steelers for fourteen seasons, from 1971 to 1984, first as a tight end and then as a tackle. He was a valued member of four Super Bowl championship teams.

There has always been a quiet dignity about Larry Brown. He is an appealing person. He has to be prodded to talk, especially to talk about himself. He laughs easily. He was often amused by those around him in the Steelers' locker room. He was the proverbial fly on the wall. He watched and he listened. He seldom started any shenanigans, but sat on his stool like a heavyweight boxer and smiled at what he saw.

Whenever I would approach him at his dressing stall in the Steelers' clubhouse, he would always smile, and ask me why I wanted to talk to him. He never saw himself as one of the main subjects for stories. But there was a quality about him that was so compelling for anyone seeking real insights into life in the NFL. It was always time well spent. Hey, this was a future business executive.

He was a fifth round draft choice in 1971 from the University of Kansas, taken with a choice the Steelers had obtained in a trade with the New Orleans Saints. The Steelers had a terrific draft class that year, also picking up Frank Lewis of Grambling and Jack Ham of Penn State with their first two selections, as well as Steve Davis, Gerry Mullins, Dwight White, Craig Hanneman, Ernie Holmes, Mike Wagner and Al Young. It was a class that continued the Steelers advancement toward fielding a first-class football team under Coach Chuck Noll.

Brown grew up in Starke, Florida, located about 40 miles west of Jacksonville and 26 miles east of Gainesville. It's a town of about 8,000 residents. His father, Willie Brown, worked at a DuPont plant, and they mined minerals that went into their products. His dad spent time in a quarry digging pigment for paints. It was a dirty job.

Brown was one of the mainstays of the Steelers' strong but too often uncelebrated offensive line. It was not until 1983 that Brown was chosen to play in the Pro Bowl, an honor that eluded Mullins, Jon Kolb and Sam Davis.

Brown and former teammate J.T. Thomas were partners in the restaurant business, owning and operating 13 Applebee's Neighborhood Grill and Bar establishments, mostly in the southwestern end of the state.

They had outlets in Robinson Township, Scott Township, West Mifflin, North Hills, Edgewood, Peters Township, Johnstown,

Jim O'Brien

Newest Steeler Hall of Fame inductee John Stallworth enjoys seeing former teammate Larry Brown, seen in action below, against New York Jets.

Larry Brown

Morgantown, Wilkins Township, Altoona, Washington and Canonsburg. Their corporate offices were in Swissvale, near one of their restaurants in the Edgewood Town Centre. They were exploring the possibility of opening another outlet in State College. When Brown and Thomas were initially teammates with the Steelers, they had both lived in the Mt. Royal Towers that were visible from windows in their offices at the western end of the building.

Brown had been married to Vanessa Thornton for 29 years, and they have made their home in Carnegie throughout their marriage. She hailed from McDonald, Pennsylvania and was a graduate of the University of Pittsburgh and the University of Pittsburgh Law School. She managed litigation for Allegheny Technologies. Some found Vanessa Brown more of a formidable figure than Larry Brown. You didn't want to mess with Vanessa. Larry was a lamb by comparison.

Larry and Vanessa both lost their mothers within a month of each other four years earlier. Her father William Thornton, known as "Poss," was a well-known figure in McDonald. His death earlier in the year was a setback for the community. The Browns had two children, Ron, 32, and Tiffany, 27.

When I told Larry I was pleased in my interviews with some of the current players to find young men who were personable, respectful, solid and eager to make their mark with the Steelers and with the people of Pittsburgh.

"I've had good experiences with some of the young players I've met at various events," allowed Larry Brown. "Everybody is quick, including myself, to say how different players are today. So it's good to hear you say positive things about them. You hope they will understand their roles and make the most of their opportunities. It's a demanding life, but it's a good life. It can open the right doors."

Larry Brown:

I felt badly about Tony Dungy losing his job as head coach at Tampa Bay. Tony deserved better. He'd done a great job there, better than anybody before him. But it looks like he ended up with a better job for more money in Indianapolis. Someone's always going to want Tony. The Colts' offensive coordinator, Tom Moore, is an old friend of Tony's and someone he was worked with successfully before. They were together at the University of Minnesota and with the Steelers. Tony was very popular when he played with the Steelers (1977-78). Everybody liked him. Everybody on our team was saddened when he was traded to the 49ers at training camp (in 1979).

I was also disappointed that Marvin Lewis didn't get the job in Tampa Bay once it was open. It looked for awhile like Marvin was the guy they wanted, then the owners went against the general manager's thinking, and changed their minds. At the last minute, it seems. Maybe Marvin ended up better off, too. He left Baltimore where he was the defensive coordinator for a Super Bowl championship team two years earlier to become the best-paid (around $850,000 a year plus incentives) defensive coordinator in the league at Washington. He's what the Redskins need. Their new coach, Steve Spurrier, is coming from Florida with a reputation as an offensive genius. Marvin gives him a guy who really knows defense and, just as important, knows the National Football League. It could be a perfect fit. I know Marvin was highly respected and liked when he was an assistant coach on Bill Cowher's staff (1992-1995) here in Pittsburgh. He looked after the linebackers for the Steelers.

Marvin grew up in house next door to my wife's family in McDonald. So I watched him grow up. My wife's brother, Kevin, and Marvin were good friends. McDonald is a small community and it has an even smaller black community. So everyone there was excited when there were news stories speculating that Marvin was going to be hired as the new head football coach in Tampa Bay. The town already claims one head football coach in the NFL in Marty Schottenheimer. Marty went from McDonald to Pitt, just like my wife, and then to the NFL. He's had several coaching jobs in the NFL. Everyone in McDonald knew Marvin well and everyone liked him. He was just that kind of person. There were stories on the radio that he had the job. Then there were stories saying it wasn't so, that there was a snag. They were setting up celebrations in McDonald. I was talking on the telephone one day with someone from McDonald and they thought it was a done deal. I told them to hold up, that I had heard something that it might not happen. It was confusing. It was so bizarre. They thought it was a done deal. Then it fell through. The owners wouldn't go along with the general manager's choice. It hurt to hear that. Knowing him personally, I thought Marvin would do a great job and I thought he deserved a shot like that.

Marvin never forgot where he came from. He called my wife when her dad died. And he died during the playoffs (in January of 2002). He took the time, when so much was going on around him and there was such a demand on his time, but he was always like that. That meant a lot to us.

Marvin Lewis is special. I think he's a guy who cares a lot about what he's doing. I remember the kid who went off to college. He was a running quarterback for McDonald. He went off to college in the West, at Idaho State, I think. I remember when he came back. He was interested in coaching. I remember he wanted to watch film all the time. He got a chance to do that. He coached somewhere out West, and he got himself started in the coaching business.

He was very much a student of the game. He went after it. He has a passion for it. It's something you pursue, at first, not for the money, but because you just want to do it. It's a calling. It's who you are. Marvin has been recognized as one of the top coordinators. It's only a matter of time before he becomes a head coach somewhere.

I knew Tony well, too, and I saw him grow up as well. Tony was very similar in manner to Marvin. Not to roll them all in the same ball or anything, but there are a lot of similarities. Marvin is very passionate. He's not as demonstrative as Bill Cowher on the sideline. Marvin is a competitor and he plays tough. His defense is a reflection of him. It's hard-nosed and tough. That's what he's coaching.

"People saw their success through the team's success."

You have to look at yourself and see what you see. I played for the Pittsburgh Steelers for 14 seasons. I played two different positions. I was a tight end when I first got here from Kansas, and then I became a tackle. I respected the Rooneys and Chuck Noll. I saw them as being fair. They certainly were fair to me. The Rooneys were tough in negotiations. But I thought they were fair. I could see what they were trying to do. There were personnel issues. They put the best people in positions where they could succeed. They had to determine the proper compensation. I deal with the same issues in our restaurant business. Wanting and appreciating good employees is the basis of our business. You want to build the best company and you have to run a business. Those decisions are yours to make. There's no question about it that there are parallels in running a football team and a restaurant business. You need the right people to be a winner.

You're dealing with similar things. There are tough decisions to be made. If you were putting a profile together for a championship team there'd be many of the same qualities you'd be looking for and assessing.

In hindsight, you can see much more clearly than you could when you were playing. It's hard to put things in perspective when you're involved with it. Chuck Noll and his coaches were good at assessing and assembling talent. Gerry Mullins was a tight end in college just like I was. But they moved him to tackle and guard and he was great at it. They had to put him in when there were veteran players ahead of him who were better at the time. You have to put the player in before he's as good as the guy who's there. That creates some conflict. They have to give him some time to learn and develop.

All of us were selfish to a degree, but we learned to sublimate that for the good of the team. In time, people saw their success through the team's success. I think, without exception, people were working for team goals. At the time, that's how you made extra money. At that time, you could make as much in the playoffs and in the Super Bowl as you made during the season. Having done it before, they wanted to do it again. The team gained national attention and the spotlight shone on everybody.

Chuck used to talk about getting on with your life's work. So a firing is not always a bad thing, not for the company and not for the person. Maybe there's something else out there where a person will be happier and where they will make more money. So it's not necessarily a bad thing for the company or for the person.

"It hurt to see what happened to Joe."

There were some controversial decisions made about the players when I was with the Steelers. Looking back now you can see why some of the decisions were made. You realize now why this guy should play or that guy should play. I hate to use cliches, but it was usually about team chemistry. A player may not be better than another player, but he may make the team better. Bruce Van Dyke was a good player, but they thought Gerry Mullins would be a more valuable player in time, that he'd fit better. That was an example of a controversial player personnel decision. Players would take sides about the wisdom of such moves.

Joe Gilliam, for instance, was a wonderful talent. Joe was a very likable person. Everybody liked him. He was very talented. They decided to go with Bradshaw, over Gilliam and over Terry Hanratty, who was also popular and had his support group as well.

It hurt to see what happened to Joe. Then to have him die so soon after we'd all seen him at the last game at Three Rivers Stadium. It seemed like he had gotten his act together. I spent some time talking to him. I was impressed with how he looked and how he was talking. I had seen him before that and he seemed so much better. He seemed to be recovered.

He seemed hopeful. He was talking about his daughter. He made a point of how long he'd been sober or free of drugs, and how challenging it was. You were impressed and believing it. So I was somewhat shocked to learn that he had died from an overdose of heroin. I might not have been if I hadn't spent time with him two weeks earlier. I had mixed feelings about what happened. He seemed like a different person. Addicts, they say, have a lot of con in them. I could never understand why anyone got hooked on drugs. There was never an attraction for me. It wasn't a seductive kind of thing for me. But it's a seductive kind of thing for other people. I've seen that, in sports and in the restaurant business.

I've had success in sports and I want to have success in life. The script is still being written. You have different kinds of success along the way. At the end of the day, philosophically, it's about the journey. You're living your life; you're learning as you go.

It all comes down to the person. It comes down to the quality of your life. It's about how you were impacted and how you impacted others. It's not something that's quantifiable. How many people did you touch?

I am a product of my family and the teachers and coaches I was exposed to. I take a tremendous amount of pride in what I have accomplished and what I hope to accomplish.

The way I see and feel about people is based on what I learned from my parents. My mother and dad taught me so much. My mom was more verbal than my father. My mom talked. I think I have the ability to see through things and reduce it down to a person's qualities. I am interested in the fundamental person, not someone who is going to be over-enamored with what they might do. I am interested in performance, the accomplishment.

I interview a lot of people for positions with our company. Sitting across a table from someone you can pick up a lot, just talking to somebody. They're tying to impress you, at least that's the idea. You'd be amazed at what people will think would impress. Some people kill themselves with what they say in an interview.

"We have to take care of our guests."

I miss the joy of playing. What I miss the most are the guys. We had some real characters in our clubhouse. We had some guys with a great sense of humor. Some of the nicest times were in that locker room. I don't golf, but I go to the golf outings when the guys are there, just to be around them again. I appreciate their company. I don't know how to golf well, and that probably keeps me from playing, too. I don't want to embarrass myself. Plus, it takes so much time.

I remember going to the Dupont plant where my Dad worked and sitting down and listening to them talk about their life experiences. I'd just sit there and listen. It was captivating.

I thought Noll was a good teacher. He drew on what he had learned from the coaches he had, and the coaches he had worked with. He stressed the fundamentals and basics. When things went off course, he would have us go back and work on the fundamentals at practice. He thought the best way to address it was to go back to the basics. It's the same way with us. We have to have fresh food. We have to take care of our guests. We get into some bells and whistles sometimes and we get off course. You need to remind yourself of what you need to do to take care of the customers.

If we had a few bad games in a row we'd go back to basics and that's what I do in our business. We go over the fundamentals. J.T. and I use sports analogies when we talk to our staff and to our store managers. It might drive the guys nuts, but it's a common language. You can make a point with such analogies, about working as a team and chemistry and stuff like that.

There's new technology, of course, but some of the fundamentals still make good sense. They still work.

"I always had summer jobs."

I worked as a kid. When I was 12, a friend and I invested in a lawn mower, and we worked the neighborhood. I cleaned up a dairy store for a year. I always had summer jobs. The expectations at home were there, for sure. My dad found those jobs for me. I was one of seven kids. My two sisters both worked at home, helping out and cleaning what they could, and all the boys had jobs. My mother worked. The money we earned was used to offset some of our personal expenses. My family also had a strong sense of religion.

I got my greatest satisfaction from what others said about my performance. In any profession, there are tough endeavors. It's very competitive. You need some self-confidence. You also need some feedback. It gives you some sense of credibility. You need that validation. I didn't get much of that from outside. You still need something to feed off. You need to know there is respect from your peers.

I felt a kinship with my teammates on the Steelers. There was a collective sense of accomplishment. As young men, our perspective isn't what it would be now. Now you can see just how lucky we were. We had a gift and we put it to good use.

It's the kind of thing older people have been telling you all your life. You may say something today that someone, it could even be your children, may hear and not act upon, but if it's a valid point they'll draw on it later.

As much as I'd like to tell you that as an 18-year-old I formed my life's philosophy, that simply isn't so. But those things are built into you. Those values. What you think is right. What I will or won't do. Those things are shaped in you early. We're a product of every step we've taken along the way. Certainly, I grew a great deal during my days with the Steelers. And not just in a physical sense.

I knew what I wanted to be. If I ever have a legacy, I want it to be that I never intentionally hurt anyone.

I think there was something special about the Steelers' teams I played with. It's special when you have a gathering of that kind of talent. But other teams had talent. On paper, some other teams looked so powerful. But they lacked something. Nothing is perfect, but we came close to it.

The organization, the coaching, the players, and our ability to work together. That was special. You could look around the locker room and see so many great players. You didn't worry about it when someone in the starting lineup was missing because of an injury. You knew you still had a great team on the field. You always felt the team could get along without you. That was humbling. We won Super Bowls with key players out. You wouldn't want to live without them too long, but you could win without certain players.

You admired them for different reasons. It might be for sheer talent. It might be the way they conducted their personal life. Frank Lewis and I were roommates at the beginning, and I thought the world of him, as a player and as a friend. Lynn Swann's locker was next to mine, and he was special. So were Stallworth and Shell.

So was Jon Kolb. I worked out with him, and he taught me a lot about weight lifting. He took me on as a personal challenge when I needed to build myself up as an offensive lineman. We worked as long as we had to work to get what we needed to get done. Mike Webster worked as hard as anybody I ever worked with. When you look back to Willie Mays, you know there are people who may have stayed too long. Maybe Mike did that, too, but he worked so hard and put in so much time and effort, I guess it was his call when he wanted to give it up. I guess he earned that.

There were guys like L.C. I looked up to him a lot. I worked out every day against L.C. It was a combative situation. He made me work that much harder. Maybe Ernie and Dwight were more unpredictable than L.C. and Joe Greene, but L.C. was an honest workout. Dwight may have been more intense, and maybe L.C., because of his size, felt he had to save himself for Sunday. But he was tough.

I saw him once go up against Bob Brown of the Raiders. Brown weighed over 300 pounds. He was awesome. L.C. was about 230 then. Every play, L.C. never gave up. He just kept coming at the guy. He didn't try to avoid him. His stature just started to rise with me after that.

That's the beauty of football. You really see what the guys around you are made of. You could see this in your teammates. This guy answered the call. And, at the top, you had to admire Chuck Noll. You have to give Chuck credit as a manager and as a coach. He deserves credit. He dealt with a lot of different personalities and changes, and there were some tough decisions to be made, and you had to respect that.

How blessed and lucky we were, when it all meshed together. It's not something you should dwell on, not something you should brag on. It tells you that you were fortunate to be a part of that. At the same time, it doesn't define your life. It can be part of a very important segment of it. You can draw upon it now, and all those experiences. You were stretched to the limit physically and emotionally, and you lived through it.

You tend to have more hope that you'll survive this, too. You look at tough things ahead of you. You don't have to let it overwhelm you. People have to go back to basics, and remember what they did to get where they are today.

I was always nervous, always before a game. If I didn't feel it before the game, it would bother me. If I didn't take a guy seriously; if I saw film and I didn't think he could deal with me, I'd find myself struggling and have a difficult game. I'd get banged up when that happened. I was better when I respected my opponent. You always should do that.

1983 Pro Bowl lineup includes lovely host from Hawaii and five Steelers, left to right, Jack Lambert, Donnie Shell, John Stallworth, Mike Webster and Larry Brown. It was an overdue acknowledgment of Brown's ability.

Jack Ham
He understood the game

"I got into the Hall of Fame on the shoulders of a lot of people."

Jack Ham may be the most heralded of all the Steelers of the '70s. None have been accorded more honors for their efforts than the classy left linebacker from those four Super Bowl championship teams. Terry Bradshaw and Lynn Swann enjoy more national exposure, but Ham has done quite well as an analyst on radio and television for professional and college football coverage. No one has kept busier than Ham has in various enterprises through the years.

He is a point of pride to Penn State University and with the Pittsburgh Steelers and his respective coaches, Joe Paterno and Chuck Noll.

Ham is president of Nationwide Drug Testing Services, Inc., of Pittsburgh, which implements a drug-free program for many small and large businesses. He is also general manager of coal sales for Cooney Brothers Coal Company of Cresson, Pennsylvania. He often travels to Cresson and then onto his hometown of Johnstown to visit with his mother. He played his high school ball there at Bishop McCourt. He'll do some yardwork for his mother while he's there. He's still the dutiful son. He's been with Cooney Brothers since 1983, the year after he retired. Before that, he also worked for five years with the sales department of Neville Coal Company.

I visited Ham in his offices at the Airside Business Park on the site of the old Greater Pittsburgh International Airport in Moon Township. It's located on Lindbergh Drive, near Beers School Road. Just about every airport in the country has a street named after Charles Lindbergh, the heroic air pilot. Ham and I got together there on February 20, 2002. Ham was about 15 minutes late for our appointment, so his office manager, Terrie Cook, seated me in his office to await his arrival.

I had an opportunity to check out the pictures and sports memorabilia that decorate his work area. There were as many golf artifacts as there were football souvenirs, similar to the offices of L.C. Greenwood and J.T. Thomas. There was a neat stack of copies of *Golf* Magazine.

The item that caught my eye was a glass-enclosed clipping of a story from the *Pittsburgh Post-Gazette* about Ham being named to the "Insider's NFL Dream Team" in 2000. There was only one team chosen by the 36 voters for the Pro Football Hall of Fame and Ham was on it, along with former teammates Mel Blount and Mike Webster. John Unitas, who grew up and played high school football in Pittsburgh, is the quarterback of that team. Unitas was drafted by the Steelers, and cut as a rookie prospect in 1955.

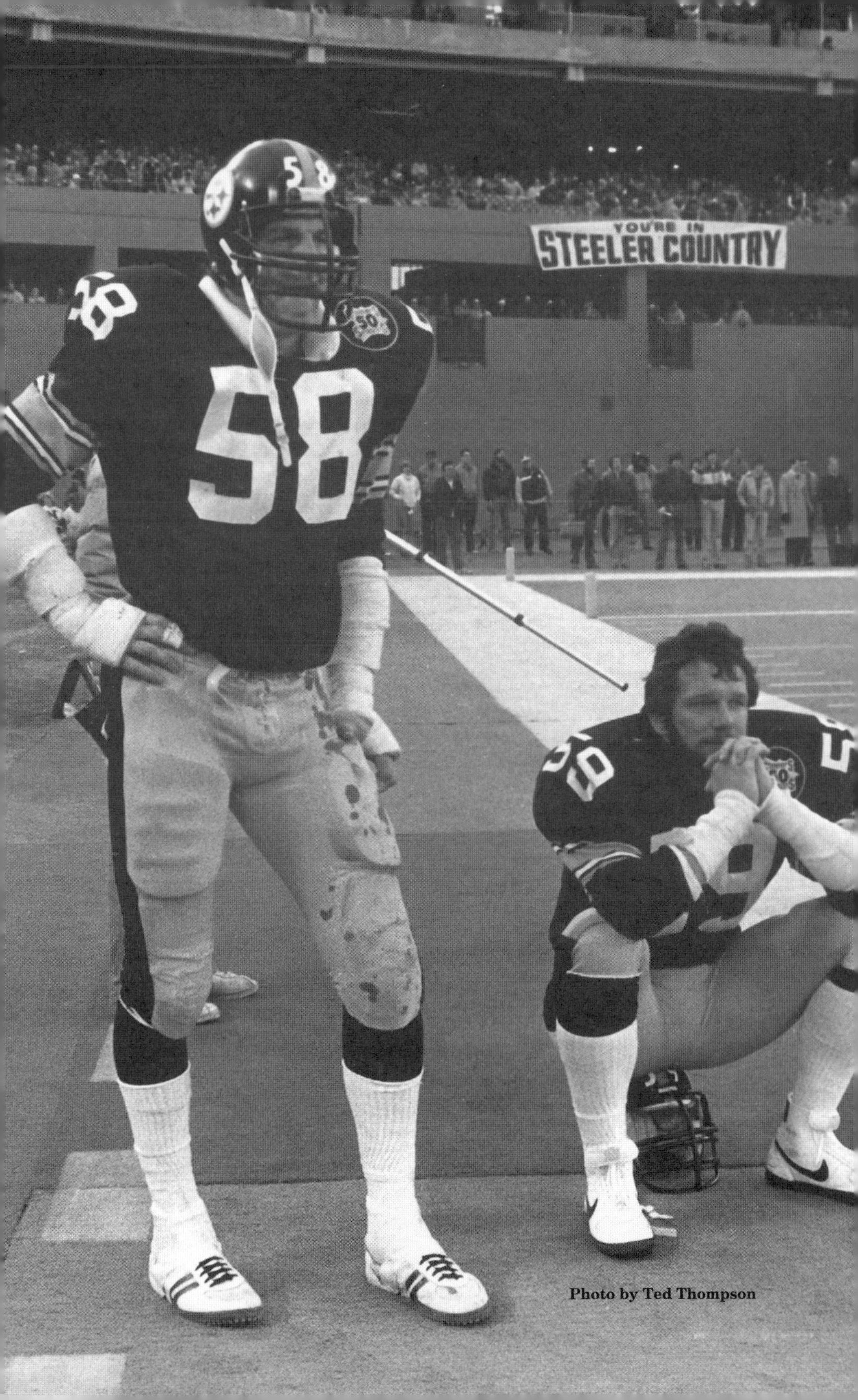

Photo by Ted Thompson

Ham was inducted into the Pro Football Hall of Fame in his first year of eligibility in 1988, and inducted into the National Collegiate Hall of Fame in 1990. He was selected to the Silver Anniversary All-Time Super Bowl team that same year. Since then he has been selected to the NFL's 75th Anniversary All-Time Team, and *Sports Illustrated's* All-Time Century Team. His credentials are impeccable.

Ham was hobbling a bit when he entered his office, apologizing for his tardiness. He said he had been delayed at a rehabilitation session for an injured ankle. He had hurt it playing pick-up basketball. It was his left foot, the same one as I remembered that kept him out of the 1979 playoffs and the Steelers' Super Bowl XIV triumph at Pasadena, California in January of 1980. That was the Steelers' fourth Super Bowl victory in a six-year span.

"I can't complain," said Ham. "I know accountants who have more physical problems than I do. But football does exact a price."

Ham stands 6-1 and weighs 222, his playing weight. His salt and pepper beard gives him a different look from his playing days. He would be 52 two days before Christmas.

I had arthoscopic surgery on my left knee a few months earlier to repair torn cartilage. I had injured it playing in a pick-up basketball game at my high school gymnasium. I told Jack that, as much as I hated to do so, I was retiring from playing basketball. At 59, I was giving up the game. I decided it was better to be able to walk without a limp at 60 rather than risk further injury. He smiled. No one ever wants to stop playing games. So we compared basketball war stories for a while to warm up for our interview session.

Joe Greene once gave Jack Ham a game ball when Ham wasn't sure he deserved one. "He's so good," said Greene, explaining his decision, "you just take him for granted. We shouldn't. His game is as low-key as he is."

Mike Wagner, who's been a close friend of Ham ever since they first broke in together in 1971, had this to say about him late in their careers: "Jack just totally controls his area of coverage. Teams don't exploit him anymore. He's always impressed me with his anticipation and his knowledge of what the other team is trying to do.

"He gets himself into position, and attacks the blocker before they can get to him. Greene and L.C. Greenwood control the line of scrimmage. I used to play over on that side more, and very little garbage leaked through. Sometimes in our huddle Jack seems to be sleeping. He's so low-key. Teams run at that side because they can't believe it, or they've got to balance their offense. They can't run left all the time."

Woody Widenhofer, the defensive coordinator of the Steelers back then, said, "They take it for granted that the guy plays a great game. They're so used to him performing well."

I'll never forget another facet of Jack Ham. When I was covering the Steelers for *The Pittsburgh Press* from 1979-1982, I thought Ham and Jon Kolb were tough interviews. It wasn't easy to get them to talk or share their thoughts, or, sometimes, just to say hello. They seemed aloof, unfriendly. When my brother died in 1982 they were the first players on the team to approach me and offer their condolences. That taught me a lesson about judging people too quickly.

That 1971 draft class was special

Jack Ham was one of the greatest outside linebackers in pro football history, and retired after playing 12 seasons (1971-1982). He was not as colorful as some of his teammates, but was always one of the most popular players among the fans. They appreciated his accomplishments on the field and his quiet class off the field. Being Polish and a Penn State alumnus helped his popularity rating.

His peers and the media acknowledged his all-around ability. They made him an All-Pro selection for nine straight seasons. He was the only unanimous defensive choice on the NFL 1970's Team of the Decade. He was elected to the Pro Bowl eight years in a row (1974-1981), establishing a record for linebackers that was tied in 1982 by teammate Jack Lambert. In 1975, Ham was named the NFL Defensive Player of the Year by *Pro Football Weekly* and *The Football News*. His most impressive statistic is his 32 regular-season interceptions which is the third highest in NFL history by a linebacker. Twice he led all NFL linebackers in interceptions and his total is fourth in Steelers history.

He also added five post-season interceptions, which is a team record. Two of those interceptions came in the 1974 AFC Championship game against Oakland, one of the biggest victories in Steelers' history. The first one stopped an apparent Raiders' scoring drive and the second he returned 24 yards to the Oakland 9-yard line to set up the winning touchdown. The Steelers went on to win their first Super Bowl two weeks later.

Ham joined the Steelers as a No. 2 draft choice in the 1971, one of the most productive draft classes in the team's history and one of the best in NFL history. Thirteen of the 22 selections that year made the team and nine of them were regulars at one time. Six of these players, including Ham, were starters on all four Super Bowl teams. The only draft class that eclipsed that one was the 1974 class that included four future Hall of Fame performers: Lynn Swann, Jack Lambert, John Stallworth and Mike Webster. While more spectacular perhaps, it was not as deep as the 1971 group.

Ham became a starter at the beginning of his rookie season. He clinched a regular position with a three-interception performance against the New York Giants in Yankee Stadium in the final pre-season game that summer.

In 1972, he made the All-Pro team for the first time when he had a career-high seven interceptions. He began his string of Pro Bowl appearances the following year and was the only NFL linebacker chosen for those eight straight seasons.

During the football season, Ham serves as color analyst for the Penn State Radio Network — with Steve Jones doing play-by-play — and for KDKA-TV covering the pre-season games for the Pittsburgh Steelers since 1999. He also works for Westwood One covering NFL games on weekends. He also had a show on ESPN Radio 1250.

Ham has a home in Sewickley, next door to Lynn Swann. Jack has been married for 26 years to Joanne Ham. In the beginning, she was a teacher in the Upper St. Clair School District. She has a master's degree in anthropology and biochemistry. She had thought about being a veterinarian. In recent years, she has been an instructor in corporate training for Achieve Global. She's writing a children's book. It's not about Jack, or a beanstalk.

Jack Ham:

At the time I was playing for the Steelers, I didn't realize how good some of those guys were. You go through it and you're not rating your teammates. You're just playing with them. As the years go by, you sit back and reflect on those championship seasons and it becomes clearer. You didn't know you were as good as you were.

I had Joe Greene and L.C. Greenwood in front of me and Jack Lambert to my left, so I was surrounded by the best ballplayers you could possibly have on your side. I'm smart enough to know that I wouldn't have gotten all the honors I did without the support I had around me. I've gotten these accolades on the shoulders of a lot of other people.

If I had been with the New Orleans Saints I wouldn't be in the Hall of Fame today. I thought Archie Manning was a great quarterback, but he has no Super Bowl rings.

Without the guys around me, I wouldn't have been able to drop off in pass coverage as much as I did and get all those interceptions. Teams were playing catch-up football against a great team. They weren't trying to pound the ball at us. I didn't have to take on too many offensive linemen. I played 12 years, but I wasn't on that field as much as I might have been for a poorer football team. Our offense could control the ball and keep us on the sideline. Playing 50 plays a game instead of 60 to 70 plays saves a lot of wear and tear on your body. This year I think they needed 54 plays a game defensively, and that helps. You have a whole lot less chance of getting banged up.

Among my assets were my quickness and being able to read and diagnose plays quickly. I learned a lot of that from Andy Russell. Talk about being a good fit. He had been there for six or seven years when I arrived and just being able to learn from a guy like that was a big boost for my career.

At 225 pounds out there, you'd better be smart if you're going to survive. I don't think a lot of players realize how important it is to work in the classroom as well as in the weight room. I knew what I was seeing out there from going over film and chalk work with the coaches. They put it up on the board and taught us what to look for. We always had good coaches, and it began with Chuck Noll. He knew what needed to be done if we were going to have a winning program.

I firmly feel that the best thing that ever happened to our football team was when the New York Jets upset the Baltimore Colts in the 1969 Super Bowl. That was the game Joe Namath guaranteed that the Jets — the AFL champions — would win the game. Chuck Noll was an assistant to Don Shula with the Colts, and I think it left a lasting impression on him about how you have to approach games and make sure you are properly prepared and not to take anything for granted. There was no way the Colts should have lost to the Jets. Noll came to the Steelers that same year and he knew from the start just how he wanted to handle things, and the kind of players he would need to produce a winning football team.

Chuck had the ability for the big games to push the right buttons. He knew how to prepare a team for a big game. He knew when to push and when to back off. It can hurt you to practice too much. He was always a big believer in getting the most out of a practice session, but he thought there was a point of diminishing returns. He gave us three days off before our first Super Bowl. The Vikings had been there twice, but Noll had us ready like we knew what it was all about, too.

I remember before our AFC championship game with the Raiders in Oakland in 1974. They had played the Miami Dolphins the week before and John Madden made the remark that the two best teams had met in that game. Noll would not let us forget that oversight. Joe Greene said he never saw Noll get so riled up before. I never saw him that mad. The veins were popping out on his neck. I saw him mad after games. I saw him mad at Tuesday meetings when we'd review game film and he'd be livid. But never before a game. I'll tell you something: we don't win it without Chuck Noll.

> "What makes this game so unique is it's not just you. You want to play well because you don't want to let a teammate down. I didn't want to let down Joe Greene or L.C. Greenwood who played in front of me. I made sure I did what I had to do — my responsibility. That's the way I felt about this game. That's why I really loved it so much. That's just the feeling our team had."
> — Jack Ham

"I wasn't looking for a coach
to be my buddy."

I thought Joe Paterno was gone during my sophomore year at Penn State. The Steelers wanted him. He went for the interview, but he turned them down. They hired Chuck Noll instead. I can't see Joe Paterno in the NFL. College football is what Joe Paterno is all about. He's a perfect fit for Penn State and college football.

Later on, Joe was going to Green Bay to interview for that job. I think New England, the Giants, Pittsburgh and Green Bay all came after him at one time or another.

He had other opportunities. I think it was wise on his part not to go somewhere. Joe was meant for college football. He was my No. 1 choice when I was coming out of high school in Johnstown; that's for sure. For a 17-year-old or 18-year-old kid, he puts things into perspective for you very quickly. In my senior year I helped baby-sit his kids on an airplane trip and it may be the reason I don't have any children today.

You were always aware of where Joe was on the field. Joe could be 50 yards away and he'd jump on someone. Maybe that's why his glasses are so thick. I think they are binoculars or lenses for a telescope. He sees everything that's going on. He has peripheral vision. You didn't know him personally. At times, you were afraid of him. I got to know him better after I came to the Steelers. I'd see him at different functions and we'd talk, and it was a different kind of exchange. I went on some trips with him for Nike, and I got to know him better.

I've always had the utmost respect for him, but we had no real relationship when I was playing for him. I see where guys say they hated Joe Paterno. I wasn't one of them. I wasn't looking for a coach to be my buddy.

It was the same thing with Chuck Noll. It was very business-like. In my rookie year we're playing the Bears in Chicago in the season-opener, and I'm starting for the first time. There was no pep talk. His attitude was there was nothing I'm going to tell a football team five minutes before a game that's going to make a difference.

He was not into screaming before a game. If you're going to be a good coach, or a good leader, you'd better be yourself. If Noll tried to be a rah-rah guy it would have been so phony.

I was never into screaming, either. If Ray Lewis feels he needs to do that to be effective for the Baltimore Ravens that's his business. We had players do that. What's really important is that we had smart players. They didn't make too many mental errors. Back then, players didn't run around jumping up and down and bumping their chests into each other the

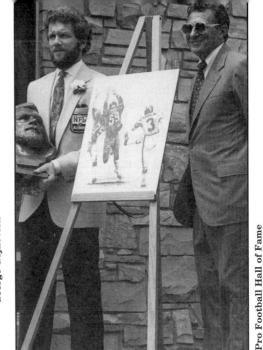

Ham was introduced by Penn State coach Joe Paterno at 1988 Pro Football Hall of Fame induction ceremonies.

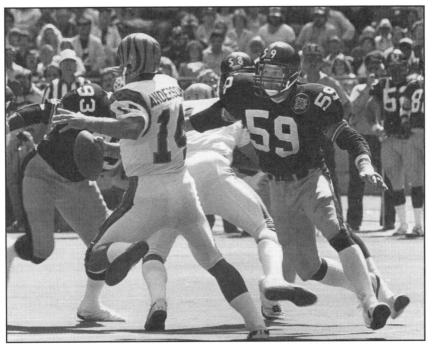

Jack Ham (59) closes in on Cincinnati Bengals' quarterback Ken Anderson.

way they do now. I didn't need anybody hitting me on the shoulder pads to get me prepared to play.

It's okay if the guys are pumped up. I don't like that choreographed junk, though. I know it's a different breed, but I don't have to like it. I don't expect guys to just hand the ball to the officials when they score a touchdown, but that's what Jim Brown, Walter Payton and Barry Sanders did. And they were pretty good. I hated it when Terrell Owens of the 49ers went out to midfield to spike the ball against the Cowboys. That was way overboard. All the players from my era and today know what's over the line.

I like the Steelers linebackers today. Jason Gildon has been performing at a high level for a number of years. I hope they sign Joey Porter. He's getting very good. I read that it doesn't look good for them signing Earl Holmes. He was very effective for them, too. But they survived the loss of Lavon Kirkland, so you can replace people. Kendrell Bell came in as a rookie and was great in Kirkland's place. He made an immediate impact. They seem to have a nice blend of youth and experience. I'm sure Holmes helped Bell, telling him where to line up, and so forth. And Kirkland had already seen his best years.

The position is different today, so it's not like comparing a quarterback of my day with Kordell Stewart. The outside linebacker has different responsibilities because they play a lot different scheme today. I like Joey Porter. It seems like he keeps getting better and better, playing smarter and more comfortable out there. I've watched him coming into his own.

I was not a Jason Gildon fan at first, but now he's doing it every day. They have good speed at that position. It helps them blitz effectively.

These guys are impressive, but I don't want to hear that Jack Lambert and I would be too small to play today.

These guys work at football on a full-time basis. That was not the case when I first came here. Our off-season was really our off-season. I worked for a coal company in the off-season. I wasn't lifting and taking nutritional supplements. Jack Lambert wouldn't be 218 today. He'd be 240. I'd be heavier. You can play outside at 240.

Goal-wise, I didn't come into this league to be an all-pro. I wanted to be on a winning team, like I was used to at Penn State. I sure didn't want to be on a losing team. I never experienced a losing record and didn't want to in the pros, either, but that's what happened here my first year. I enjoy the team aspect of the game, going for championships in the playoffs and winning Super Bowls. Those are the fun things to me. All-Pro . . . that's after the fact.

"The root of the evil is money.
It's what's ruined the romance."
— Jack Lambert

"Franco wasn't the greatest practice player."

I remember when Franco Harris came to the team the year after I did. I had played with Franco at Penn State and I knew how good he was. We had Lydell Mitchell in the same backfield as Franco at Penn State, so we were loaded there.

The Steelers had a bad experience with a Penn State back before we got there. Bob Campbell didn't pan out for them. He dropped punts and fumbled the ball. Some of the veteran players were down on Franco from the start with the Steelers.

When he came into camp some of the veterans and press guys were ready to put him in the same grouping as Bob Ferguson and Dick Leftridge, two running backs from Ohio State and West Virginia who had failed miserably with the Steelers.

Franco wasn't the greatest practice player and that only added to the doubts about his ability. Then we played an exhibition game in Atlanta and Franco ran about 80 yards for a touchdown and that's when everyone knew he'd be fine.

Franco just had his own schedule. He and L.C. might have been the two worst practice players in the team's history. They moved to the beat of their own drums. Franco saved himself for the real stuff. He walks better than most old running backs these days.

We had a great set of running backs in Franco Harris and Rocky Bleier. I met Rocky in 1971, and I thought he had a tough situation. But he made it. In '76, when he got the thousand yards, I never saw 44 guys pulling so hard for one guy to get an individual goal like that. Everyone roots for Rocky. He's that kind of guy.

"I know who the good players are."

My schedule gets pretty demanding, but I'm doing what I love to be doing. My itinerary gets tight at times. Sometimes it gets a little hairy. The kickoff is at 12:10 at Penn State and I have a 3:50 flight out of there. I've been able to make it, but the drive to the airport gets demanding. I do a college and pro game every weekend for 18 weeks. Westwood One has been great. They do their best to accommodate me. They try to give me assignments that make logistical sense.

I know who the good players are and I know who the weak links are, especially on defense. I see things the way I did when I was playing linebacker. I can see what's coming. It helps me analyze what's going on when it's my turn to talk. I try my best to make my points quickly and get out of the way of the play-by-play man. I want to complement him, not compete with him for airtime. I'm just helping out, adding my two-cents' worth. I work a lot for Westwood One with Harry Kalas out of Philadelphia and Dave Sims out of New York. We're a good mix. With Penn State, I work with Steve Jones.

Since you asked, I must tell you I don't know the whole story on what's going on with Mike Webster. I was at a cocktail party at the Sunnehanna Country Club in Johnstown, and I saw Webby there. I went up to him and said, "Thanks for coming." He snapped at me, "I didn't come here for you!"

"I didn't mean it that way," I said.

He wouldn't let it go at that. He was argumentative, and I had to walk away. I didn't want to get into it with him publicly. It would be embarrassing for both of us. I didn't know where he was coming from. I'm from Johnstown and I was just happy to have him there. I hope he's getting along well. He showed the way when he was with our team.

Jim O'Brien

John Steigerwald shares KDKA-TV microphone with Jack Ham during Steelers' 2000 pre-season schedule.

Leo Nobile
Patriarch of the Pittsburgh Stealers

"I played with some great ones."

L eo Nobile blocked for "Slingin' Sammy" Baugh and tackled "Bullet Bill" Dudley and was a teammate of Jerry Nuzum, Johnny "Zero" Clement, Elbie Nickel, Fran Rogel, Jerry Shipkey and Bill McPeak. He was a two-way guard in the National Football League for three years, the first (1947) with the Washington Redskins and two of them (1948-1949) with the Pittsburgh Steelers. He stood 5-11½, 195 pounds in his prime. He fell one year shy of the necessary four years then needed to qualify for an NFL pension.

He had dark wavy hair and a noble Roman face that was perfect for a gladiator or football player. There's a memorable photo of him wearing a leather helmet, his face soiled black, that appeared in *Life* magazine. It's a perfect portrayal of a tough sport. They didn't wear face-guards back then. The photograph was the work of Arthur Rickerby of Acme Photos.

At age 80, Leo Anthony Nobile was the oldest of the Pittsburgh Steelers I visited to interview for this book. He gets excited talking about those halcyon days at Forbes Field. He played with and knew a lot of people who are now enshrined in the Pro Football Hall of Fame. He has scrapbooks to prove it. He also cherishes the memories of his Steelers teammates. He is proud of his Italian heritage and his achievements in athletics and in the community.

"Fran Rogel was a fraternity brother of mine at Penn State," noted Nobile. "We were in Kappa Delta Rho together. I bought my first car from Jerry Nuzum. I knew a lot of Steelers personally through the years."

Rogel was in an assisted-care residence, St. Barnabas, in the North Hills of Pittsburgh, and not faring well. He would die in early June. Nuzum had died the previous year. Nobile knew he was lucky to be able to still drive his car, and get around with the aid of a black cane. He still had an adventurous spirit.

While I was working on this story, Byron R. "Whizzer" White, who had starred at the University of Colorado and with the Steelers, died at the age of 84. He had served as a judge on the Supreme Court for 31 years, and had retired from the court nine years earlier. He died in a Denver nursing home on April 15, 2002. White was the highest-paid player in the league when he signed as the No. 1 draft choice of the Steelers in 1938, getting the munificent sum of $15,500. He had been one of the most decorated players in college football history. He led the league in rushing and was named the NFL's Rookie of the Year. He left after one season, as he told Art Rooney he would, to go to Oxford University in England as a Rhodes Scholar. He was named to the Supreme Court at age 45 — the youngest to be so honored — by President John F. Kennedy.

Soon after, two other backfield stalwarts who had short but successful stays with the Steelers, Sam Francis and Joe Geri, also died.

"You're welcome to join us any Thursday."

Nobile lives with his wife, Ann Ryan, at their comfortable split-level red-brick and white paneled home in Coraopolis, near Robert Morris University. He was previously married to Catherine for 40 years and they had three children. He met Catherine during his student days at Penn State. As part of his scholarship, he had a choice of eating at a restaurant or a fraternity house, and he opted for a restaurant. He felt it would give him greater flexibility time-wise. He ate at the Allen Crest Tea Room and Corner Room. Catherine was the hostess there. One day he got up the nerve to ask her for a date and they were later married. His second wife, Ann, disclosed to me that she had been a nun — a Sister of St. Joseph — for 20 years. She met Leo after she left the order. They had been married for 11 years when we met.

They had three cats — Mario, Sylvia and Momma Cat — and a dog, a mixed poodle named Puppy, when I interviewed Leo. They later added a Maltese male puppy named Silvio. "He gets into the darnedest trouble," said Nobile in a later telephone conversation.

When I visited Nobile at his home on Wednesday, February 20, he and Ann were entertaining two of their dearest friends, Diane and Lloyd Voss. Nobile and Voss had gotten to know each other through their involvement with the Steelers Alumni. Shortly after Diane and Lloyd left, Ann put out some crackers and chips for me, and a Diet Coke. I was ready to go to work. Two of Leo's daughters, Beth and Natalie, showed up when I was there. He has another daughter named Michelle. The Nobiles joined us when I was visiting the Vosses a month later at their home in Scott Township.

At our second meeting, Leo and Ann said they were about to drive down to Florida where they have a getaway home in Jacksonville. While there, they also visited his sister, Dolores Hopkins, who had a home in Davie, 12 miles from Fort Lauderdale.

Leo Nobile grew up in Ambridge and remembers as a youngster when Italians weren't welcome in certain parts of town, and had to walk on specified sidewalks to avoid trouble. Even so, he returns every Thursday morning to his hometown and has breakfast at K&N Restaurant on Merchant Street, where he used to hang out when he was in high school. He says he sits in the same booth.

"If I had paid a quarter for every hour I had my ass in that booth I'd own that restaurant by now," said Nobile. He said he and his buddies on the Ambridge football team sat in that booth for two hours after nearly every practice before heading home for dinner.

Proud Pittsburgh Steelers Alumni officer emeritus Leo Nobile and wife Ann Ryan live in Coraopolis, but return to his hometown of Ambridge for lunch on a weekly basis. A Penn State grad, Nobile was a watch-charm guard for the Washington Redskins (1947) and for the Steelers (1948 and 1949).

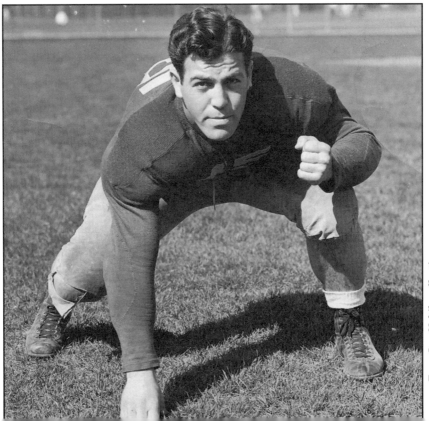

He says he has the same meal each time he's there: three pancakes, juice and coffee. "You're welcome to join us any Thursday," he said.

From Ambridge, Nobile went to Penn State where he played for Bob Higgins, who preceded Rip Engle and Joe Paterno as the head coaches of the Nittany Lions. Marty McAndrews handled the freshman team that went undefeated. Nobile was joined by Harry and Dave Alston from Midland, and Red Moore of Rochester on that freshman team. Nobile is proud of his football background.

There were photos framed on the wall and other Steelers' memorabilia in the corner of the living room where he was sitting. One showed Nobile flanked by former Steelers owner Art Rooney and former Pittsburgh Mayor Richard Caliguiri.

He has a plaque denoting his induction into the Pittsburgh chapter of the Italian-American Sports Hall of Fame.

Nobile seldom leaves his home, driving his 1993 champagne-colored Cadillac Sedan DeVille, that he is not wearing a blazer or shirt or jersey or jacket that has the emblem and script of the Steelers Alumni or the NFL Alumni emblazoned on his breast. He served as president of the Pittsburgh Steelers Alumni for seven years.

He regularly attends all pro football alumni meetings and get-togethers. He enjoys seeing the likes of Ernie Bonelli, who came out of Pitt to play halfback for the Steelers in 1946. He also recalled Carl Nery, who came out of Duquesne University to play guard for the Steelers in 1940 and 1941. Bonelli and Nery both were living in Mt. Lebanon. Nobile was a teammate of Val Jansante, an end from Duquesne University, who was still living in his hometown of Bentleyville.

Another Duquesne grad, Ray Kemp of Cecil, who was on the Steelers — or Pirates — in the first year of 1933 died during this period. Kemp was the first black ballplayer on the Pittsburgh pro team.

Nobile had the best scrapbooks I had seen since Betty Prince brought out several scrapbooks about her husband, Bob Prince, the legendary "voice of the Pittsburgh Pirates," when I visited her townhouse in Mt. Lebanon a few years earlier while working on Bob's biography *We Had 'Em All The Way*. I love looking at those old newspaper clippings.

When Nobile was playing ball for the Steelers, he was a big fan of fellow Italian favorites at Pitt such as Lou "Bimbo" Cecconi, Carl DePasqua and Lindy Lauro.

There were great football personalities pictured and written about in yellowed newspaper clippings in those scrapbooks belonging to the Nobile family. Leo couldn't remember who kept those scrapbooks for him.

There were pictures and stories of a game between the Redskins and Rams before a crowd of 80,889 at the Coliseum in Los Angeles, matching quarterbacks Sammy Baugh of the Redskins and Bob

Waterfield of the Rams. Waterfield was married to curvaceous movie star Jane Russell. There were also photos of two other famous quarterbacks, Sid Luckman of the Chicago Bears and Paul Christman of the St. Louis Cardinals. They are all fabled figures in football history.

The Steelers were coached by John Michelosen, also from Ambridge, during the two seasons Nobile was on the ballclub. Michelosen had succeeded his mentor, Dr. John B. "Jock" Sutherland, following his death of a brain aneurism in a Kentucky farmfield following the 1947 season.

The Steelers had posted an 8-4 record during the regular season, with a 5-1 home record, in Sutherland's last season. They lost to the Philadelphia Eagles, 21-0, in an Eastern Division playoff game. That was the last time the Steelers were in the championship playoffs until Chuck Noll's Steelers got to the AFC championship game in 1972. When the Steelers defeated the Oakland Raiders, 13-7, at Three Rivers Stadium on Franco Harris' "Immaculate Reception" it was the first playoff victory in the 40-year history of the franchise.

Under Michelosen, in Nobile's two seasons with the Steelers, they were 4-8 and 6-5-1. There were NFL teams then called the Los Angeles Rams, Chicago Cardinals, Boston Yankees and New York Bulldogs. The Steelers regularly played the New York Giants, Washington Redskins, Chicago Bears, Philadelphia Eagles, Detroit Lions and Green Bay Packers.

Nobile remembers signing with the Steelers for a $1,500 bonus, contingent on playing 50 percent of the plays. His Steelers' salary was $3,850 the first year and $4,500 the second year.

He worked nearly 30 years for Alcoa before retiring from there in 1978. He then went to work as an activity director at the Western Penitentiary in Woods Run. He managed to get Art Rooney to donate football equipment once used by the Steelers. The prison team looked spiffy in their Steelers' uniforms. "We played all home games," said Nobile with a wide grin, "and we were known as the Pittsburgh Stealers."

It was during his days at Western Pen that I first met Nobile, usually bumping into him at the Allegheny Club at Three Rivers Stadium.

He had a theatrical look about him. He wore his sideburns long and wide. Since his hair turned gray and thinner his sideburns are not as prominent as they used to be. Once upon a time he looked like one of those hanging judges in one of those old British movies.

On the day I visited his home, he was wearing a bright red blazer with an NFL Alumni patch over his heart, a white shirt and tie, and his cat Sylvia was on his lap, or the arm of his chair. He petted Sylvia as he told me his stories. Two months after my visit, Sylvia was missing for three days and Leo was saddened by her absence. Then Ann found Sylvia locked in the garage. Leo was so relieved. He loves all their pets so much.

127

Leo Nobile:

I went to the Steelers' office one day and asked if I could see Mr. Rooney. I told the secretary I was a former Steelers' player. I told her he probably didn't remember me, but I would appreciate if he could see me for a few minutes. And, in a short time, I got to see him.

When he saw me and heard my name, he said, "I think I remember you. I think you came to us from the Redskins. Didn't you play at Penn State?"

So he did remember me; that made my day. I told him about our situation at Western Penitentiary. I said, "We have a football team, but we don't have a football or any equipment. All we have are bocce balls." He gave me helmets, shoulder pads, shoes, balls and practice jerseys. We filled a van with the stuff. That's how the Pittsburgh Stealers came to be.

We also had competition in the prison in volleyball, basketball, bocce, baseball, boxing, tennis and weight-lifting. Some of the guys suggested I let them try pole-vaulting, but we dismissed that idea. You get the picture?

When I was with the Redskins, we went to training camp in California. It was at Occidental College in Los Angeles. Sammy Baugh was in his heyday. Sammy Adrian Baugh, I'll never forget him. He was one of three players on our team from TCU. We also had Dick Todd and Kyle Aldrich from TCU. Baugh was one of the all-time greats. And he was a great guy. He'd run out on the field by himself, with a couple of cheerleaders around him. The Redskins had their own marching band. And everyone in it dressed like Indians, with war bonnets on their heads. They were beautiful costumes. Some people came to the games just to see them perform and go through their steps. It was a real point of pride to the club owner George Preston Marshall. He's in the Hall of Fame, too. He was one of those guys, like Art Rooney and George Halas and Curly Lambeau, who put the league together. They were the pioneers of pro football.

Marshall wasn't around the team that much. He spent a lot of time at the racetracks. He made the money and we got paid on time. I was making $350 a week with the Redskins.

I was a rookie the same year the great receiver Hugh "Bones" Taylor came to the team. He and Baugh became quite the passing combination.

When I joined the Steelers they held their training camp at Alliance College in Cambridge Springs in northwestern Pennsylvania.

My father was a tailor from Calabria, Italy. His name was Genaro, and they called him Jim. He never saw me play pro ball. He spoke in broken English with an Italian accent. He used to tell me to knock 'em down and pick 'em up. He was a tailor at Davis' Department Store in Ambridge. He got a day off to see me play once against Midland High School. His boss gave him the day off so he could see me play.

I was clipped from behind on the kickoff for the second half and couldn't play anymore. They tell me my dad kept asking everyone around him after that, "Where's my boy?" He never came back for another game. He said he was bad luck.

I went into the military service in 1943 during World War II. I was in the Army for 2½ years. I was with an artillery unit at Fort Bragg and then I went to the South Pacific. Harry Truman was our President at the time. I was a radio operator. I got a Morse code message one day that said 28,000 Japanese had been killed when a bomb was dropped on Hiroshima. I thought I better go see the captain of the ship and report this, but everybody thought there had been a mistake. That couldn't be right.

I remember we were on this island near the Phillipines when we got a package that included some Fort Pitt beer from back home in Pittsburgh. We were all excited about that.

Simple little things meant a lot in those days.

The same was true with our pro football experience. We sure as hell weren't playing for the money. We sure enjoyed playing the game. When I was a kid, if someone said we were going to a game at Forbes Field that was unbelievable. And here I was playing professional football on that same field. They had a Leo Nobile Day at Forbes Field and all the folks from Ambridge were there.

Sammy Baugh was the best ballplayer I ever played with. In comparison to the other people I played ball with in high school and in college and the pros, he was like two or three steps above them. He just had this manner about him. A quarterback is supposed to know where everyone is on the field, and he had that down pat. He treated me swell. I don't know whether he knew the abilities of the ballplayers or not, but it didn't matter with him. When I signed with the Redskins, I had some questions about my own ability. In my own mind I wasn't sure I had the size to play pro ball.

We all lived in the same hotel in Washington D.C. We had to pay our own bill. There was a wealthy gentleman who lived in the hotel. His name was Sir William K. Ryan. He was from a railroad family. He'd come downstairs for dinner about the same time we were returning from practice. He'd take different ballplayers to dinner and he always picked up the tab.

He had a limousine and every so often he'd take us to the airport and we'd fly off to some place like Virginia Beach and go to some great restaurant. He'd sign the check. There'd be two or three of us players, and every time he'd take us to a different restaurant. We used to wonder where the hell he got all of his money.

We'd come back and we'd go to the hotel desk and the woman there would give us each a few $50 bills he'd left for her to give us.

I was happy to be coming back to Pittsburgh, though, when I learned I had been traded to the Steelers after one year. I was excited about the idea of playing at Forbes Field that had always been such a big deal for us when I was a kid. I was a real celebrity in Ambridge.

My coach at Ambridge was a guy named Moe Rubenstein. He had about a dozen guys who went on to play pro ball. He got maybe 100 of them college scholarships. He lived about a block from the high school and was really dedicated to the program.

People have always treated me well. When I was at Penn State we all had local businessmen as our sponsors. The guy who sponsored me owned the Allen Crest Tea Room. It's still there.

A teammate of mine at Ambridge was supposed to go with me one day to visit Ohio State University. His name was Ray Ulinski. We were so naïve we ended up in a car with guys who were recruiting for Penn State. They drove us to State College and we liked the place and decided to go there. At first, we thought we were in Columbus. What did we know? We just filled out papers and signed our names and the next thing we knew we were going to Penn State. It worked out fine.

That Ray Ulinski had an older brother, Eddie. He was the first kid to come out of Ambridge and make it in the pros. Eddie played with the Cleveland Browns and Ray played with me with the Steelers. The guy who was taking us around was a fellow named Shag Wolosky from Brownsville. We saw a statue of a Nittany Lion near Old Main, and we asked him what it was. When he told us it was a Nittany Lion we knew we were at Penn State. Shag said we'd be too embarrassed to tell anyone what happened.

Michelosen scouted me when I was with the Redskins and talked to me about the Steelers. He was from Ambridge, like me, so I felt comfortable coming with him. I lived on Coltart Street in Oakland when I was with the Steelers. I rented it from a Polish man. It was a two-story home. I could walk to Forbes Field where we practiced and played our games. Some times we practiced at South High School.

I have only the best of memories of those days.

Lloyd Voss
One of Lombardi's boys in Green Bay

"I just wanted to play."

I knew Lloyd Voss was going to be a good interview. He had played for Vince Lombardi in Green Bay, and I wanted him to talk about that, and he was in Pittsburgh when Chuck Noll was named to replace Bill Austin as the coach of the Steelers. He knew the best of times in Green Bay and the worst of times in Pittsburgh.

His timing couldn't have been worse. He left both teams just as they were about to get great, just as they were about to rule the National Football League. To hear Voss talk, though, he never had a bad day during his pro football career. This is a Minnesota farm boy who feels he's been blessed throughout his life. He was a tough defensive tackle, 6-3, 265, and he played alongside Joe Greene, L.C. Greenwood and Dwight White before Fats Holmes joined them.

He had turned 60 on February 13, 2002, though he thought he was 59. "I feel like I'm 45," he said.

I had not talked to him at any length in nearly 30 years, but I remembered seeing him at Ray Mansfield's funeral a few years earlier. He was openly crying in the middle of the room at the funeral parlor. Tears were streaming down his rosy cheeks. He was wiping them away with the back of one of his huge hands. There were several Steelers who moved in and out, and stayed awhile, at the L. Beinhauer & Son Funeral Home on Washington Road in McMurray that day, but none was as visibly moved as Lloyd Voss.

He was in the midst of several former Steelers when I saw him. One of them was comforting him; I forget which one, maybe Bruce Van Dyke or John Banaszak. Nearby, Jack Lambert looked pale and somber by comparison, his hands deep in the pockets of a dark trench-coat.

I like men who can cry, especially big guys who have tested their mettle in the tough world of pro football. Lombardi could cry. I remember Noll wept the day he announced his retirement as coach of the Steelers. Paul Brown and Tom Landry were thought to be stoic, but they both cried when their coaching careers came to an end. These were emotional men. Sometimes they cried because they were so happy. They had big hearts and when their hearts were heavy with grief they could give in to tears. There was no shame in showing one's feelings. Voss loved Ray Mansfield; they were more than former teammates, more than just friends.

They had both pulled potatoes and asparagus and beets and onions out of the ground on farms as kids and they knew what it was like to get their hands dirty. They worked in fields before they played football on them. They knew how their parents were always worrying

Early front four in Chuck Noll's tenure included, left to right, Dwight White, L.C. Greenwood, Lloyd Voss and Joe Greene.

Lloyd Voss

From the Lloyd Voss collection

Lloyd Voss spent some tough days with Steelers of the '60s. Remember these uniforms?

about the weather. They knew that pro football was a better life than what their folks had known. They had much in common; their bond was made of steel cable. They loved their beers and cheeseburgers and good cigars and good music and good times together. Most of all, they loved being with football players, sharing war stories and dirty jokes.

When I interviewed Voss for this book on March 7, 2002, I wasn't surprised when he shed some tears on particular topics. I smiled because I anticipated them. I wanted his heartfelt feelings. He smiled back, laughing through the tears. He knew himself. He knew he cried easily, more so with advancing years, like most of us. He dabbed at his reddened eyes from time to time. He was having a good time. "I'm very sentimental," he said. I could see his wife, Diane, nodding in agreement from a seat nearby.

Following his pro football career, Voss worked 23 years with the Allegheny County Parks & Recreation Department, and spent a great deal of time at South Park. He spent the first three years downtown at the City-County Building. He and Jerry Bergman, then an NFL referee from the North Side, were looked after by County Commissioner Tom Foerster, an old friend of Art Rooney. Dick Phillips, a college basketball and football official, was the superintendent of recreation during that same period.

Voss spoke about South Park and the old white stone building that served as the Steelers spartan locker room during their days at the Fair Grounds. It's quite a contrast to their current set-up at the UPMC Sports Performance Complex on the South Side. Nowadays, they could hold an auto show or boat show in their spacious dressing quarters.

Bill Cowher ought to bus his ballplayers out to the Fair Grounds some day so they could see how good they have it by comparison. The old white stone building was leveled about five years go, but they'd get the picture. Despite its primitive state, Hall of Famers like Bobby Layne, Ernie Stautner and John Henry Johnson once dressed there, so it didn't keep them from playing as well as the best of them.

"I'm not sorry I was sent here."

On the morning I was scheduled to speak to Lloyd Voss, it came back to me that I had first talked to him in 1974, when he came out of retirement to play for the New York Stars of the World Football League. I had forgotten about that when I first called him. It came to me as I was awakening that morning. I was working for *The New York Post* then, and I had a fondness for new leagues. I had covered them all, from the ABL to the ABA, from the Rens to the Pipers and Condors, from the Floridians to the Nets. I covered Pele and the Cosmos when the North American Soccer League came in, and then a box lacrosse league. I covered the New York Islanders before they even had a nickname, before they won four consecutive Stanley Cups. I covered jai alai in Miami and alligator wrestling in the Everglades when I worked at *The Miami News*. There were always interesting and offbeat characters in offbeat leagues. Boxing was full of them. The Stars played at New York's Randall's Island in a shabby city-maintained stadium normally used by schoolboys. It was New York's answer to the George Cupples Stadium on the South Side of Pittsburgh. The Stars moved to Charlotte at mid-season. It wasn't working in New York.

I could picture only a part of the poorly lit locker room — bare light bulbs against a dark ceiling — where I had interviewed Voss in New York after a game, or a practice, I'm not sure which. I still have the newspaper clipping of the story I wrote about him somewhere in one of the scrapbooks my mother kept for me in those days. They're in my basement.

Voss was on that team, and so were Gerry Philbin, George Sauer and John Elliott who had been a part of Joe Namath's New York Jets when they won the AFL title and the Super Bowl in the 1969 season. As it turned out, Voss remembered me interviewing him in New York. Tom Moore was an assistant coach on the offensive unit with the Stars. Moore would be the receiver coach of the Steelers on Chuck Noll's staff when I came home to Pittsburgh in 1979. Now he's the offensive coordinator on Tony Dungy's staff at Indianapolis. Moore had coached at Georgia Tech with an old friend of mine, Dick Bestwick, and I would use that mutual friendship as an ice-breaker. I know I spoke to Moore and interviewed Philbin when they were with the Stars. It seems so long ago, scenes filed somewhere in the back of my mind. Bob Gladieux, a running back from Notre Dame, and Tom Sherman, a quarterback from Penn State, were also New York Stars, as I recall.

In his first two years (1964-65) in the National Football League, Voss had played for Vince Lombardi, and then he played for Bill Austin and Chuck Noll in Pittsburgh. The Packers won the first of a string of National Football League championships in his second season. He was a backup defensive lineman for the Packers. Austin was an assistant coach on Lombardi's staff. When Austin succeeded Mike Nixon as head coach of the Steelers in 1966, he made a trade to obtain Voss. He thought Voss could help him in building a winning team in Pittsburgh.

As a result, Voss missed out on being a part of the Packers' run as one of the greatest powers in pro football history. And, at this end, he missed the start of the Steelers' championship run in the mid-70s. He was a bridge between the glory days in both river cities. He doesn't look back. "I wanted to start, and I had a chance to play in Pittsburgh," he said. "I had a good stay here. I've never regretted it. No, I'm not sorry I was sent here. Maybe I helped some of those guys get ready to win all those Super Bowls here."

The Steelers were 2-11-1 in Austin's last season in 1968 and they were 1-13 in Noll's first season in 1969. How much fun could that have been? You'd have to meet Lloyd Voss to appreciate how he appreciated that period, and has only positive thoughts about it.

Lloyd's wife, formerly Diane Kruger, was the best hostess I have ever had during a home visit for an interview. She's in my Hall of Fame from now on. She offered fresh fruit and cheese and crackers and wine, and had a candle display lit on the dining room table. It was all displayed with care, even white cloth napkins. She put out that kind of spread on two separate occasions. I was not used to such treatment. Usually, I have to ask for a glass of water or a Diet Coke to keep me going. Lloyd, I learned, had originally met Diane when he hired her as a nurse to look after his ailing father back on the family farm in Minnesota. His mother and sister had died and his dad was living alone. Diane was living in Luverne, about seven miles from Magnolia. She was not into sports and had never heard of Lloyd Voss. His first wife, Jane, died in 1995, after they had been married for 27 years.

It was easy to detect that Diane did a good job of looking after Lloyd. She had him spoiled and he loved it. I liked her right away. Like Lloyd, she was for real. Lloyd was lucky to have found such a nice person to fill a void in his life. Diane was a widow and was looking for someone to share her life as well when they met.

There was a large portrait of Voss in his Steelers uniform on display over the mantel in his living room. There were more photos on the walls along the stairway leading down to the family room in the basement of his well-kept two-story red brick home in Scott Township, not far from a cemetery. There was an aerial view of the family farm out in Minnesota. It was on the wall to the left at the top of the stairs. The game room was full of photos and montages from his playing days. They showed Voss assailing some quarterback or tackling some running back. There were several photos and drawings of Vince Lombardi. There was a lamp with a light affixed to the top of his Steelers' helmet. My wife would never let me have that in our house. It was his personal Wall of Fame. It's like that in Rocky Bleier's home, about two miles away in Mt. Lebanon, only there are children's toys and games spread across the floor in the Bleier basement room. Lloyd's kids and Diane's kids live elsewhere.

There were photos and his football jersey from his days at the University of Nebraska. The bright red offered quite a contrast to the black and gold motif of most of the room.

They reminded Voss of his life in football. We retired to his family room to talk about those days.

Lloyd Voss:

I remember at the end of my rookie season in 1964 we played the St. Louis Cardinals in the Playoff Bowl at the Orange Bowl in Miami. That was a game for the runners-up in each division of the National Football League. In 1965, we won the world championship in Green Bay. We beat Cleveland for the title.

I remember that morning like it was yesterday. I lived in a duplex in Green Bay. I always slept with a window open. Around 7 a.m., I could hear someone shoveling snow outside. I looked out the window. It was snowing, really snowing. I said, "Oh, boy, this is going to be a helluva day."

Here's something that happened in Green Bay. My nose was always getting cut open by the bar on my facemask. Lombardi had an equipment salesman get me a specially made double-strap chinstrap. That was the first one that was ever made. Now it's pretty standard stuff.

Playing for Lombardi was a great experience. He was a fundamentalist, and we worked and worked to get things right. Training camps were hell. His philosophy was that there were three key things in your life: your family, your religion and Green Bay Packers football. He was a very temperamental guy. He was an Italian. He could change personalities or moods in a second. He loved to laugh. If he saw something he didn't like he'd explode.

We played half of our home schedule in Milwaukee. We'd take the train down from Green Bay on Saturday. We'd take two buses back to Green Bay. We'd stop at this bar to pick up some beer on the way back. It was always the same place. He'd go in with a two-wheeled dolly and bring out two or three cases. He'd toss the beer onto the bus, two per man. If we lost, he'd say, "I should give you oranges! He and his wife Marie would sit beside each other in the first seat behind the bus driver. It was a two-hour bus ride back to Green Bay. After a loss, he wouldn't talk to her all the way home.

When he traded me, I was called to the front office. They gave me some traveling expenses. Lombardi didn't tell me I had been traded. Pat Peppler was director of player personnel. He told me I was traded before I went to see Lombardi. I bumped into Lombardi in the hall. He had tears in his eyes when he talked to me. He wished me good luck.

Bill Austin was the guy who tried to sign me when I was a senior at Nebraska. The National Football League and the American Football League were fighting over college players, doing their best to outdo the other and get everyone they wanted signed as soon as possible, even before the NCAA permitted them to do it.

I was drafted No. 1 by Green Bay and No. 2 by the New York Jets of the AFL. I could have made three times as much money if I'd gone with the Jets — that was before Namath — but I wanted to play in the NFL. Green Bay didn't mean anything to me. I didn't even know where it was. I knew Magnolia, Minnesota and Sioux Falls, South Dakota.

When Austin came to Pittsburgh in 1966, he traded for me. We had just finished two-a-days at St. Norbert College, where we trained in DePere, Wisconsin, just outside of Green Bay. The college team — they were called the Green Knights — wore the same colors, green and gold, as we did. The Steelers' training camp was at Kingston, Rhode Island that year. In Green Bay, I had played on all the special teams and I was a backup lineman behind Willie Davis and Lionel Aldridge. Davis is now in the Hall of Fame.

I was not upset about going to Pittsburgh because I was going to play ball. Austin failed because he tried to be Lombardi. He ran the same offense. He tried to be the same disciplinarian. It took awhile for the players to discover that he wasn't being himself, and that he wasn't consistent. He traded guys the third year who didn't buy into his ways, like Roy Jefferson and Marv Woodson. By the third year, there were problems. We had a lot of turnover. When Dan Radakovich came in as the defensive line coach in 1971, he wanted more speed in the defensive line, and my playing time was cut considerably. I remember Radakovich as a screamer.

Joe Greene was a player. He had good size, great quickness. He was young and, at times, he didn't play the defense as it was designed to be played. He took it upon himself to do what he wanted to do. We had a good defensive team when I was there. That defensive team, when they were playing in the Super Bowls, had tremendous personnel.

I loved working for Art Rooney. He was a great guy. I was making about $15,000 when I was playing for the Steelers at the start. One day I went in to sign a new contract. I kept track of how I graded out. Fran Fogarty was the business manager and he was going to offer me the same amount of money as I had been paid the previous year. Mr. Rooney was there when I was talking to Fran. He was sitting back there, working on his cigar.

At one point, I said, "Fran, I graded out best of the defensive linemen and I think I deserve a raise."

He said, "We can't do that."

Art Rooney piped up and said, "Fran, give it to him." So I went up to $17,000 in 1967.

After I quit playing, I really didn't follow it that closely.

I go back to Green Bay for reunions. They're better about that sort of thing than the Steelers. I'm getting set to go to another reunion there this September 10. They want everyone who played for Lombardi for this one.

I never expected to play pro football. I never expected to go to college. I grew up in Magnolia, Minnesota in the southwest end of the state. We call it the Tahiti of the North. It's about 35 miles east of Sioux Falls, South Dakota, and about 240 miles from Minneapolis. It's 9 miles from the Iowa border.

Lloyd Voss has photo displays and mementos of his days with the Steelers and Green Bay Packers in his Scott Township home. In photo behind him, he and Chuck Hinton (64) are closing in on Washington Redskins' quarterback Sonny Jurgensen. He takes pride in playing for Vince Lombardi.

"Pride is developed from a winning tradition."
— Vince Lombardi

My dad — we called him Hub — owned a 300-acre farm. He had some beef cattle, along with hogs and chickens. We did our own slaughtering. And we grew our own food. We had a big garden. I'd come home from practice and I'd have to gather the eggs. Those chickens were something. They'd get clucky and they'd peck you when you reached in to get the egg. I had a foot-long stick and I'd smack 'em if they pecked me. I buried a lot of chickens in my day in a graveyard out in back of the barn.

I graduated in a class of 17 kids. In my junior year, we were the last six-man football team in the state of Minnesota. If we played a bigger school that usually played 11-man football they played six-man football against us. In my senior year when we went to 11-man football, we had to strong-arm some guys to play because we wanted to be able to play. And we needed more players.

I was recruited to play at the University of Nebraska. I remember one day at school being told to go to the teachers lounge. There was a coach there from Nebraska to see me. They wanted me to come down to Lincoln to check out the school. I got letters from Notre Dame and small schools like North Dakota State and South Dakota State.

Minnesota came after me, too. I was on the track team and I went to the state championships. They were held at the University of Minnesota. I threw the shot and discus, and I was there for the discus. Dennis Crawford, who was the offensive line coach at Minnesota, met me there. He took me to see Murray Warmath, the head coach.

Coach Warmath was sitting behind his desk. He's got his feet up on the desk. He's got a big ol' cigar in his mouth. It was like something out of a movie. He welcomed me. He had a big Southern drawl. He said, "Turn around, boy, and pull up your pants legs." I'm wondering what he's doing. Is he buying a horse? He was checking out my calves. I told myself, "That's it. I'm going to Nebraska."

I played for the South team in the state all-star football game and I roomed with Larry Kramer. Minnesota and Nebraska were recruiting Larry, too. We both went to Nebraska. Right after I left for Nebraska, Murray Warmath and Dennis Crawford pulled up to my parents' farm in their car. My mother told them I left a half-hour ago for Nebraska. We played Minnesota in my junior year at Nebraska and we kicked their ass. I felt good about that.

I was 6-3, 200 pounds when I reported to Nebraska. I was a tight end my freshman year, and the next fall I moved to offensive tackle and defensive end for the next three years. In my junior year, we played in the Gotham Bowl. That was at Yankee Stadium in New York. We won that game. In my senior year, we won the Big 8 and played Auburn in the Orange Bowl and we won that one, too. Bill Jennings was our head coach. Bob Devaney came down from Wyoming and joined his staff. Then he became the head coach at Nebraska. Tom Osborne was a graduate assistant coach that year.

We had a reunion of that 1962-1963 team in April of 1999. Bob Brown, the big offensive tackle for the Philadelphia Eagles and Oakland Raiders, was on our team. We played an unbalanced line and Kramer, Brown and myself formed the defensive line.

We had the horses. There were 18 guys off my senior team who went into pro football. That 1963 season was the beginning of powerhouse teams at Nebraska.

"Coming to Pittsburgh was like a nightmare."

The stadium and practice facilities at Green Bay were first-class for that era. It was nothing like it is now, but for its time it was pretty good. Then I come to Pittsburgh and we're practicing at the Fair Grounds at South Park. It was like going from the penthouse to the shithouse. There were five or six toilets and half of them had seats. Half the showerheads were missing, too. I had a window behind my locker and if it snowed you had to wipe snow off your dressing stool. The windows didn't close all the way.

We dressed in the basement of the building. The coaches' offices were on the first floor. On the second floor, there were two big rooms. One was for the offense meetings and one was for the defense meetings. Plaster was coming off the walls.

Coming from Nebraska, which had first class facilities, to Green Bay was probably a step up in that regard. Coming to Pittsburgh was, well, like a nightmare. You'd go down on the field at the Fair Grounds, and you had to be real careful. They had the Allegheny County Police horses stabled there. They let the horses out on the field to get some exercise and to graze in the grass. If you'd put your hand down in a three-point stance, you'd better watch where you put your fingers.

If you wanted to play, though, they gave you the chance to play. Some of the other defensive linemen who were here when I came were Ben McGee. Chuck Hinton and Ken Kortas. The defensive line coach when I got here was LaVerne Torgeson. I used to run with Bruce Van Dyke and Ralph Wenzel.

Bill Saul was the middle linebacker. He was something. At the linebacker position, we got Rod Breedlove from the Redskins and John Campbell from the Colts. We had Marv

Woodson, Clendon Thomas, Brady Keys, Paul Martha and Willie Daniels in the secondary. I remember those guys.

I played in the All-Star Game in Chicago with Martha, and also in the All-American Game in Buffalo. We played here together, then he was traded to Denver in 1971. He was one of the hardest-hitting backs in the league. He hit people so hard he almost knocked himself out.

Saul was, let's say, well-endowed. He'd come out of the showers with a towel over his head, and he'd holler out, "Guess who?" Saul was quite a ballplayer, and he was always good for a few laughs.

After practice at St. Vincent's, we'd go to the 19th Hole. We'd have fun over a few beers. Lloyd and Paul and guys like that would get into chugging contests. Saul looked like Lurch on TV. He'd pour a beer into a glass, and he could get his mouth completely around the top of the glass. He'd just tip it back and empty it in one gulp. It was quite a show.

Martha was amazing. His father-in-law was the president of U.S. Steel. During the off-season, he'd be straight and narrow. When he was with us during training season, he'd let his hair down and had a pretty good time. He and Saul would sneak out after room check.

When practice was over at St. Vincent's, we'd go out and have a few beers at the 19th Hole. We'd come back for meetings and then we'd go back to the 19th Hole. Curfew was at 11 o'clock. Sometimes Bill and Paul would get into a wrestling match in their room. Shortly after 11, you could hear them going at it.

During the season, when we practiced at the Fair Grounds, we'd go to the South Park Inn and to Al's Tavern.

When Austin was the coach, we played back-to-back pre-season games in Portland, Oregon. Austin had gone to the University of Oregon. We were housed in this building that had a fire escape. At the bottom there was a chute that emptied into a big garbage can. Paul and Bill broke curfew quite a bit. I remember this one warm night in August. Andy Russell and I were roommates. We heard Paul and Bill sliding down that chute into the garbage can. It sounded like a bowling alley. They got caught. One of the coaches was out there watching to see if anyone was breaking curfew. I can't remember which coach, but he got 'em.

We had some interesting guys then. I remember we had a tackle named Charlie Bradshaw. His hair was almost white. They called him "Mr. Clean" because his jersey never got dirty. A lot of people don't know what a good offensive tackle he was. He stayed clean because nobody could knock him down. We had another good tackle named Dan James. Dick Hoak was one of our best running backs. He was a nice guy, a

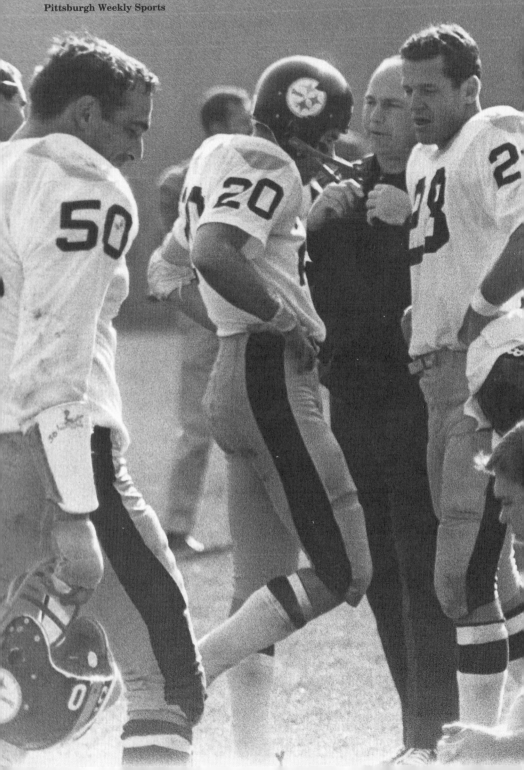

Lloyd Voss recalls teammates such as Bill Saul (50), Paul Martha (20) and Clendon Thomas (28), seen here with assistant coach LaVerne Torgeson.

Pittsburgh Weekly Sports

quiet kid. He's been with the Steelers ever since. Now he coaches the backs.

I remember Ray Mansfield. We were pretty close. I remember we all went to Froggy's downtown following his funeral. Ray's partner in the insurance business was Chuck Puskar. He went to his apartment and got a guitar. We all got lit up pretty good on those drinks they serve at Froggy's. Chuck's son, Chip, is a helluva singer and he started singing a song about "there's a time to live . . . and a time to die." We were all crying.

A lot of different thoughts and stories come to my mind...

I got to know O.J. Simpson intimately when he was a running back for the Buffalo Bills. Andy Russell was the linebacker behind me on this one play. We run a stunt where Andy is going to rush inside and I am going to go outside. They ran a sweep to the left with O.J. getting the ball. Then O.J. reverses field and comes back my way. I know I have to have containment, and keep him inside. I have to tackle him. I've got one leg with my right arm. My left hand has got him by the crotch. I knew what I had, but I had to hold on tight. I wasn't going to let go. Otherwise, he'd break the tackle and get away from me. When he got up, I said, "O.J., I'm sorry about that." He smiled at me and said, "That's OK, man." I should have squeezed harder and put him out of the game.

Andy Russell and I roomed together for six years. He was a great guy and a good friend, but we weren't that close after our playing days. Just traveled in different circles. No problems. He was very smart, very intense and had good instincts for the game. He was good at recognizing different formations, knowing tendencies, knowing what plays came out of those formations. It was a big help.

I remember what it was like after Ernie Holmes got arrested for shooting at Ohio state policemen who were flying over him in a helicopter After that, I'm sitting on the stool next to him in the locker room and wondering when he's going to go off again.

I went to Denver in 1972 and Van Dyke went to Green Bay in 1972. I think Van Dyke lives out in South Strabane. I still get invited by Denver to player reunions, and I only played there for one year. You have to pay to get there, but it's a great time.

I didn't play ball in 1973, but I got a call from Babe Parilli when he became the head coach of the New York Stars. He knew me from his days in Pittsburgh and Green Bay. Now I'm going to a reunion of the Stars in Charlotte. It'll be great to see the guys again.

Even so, I feel more like a Steeler than anything else. I like Pittsburgh. That's why I've stayed here. I have three children who live in the area, and I enjoy seeing them. I go to the alumni golf outings and get-togethers here. I've become a close friend of Leo Nobile through the Steelers Alumni organization. I like Mel Blount; he's a heck of a guy. I've gotten to know Robin Cole, who's the president of the group now. They're all good guys. I like Rocky Bleier. He was just coming back from Vietnam when I was sent to Denver. He's quite a story.

It's been great here. I didn't go back to Minnesota because I didn't like working a farm, and Magnolia is a town of only about a hundred people. There's nothing out there. The closest town is Sioux Falls. Even today, there's maybe 40,000 there. There's more to do here. We live in a great location here.

I stay home most of the time now. We go back to Minnesota to see Diane's family from time to time. We go to Maryland once in a blue moon to see my old teammate, Ralph Wenzel. We were real close. It would have been nice to play on more championship teams. When you win the Super Bowl you have a team that has a lot of talent. When Pittsburgh was winning — those Steelers of the '70s — they had more talent than those great teams of the Green Bay Packers.

Lombardi and Noll had two different personalities. Noll was a quiet guy. Like ice at times. You never really knew what he was thinking. Lombardi was just the opposite. When I was at Nebraska, Bob Devaney was like a father image. He wasn't a screamer. Neither was Noll. I liked it better that way.

Why was Noll so successful? He had great personnel playing for him. He was a great coach. The only thing I know about Cowher is seeing him on the sidelines on TV. I don't think I could have played for him. He's a screamer.

Lloyd Voss (65) was a valued member of New York Stars of the World Football League (WFL) in 1974, when they played at Randall's Island.

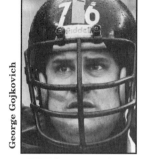

John Banaszak
W&J coach believes in basics

"I'm in it to help the kids grow up like I did."

There are lots of photos of past athletes on display in the halls and office walls in the Henry Memorial Center that houses the athletic department at Washington & Jefferson College in Washington, Pennsylvania, about 25 miles south of Pittsburgh.

There are team photographs of football and basketball and soccer teams, among other activities, some of them dating back more than a hundred years. They have done a better job in this respect than many schools, including my alma mater, the University of Pittsburgh, in preserving their past.

Scott McGuinness, the second-year sports information director at W&J, says there are more of those vintage photos in the school library, but most of them are not identified.

I saw some team basketball photos from the mid-to-late '50s that had a familiar face in them. Bobby Bowser was a starting backcourtman at W&J when I was a teenager. He was from my hometown of Hazelwood and he played basketball with us younger guys at the playground at Burgwin Recreation Center near his home in the Glen-Hazel projects. He was one of the first college basketball players I ever met. Playing in games with him was a big deal. For me, he will always look like he does in those team photos.

John Banaszak, the head football coach at W&J, was showing us around, including a tour of the 1200-seat basketball arena. We walked over two shuffleboard outlines on a cement floor. I wondered when anybody last played shuffleboard there. Banaszak pointed to some of the earlier photos in the hall outside his office, including a great horizontal shot of the 1911 W&J football team, about 30 players lined up shoulder to shoulder in single file. They are classics. "I love this stuff," said Banaszak. "Someday, a hundred years from now, someone will be looking at a photo of our team, and saying how funny we look."

That team photo is sure to draw attention because the 2001 team went undefeated in the regular season, posting a perfect 10-0 record, and finishing the post-season playoffs with an 11-1 record. They lost in the second round of the NCAA Division III playoffs at Widener, 46-30. With the players expected to return, W&J would no doubt be rated as one of the best Division III teams in the country in pre-season polls.

Maybe they will be mentioning Banaszak, who would turn 52 in August, 2002, in the same breath as some of his legendary predecessors at W&J. Then again, an ill wind was blowing Banaszak's way at W&J, that threatened his stay there.

John Banaszak (signature)

Photos by Jim O'Brien

Andy Russell's 26th Annual Celebrity Classic drew, left to right, Randy Grossman, John Banaszak, Glen Edwards, Mel Blount and Chuck Noll to The Club at Nevillewood in May, 2002. Luncheon gathering, included, left to right, John Banaszak, Gordon Gravelle, Andy Russell and Rocky Bleier.

Banaszak would not discuss the problems or differences of philosophy I had heard through the grapevine that he was having with the school and athletic department administrators when I visited him on Wednesday, February 27, 2002. "This is a great school and I have a great team, and we're pointing toward another great season," said Banaszak.

It seems a shame because Banaszak couldn't be a better fit for the Prexies. On the surface, it would seem it should be a perfect marriage. None of the greats they talk about at W&J have done better than Banaszak. I've heard him speak on half a dozen occasions, and always thought he represented the Steelers and W&J so well.

Earle "Greasy" Neale, later a famed NFL coach, guided W&J to a 10-0-1 record in 1921, the tie a scoreless affair with California in the Rose Bowl on January 2, 1922. There are still signs acknowledging W&J's Rose Bowl appearance on display at Henry Memorial Center. Neale and Walt Kiesling coached the infamous Steagles, a combination of the Steelers and Eagles, in 1943, during World War II, when home games were divided between Pittsburgh and Philadelphia. So Banaszak is the second W&J head coach with a Steelers background.

John Heisman, for whom the Heisman Trophy is named, coached the Presidents to a 7-1-1 record in 1923. Andy Kerr, who went on to greater fame as the football coach at Colgate, led W&J's football team for three seasons (1926-28) to a 16-6-5 record.

Wilbur "Pete" Henry, an All-American lineman at W&J who was also called "Fats" Henry, is honored by the campus gym's name. Henry had a 4-9 overall mark for the 1942 and 1945 season. There was no football played at W&J in 1943 and 1944 because of World War II.

John Luckhardt, who coached the team from 1982 to 1998, posted an impressive 137-37-2 (.784) record. It was Luckhardt who doubled as athletic director and brought Banaszak to W&J in 1994, as a defensive coordinator and baseball coach, and then turned the football program over to him. After three years, Banaszak had a better winning percentage (.828) with a 29-6 record.

Luckhardt left W&J in 2001, as did Dr. Howard J. Burnett, the school president. Both retired after distinguished careers on the campus. They were a winning parlay. There was a new president and athletic director at W&J, and it remained to be seen how this change in administration would impact the future of the football program. Burnett had been a big booster of having a first-rate football program to call positive attention to the school.

The Cameron family of Coca-Cola distributing fame made a $2.5 million gift in 2000 to the respected liberal arts college to upgrade its football facility, formerly College Field. It's now called Cameron Stadium and it's one of the most impressive facilities in all of the NCAA Division III ranks.

George Gipp and Knute Rockne of Notre Dame even strode across College Field in former days.

"Deacon Dan" Towler, the school's most famous football player, had visited the campus for different special occasions several times in recent years. Towler died at age 73 on August 1, 2001. He had looked hale and hardy when I had last seen him and spoken to him at the Super Bowl XXXV in Tampa in January of the same year. It was a year when a lot changed in the W&J football tradition. I had also seen Banaszak with Towler at several W&J sponsored gatherings at the Southpointe Golf Club in Canonsburg where the Piatt family holds forth.

The rich tradition is not lost on Banaszak. He has enjoyed being the coach at W&J. He did, however, apply for and get interviewed for a job opening at Mercyhurst College in Erie a few months earlier, but was not hired. I remember how surprised I was when I read that news item in the *Post-Gazette* because it appeared that Banaszak had an idyllic job at W&J during a time when there was much construction on the campus, and the best seemed to be on the drawing boards. I had heard Banazak say only the year before, "I have the greatest job in the world." He remained at W&J where prospects were strong for another stellar season. His name did come up again when California (Pa.) University was looking for a football coach in the spring of 2002. Duquesne's Greg Gattuso and Luckhardt were also interviewed for that position. Luckhardt believed his health had improved to the point where he could return to action. Gattuso may have wanted to move up to a different level of competition. Luckhardt landed the Cal job.

Banaszak began coaching at W&J as a volunteer assistant in 1993 and moved up to become the school's defensive coordinator as well as head baseball coach. "John's doing a great job," allowed Luckhardt, "he's tremendous."

Banaszak has a spacious but spartan office in a corner of an office complex for the football coaches on the second floor of the Henry Memorial Center. There are framed photos and art renderings on the wall behind his desk drawing attention to his glory days as a player with the Pittsburgh Steelers. He was a standout defensive lineman for the last three of the Steelers' four Super Bowl championship teams, who are pictured on the wall.

There were three white bricks on his desk. Banaszak likes to use bricks as symbols in his weight-lifting program at W&J, as he has added the bricks Luckhardt laid there in establishing one of the strongest and proudest small college football programs in the country.

There was a framed sign at the forefront of his desk calling attention to the 10-0 season. It was given to him by John Waldron, an advertising executive who was a member of the "Banaszak Bunch," his fan club during his playing days with the Steelers at Three Rivers Stadium.

Waldron, who survived a kidney transplant and remains a dear friend of Banaszak, wrote "Excellence is never accidental. Nor is it inadvertent or fortuitous or coincidental. No. Excellence is the predictable result of discipline, training, desire, daring and flawless execution under pressure. Excellence then was perfection, realized on a battlefield in western Pennsylvania on a gray Saturday in November." Banaszak is a big admirer of Waldron, who showed a lot of courage in the face of a life-threatening illness.

Banaszak gives a presentation ("Be A Champ") to many schools, civic organizations and parent groups, in addition to his corporate presentation ("You Were Hired To Be Successful"), which is given to sales and marketing groups. The Cleveland-born Banaszak graduated from Eastern Michigan University with a B.S. degree in health, physical education and recreation. He was living in McMurray, closer to the city in Washington County, with his wife of 31 years, Mary, who was the executive director of Greenbriar Treatment Center. They have three adult children, Jay, Carrie and Amye.

Banaszak began his pro career as a free agent in 1975. Before he went to college, he was in the U.S. Marines for two years (1969-1970). He was one of only three rookies who made the defending Super Bowl championship team. Dave Brown and Mike Collier were the other two rookies who made it. Banaszak was primarily a special teams player seeing only spot duty as the Steelers won another championship in Super Bowl X.

He started five games in the 1976 season during the greatest stretch of defensive play in the history of the NFL. The Steelers began the season 1-4 and won their last nine games while giving up only 28 points and registering five shutouts to win the AFC Central Division title. In 1977, Banaszak was moved to the starting right end position. After Steve Furness sustained an injury, Banaszak was moved to the inside tackle position where he stayed until a knee injury forced him to the injured reserve list for the remainder of the season.

Banaszak came back in 1978 and started 45 regular season games through 1980. He started at defensive end on two Super Bowl championship teams — XIII and XIV — during this stretch. In Super Bowl XIII, Banaszak was credited with two sacks, a fumble recovery, six tackles and a tackle for a loss, which gained him Defensive Player of the Game honors in the 35-31 victory over the Dallas Cowboys.

In the following Super Bowl, Banaszak had one sack and five tackles in the 31-19 victory over the Los Angeles Rams. That game was played, by coincidence, at the Rose Bowl in Pasadena. After his eight-year stint with the Steelers, Banaszak moved on to the USFL, where he played two seasons (1983-1984) with the Michigan Panthers, and was a member of the USFL's first championship team. He finished up with the Memphis Showboats as a player/coach, mentoring a young stud named Reggie White, who would later make a name for himself in the NFL with the Philadelphia Eagles and Green Bay Packers. He also worked with former Pitt basketball player Sam Clancy, who went on to star with the Cleveland Browns and Seattle Seahawks. "What a character," Banaszak said. "Sam was a beautiful guy."

Banaszak has borrowed much of his strategy and coaching philosophy from Chuck Noll, a Hall of Famer after his 23 years at the helm of the Steelers, and defensive assistant coaches Bud Carson, Dan Radakovich, George Perles and Woody Widenhofer

When I told Banaszak something about Noll coming to practice following a game with notebooks filled with things he wanted to convey to his charges, Banaszak said, "So that's where I got that from. Now I know. I bring mine in on Sunday."

John Banaszak:

We play a very aggressive, hard-hitting defense at W&J, the same way we played with the Pittsburgh Steelers. We may not be as talented, but we're as enthusiastic. My book on football has only three chapters. I promise my young men that I'll work as hard as I can possibly work. I'll coach with as much enthusiasm as I can possibly muster. And we play to have fun. This is not life or death, but it's pretty close to it. I coach to win.

I think winning is important. I think winning is the reason I'm here today. Winning is not the only thing, as Vince Lombardi said, but being a champion is. I want my guys to be champions on the field, in the classroom and with their family. Working hard, having fun and winning is what I'm all about.

After what I went through six years ago, when I thought I might lose my leg or even my life when I had a life-threatening infection following knee surgery, I'm probably more laid-back now.

I know I've been criticized for being so animated on the sideline, but that's me.

My family and my happiness are paramount in my mind. I'm not into coaching for ego reasons. I'm in it to help the kids grow up like I did. I appreciate my wife Mary and our kids more than ever. I wouldn't trade them for anything. I love my life and my wife a little differently after what I experienced. I have learned to count my blessings.

"It never ends."

What do I know now that I didn't know then, back when I was playing for the Steelers?

I know that we were the greatest football team that ever played the game and that it became a lifelong experience. It never ends.

151

We are separated by anybody else who ever played the game because of the success we had on the football field. It has been transformed to so much success off the field. We have had so many positive experiences off the field.

In my wildest imagination, I never knew it would last this long. I know how important it was to win championships. Never did I think it would last this long.

I see Mr. Rooney in that art print there on the wall. I think about him a lot. I wonder what it must have been like for him in the early days. I think about the struggles that he had keeping the team afloat, trying to win. I know how passionate he was about that. He didn't like all that losing, all those .500 seasons. He and his son, Dan, make that one move, hiring Chuck Noll. Finally, they got a break.

Chuck is the guy who put it all together. I'm proud to have a lot of Chuck Noll in me. I remember how important he thought preparation and practice were. He'd say, "Whatever it takes is what we do here."

I always thought he was such a good organizer. He could put it all together and he did. All those egos flying around the locker room. To be able to control that and focus that. His coaching staff was a model of what it should be like. He listened. That coaching staff didn't always agree. They fought for what they believed. It certainly was not a monarchy.

It's still that way. Chuck will still listen. He'll ask me questions about my team when I see him. He'll ask me what our training camp was like. He'll say things like, "Did it work last year? It will work again. Don't change just because other people are changing." He's still knowledgeable. You can still learn from him.

"You never get a second chance to make a first impression."
— Chester Banaszak

My teammates have been very supportive of what I've done here at W&J. I have been fortunate to coach in the Pittsburgh area, and be able to call upon some of my teammates to come out here and talk to my kids. Some of the greatest players in Steelers' history have been on this campus to talk to my kids.

Mel Blount, Franco Harris, Rocky Bleier, Gerry Mullins, Mike Wagner and Randy Grossman have been here this past year. Ted Petersen and Robin Cole have been here often enough that they're like coaches. When you look at the credentials of people who have been on campus it's impressive. I've had a lot of Super Bowl rings on this campus the past year. Our kids have benefited from that.

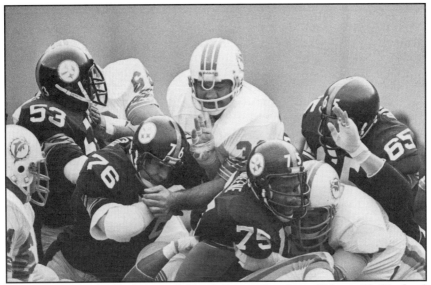

Miami Dolphins Hall of Fame fullback Larry Csonka collides with Steelers' Dennis Winston (53), John Banaszak (76), Joe Greene (75) and Tom Beasley (65). Below, Banaszak celebrates big stop, along with, left to right, Greene, Ron Johnson and Beasley.

"This will remain the land of the free as long as it is the home of the brave."
— Veteran Elmer Davis

I listen to what those guys have to say to my kids. I'm in there, too. The messages are important backups to what I have to say on a daily basis. Our kids hear it from a different perspective. Our kids aren't thinking about playing pro football.

My goal wasn't to motivate them to win football games. I thought it was important for them to hear from some of the greatest people who have played this game. On this level, this is more than football. I want to prepare them for life after college, for their careers.

I think our kids play the game with a lot of class. They celebrate with each other and with their coaches, and they conduct themselves properly on and off the field. Being a champion is important, I'm always telling them that. I want them to be champions in the classroom. I want them to show their professors the respect they merit. I want them to be champions to their parents. I told them to send their moms cards for Valentine's Day. I tell them to call home. That's important. Being a champion . . . I tell them that will last forever.

I took some of our kids to Children's Hospital last year. They visited with the kids. Here, I have a picture of that. See these kids, these patients at Children's? There are your champions.

My dad, Chester Banaszak, told me a long, long time ago that you never get a second chance to make a first impression. That might be the most important reason I'm here. I was drafted by the Steelers, but I made a good impression when I came to St. Vincent's as a free agent.

What I'm dealing with here is the future. I have about 125 young men. It's their future, and we will take that very seriously. And we'll win a few football games along the way.

I mentioned John Waldron, whom I first met because he was part of the "Banaszak Bunch" at Three Rivers. He needed a kidney transplant. After he was operated on, a little nurse had to climb up on a chair to check him out. She shined a light on his eyes, and to see if he was jaundiced. She said, "Most excellent." I've golfed with him, and he's told me that story. And that's why I have a "Most Excellent Award" here at W&J. After our games, I go around the clubhouse and I go up to somebody I think really made a contribution to our effort that day, and I whisper in his ear, "Most excellent."

Last season was only the sixth undefeated football season in the history of the school. It's something we're very proud of. It's all a contradiction. Never in my wildest imagination did I think 25 years ago, when I was part of the Pittsburgh Steelers championship teams, that it would last this long.

154

We won four Super Bowls in six years. When I talk to my kids, it's what they did off the field that really impresses me. It's what we've made of our lives. The City of Pittsburgh still holds us up on a pedestal no one else will ever reach.

"This is a team of individuals."

I know the Steelers had a good season this year, and there was a lot of talk that brought back mentions of our team. But this is a team of individuals. It's hard to compare them to our teams, and what we had. There are some obvious differences. These athletes are bigger, faster and stronger than we were. Athletically, they are superior to what we were on the football field. Their training regimen is completely different and it's a year-round thing. The facilities are different. Their development is different. I think their outlook and their attitude is different, too.

The one thing that sets us apart from the current Steelers is that we were a football team. I played with nine players, a coach and two owners who are in the Pro Football Hall of Fame. As I sit here at my desk in front of this computer, I can go on-line and call up an e-mail message that was sent to me by John Stallworth. It was 20 years ago that John and I were teammates. But we're still teammates through life. I'm so happy that he's been elected, at last, to the Pro Football Hall of Fame.

After the AFC championship game, we were at Morton's of Chicago Steak House in downtown Pittsburgh. There were a half dozen of us there, with our wives, and it was great to be with some of my former teammates. Next door to us at Morton's was Kordell Stewart. He was there with family and friends. No teammates.

That's not the way we were. The party we had after the AFC championship game in 1979 was going to happen whether we won or lost. We would have gotten together at Jack Ham's house. Only a handful wouldn't be there. Most of the guys would be at Hammer's house.

I'm not close to what they do now, but I hear rumors and stories that they don't socialize much with each other. I hear they don't spend much time with each other off the field. That was something we did. It was important to team chemistry. We liked each other's company.

The times are different. Maybe it's the money that changes everything.

There's a big difference in the makeup of the team now. Our '75 team was completely homegrown. All the players were drafted or signed as free agents coming out of college. That will never be duplicated. I don't think the players think of themselves as Steelers like we did. When you have players signing with other teams when they become free agents you don't have the same kind of loyalty, or feeling for one's team. It's a different era.

Being part of the ceremonies for the last game at Three Rivers Stadium was fun. It was great to see all the guys again, as it was when we had the reunion at the convention center three years ago. It brought back a lot of memories. A lot of things went through my mind.

It's what's reinforced. You understand what it takes to be successful. You know what you need to win championships. "Whatever it takes" is a phrase that still makes sense. Whatever it takes to prepare, whatever it takes to win, whatever it takes to be a champion. That covers everything.

Chuck was so big in that area. He emphasized that the preparation was more important than the day of the game. Sunday was fun day. At practice, he said to make sure you were a better football player when you leave the field that day. He wanted you to finish every practice, to finish every play. He gave you positive reinforcement. It's what I want to get across to our kids. We walked the walk back then; no doubt about that.

We were tough, physically and mentally. We were cocky. And we backed it up.

We don't live in a perfect world. When you've got as many individuals as we did on those championship teams, things don't always go the way you wish they would. I wish Steve Furness were here. We were close friends and now he's died. We were doing business with his artificial turf firm when he died. I'd seen him the week before he died and he looked terrific. You want to talk to him again.

I'm recruiting Ray Mansfield's nephew, Tom, from Seattle, Washington. What do you think that's like? This is the son of Ray's brother, Ted. Ray was so much the spirit of our early teams in the '70s, and he remained a part of our lives after he retired as a player. He was always getting us together for one event or another. When I open up my drawer, I see things that remind me of these guys.

I think about Joe Gilliam. He got hooked on drugs and he died from it, right after we'd seen him at the last game at Three Rivers Stadium. We thought he had cleaned up his act, that things were going to be OK for him. Sam Davis is really a tragedy. I feel terribly about what happened to him, and the condition he's in. I have to make an attempt to see him. I spoke at South Allegheny's football banquet and someone called Sam's situation to my attention. I know Sam's still out there at a nursing home in McKeesport.

156

I know from the reunion we had three years ago that some of my teammates have struggled and that they've had some hard times. Guys like Glen Edwards. It's not a perfect world. There's Mike Webster. Webby slipped my mind. There's a real tough one. We know what he needs to do, regarding his addiction to pain-killing drugs, but he's let a lot of people down with what he's done, or not done. I don't know what to say about him.

It's sobering stuff, for sure. I gotta believe that the best days of their lives were spent with us. Webby was my roommate for two years. I know how much fun he had. Today's the dark side, but I'm going to remember the bright side of the things we shared in the best times of our lives. Sam and Webby were so great. They were such good guys. They showed the way for the rest of us. I wish we were all experiencing great things in our lives today. But that's utopia. That's not the real world.

From Washington & Jefferson sports information office

John Banaszak succeeded legendary John Luckhardt as successful coach of the Washington & Jefferson football team. Luckhardt was hired to coach California (PA) University in 2002.

Edmund Nelson
The insurance man

"My goal is not to get hurt."

I felt sorry for Edmund Nelson and the Steelers. I knew they were in for a long night during the warm-up session for an exhibition basketball game at Seton LaSalle High School on February 28, 2002.

They were up against the so-called South Hills All-Stars in a game to raise funds for the Seton-LaSalle girls' basketball team. The gym was packed to its 800-seat capacity early and everyone was in for a good time. Except the Steelers, that is, but even they left smiling.

The Steelers showed up with only seven players, and three of them were alumni. The former players were Louis Lipps, easily their best basketball player, and Edmund Nelson and Bryan Hinkle. These three were also their best-known players. The current Steelers included rookies Rodney Bailey, Justin Kurpeikis, Mathias Nkwenti and Chris Hoke. They all played on the Steelers special team units — when somebody is kicking the ball — and that was a tip-off to the Steelers' dilemma in this basketball game.

Nelson was wearing a black wool stocking cap during the warm-up session and when he was sitting on the bench. He had been complaining about a head cold. He blamed it on the basketball games he had been playing of late with the Steelers. "You come out of a hot gym into the cold and you're vulnerable," Nelson said.

"I really like to play; I just wished I had felt better," he added. "My knees hurt and I was sick. I was having a hard time out there."

Tom O'Malley Jr., the manager of the Steelers basketball team, had been having difficulty finding enough current players to stock a basketball team. Most of them were out of town. So he called on some former players in a pinch.

Ted Petersen was one of them. He had played some games that same week. Petersen turned yellow the day after his last appearance and had to leave work as a physical education instructor at Trinity High School at mid-afternoon he felt so lousy. He'd hurt his knee and he just wasn't feeling so hot. "I obviously wasn't in shape to play basketball," said Petersen when I mentioned that to him during a visit to his school.

Nelson normally looks good in hats. He even wears them on camera when he is critiquing the play of the Steelers or conducting a sideline interview on TV. But this was different.

The South Hills All-Stars starting lineup consisted of five women. "That was the first time in our long history that's ever happened," said O'Malley, who grew up in Castle Shannon and heads the office at the Bob Purkey Insurance Agency in Bethel Park.

Photos by Jim O'Brien

Edmund Nelson with his wife, Cynthia, at Andy Russell's 2002 Celebrity Classic, and with Bryan Hinkle on 2002 Steelers' basketball team. Nelson was suffering with a head cold and kept his head covered during no-contest outing at Seton-LaSalle High School.

O'Malley used to help Baldy Regan manage and promote the Steelers basketball team and books an ambitious winter schedule throughout the district.

For this game, O'Malley should have brought Kaye Cowher, the wife of the Steelers' coach, who was a first-rate basketball player at North Carolina State University where they first met. Kaye and her twin sister Faye also played for the New York Stars of the Women's Professional Basketball League.

"I don't know how Baldy and I managed to do this all those years without cell phones," said O'Malley. "You have to make a lot of calls to round up a team and get them to the gym on time."

Wayne Herrod, who sells cars by day and helps coach scholastic basketball teams at night, promoted the game and asked O'Malley and the Steelers beforehand, "Please take it easy on our girls."

Three of the five women were Seton-LaSalle alumnae, including former pro star and two-time Olympian Suzie McConnell Serio, who now lives in Upper St. Clair. She was two days away from coaching her Oakland Catholic girls' basketball team to a WPIAL AAAA championship victory over Upper St. Clair. Melissa Shell and Kelly Mazza both played college basketball, as did Mt. Lebanon's Kim Seaver. Dawn Zerman played at Kent State and some pro ball in Europe. Her fiancee Gary McCullough, who also played, teaches in Upper St. Clair and is a member of Jim Render's outstanding football coaching staff.

The South Hills All-Stars included two terrific local high school basketball coaches, Tim McConnell of Chartiers Valley and Rick Bell of Canon-McMillan, formerly of Peters Township. Bell brought along his volunteer assistant coach, 6-6 Doug West. "That's why I really was invited," said Bell. "They knew I'd bring Doug with me."

West, who resides in Nevillewood, was a star performer at Altoona High School and Villanova University prior to an 11-year NBA career, finishing up with the Minnesota Timberwolves only two or three years earlier.

The All-Stars were coached by Greg Gattuso, an alumnus of Seton-LaSalle and Penn State who normally coached the football team at Duquesne University. He didn't know the hell that was in store for him in the coming month. The other coach was Jerry Conboy, one of the finest basketball coaches in the area, who was coaching the girls' basketball team at Seton-LaSalle.

Within a few weeks, two of Gattuso's football players at Duquesne University would be arrested and charged with the murder of another young man in a bizarre drug-related tragedy. Gattuso understandably had a tough time dealing with that. The victim was wrapped in a chain with a 60-pound weight attached and dumped from a bridge into a river.

I ran into Rodney Bailey, a defensive lineman from Ohio State, two nights after that basketball game, in Columbus, where we both spoke to the Pittsburgh Club of Columbus. He said, "I never saw such a good basketball team, men and women, since I've been playing in these games. That West went over me twice for thunder-dunks. I was just trying to get out of the way so I wouldn't get hurt."

The dunks by West turned on the crowd as much as the Seton-LaSalle cheerleaders. The South Hills All-Stars raced off to a 34-17 lead, and won going away, 86-47. Suzie and Tim McConnell were setting the pace for their units in leading full-court pressure. They were creating steals and racing past the Steelers like punt-returners for the Baltimore Ravens and New England Patriots.

It was a fun evening, but it wasn't pretty.

Nelson said Tim McConnell got carried away with himself. "Suzie has a competitive edge, but she knows how to have fun out there, too," Nelson said. "She was pushing us around and being playful, while trying her best to beat us at the same time. She's fun.

"But her brother was playing like he was trying to make the NBA. I wish I had felt better so I could have gotten a piece of that little bugger. I hear he's a good coach, so he should know better. The people are there to see the Steelers and to get some autographs. They didn't come out to see Tim McConnell. You can break a good sweat and have some fun at the same time. My goal is not to get hurt. It was always that way in those basketball games. Sometimes we'd go to some high school where a teacher was trying to show the students how tough he was. That's silly. You don't want any problems. And you don't want to upset any of these young guys on the Steelers. They can hurt you without really trying."

Nelson is a graduate of Auburn University with a B.S. in personnel management. He has been an agent for State Farm for 12 years, and has qualified seven times for the insurance company's Millionaire Club. Like a good neighbor, as the company theme goes, Nelson is there for you.

There are some framed awards in his offices at South Hills Village. In 1981 he was the defensive MVP in the Blue-Gray Game. In 1982 he won the Cliff Hare Award as Auburn's Scholar Athlete. In 1986, at the height of his six-year (1982-1987) career with the Steelers, he was named the Miller Lite/NFL Defensive Lineman of the Year.

He has gotten heavily involved in radio and TV coverage of the Steelers. He has served in recent years as an analyst for Infinity Broadcasting, and has done pre-game and post-game shows on KDKA Radio. He has also done sideline reporting for KDKA-TV on pre-season games. He has been a panelist on the fast-paced #1 Cochran Sports Showdown and an analyst on a playoff special, both on KDKA-TV.

He teamed up with Bob Pompeani, Mark Bruener and Ed Bouchette on KDKA-TV for coverage of the 2002 College Draft. He was understandably excited when the Steelers selected Kendall Simmons, an offensive lineman from Auburn University, Nelson's alma mater. He, too, was a War Eagle. Simmons stood 6-2½, 311 pounds and played tackle in college, but was selected as a guard by the Steelers.

161

"I was ecstatic, of course," Nelson said. "Oh, oh, here we go! I had stood next to him at the Auburn spring game a week or so earlier. I was there to be introduced at halftime with some other old War Eagles. So I'm sure he knows me, too. He's not that tall, but he's real stocky. He's a mean-looking dude.

"Right away, there was a question as to why the Steelers would draft a lineman when they're pretty well stocked there. When you think about what the Steelers do best, though, it makes sense. Good offensive and defensive linemen are hard to come by. There were lots of good skill position players available in the draft. So I think it's a good pick."

I had paid a visit to his office on Wednesday, February 13. It was a cold, blustery morning and Nelson said he was freezing from walking through the parking lot at South Hills Village. He warmed up in a hurry in his office with a coffee and carrot cake muffin.

Edmund Nelson:

God takes care of those of us who don't know how to take care of themselves. State Farm tried to recruit me to return to Auburn to be an agent. My wife, Cynthia, is from Auburn, but she didn't want to move back. So I continued to look for work here. I had all these business cards from people who gave them to me when I was playing for the Steelers and said to call them when I was ready to go to work. They told me to call them whenever I needed something. So I did. But I couldn't make a connection for a job. Those people weren't as enthusiastic about talking to me as they were when I was still playing for the Steelers.

An ex-player is not nearly as loved. It's not even close. It wasn't a shocking revelation. I knew better than that.

A man named James Daniels had been an assistant at Auburn when I was there. He was at training camp with the New Orleans Saints as part of the NFL's program to identify and develop black coaches, when I was with them in 1988. He's now an assistant with the Atlanta Falcons. He remembered me and recommended me to State Farm. They wanted to train me to manage an office in Auburn.

He told me to get in contact with State Farm officials in this area. I took an aptitude test and passed it. One of the guys I met that way was Ralph Campanelli. He had a State Farm agency here, and he was also a successful football coach at Canon-McMillan High School in Canonsburg. I went to work for him in a building in South Fayette

I've been with them for 12 years. I moved here in 1995. I've been living in Upper St. Clair since 1986. It couldn't have worked out better.

162

"It's getting better and better."

My mother and father are still living. One year we had eight home games at Auburn and my parents were at seven of them. That tells you in a nutshell the kind of support I had.

My mother's name is Mary. I learned how to manage money from my mom and how to present myself to the public. She was a teacher for pre-school children. She was always on us about standing tall and enunciating when we spoke. My dad, whose name is Darlee, showed me how to shake hands firmly and to look people in the eye when you meet them and when you talk to them.

My dad had retired from the military after serving for 20 years. He was a warrant officer. I was an Army brat. We lived in Europe twice. We settled in Tampa when I was eight. I was the youngest of three boys. My brothers are Darlee Nelson Jr. and Harold Nelson. We were all born in Live Oak, in north central Florida, about 75 miles from Tallahassee.

Both of my parents told me not to follow others blindly. They'd say, "Hey, if Johnny jumps off a bridge are you going to do that, too?" I found myself saying that to my kids. I'll think, there I go sounding like my parents. You can't do everything everyone else does, and that's OK. They led me to believe that was OK. They taught me how to be strong so I didn't want to do what others were doing if I didn't think it was right. I learned so much from my parents.

I grew up in the '60s and '70s, and the single parent population wasn't what it is today. But my dad was away in the Army at times and it was up to my mother to look after us. My mother is a very strong person. She had to deal with three strong-minded boys.

My dad was away in Vietnam and my mother was having a tough time with my older brothers and she wrote to my dad in Vietnam about it.

My dad wrote back and, in a nice way, threatened my brothers with their lives. He said, "I will kill you if you don't shape up." My mother did not spare the rod. She did what she had to in order to keep us well behaved.

If she hit me I deserved it. I can only remember one beating by my father. Once he did it I said to myself, "When Dad's home I'm going to be good." Today, if you hit a child in public you're liable to have CYS at your door that same day. And your children will be the ones who report you! I wouldn't be who I am today if I hadn't been disciplined by my parents.

Kids today, when their parents are talking, interrupt them all the time. If I did that I'd get slapped. My mother thought we should be seen and not heard. We were raised to behave in restaurants and public places. Today, too many parents expect the teachers and coaches to handle all the discipline. That's not the way my wife and I do it.

I didn't have any sports idols when I was growing up. My dad was my idol. I tried to pattern myself after him. He went to work every day and he came home at night. He supported his family and he was the kind of person I wanted to become. He believed you had to start off every day with enthusiasm.

I love what I do. And it's getting better and better. I know a lot of people who don't like what they're doing, who dread each day. I do what I want to do. The hard part is out of the way. I paid my dues in this field. Most of my business now is referrals. Word of mouth is my best advertising. I made all those cold calls and now I am reaping the benefits of that hard work. I have a lot of repeat business, too. Something will happen in their life and they will call me.

"He gave you that look."

I look back proudly on playing for the Pittsburgh Steelers. I wouldn't trade it for anything in the world. I played for the world's greatest coach. That was Chuck Noll. He had his moments when he was tough to live with, but he knew what he wanted. He gave you that look and you better get your act together.

He commanded your respect. By the time I got here, he had already won four Super Bowl rings. He earned everyone's respect. I played seven years in the National Football League, six of them here.

I got cut by New Orleans and New England the next year, and ended up playing in a playoff game with Cleveland.

Marty Schottenheimer was the coach. That was the last game I ever played. I'm not proud of it. Some of the funniest things that ever happened to me happened during that year away from the Steelers.

I was playing in a game for New England. I came in during a goal line stand and I lined up against Max Montoya of the Cincinnati Bengals. Boomer Isiason was their quarterback and Doug Flutie was our quarterback in that game. Boomer backed off the line a few times and, finally Max asks me, "So, Edward, how's it going?" I said, "Fine, everything's all right." The rest of the guys looked at us like we were crazy. It was so cold that you could see your breath before your eyes. I guess that was Max's way of warming things up a little.

I remember something funny that happened when I was with the Steelers. Ron Johnson, one of our cornerbacks, came up and cold-cocked Jack Lambert. He hit Lambert in his

EDMUND NELSON

kidney with his helmet. He had his eyes closed and he just dove into a pile of players.

Jack rolled over and he said, "God dammit, Ron! What are you doing?"

Jack had to go out of the game. As we went into a huddle, I said to Johnson, "What the hell's wrong with you?" He starts screaming at me. We're arguing out there. I said, "What are you doing? You just put Jack out of the game!" We were going at it so hot and heavy that the referee had to separate us.

That was typical of our defense, though. We hit hard. We played some good defense in the '80s.

One time we gang-tackled this guy on his own sideline. When he went down, Donnie Shell, our safety, comes running up screaming, "What are you guys doing? Hold him up so I can get a piece of him!" We were right there in front of the guy's teammates. Donnie didn't care. "I'm not running all the way over here if you're going to do that," he hollered.

That was typical of our attitude. When we tackled somebody we weren't happy unless we had six or seven hats on them.

"L.C. should be in there."

I thought L.C. Greenwood should have gone into the Pro Football Hall of Fame before Lynn Swann. I played with Lynn Swann and I played with John Stallworth. I always thought John should have gone in first. Lynn made all the big plays in the big games, but John made more catches over a longer period. L.C. should be in there. I think it helped Lynn that he was still in the media limelight.

Terry Bradshaw had to be a big reason for the Steelers' success in the '70s. I played with the Steelers in Bradshaw's last two seasons here. His elbow was hurting then and he had this game against the Jets when he came in and we went down for two straight scores. He really took over on the field. He was the greatest leader at quarterback. You could just see the confidence he had. With him in there, we just rolled over them at Shea Stadium (34-7) in the next to the last game of the season.

When he was in the huddle he made a difference.

There were still some of the great players here when I came in. We still had Mike Webster, Jack Ham, Mel Blount, Jack Lambert, Donnie Shell, J.T. Thomas and Larry Brown.

When I first came into camp, I see this big human being on a table, and Ralph Berlin is rubbing him down. I said, "Who's that?" They told me, "That's Boss Brown." Larry Brown was a big man in those days. When I saw Mel Blount I thought he was a linebacker. He said, "Hey, Rook, you can call me Supe." Then he smiled at me and said, "Do you know why they call me that? It's short for Super." He's looking down his nose at me. I'm thinking, "If the defensive backs are this size in the NFL I have no chance to make this team. In truth, though, from the beginning I was dead-set on making the team. I was a seventh round pick, but I was sure I was going to make the team.

I came to camp in a 1970 Chevy. I had it packed to the hilt. The guys got all over me about that. It was filled with clothes, an air-conditioner, pots and pans, everything I'd need for the whole season. One day Stallworth asked me, "Why do you have all that stuff?" I said, "I'm not going back home. I'm staying." They had their attitude and I brought my own attitude.

I knew from my first game what I had to do if I was going to play for the Steelers. We opened the pre-season against New England at Knoxville when the World's Fair was being held there. There were 93,000 fans in the stands. I had played Tennessee there when I was at Auburn. I played that game the same way I played as an Auburn War Eagle.

I had to start and Lambert snapped at me after the first play. He said, "Rook, you've got to come off the ball faster or you're going to be over there on the bench with Chuck Noll!" They were an intense bunch of guys. I fit right in. I was intense, too.

I know the people were absolutely sick over the Steelers' loss in the AFC title game this year. The guard from the Super Bowl teams had changed by the time our team went to the AFC championship game in 1984. Miami knocked us out. We were right there on the brink, but we didn't have quite the leadership on the team to get it done. We worked hard and we played hard. We were a bunch of overachievers.

The team this year had the talent and the wherewithal to go all the way. I think they took New England lightly. Cowher hates it, I know, when anyone suggests his team is flat. But when you're making comments about making reservations for the Super Bowl in New Orleans you're asking for trouble.

"My job is to go out and play middle linebacker the best way I can. I don't get paid to counsel people; that's a mistake a lot of players make. I take care of my position as best I can. The way to lead is by example. I set high goals. I want to make All-Pro, be the defensive player of the year and go to the Super Bowl and win it."
— Jack Lambert

Craig Wolfley
Finding Faith is blessing

*"People don't appreciate
a good sweaty locker room."*

Craig Wolfley turns up in some interesting venues. I caught Wolfley working the corner in Golden Gloves action with his Wolfpak Boxing Club team at his Martial Arts & Sports Complex in Bridgeville and at the David L. Lawrence Convention Center in downtown Pittsburgh. He offered a poetry reading at a "Poetry in Sport" program at Carnegie Hall in Oakland. He was part of a radio broadcast team that covered the NFL draft at the Steelers' offices at UPMC Sports Performance Complex on the city's South Side.

At the age of 43, he competed in a professional boxing match with Eric "Butterbean" Esch, and he got his nose broken by his buddy, former Steeler lineman Tunch Ilkin, in one of their weekly sparring matches.

"We had to quit sparring for awhile," Wolfley allowed in May, 2002. "Our bodies are breaking down."

Wolfley was hopeful there was another boxing bout in the near future, but his friends were hoping and praying he'd put that foolishness behind his broad back. After all, the Wolfpak — isn't that a great name? — needs its leader.

Wolfley was everywhere in March and April, associated with sports in every possible manner, extending his love affair with physical challenges of all kinds, demonstrating his diverse talents.

He had three fighters from his team in the Pittsburgh Golden Gloves championships at the Convention Center and they all won titles. It was a perfect night for Wolfley's proteges. Coaching his pugilists to three-out-of-three titles is nearly as good as Chuck Noll's Super Bowl record. The Wolfpak won the team title. I was at ringside with Tony Ferraro, a sales executive with the Pittsburgh Brewing Company, one of the sponsors for the Golden Gloves. Ferraro is quite the fight fan. He'd taken me earlier to another fight show at the Omni William Penn where I had an opportunity to meet Paul Spadafora, billed as "The Pittsburgh Kid," and perhaps the most exciting pugilist from the Pittsburgh area since the late Billy Conn. Spadafora gets sponsor support from Joe Piccirilli and Pittsburgh Brewing Company.

Wolfley didn't fare as well in his own boxing outing, getting TKOd midway through the fourth round on the eve of Super Bowl XXXVI, but he took pride in just putting his game on the line at his age. When he was at the Convention Center that night, we spotted Wolfley in the company of boxing commissioner Andy "Kid" DePaul, one of the city's best boxers in his heyday and a great ambassador for the sport. Wolfley was speaking to a lot of guys with flattened noses,

Craig Wolfley 73

Photos by Jim O'Brien

Craig Wolfley has some fun with WDVE's Jimmy Krenn, and gets serious in corner with one of his Wolfpack pugilists in Golden Gloves tournament.

soaking up everything he could learn about boxing. He says he reads a lot of books and watches a lot of fight films, eager to pick up anything that might help him and his fighters.

The flip side of his physical efforts was his rendering of a poem at Carnegie Hall with the likes of Lynn Swann, Nellie Briles, Nellie King, Myron Cope, Bruno Sammartino, Jay Caufield, Sally Wiggin, Jim Roddey and Mayor Tom Murphy.

He said he was surprised to find himself in such distinguished company. Then he turned the event into a roast — shooting down just about everyone on the dais. Except Bruno Sammartino. He said when he got the invitation to attend the event it was the mention in the line-up of Sammartino that made him say, "I'll be there!" Then he read a four-line poem, the shortest offering on the program.

"Everyone was great," said Wolfley. "I never thought I'd have such a good time at a poetry reading!"

Wolfley works and gets paid doing what he enjoys doing anyhow.

He's managed to make a career out of it. He played 12 years as an offensive lineman in the National Football League, the first ten (1980-1989) with the Pittsburgh Steelers and the last two with the Minnesota Vikings.

He was selected to the Steelers' All-Century Team and to the 20th Century All-Star Team at Syracuse University. Wolfley didn't merit first-team honors with the Steelers, but it shows his popularity among the fans and media and he was a solid performer throughout his Steelers' stay. Gerry Mullins and Sam Davis were definitely the Steelers' finest two guards, but Wolfley wasn't far behind.

Wolfley has successfully competed in the World's Strongest Man and the NFL Strongest Man contests, and placed second in the first professional sumo contest on the North American continent. So it may not be too smart to challenge his qualifications for the Steelers' All-Time team.

There isn't a nicer guy in the world than Wolfley, but he gets his kicks in the strangest ways. He has his black belt in free-style Jiu Jitsu, and has over 19 years of training in martial arts, including western boxing, kick-boxing, Muay Thai kick-boxing ("that's what Bruce Lee does"), Jun Fan Trapping, Grappling and Kali.

Wolfley was one of the original founders of the Power Punch program taught to professional and amateur football players and teams throughout the country. He conducts a summer program.

Craig and his wife, Faith, a former karate champion, own and operate the Martial Arts & Sports Complex in Bridgeville. Their facility offers martial arts training, fitness kickboxing programs, kids' karate and specific athletic training. It's about 2½ miles from their home in Upper St. Clair. They live just a block away from my home. Faith was captain of the karate team while serving in the U.S. Air Force at Biloxi, Mississippi and then at the U.S. Air Force Academy in Colorado Springs, Colorado. Craig and Faith take turns looking after the place and C.J., their two-year-old son, at home during the day, and

Craig works at the facility until 9 each evening. Faith is so enthusiastic about everything and fun to be around. I've caught Craig watching cartoons on TV with C.J. in their family room. I feel safer having them in our neighborhood.

A boxing ring dominates the large room, along with physical exercise equipment and weights. The walls are lined with full-length mirrors to the students can see themselves in their workouts.

Their children, Megan, 17, and Kyle, 15, are students at Upper St. Clair High School. Faith was expecting another child. "We think it's going to be a girl," said Wolfley. "That will be great."

Not only did his best buddy break his nose, but Craig's wife, Faith, left a black and blue mark around his eyes from a deftly delivered kick when they were fooling around in a kick-boxing sparring session at their gym.

"She just kicked me upside my head," said Wolfley. "It's tough when you're wife does that to you."

Women have been giving him a tough time most of his life, it seems. He recalled a story from the day he was taken in the NFL draft. "I remember how silly it was," Wolfley said, describing the scene in his suburban Buffalo home on Draft Day 1980. "For some reason, my youngest sister, Joy, gets the call. She must've been 16, 17. She was a real turkey then. She's sitting there on the phone with her thumb down and this sad look on her face. She hands me the phone, saying, "I dunno, some guy named Chuck from Pittsburgh..."

That guy named Chuck from Pittsburgh, of course, was Chuck Noll, who had won his fourth Super Bowl in six years just a few weeks earlier. The Steelers had just drafted Wolfley on the fifth round. That was four rounds after Mark Malone, a quarterback from Arizona now at ESPN, and one round before Tunch Ilkin, a broadcast partner of Bill Hillgrove and Myron Cope on Steelers broadcasts and a sparring partner of Wolfley these days.

Wolfley was a late addition to a WBGG (970 the 'Burg) radio team covering the 2002 college draft in mid-April. Wolfley was happy to be included. "You're talking about your favorite thing, football, with your best buddy, Tunch," said Wolfley. "You're eating fine food. And you're having a great time. What's not to like? You're eating free food and getting paid for it. What could be better? America's such a great country."

The feeling is mutual, to hear Ilkin. "He's so creative and has such a natural flair for radio and TV," said Ilkin. "I think he has a great future in this business. He's great to work with."

Wolfley participated with Ilkin in the Light of Life Mission Walk along the Allegheny River on the North Shore on Saturday, May 4. Ilkin heads the board for the shelter for homeless people near West Park and Allegheny General Hospital. The walk was held the day before the Pittsburgh Marathon. "We walked 15 miles and I was worn out," said Wolfley. "It gave me a renewed appreciation for the marathoners."

171

Wolfley was scheduled to work as a sideline reporter with WDVE for the 2002 schedule, working home and away games. "He's relaxed and funny and a good storyteller," commented Cope when I asked him about Wolfley at a chance meeting at Atria's Restaurant & Tavern in Mt. Lebanon shortly after the announcement. "I think he'll add to our broadcast. He and Tunch feed off one another."

Jim Godwin of J. Allan Steel Company said he enjoyed listening to the Steelers' show featuring Ilkin and Wolfley, and enjoyed them both on draft day as well. "Wolfley is funny as hell," said Godwin. "He told a story about fighting Butterbean Esch, and he had me in stitches."

Wolfley sat down on a soft couch in the dressing room in a corner of the complex and discussed his life and times in the football arena.

Craig Wolfley:

Football takes its toll. You never escape its wrath. I have my share of aches and pains, but I'm luckier than most. I still get around pretty good. I have my martial arts classes, box a little, still lift weights, watch what I eat, and try to stay in decent shape. But nothing I do gives me the rush I used to experience when I was playing football. There's nothing to replace that.

The biggest challenge I faced when I was finished in the NFL was figuring out what I was supposed to do with the rest of my life.

It's quite a turn-around. What's the juice in a sales competition versus being part of a touchdown drive in the AFC championship game? Everything else seemed to pale by comparison.

At 31, you're done as far as football is concerned, and you've accomplished all that you ever wanted to do. Suddenly, you're left with a big void. It's like coming down from the Rocky Mountains and living in Iowa. All of a sudden, there are lots of flats. Going through a divorce also challenged me. I don't want to get into that too much, though. Suffice to say there were two great losses in such a short period of time.

I was married to Beth for 11 years and we had some great years together. But there were always problems in our relationship. A divorce takes two people to bring it about, so I'm not blaming anybody. My leaving football only brought a lot of the problems to the surface.

One day I was talking to Beth about how I felt. This was shortly before she left us. I said, "I don't know what to tell people anymore when they ask me what I'm doing. I don't know how to respond to people. What am I?" And Beth came back, "You! What about me?"

There's a study that's been done by the NFL Players Association and it shows that 75 per cent of the NFL Alumni end up divorced. I'm sure it's still that high. Within a year of my retiring, Beth left. We're at peace with each other now, and try to do what's good for the kids. I'm grateful for that.

Thank God I found Faith. I've got a great wife — yeah, her name is Faith — who shares so much with me. We have been together the past six years. We share many of the same interests. There's been a real bonding right through some difficult times. Being a Christian is important to me, so it's perfect that I have a wife named Faith.

It's like she was meant for me. Her middle name is Dale and that's my younger brother's name. My oldest sister's name is Linrae Faith. I also have a younger sister named Joy. So Faith fits right in.

You know my brother Ron. He was a running back at West Virginia. He played for the Cardinals, the Browns and the Rams. He played for the St. Louis Cardinals at the beginning and the St. Louis Rams at the end. So he started and finished in the same city with two different teams. That ought to win you a beer some night when you're playing sports trivia.

I look at Faith. She's probably one of the greatest gifts I've been given in my life. Her strength and character have helped me through some of the darkest times in my life. No one quits on Faith. Not the kids, not her husband; even when he wants to. She's truly a gift from God.

"It was a whale of a fight."

During the past six weeks, I was training for and competing in fights. I felt more alive than I've been in a long time. There was a buzz and a juice that I enjoyed. I really dug it.

I fought Butterbean Esch on February 2, the day before the Super Bowl. The fight was at a gambling casino in Gulfport, Mississippi. It lasted three-and-a-half rounds. It was a whale of a fight. I think I cracked my nose. That's why they stopped the fight 90 seconds into the fourth round. It was bleeding pretty good. So I lost on a TKO. Yeah, I'd do it again. Show me another guy in his 40s who can go out there and do that. Sure, I'd do it one more time.

Actually, I think Tunch cracked my nose to begin with, and Butterbean just re-cracked it, so to speak. Tunch and I spar once or twice a week, sometimes three nights in a week, depending on our schedules. We have a great time in that ring.

It's important to find out what God's will is in your life. I enjoy teaching martial arts and training athletes and fighters.

With the broadcasting and analysis of the Steelers I've been doing the last three years on radio and TV, it's brought me back full cycle. I'm around football and the Steelers again. I get to see my best friend Tunch Ilkin more often — he's like a brother to me — and that's always special.

Being around the guys is tremendous. People don't appreciate a good sweaty locker room. I missed that.

There's something else that's really happened to help in that transition. That was the day my third child was born. I look at it as a great healing process. That happened on April 25, 2000, when Faith gave birth to C.J. He's Craig Jr., but we call him C.J. Did Faith tell you she's pregnant again? We're excited about that, too. We've had custody right along of my daughter, Megan, who's a junior at Upper St. Clair High School, and Kyle, who's a freshman there. We've got a great family. My nephew Ron Blue lived with us for a year when he was a senior at Upper St. Clair High School and now he's on a scholarship for football in his second year at Bowling Green University.

I'll tell you how I got into martial arts in the first place. It began about 20 years ago. In my second season in the league, I went up against Randy White of the Dallas Cowboys. He trapped my hands against my chest all day. Then he went around me. Play after play. On one play, the last thing I saw was Terry Bradshaw's feet going up in the sky. I think I helped Randy White get into the Pro Football Hall of Fame that day. I knew he was into martial arts.

In the off-season, I looked for a martial arts instructor, someone who could show me to use my hands more effectively. I found a guy named Sarge Edwards in McMurray. Tunch and I started training with him. It helped us both. Tunch later taught it to a lot of pro players as a consultant coach with several teams.

"It's where I'm supposed to be."

I think Russ Grimm came in and changed the perception of what they were able to do and had to do. He brought with him leadership. Now they're going out and kicking butt. He was a key guy with the "Hogs" when the Washington Redskins were winning Super Bowls. He has some Super Bowl rings. Grimm brought a mental approach that's apparent now. They're into butt-kicking that had been lacking. I thought Kent Stephenson was an excellent line coach, but Grimm gets more respect right off the bat because he played in Super Bowls and Pro Bowls. He had a reputation. That automatically gets their attention. He's very demanding. He knows how he wants things done and he's not satisfied with anything less.

174

You're expected to know your assignments and to carry them out. He taught an aggressive style of run blocking and pass blocking. He has you attacking. He's brought out the best in all of them. He's tapped into their strengths.

Across the board, they're playing better. The new center, Jeff Hartings, has worked out fine, once he got used to the difference between playing guard as he'd done in Detroit and playing center for the Steelers. You can't take away from Dermonti Dawson's greatness. He was like Mike Webster. He was equally great. Just lining up and working out with Mike Webster was one of the great aspects of my playing experience. But we all wear down. Dawson was no longer physically sound, and wasn't able to play the way we knew he could play.

Mentioning Mike Webster hurts now. His problems have caused me more heartache than you can imagine. It's scary. Yeah, everybody falls from grace. Some of us fall softly and some of us fall hard. No one gets out free.

I just haven't seen him and we used to be so close. The last time I saw him was at a Paul Spadafora fight at Station Square last summer. He was there, selling and signing some shirts and merchandise. He just looks at you now with that 1,000-yard stare. It hurts. He was my mentor; he was one of my heroes. When I was playing, I wanted to be like Mike. And that meant Mike Webster, man, not Michael Jordan.

When I was a kid, growing up in Orchard Park, I was a big fan of the Buffalo Bills. Their stadium was right in our town. In my junior year at Orchard Park High School, I went to school with the daughter of one of the Bills' assistant coaches. He arranged for four of us to visit the Bills' locker room. I can still remember going through this row of lockers and all of a sudden there's the Juice, O.J. Simpson himself. That was like the greatest thing in the world. I was just in awe standing there, staring at him.

Who would ever expect what would happen with him and the death of his wife and her friend? Who would ever expect that same person to be in that Bronco chase? I'll never forget sitting in my chair at home, watching that; not believing what I was watching. What was going wrong?

I was so astounded. So two of my heroes have fallen. What happens when your heroes have feet of clay like that?

That's why it's important to know who you are when you go into the pros and who you are when you come out.

This game exacts a price. The game is exciting and rewarding. It challenges you in every aspect, spiritually and physically. It demands a great deal.

After 11 years of living the dream, there's a great sense of loss and belonging. One of the things that lead to self-destructiveness is that, suddenly, you have no purpose. Or you feel that way, anyhow. You've gone through a period of time where you always knew where to be and when to be. You had a schedule. Suddenly you look around and — wow! — you have to develop your own day. Nothing has the juice like a Sunday afternoon game.

It can be difficult to find satisfaction and meaning in your life after football. Few of us can step out and do it well. The rest of us have to stumble along and find our way.

I wasn't interested in coaching football. I chose to step away. I didn't want to be a coach. I didn't want to be a part of that. This place is about two-and-a-half miles from my home. It couldn't be more convenient. Yet I'm in a different world when I'm here. It's where I'm supposed to be.

You have to find something to do. Your NFL pension doesn't start until you're 55, unless you opt to take a lump sum from it now. But you don't want to do that. Some guys have, though. They had to.

"The locker room's your house and family."

Two years ago this team was a group of players. This year they really cared about each other. There was a different feeling in the locker room. There was a difference. For a football player, the locker room's your home and family. There was an emergence of key players like Kordell. I think the coaching staff, so many of them former pro players, really added to the program. Plaxico improved tremendously from his rookie year, and he can improve even more. Hines Ward provides great leadership by example. The early strong start by Jerome Bettis helped them get off on the right foot, after that first game in Jacksonville.

Casey Hampton and Kimo and Aaron Smith did a great job on that defensive line. They had a stellar group of linebackers and defensive backs. They read well and they're intelligent. It's a unique team.

They're a good example of what Chuck Noll used to refer to as synergism — the whole is greater than the sum of its parts. But New England did, too. Perhaps a touch better.

I came here in 1980, right after the Steelers had won their fourth Super Bowl in six years. They were the NFL team of the decade during the '70s. They had made the playoffs in eight of those years. They left long shadows. They were greats in their time. Many of them were still here when I arrived. I thought I would be part of a continuance of that excellence. Tunch and I both came in that year, along with Mark Malone and Bill Hurley, and we were excited about the company we were

176

Craig Wolfley (73) leads the way as blocker for running back Walter Abercrombie (34), and lines up behind his idol, Mike Webster, for "gut check" run around the practice fields at St. Vincent's College, followed by, left to right, Pete Rostosky of Bethel Park, Gary Dunn and Terry Long.

keeping. Yes, we missed out on something. We've stayed close and it's still a subject for conversation.

We had great expectations. I remember Joe Greene with his four Super Bowl rings talking about "One for the thumb." I was all for that. It never happened, but I'll never forget seeing him wearing all those rings.

One thing that stands out is the face of the faceless. So many of us never have a chance to win a ring. Look how everybody wanted John Elway to get that ring, but there are so many of us with less celebrity than an Elway or a Marino who have no ring, either.

"We're twin brothers from different mothers."

There's also a prevalent feeling that so many of the Steelers have been successful after football. But there's a whole horde of guys who've fallen hard, or had serious problems. You had Steve Courson and Mike Webster and Sam Davis, for instance, with serious health issues. They've had a tough time in many ways. I feel for them. I worked and learned alongside them for years. They helped me in so many ways.

Tunch and I talk about that. Then there's Tunch Ilkin, yes. Our friendship is one of the best things that have ever happened to me. It's a fantastic friendship. He's a brother through and through. There's the quote he said, "We're twin brothers from different mothers."

Jon Kolb was a big influence in my life. Kolb had rock-like fortitude. If you ever wanted a picture of an offensive lineman it was Jon Kolb. He was able to weather storms on and off the field. He was so straightforward. He was able to stay the course. He's coaching football at Grove City College now and he hasn't changed a lick. If you want to see a 51-year-old man in remarkable condition you want to check out Jon Kolb. I learned so much from him and Larry Brown and Sam Davis.

Larry Brown carried himself with such grace. That is unusual for an offensive lineman. He was a wolf in sheep's clothing if I ever met one. He was a gentleman off the field and an absolute killer on the field.

Mike Webster was the personification of what it meant to be a Steeler. He was everything you could imagine a Steeler being. He was a professional's professional. He studied long and hard. He knew what everyone on the offensive line was supposed to do, and recognized every defensive set. He was the "quarterback" of our offensive line, calling out all the adjustments and assignments in an instant. He had courage that defied belief. He was the greatest example of leadership, and his non-verbal communication skills were exceptional. If there could ever be a complete paradox he was it. His presence

178

was so forceful it just pulled you along. Then, soon after he got out of football, he ran into so many personal difficulties. He and wife split up and you heard the stories about him sleeping in his car and in a bus station. It's mystifying to all of us.

I missed the heyday of those guys working out and lifting weights at the Red Bull Inn in Washington, but I caught the tail end of it, and it was like going to graduate school. It must have been something. You had Brown, Webby, Kolb, Ted Petersen, Steve Furness or Furney as we called him. Steve Courson came from time to time.

Then there was Chuck Noll. He was just so great as a coach. And now I know what a genuine guy he is outside of football. Now you can just enjoy him. He's the only guy who ever intimidated me the way he did. To me, he was ten feet tall and bulletproof. I understand now that to survive as a coach for 23 years you have to do certain things a certain way. He couldn't be your buddy; he couldn't be your pal. He never would have survived. I understand now how much he cared for the guys who played for him.

He didn't wear his feelings on his sleeve. He didn't let it show. I truly believe he was one of the last coaches who taught you as much about life as he did about football. It's hard to give advice to dot.com guys anymore.

I see some of these young guys and I have to shake my head sometimes. I still like them and admire their ability, mind you. I don't think there's a respect for the history of the game. Or what went down before they got here. That's why Tunch and I took particular glee in giving out the Old School Award. We started that ourselves. We give it to the player who best demonstrates the virtues of the old school players. We do that each week on our show on 970 The Burg. We also have a Must've Played Before Helmets Award. You have to have a screw loose to qualify for that one. We don't lack for candidates for that award, either.

When Tunch and I came here the older players took us under their wings. They were from the old school. Those guys taught you how to live, breathe, talk and walk like a Steeler.

You were a rookie and they reminded you of that often, too. There was no doubt about where you stood in the food chain when you came in. When you got that permanent nameplate over your locker you felt like you had arrived. You were a survivor. It was a simple wooden nameplate, but it was like a plaque for a young player. Because of the money they're paid and the signing bonuses they receive the rookies don't feel too humble when they arrive nowadays.

I still have my Steelers' nameplate. I have my Vikings' nameplate, too, but it's not as big a deal. My Steelers' nameplate is one of the greatest things I took home with me.

179

Randy Grossman
He knew how to play the game

"All of a sudden . . .
you're the ordinary man."

It was Thursday, March 21, the first full day of Spring in 2002. It was a blustery day in downtown Pittsburgh. March had come in like a lamb, as the saying goes, and it was leaving like a lion. Temperatures this day would drop within a few hours by 20 degrees from 49 to 29 degrees, and it seemed even colder. A cold, arctic air mass had placed the Northeast back in the icy grip of winter. The wind was blowing in from the three rivers. The rivers were running high and fast, with ice chunks riding the waves, and communities in low-lying areas along the Allegheny and Monongahela and Ohio Rivers were warned that flooding was possible. It had been raining a lot the past few weeks. The late Art Rooney used to say that when the spring showers came when he was a kid, if you spit in those rivers they would overflow in his neighborhood on the North Side.

The city was warmed somewhat by the fact that the University of Pittsburgh men's basketball team had just defeated Central Connecticut and California in the NCAA tournament played at Pittsburgh's Mellon Arena. That 8-team tournament drew lots of out-of-town visitors to the city for a long weekend. Pitt would be playing that same night against Kent State in NCAA regional finals at Rupp Arena in Lexington, Kentucky. The Panthers were the talk of the town. I was looking forward to watching their game on TV. They would lose in overtime in a game that reminded me of the Steelers' loss to the New England Patriots in the AFC title game. Many of Pitt's fans were assuming that Pitt would whip Kent State and then might be in over its head with Duke in the regional final. Pitt and Duke both were defeated that night. So much for the smart money. Kent State played defense as well as Pitt did, and stifled their offense. That's all she wrote. The Panthers couldn't play their own game.

Before the workday was over it would be snowing. Joe said it would. So advised by WTAE's weathered weatherman Joe DeNardo, I knew to don a black trench coat and a gray scarf before departing my suburban home to visit former Steelers tight end Randy Grossman, a financial advisor, at his Advest, Inc. offices on the 34th floor of Oxford Centre. I parked in a year-old garage between the city's jail — why did civic leaders allow a jail to be built in such a desirable highly visible spot along the Mon and the Parkway East? — and the new PNC corporate office building. The jail is the better looking of the two buildings.

I walked toward Grant Street. En route, on Ross Street, I passed an impressive mural paying tribute to the city's great baseball players of the past — Wagner, the Waner brothers, Traynor, Maz, Clemente,

Randy Grossman meets up with former coach Chuck Noll who represented Pittsburgh Vision Services at West Penn & National Collegiate Tennis Tournament in Mt. Lebanon. Below, Grossman at Advest, Inc. offices at Oxford Centre in downtown Pittsburgh.

Photos by Jim O'Brien

The Bulls and Bears in the Market

THE NEW-YORK HISTORICAL SOCIETY, NEW YORK CITY

Stargell and Gibson — that had been painted a year earlier on a support wall under the Boulevard of the Allies. I passed the Chinatown Inn, about the only remnant remaining of the city's once-distinctive Chinatown district, and made my way to Grant Street.

Once on Grant Street, I could see the City-County Building, with the statue of the late Mayor Richard Caliguiri, in the center before the stairway. There would be snow on his head and nose and shoulders when commuters passed it on the way home after 5 o'clock. I knew Dick Caliguiri when we were both teenagers. I was 14 and he was about 19 when he was looking after his father's bowling alley on Second Avenue, the main street in Hazelwood. I was then the sports editor of *The Hazelwood Envoy*, a bi-weekly newspaper, and would stop at the bowling alley to get high scores for the previous week to run in the sports section. He lived in Squirrel Hill and had graduated from Taylor Allderdice High School. He went from working in the parks & recreation department of the City to become a member of City Council and, eventually, the mayor. He was a most popular and effective mayor. The city was saddened when he died of amyloidosis.

When Caliguiri was the mayor in 1979, I visited him in his offices at the City-County Building. He provided an introduction essay, and even talked me into amending the title for a book that would be called *Pittsburgh: The Story of the City of Champions*. It was a book that Pittsburgh artist and graphics specialist Marty Wolfson and I teamed up to edit and publish, the first in the "Pittsburgh Proud" series of books.

I had interviewed Grossman for one of my earlier books, *Whatever It Takes*, which was no longer available. It had been ten years since I had last done an in-depth interview with him. Back then, he was working as a financial advisor at Kidder, Peabody, a prestigious firm that no longer existed. Chuck Noll used to say that "the only constant was change," but that didn't make it any easier to deal with it. Too many companies and corporate logos — like Gulf, Koppers, Westinghouse — had disappeared from the downtown scene since I had returned to town in 1979.

The Oxford Centre is a 45-story glistening silver-shelled building that is home to some star tenants. Chip Ganassi, the auto racing magnate whose cars have won the Indy 500, has his offices there. The prestigious Buchanan Ingersoll Law Firm claims eight floors. Klett, Rooney, Lieber & Schorling, the law firm that has the Steelers' future leader, Art Rooney II, among its partners, is there as well. The Scaife Foundation is a prime tenant. Retailers include Hardy & Hays and Emphatics. The Rivers Club is there. The building opened in April of 1983 in the midst of a mini-Renaissance that added several impressive skyscrapers to the city's skyline during Mayor Caliguiri's reign.

The Oxford Centre was owned and operated by the Oxford Development Company. Its chairman and president, Ed Lewis, once said of Pittsburgh, "I like the scale of the city." It was a city of big companies, once the No. 3 corporate headquarters in America, but it had a small town quality about it. You could walk from one end of the downtown district to the other end, something I could never do during the nine years I worked in New York City. Pittsburgh was more manageable. It had no bigger fans than Ed Lewis and Randy Grossman. "I love Pittsburgh," said Grossman. "I'm glad I came here, and I plan to stay here. It's been good for me in so many ways."

There was a gentleman in a tuxedo playing a grand piano in the lobby of Oxford Centre. Nearby, there were three women volunteers selling bright yellow daffodils — a sure sign that spring had arrived — to raise funds for the American Cancer Society.

It cost me $4.50 to park in that indoor garage for a little over two hours, versus $10 in a lot across the street from Oxford Centre, or about $30 in midtown Manhattan. Pittsburgh was a lot less expensive than New York, Chicago or San Francisco. A rich woman once remarked that she feels clever when she saves money.

Getting to Grossman was akin to running for a first down against "the Steel Curtain" defense of the '70s. I had to show identification at a desk in the lobby, sign in, put an identification label on my coat, and pass three security guards standing by the entrance to the bank of elevators. "I'm gonna ax you to see that on the way out," a woman who probably pronounced Pittsburgh as Pixburgh told me as I went by. It was a reminder of September 11, and how much freedom we have sacrificed since that fateful day when Terrorism became the talk of every town in America, maybe in much of the world.

"You can never step in the same river twice."

It was good to see Grossman. His head was shaved close, like the greens at The Masters in Augusta, like his former teammate Andy Russell. His hair wasn't as white as Russell's, but it must have been just as sparse, especially above the forehead. He was wearing a well-starched white dress shirt and dark paisley tie, dark slacks and a welcoming smile when he came to get me in the waiting area of Advest. He looked the part of his current position.

I was 15 minutes early for our appointment, so I'd had time to check out some of the Advest literature in the lobby. Their mission statement goes like this: "To be the best at helping people build wealth, primarily toward retirement, through the highest quality, most effective professionals in the industry."

In reflecting on the ever-changing financial services industry, Daniel J. Mullane, the president of Advest, referred to an old saying, "you can never set foot in the same river twice." It seemed appropriate to seeing Grossman and many of his teammates ten years after our last interviews, and more than 20 years since most of them had last played for the Steelers. In some ways, they were the same, of course, but in other ways they had changed. They were older, wiser and more willing to share their innermost thoughts on the Steelers and their stays in Pittsburgh.

At Advest, a national investment firm based in Hartford, Connecticut, Grossman was a member of a nation-wide team of 500 financial advisors under the corporate umbrella. He had been in the restaurant business once upon a time after retiring as a player, as an owner with Bobby Rubino's Ribs at Station Square, but he had been in the financial counseling business since 1989.

He was born in Philadelphia on September 20, 1952, so his next birthday would be the Big 50. The Jewish version of the Afro hairdo and dark mustache he wore when I started covering the Steelers for the 1979 season were gone. He still had the four Super Bowl rings he'd earned during his eight seasons (1974-1981) with the Steelers, and he was still a cerebral, thoughtful spokesman. He still had the same — ahem — dry sense of humor.

He was officially listed now as a Securities and Exchange Commission registered representative, investment advisor and retirement planning specialist with Nussbaum Partners at the investment firm of Advest, Inc. Since my visit, he was proud to say he had met all requirements and had become a certified financial planner (CFP). He specialized in providing investment consulting services to charitable organizations, pension plans and individuals.

The retired workers of LTV could sure use a guy like Grossman to steer them through troubled waters. The LTV Corp. had recently declared bankruptcy, and would no longer make good on its pension promises. It would affect several thousand people in Pittsburgh and Western Pennsylvania, who once worked at J&L and later LTV on the South Side, Aliquippa and in my hometown of Hazelwood. I'm sure I knew a lot of them. Those guys had a great benefits program, but now it was gone up in smoke. A bankrupt Bethlehem Steel would soon do the same. It reinforced the feeling that I'd done a smart thing by establishing my own pension program while still a student at Pitt in the early '60s. I have Beano Cook and Jack Henry, an old sportswriter turned securities broker, to thank for that.

As a schoolboy in Philadelphia, Grossman gained all-state recognition as a football player. He attended Temple University on a football athletic scholarship and majored in business administration. He received All-East and All-America mention in his senior year of 1974.

He signed as a free agent with the Steelers that year. One of his many career highlights included catching a touchdown pass in Super Bowl X against the Dallas Cowboys. A classic overachiever, Randy was a sure-handed, clutch possession receiver, who averaged 13 yards per reception over his career. He was also a fine blocker and made a good impression as a rookie with his spirited play on special teams.

He has a nervous cough, but he is an effective public speaker in the areas of estate planning, investing and personal motivation. He lived for years in Squirrel Hill, but recently relocated to Indiana Township in the North Hills with his wife, the former Barbara

Kierski, and three children, Oliver, Lucy and Sarah. Oliver, 27, and Lucy, 21, were children from his first marriage, and Barbara had given birth to Sarah, 6, a year after they were married. When he told me Oliver was on his way to Alaska, I mentioned that I had spent ten months there as an information specialist with the U.S. Army's Arctic & Cold Weather Training Center, at Fort Greeley, somewhere on a glacier between Fairbanks and Anchorage. Now we were swapping war stories. As it turned out, Oliver stopped in Washington, and then changed his mind about going to Alaska. Instead, he went to Friendsville, Maryland to work as a whitewater rafting guide.

Grossman's remarks are filled with the language of the investment and banking community.

Randy Grossman:

I just got a call from my son, Oliver. He's in Wyoming, on his way to Alaska. He's headed for some place called Dutch Harbor, near the Aleutian Islands. He's a graduate of West Virginia University, with a degree in history, but I guess he's not ready to get a real job yet. Right now, he's doing whatever he wants to do. Last year, he was a vacation guide in Costa Rica and the Dominican Republic. His first love is whitewater kayaking. My daughter, Lucy, is a sophomore at Penn State. She's going to New Zealand later this year in a Study Abroad program. Oliver is making plans to meet up with her there. I'm sure they'll have fun.

I don't think I could handle Alaska. You were there in the military service? That must have been some experience. Cold never bothered me as a kid. My first year here, we had a playoff game with the Oakland Raiders at Three Rivers Stadium. They had a tarpaulin covering the field and they had torpedo-heating devices blowing hot air across the field. The cover came off the field in one corner and the turf was frozen solid. I think I suffered some minor frostbite injury during that game. Ever since then the cold and I are fine as long as I'm dressed warmly.

That's one way I am reminded of my days with the Steelers. Some of those guys who tell you about their injuries, the ones who played in the 80s, are in for an enlightening experience. They don't realize the impact yet. The older you get the biggest interest is charged to your body's condition. I played a crossover position as a tight end. I was a receiver and a lineman. It's the linemen, the guys in the trenches, so to speak, on both sides of the ball who really pay the price. The physical demands on linemen on either side of the ball are immense.

The guy who is most amazing to me is Bruce Matthews, who played guard for the Houston Oilers and the Tennessee Titans. He's been there like 20 years, playing on the line, and I can't begin to comprehend how his body has held up. It's really just amazing, just amazing. (Matthews would announce his retirement in June of 2002.)

We had compound success with the Steelers, first as players and then in the real world. Outside of the aches and pains and physical problems, the byproducts of that success are not a negative. Oh, yes, there is a significant letdown from the adoration and respect that comes with notoriety and celebrity. All of a sudden you're the ordinary man, and you may carry over some of the notoriety and celebrity. Certainly guys like Terry Bradshaw, Joe Greene, Lynn Swann, Rocky Bleier and, to a lesser degree, Franco Harris and Andy Russell have remained high profile people and continue to draw benefits from their football-playing days. Several of those have not had to get too acquainted with life in the real world.

There's Chuck Noll's line about getting on with your life's work. Most of us, who were not big stars, are grunting along like everybody else. You get more famous and less famous at the same time. Your fame becomes greater or less. With the people who know you, well, you just get better with age. With kids, your significance as a Steeler diminishes. They ask you questions like "Are you famous?" or "Were you famous?" or "Are you someone?"

I was 6-1, 215 when I reported to the Steelers. Some would say I wouldn't be big enough to play tight end and compete in the NFL today. There's a fallacy in that sort of thinking, though. The essential game has not changed regardless of the different things they do now. It's still one side beating up the other side.

Yes, they are bigger and stronger and faster today. But we were bigger and strong and faster in our day, too. The future guys will be bigger and stronger and faster than the guys who are playing now. It's an evolutionary process. Jack Ham and Jack Lambert would be bigger and stronger and faster today; that's all. I'm quite confident they could compete in any era. They wouldn't be the same size. To think otherwise is ludicrous thinking. It's still the same. The talent is pretty even across the board these days. The team that is best prepared and best schooled in the proper techniques, and executes the best, will win. That was always Chuck Noll's focus. To say a player now is better than a player then doesn't hold water. They're the same. Sometimes someone comes out who sets a new standard — like Michael Jordan or Mario Lemieux — and they're not the same as everyone else. Other than them, superstars in sports still perform at some relative level.

What do I know now than I didn't know when I was playing for the Steelers? I know what an adult knows compared to what a kid knows. You think you know everything when you're young, but you've had such a limited life experience. But, of course, my kids don't want to hear that.

When you're talking to people about their secrets for success, they'll mention hard work and dedication. But there is always a significant amount of luck in the accomplishment as well. If they don't acknowledge that they're not being true to themselves.

"Mr. Rooney still remembers my children."

I was amazingly fortunate throughout my athletic career. I was always in great organizations, through junior high and high school, college and here. The Rooneys epitomized the environment I was fortunate to have.

When I was playing for the Steelers we'd have a light practice on Saturday morning, and you were allowed to bring friends and your family to Three Rivers Stadium during that session. All the rugrats were running around the outskirts of the field. Oliver was too young to come with me for most of my career, but he came toward the end. Oliver was six years old when I retired. He met Mr. Rooney a half dozen times during my last year with the team.

I was retired for four or five years and I had occasion to visit the Steelers offices at Three Rivers. I had to go over there for something. Art Sr. was walking around in the hallway, with his cigar, of course, and he saw me coming. He stopped and shook my hand and said, "How's Oliver doing?" That as much as anything epitomizes the true caring he had for his players and their families. You're five years removed from the team and Mr. Rooney still remembers my children.

It's always impressed me so much how every organization reflects the top management. The whole group of players who were my teammates parroted the great confidence and pride and capability of the Rooney family. It was a special group.

I think Dan Rooney is such an amazing beneficiary of his father's personality, in a different way. He's not as outgoing and gregarious as his dad was, but in basic ways he's so similar. The Rooney family is financially successful. They're not like what you'd expect of people in their situation, however. They're not like the second or third generation wealth I've encountered in my investment career. They work as hard as anyone does. Dan is that way; young Art (II) is the same way.

187

What did I learn from them that I've molded into my own way of doing things? When you're there I don't think you consciously pick up on it. It's just a tone that is set. Whoever is on top has an effect on those below them. It wasn't as if I did anything differently, but it definitely shaped the character of the team. Chuck melded into that. It's kinda funny now to see the difference in personalities at the top. Chuck and Dan were so similar in their style and approach to things. Chuck and Dan seemed so much alike. Bill Cowher and Dan appear to be so different. It just shows there are different ways to get success. Certainly, Bill's been successful. I wouldn't want to compare Chuck with Bill. I'm not there at practice; I'm not on the sidelines. It would be unfair for me to try to compare them.

"I can't think of a nicer place to live."

I spent the first 21 years of my life in Philadelphia and now I have been in Pittsburgh for 28 years. Pittsburgh is a small place geographically, but it's an amazingly dynamic place. It impresses me that the corporate chieftains here seem reflective of the Western Pennsylvania mentality, regardless of where they came from. There's a positive perspective, but a quiet hard-working mentality. They follow through on that.

Philadelphia was originally the financial capital of the country. Now you have PNC and Mellon Bank, or Citizens Bank, swallowing up Philadelphia in that regard. The banking headquarters are here now. How did that happen?

I love Pittsburgh. I love Western Pennsylvania. I couldn't imagine living in Philadelphia now. I grew up there and loved it as a kid. Some people don't think Pittsburgh is cosmopolitan enough, as pertains to restaurants and theaters. I must live a totally sheltered life. I don't know what they're talking about. Unless these people are eating out every night, and looking for gourmet entrees at every setting, I don't know what they mean. There's more than I can take in as far as the restaurant and theater experiences are concerned.

I can't think of a nicer place to live. The weather could stand some improving, but other than that...

"They're the mother hens of the locker room."

I came into the National Football League in the era of indentured servitude. I signed as a free agent. I don't know who pointed me out or recommended me to the Steelers, but I am grateful to that individual.

188

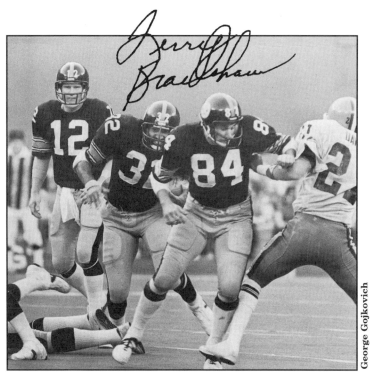

George Gojkovich

Randy Grossman (84) leads the way for Franco Harris (32) who gets handoff from Terry Bradshaw (12) in contest with Cleveland Browns.

Lou Malkin, Vinard Studios

Steelers roast for benefit of Pittsburgh chapter of American Diabetes Association in 1980 featured, from left to right front row, Cliff Stoudt, Jim O'Brien, Randy Grossman, Bennie Cunningham, Theo Bell and, in the rear, Lynn Swann, Jim Smith, Stan Savran, Calvin Sweeney and John Stallworth. Stallworth followed Swann into the Pro Football Hall of Fame in 2002. Grossman had more hair on his head than anybody on team in those days.

I do know that they sent Ralph Berlin, the team trainer, to Philadelphia to sign me to a contract. Ralph tells the story that when he came to see me he excused himself to call back to Pittsburgh to make sure I was the right guy. He must not have been that impressed when he saw me. When he came to sign me, he was wearing a three-piece pinstripe suit, with a watch chain dangling from the pocket. He was wearing dark glasses and he had a big cigar in his mouth. I took him to be one of the owners of the Steelers. "They must really want me," I thought to myself, "for one of the team owners to come and sign me." When I got to St. Vincent's that summer, I went into the locker room and I saw this same guy in short pants and a T-shirt that didn't quite make it to his belt. The only thing the same was the cigar. And the bravado was still there. I was told he was the trainer. I thought, "I'm in trouble." That turned out to be a good thing. He sorta had a vested interest in me. He signed me, so he worked hard to keep me healthy.

Ralph Berlin was part of the Steelers' scene, an important part. So was Tony Parisi, the team's equipment manager. Parisi had played pro hockey and he knew his way around a locker room. He knew what the guys needed. The importance of the trainer and the equipment manager and their staffs — no matter the sport — can't be overstated. They're the mother hens of the locker room. I'm sure a lot of information on the players that Chuck Noll relied on came from those guys. They are on the firing line dealing with player problems every day. From a pebble in your shoe to nagging injuries, they're the source of such information. Nagging injuries are worse than serious injuries because the coach relies on the trainer as to whether a player should play or not. Tony was great. He really looked after us. You can't believe all the kinds of different needs they served. Reality hits you in the locker room. There everyone is equal among the players themselves. The only thing that sets them apart is pure performance. Some guys said Tony and Ralph treated everyone alike — like dirt — but they were only kidding. Ralph had a classic line, though, he used to put any upstart rookie in his place. "I was here before you came," Berlin would say, "and I'll be here when you're gone." If anyone was too impressed with himself, those guys put him in his place. They were everyone's reality check. As Tony put it, "Everybody stinks in the men's room." They had Chuck's full support and he let them run their own shops.

They could say things to us without anyone getting mad. It's like the relationship you have with a best friend. They can call you names no one else can. That's the kind of relationship we had with Ralph and Tony. There was respect and caring and interest in you — you knew that, evidenced by what they did for you — so it wasn't an insult whenever they said something, no matter what they said. You can't compare our locker room to any locker room. You'd have to compare it to a championship locker room. There's a difference. I don't know what it's like for boxers or golfers in their locker rooms, but there was a special chemistry in ours.

It wasn't just one or two guys. I don't know what the Chicago Bulls locker room was like when Michael Jordan was their star. With our team, there were so many guys who had to contribute at such a high level for us to be a championship team. We had backup guys who could start for other teams. Everyone wants to be recognized as the best, or one of the best. You want to get a game ball.

Joe Greene had clearly established himself as a presence in the locker room. As dynamic as he was on the field, he was as calm in the locker room. To have people like Mel Blount seated around the room, setting the standard for the high caliber we had, was an amazingly strong influence.

We had an especially young team in 1974. That was the year of the players' strike. There were a dozen or more rookies who made the team that year. The only older guys were L.C., Joe Greene, Andy Russell, Ray Mansfield, Sam Davis, Rocky Bleier and Mel Blount. Many of the top players had come in only two years earlier, guys like Franco Harris and Jack Ham.

We had an amazing rookie class in 1974. Four of them are in the Hall of Fame — Lynn Swann, Jack Lambert, John Stallworth and Mike Webster — and a fifth, Donnie Shell, was under consideration in the final voting this year. We also had Jim Allen. Shell and I signed as free agents. Terry was still feeling his way at that time. We started the 1974 season with Joe Gilliam as the quarterback. Terry hadn't yet reached the level of performance we associate him with. Yet we ended up winning our first Super Bowl at the end of that season, my first in the NFL.

I never felt safe every year as it got to cutting time. You have to have some luck. Part of my luck was the player strike. Many of the veterans were late in reporting to training camp. I had a chance to show what I could do. There were six exhibition games then, not four. Several of the other rookie tight ends got injured. Because of the strike and the late start in assembling teams the NFL rosters were expanded by two additional player spots. The Steelers kept three tight ends, Larry Brown, John McMakin and me. They normally kept two. McMakin went to Seattle the following season in the expansion draft. A lot of things fell into place for me. I didn't know where I stood going into the last pre-season game. We'd left St. Vincent's and they had us in a hotel in Pittsburgh the week before that last exhibition. I asked our receivers coach, Lionel Taylor, what I was supposed to do. "Should I be looking for a place to stay?" I asked him. Before the last cut, he said, "Go ahead and look for a place." That's when I knew I'd made the team.

"The fame is fleeting."

Andy Russell may have served as a role model for me. Not because of a close friendship, but because of his success. I saw what he'd done, and how he'd gone about getting established in business in the Pittsburgh corporate community. I saw the success he had in business and in his life's work. It was a strong influence. I can't think of anyone else. Our experience is significantly different from the primary recognizable people. For the rest of us grunts, the fame is fleeting.

I don't expect that everybody should know what I did, so I'm not unnerved when they ask, "What position did you play?" It's actually a pleasant treat to be noticed at all.

The thing I'm proudest of is my consistency. I thought that was my biggest contribution, the level of performance that I maintained. I was lucky that I never suffered any disabling injuries so I was always able to play. That was important to the team.

My favorite tight ends when I was growing up were Pete Retzlaff of the Philadelphia Eagles and John Mackey of the Baltimore Colts. Of course, every tight end thinks of himself as a wide receiver, so I liked Lenny Moore and Raymond Berry, too.

I first gained attention and respect on special teams. But I hated special teams. It's a big part of the game, though, as we saw with the Steelers in the playoffs this year. You're in the greatest danger of getting hurt.

Dan Radakovich was a big help to me. He was a tremendous technician. He was with the offensive line the time I was with him. He was the best I'd ever seen. The offensive line he coached here and the success of the running backs were both testaments to his ability. I think Chuck Noll emphasized technique and execution because he was an undersized lineman and linebacker with the Browns and he knew how important they were to his success. So he taught technique relentlessly. Size-wise, he wasn't scaring anybody.

Radakovich was one of the assistant coaches that stick out in my mind. George Perles was a good assistant, too. George Perles was tremendous. They all accomplished what they accomplished in different ways. I had high regard for Lionel Taylor, our receivers' coach. Dick Hoak, who's still there, was a great stabilizing force. And Chuck, in his own way, was a tremendous coach. He was as much an assistant coach as he was a head coach. He really, really, really enjoyed coaching. Teaching. He had great respect for technique and preparation. There was delegation, of course, but Chuck was always there as well. If he saw a problem, he'd show someone how to do it right.

Yes, there was a magic. Trying to explain the magic is like trying to explain a miracle. There is no explanation. Whether the stars were aligned and this group of individuals came together at a miraculous point in time is hard to say. This group of people came together by circumstance and chance. And, of course, there was a large component of luck.

You have to control all the things you can control, but you never know which way the ball will bounce. That's what makes it interesting.

That's why everyone is so excited about March Madness.

I don't go to the Steelers' games anymore. During the season, I listen to the games on the radio and put up with Myron Cope. I watch the playoff games on TV. If you really want to watch the games it's hard to beat watching them on TV. If you want to experience the event you have to go to the game. That's not important to me anymore.

The Steelers were a rerun of the Baltimore Ravens the year before. They can't score a lot, so they play tough defense and keep you close enough that they don't have to score a lot to beat you. I am speaking strictly from a fan's perspective. I'm not associated with the team anymore. I'm not at practice so I don't see what's going on. Like every Steelers fan I was tremendously disappointed that they didn't beat the Patriots and get to the Super Bowl. Who knows what might have happened there?

If I was a betting man and I'm not, thankfully, I'd have bet they'd go to the Super Bowl. New England deserves credit, though. Three games in a row they came from behind to win. Look what they did to the Raiders, to us and to the Rams.

It reinforces the fact that every game does matter. You must be prepared and play your best to win. And you should want to win every game. The least controllable part of the game is special teams. And it cost them the game. They won on offense and they won on defense, but they lost on the scoreboard. Special teams killed them. They did everything they needed to do to win, except for special teams. It's an important part of the game. It does come down to coaching. The hardest coaching job on the team is special teams. Most guys don't want to be there. It's potentially the most dangerous place to be. I think it's the most frightening part of the game.

It's so elementary, though. It's not rocket science. You don't have to practice it that much. You should know whom you're supposed to block and whom you're supposed to tackle. There aren't multiple formations to deal with. It's the basics. It's all mental. Everybody's fast and big and as fast and big as everybody else is. You have to have it in your mind that you're going to do it. There's nothing fancy about special teams. There were three plays on special teams that sunk the ship. If they would just line up on offense and defense they win the game. They don't have the same bravado we did when we took the field. Teams were afraid of us.

There are some things you do that you don't want to do. I was in for covering punts and kickoffs and on extra-point teams and field-goal teams. I didn't like it one bit. But I wanted to make the team. The last thing I wanted to do was make a mistake. The last thing I was going to do was volunteer for such duty, but I did what had to be done. I took pride in my performance, whatever I was doing, not just pass catching. I was considered a good blocker, too.

Sometimes you see a successful person who seems to be doing everything wrong, and you wonder why he's successful. But he just keeps going, and he just keeps after it. It has a dulling effect. He just wears you out.

Chuck Noll would come in to the locker room after a bad series of games and he'd pull his "let's get back to basics" speech out of his files. His belief was that when you're playing poorly you're executing poorly. He'd say if we have to go into this game with one play and execute it properly then that's what we'll do. It's true. Even if you know he's never going to do that. But we'd practice each play at its most basic form.

Quarterbacks today don't call the plays. They've become just another position player. They're no different from everyone else. I think something is lost there. A good quarterback, a good leader, has a sense of what's best to do. He understands what's going on out there and what will work best. Besides, it brings out his leadership qualities. I think Terry Bradshaw had more freedom to call plays than Kordell does.

Chuck Noll was our leader, no doubt about that. He was one of the primary pieces to the puzzle. He enabled us to win by assembling the players and assistant coaches. He was very involved in scouting responsibilities. He actually went out to see college players. And he did a good job in the selection of assistant coaches. His biggest contribution was as a teacher. He was truly involved with teaching how to play the game the right way, the way we could win. There were immeasurable sorts of things he brought to the table.

Chuck's focus, his controlled focus, was at the core of our success. He wasn't a fire and brimstone motivating kind of guy. There was an amazing intensity and focus, but not to the point of spilling out. It was controlled intensity. Offensively, it was just something that was marching forward. The defensive side was just a brick wall. Most of us were just bricks in the wall. The only guys I would characterize as foundation blocks in and of themselves would be Joe Greene and Mel Blount. Even their greatness was enhanced by the components around them. Joe Greene would not have been the Joe Greene we knew without Ernie Holmes and L.C. and Dwight alongside him. Mel Blount without Mike Wagner and Glen Edwards and the defensive line and backers would not be the Mel Blount we knew. Without Joe and Ernie and the stunt 4-3, Jack Lambert is a different player out there. They kept blockers away and let Lambert make the tackles. Football is such a team game. There are so many players out there. Mel and Joe were just such amazingly superior athletes and they had the mental acumen for the game.

I split the tight end spot, for the most part, with Bennie Cunningham. His biggest strength was his strength and size. A player can be at a disadvantage because of his size. The expectations can be bigger, and more is expected. He was a big tight end for his day, but not these days. He wasn't really challenged on the way up. At the pro level, he discovered he couldn't do what worked for him in college. The pro level is the great equalizer. You skim off the top and you get to the cream. Everyone is good here. Bennie could have taken his game to another level and been one of the top tight ends who ever played the game. Bennie with another team might have had a better career. How often is a tight end going to get the ball when you've got Lynn Swann and John Stallworth? And you had running backs like Franco Harris and Rocky Bleier. There's not enough plays. Every tight end in the Hall of Fame was a great receiver, not another blocker.

Looking at the current Steelers, there's no question about Mark Bruener's ability on the blocking side. I don't know about the receiving side. I don't go to practices. They don't throw the ball to him much in games, so there's no way to judge him in that respect.

He's had a chance to settle in which is rare today. It's a different time, a different place. In today's NFL, with the salary cap and free agency, I probably wouldn't have played eight years for the Steelers. I have no regrets.

It's a shame today that there's a misconception that players these days don't have to get into the real world. That may be true for the high-paid superstars, but not for the regular players. The NFL life of the average player is under four years. The majority of players still have to find a job after football. They can't live off the interest and dividends from the money they make playing football. They have to live on some kind of budget, manage their money carefully, and plan for the future. He has to be reasonable. But he's 23 or 25 and he's clueless when it comes to handling money. He wants the best house and the best car and the best clothes and jewelry. And they're looking after family and friends in some cases. Some of them don't hold on to their money too long. They should talk to me. Or Andy. Or Dwight. Maybe we could help them.

From Grossman collection

Randy Grossman is greeted by son Oliver, age 3, upon returning from Steelers' third Super Bowl victory on January 22, 1979.

Hall of Fame Steelers from the '60s

Ernie Stautner was presented by Steelers' owner Art Rooney for induction into the Pro Football Hall of Fame in 1969.

BOBBY LAYNE
Inducted in 1967

Jim O'Brien

Leona and John Henry Johnson at Hall of Fame ceremonies for Steelers' president Dan Rooney in August of 2000. Johnson was inducted in 1987 along with Joe Greene.

Dwight White
He can still walk the talk

"We cast a long shadow."

Dwight White was sitting in a chair in the middle of his spacious second-floor office at Centre City Towers, which overlook the intersection of Smithfield Street and Seventh Avenue in midtown Pittsburgh. He was sitting across from me at an expansive coffee table, talking about the glory days of the Pittsburgh Steelers. It was a sunny day and sunrays streaked through half the room behind him.

After he had been talking for about a half-hour, White rose from the chair to cross the room. He put his right hand to the base of his spine, and absolutely creaked as he walked toward the windows. He bent his knees in an exaggerated manner to emphasize his discomfort. He wobbled like a crooked old man. He complained of old football injuries that remind him every day of what he used to do for a living. Going up and down stairs is a challenge. He listed some medical procedures he had in recent years to correct the problems or to ease the pain.

"I had rotator cuff surgery on my left shoulder and surgery on my left knee to correct ligament and cartilage damage. Everything I've done is on my left side. When you're a right end that's the side that takes all the hits and nicks. I even had carpal tunnel surgery," he said, rolling his expressive dark eyes. That surgery was to relieve the pressure on nerves in his left wrist and thumb.

I thought carpal tunnel syndrome was something that was more a job hazard for a professional writer or secretary, someone who was working at a computer or typewriter every day. White could see my puzzled look at what he had disclosed.

Then he leaned forward in his chair, and placed his left hand to the carpet, curling his fingers, and assumed his familiar three-point stance, the one that used to alert wary offensive tackles that he would be coming at them before they knew what hit them. "It's from doing this so much," said White with a mischievous wink. "The old three-point stance."

There is no more animated speaker about the Steelers' glory days than Dwight White, the wonderful defensive end on that famous foursome that, at its best, also included, left to right, L.C. Greenwood, Joe Greene and Ernie Holmes. Just saying their names evokes great memories. There were other foursomes for the Steelers in the '70s, including Lloyd Voss and Ben McGee at the beginning, and Steve Furness and John Banaszak later on, but that's the foursome that gained the greatest fame. That's the one that made the cover of *Time*. The Steelers' greatness began on the front line, in the trenches. White was the smallest of the four, at 6-4, 255, but his heart and spirit were

**Dwight White holds forth
at his offices in
Centre City Towers.**

Photos by Jim O'Brien

just as large. His mouth, he must admit even now, was easily the biggest of the bunch. He was into trash talking before anyone even talked about trash talking.

White was 52 as we spoke and would turn 53 on July 30. He was born in 1949. One of his teammates, Andy Russell, turned 60 the previous year. It was hard to believe some of the Steelers of the '70s now qualified for senior discounts at movie theaters and restaurants. Or that two of them, Ray Mansfield and Furness, had died. A popular assistant coach, Rollie Dotsch, had died as well.

White's daughter, Stacey, called him on his cell phone three times during our interview. She was traveling from Hampton, Virginia to South Beach in Florida for spring break. Dad was warning her about the kind of guys and gals she'd find there, and not to go anywhere without her girlfriends. If it were up to him, she'd travel with a "Steel Curtain" escort.

There was a limited signed print of the "Steel Curtain" crew on the wall to the left of where White was sitting. There were more photos on that same wall, professionally matted 9″ x 7″ black and white game action glossy photos from his days at Three Rivers Stadium just across the nearby Allegheny River, paying testimony to what he'd done during his playing days with the Steelers. There was more of the same in the next office, where his secretary the past four years, Susan Chunko, held forth. There were city scenes, showing sternwheeler boats on one of the three rivers. There were two framed covers from magazines in the '70s — *Time* and *Black Sports* — showing White with Greene, Greenwood and Holmes. They were one of the fiercest and most famous foursomes in NFL history.

I was sitting at the end of a handsome black leather couch where White had invited me to sit, and taking notes on a long yellow legal pad. "You don't use a tape recorder?" asked White when we started our conversation, looking over his eyeglasses.

"No," I responded. "I want to talk to you. This way I will listen to what you say. We'll just talk."

This was a Thursday in mid-March, 2002, and White said the "Steel Curtain" would be participating in a sports memorabilia and card show in suburban Chicago that coming weekend. The *Chicago Sun-Times* sponsored the show in Rosemont. "We're not just known in Pittsburgh," said White. "We're still remembered fondly on a national scale." Prices for their four signatures would range from $90 to $125, depending on what item a sports collector wanted signed, according to a promotional flyer that White showed me. It would be a good payday for all of them.

White said they have about six such signing sessions a year, and they were booked for Cleveland and Edison, New Jersey in the spring. "We can't do anything during the football season because Joe is busy with his coaching with the Arizona Cardinals."

White was wearing an olive-colored button-down dress shirt. He wasn't wearing a tie, but his shirt was buttoned to the neck. That same shade, by the way, is called charcoal gold on a Jeep Grand

Cherokee I admired later that day. Charcoal gold sounds better. He appeared the same size as his playing days, maybe ten pounds more, he admitted. He still worked out; he walked on a regular basis. He looked good. He still had that toothy smile, that bad-boy-about-to-get-into-mischief look. His eyes gleamed behind glasses that were perched at the end of his nose. Once White got underway, there was no stopping him.

White surprises people who meet him for the first time, or those who hear him speak at social settings around the city. "I heard him speak at a golf outing at the South Hills Country Club when he was playing," said Dr. Bill McClelland, a retired dentist who resides at Southpointe in Canonsburg. "He was really good and quite humorous. Everyone was impressed with him."

When I looked at the list of Steelers alumni I would be calling on to do this book, I hesitated when I saw White's name. He always liked to crack my knuckles a little. He liked to preach to me, keep that ballplayer vs. villain reporter repartee going strong. He and Jack Lambert were both like that. Like dragons, they could blow fire and smoke through their nostrils as they sneered at your notebook. If they could make you a little uneasy it brightened their day. They liked to growl a little to relax you.

Remember White was called "Mad Dog" during his heyday with the Steelers. He and Lambert didn't even talk to one another, carrying a grudge dating back to a clubhouse incident in 1974 at St. Vincent's in Latrobe. Lambert, then a rookie, took offense to something White did — tossing his jock strap at Lambert's head after practice — but they had a common bond in keeping quarterbacks and sportswriters on their heels or worse.

"I knew I was smarter than the majority of players in our locker room," White had told me in an earlier interview. "Like Yogi Bear used to say, I'm smarter than the average bear."

The nickname "Mad Dog" hardly suited him now that White moved among industrial giants and corporate leaders, that he occasionally lunched at the Duquesne Club around the corner on Sixth Avenue. White, with less acknowledgment, was doing what Andy Russell had been doing over the same span as an investment banker. I thought White was more politically sensitive than I found him to be ten years earlier. He often refers to "Mad Dog," like it was a character from his 20s, or something from a cartoon strip.

White couldn't have been more pleasant or accommodating when I called him on the telephone, or when I visited him at his offices at Mesirow Financial, a Chicago-based investment banking firm. White was their man in Pittsburgh. He was downright charming during our visits. He had been in this business for just over 20 years, or shortly after he retired from the Steelers. He played for the Steelers for ten seasons (1971-1980). He pointed out that they were in the playoffs for eight of those seasons and won the Super Bowl four times. "I could have gone elsewhere to play when I retired, but ten years was long enough, and I knew I wanted to work in Pittsburgh," he recalled. "It was time — as Chuck Noll would say — to get on with my life's work."

There isn't a better interview in Pittsburgh than Dwight White. I recalled that Ed Kiely, the retired public relations executive of the Steelers, said he once asked Roy Blount Jr. who was his most surprising interview for his celebrated book, *About Three Bricks Shy of a Load*. Blount told him that White was smart and easily the most candid of the Steelers he had interviewed. Nothing has changed in that respect. White had a passion for playing football, and for talking about it. He always walked the talk. He wasn't so sure the current Steelers were doing that.

"Why not?" he said when I spoke to him of my earlier concerns about coming to see him. "You're OK with me. But I gotta keep you on your toes. You better make me look good. Somebody might write a book about you someday and they'll be coming to me for some quotes."

He had been a very consistent and durable player during his entire career with the Steelers. He sacked quarterbacks and twice intercepted two passes in a game. He was a starter since his rookie season of 1971.

In his second season, when the Steelers made the playoffs for the first time in the team's history, he led the club with career-high 10 sacks. That was especially impressive because he played outside and usually on the other team's weak side. He made the Pro Bowl that season and again in 1973.

"It was always fun to be with Dwight," said Dwayne Woodruff. "He was always the life of the party. He kept us laughing in the locker room."

White was a standout in the Steelers' first two Super Bowl victories. In Super Bowl IX against the Minnesota Vikings, he trapped quarterback Fran Tarkenton for a safety for the game's first score and the only safety in Super Bowl history. He came out of a hospital bed in New Orleans to play in that game after losing 30 pounds with a viral infection. That tells you all you need to know about what Dwight White was all about. "I can remember Dwight White getting out of a sick bed in a hospital and helping us win our first Super Bowl," said Jon Kolb. "Nobody should forget that."

In Super Bowl X, against the Dallas Cowboys, White had three quarterback sacks to his credit. Roger Staubach, no doubt, could still pick White out of a police lineup.

While he was playing for the Steelers, White sampled some job opportunities opened to him by his stature with the local pro team. He worked for the U.S. Department of Commerce, then H.J. Heinz Co., then Bache-Halsey which became Prudential-Bache, and then a small investment banking firm, Daniels & Bell, where he succeeded the founding owner Travers Bell as president and chief executive officer. Daniels & Bell was the only black-owned firm on Wall Street at the time, according to White. "I succeeded him when he died," said White.

"He was definitely my mentor. I believe he was the first African-American on the New York Stock Exchange."

White has always worked. Like me, he thought it was the best way to stay out of trouble. Our mothers had told us that so many times.

I had to shut off the interview because I knew White had a two o'clock appointment. I didn't want to overstay my welcome, or make White late for his date. I said we'd get together again and continue our conversation. He was just warming up, and I was hesitant to call a halt to his passionate observations.

We left the building together, talking as we were walking. He was hustling to get to his meeting on schedule. He crossed Smithfield Street in his dark trench coat, carrying his briefcase. It was a mild day for March. High temperature for the day was 68 degrees. "I have a few appointments this afternoon," said White as he walked away. "I might take off early and get out to walk in the park."

I could picture him walking the paths of North Park, sending the squirrels scurrying for the safety of the trees. He used to walk there and fish there with Stacey, when the family lived in Ross Park. They had since moved to fashionable Fox Chapel, but walked in North Park. So Dwight White was still moving up in the world. Here's what he had to say about his Steelers' experience:

Dwight White:

The Steelers of the '70s are what people think about in this town when they think about the Steelers. We set the standard. It's more than 20 years later and they're still talking about us. We're still the standard for comparison. It's tough for the present-day team. I think there's a very long shadow cast on this team and they can't get out from under it.

Those teams of the '70s were very special. Everybody is measured by what we did. Ray Lewis came out last year and said the Baltimore Ravens' defense was the best of all time. Hey, Ray, just shut up! They did it for one year. When Ditka was coaching the Bears and they won the Super Bowl there was talk about the Bears' defense and how they might be the best of all time. They were a flash in the pan. Just shut up!

The comparisons are unfair anyhow. The game has changed. The rules are different. The players are bigger and stronger now. Offensive linemen are allowed to grab and hold. Defensive backs can't do the bump and run like they used to. Stuff like that. At some point, I think the Steelers are going to win a Super Bowl. I'm rooting for them. But they're never going to win four Super Bowls in six years. You can't keep teams together now because of free agency and the economics of the salary cap and such. Whenever the Steelers do it they'll want to compare them with our club. But they can't.

I don't think the San Francisco 49ers of Joe Montana were the equal of our team, either, no matter how many (five) Super Bowls they won. You put our defense against the 49ers and let's see how they'd do. I'd have gone up to Joe Montana on the sideline before the game. I'd have pointed to some people in wheelchairs around the field. I'd have said, "Hey, Joe, take a look at those guys. That's where you're gonna end up. We're your worst nightmare! We're coming after you!" I'd have given him something to think about. And we'd have backed it up.

We played a 4-3 on first down. We're going to line up one-on-one and we're going to kick your ass; that's what we were saying. We all knew we could beat our man. Everybody on our front line was uniquely different. You take Ernie. He was next to me. He was unpredictable, to say the least. He was as natural a ballplayer as I ever saw. No one who was not in the trenches with us can appreciate what we accomplished. Even my defensive colleague, J.T. Thomas — and I love him dearly — was not up front in the trenches, so he had no idea what it was like up there. He can tell you stories, and sportswriters can write stories, but unless you were in the trenches you have no idea what it was all about. Greene had a great attitude and he had so much talent. He was great. L.C. was deceptively quick. He had that range. He was not a rock-em, sock-em kind of football player. He was more of a finesse player. I really can't understand why he's not in the Hall of Fame. He's been short-listed twice, but he's still not there. Someone like Dan Hampton from the Chicago Bears gets named. What is this crap? I don't understand the whole selection process. Dan Hampton was a mediocre player on a piss-poor team. They were also-rans except for Walter Payton. L.C. played great defensive line for a great football team.

When Al Davis, or Chuck Noll, was talking about the criminal element in pro football, I'm sure they had us in mind. Whatever it takes; that's what we did. I take a lot of pride in what we accomplished. What did I bring to it? I was only as good as the people I played with. I was there to carry their bags, and it was an honor. I used to tell them, "You can lose with me, but you can't win without me."

"If you die as a hero you'll always be a hero."

I was part of a very unique period in Pittsburgh. I was playing with a super group of guys. Because you're unique doesn't make you successful necessarily, but we worked well together.

It was a great experience. Just about everything I have I can trace back to that experience.

My coming to Pittsburgh, my playing experience. Meeting my wife, who has changed my life. My life after football. What I'm doing now. How I've been assimilated into this community. How I embraced this community, and think it's embraced me. I played 25 years ago, but I'm still a Steeler. I was smart to stay here. There was a saying in Texas when I was a kid. "If you die as a hero you'll always be remembered as a hero; if you die as a turd then you'll always be remembered as a turd." Something like that, anyhow. It couldn't have gone any better than it did during my playing career. I had a lot of success. And I'm proud to say I've parlayed that into business and family success.

I always saw my life as something other than playing defensive end for a football team. I had ambitions beyond football. There was great opportunity for me here to make another career for myself. I'm old fashioned, I guess, and I had some ideas about what was important. Having a family was important to me. I'm from an older-generation school of thought. It was important to be responsible, to look after your family. Seeing to it that your kids do better than you. Be a good role model. Go to work every day. I'll be married 25 years this May. I attribute a lot of my later development and maturity and being a role model to being married. It's all been part of a bigger plan. I met Karen when she was in graduate school at Pitt. She elevated my game to another level.

You have to keep in mind where I came from, and what life was like growing up in Virginia and Texas. It wasn't always pretty. I had to take a step up just to reach bottom. Back at school they thought I was the least likely to settle down to a normal life. I take that as a left-handed compliment. I continue to be a work in progress.

My wife and daughter have been positive influences in fashioning Dwight White. My daughter — her name's Stacey — still gets on me if I say something I shouldn't say. Women were never a major influence in my family before I got married. My mother had 19 brothers and one sister. My father had 13 brothers and two sisters. So men — all those uncles — surrounded me when I was growing up. Some of those uncles thought comic books were serious literature. There were some real characters in the family. I have a brother who's much younger than me who's had some problems with drugs. That never happened in our family before, and it's inexcusable. I try to help him, but I'm not patient or understanding about stuff like that.

I always played the macho part. I came from the period where male chauvinism reigned supreme. I came out of the civil rights movement and the first integration efforts in the South, so I was mad about a lot of things. I saw a lot of bad stuff first-hand. I went through boycotts and stuff like that at school. I was one of the first blacks to go to what was then East Texas State University. Now they call it Texas A&M at Commerce. There was a fellow named Louie Margot who was the sports information director at the time, and he thinks we ought to write a book about our experience. We're talking about 1967 and they had not even started desegregating the schools in Dallas, which wasn't that far from us. It was the second year of integration at East Texas State. We had over 7,000 students and 27 were students of color. And 24 of those were athletes recruited to come there. There were kids from the Bronx and Brooklyn and Queens. They had a real impact on me. We were all challenged at East Texas State. I mean we had fraternities at the school that still had Stars and Bars — yes, the Confederate flag — on the walls in their fraternity houses. It was a real challenge to find your way around there. I ended up being the first black captain of the football team. One of my teammates was Harvey Martin, who ended up playing for the Dallas Cowboys. He just died this past year. He had gone through some drug problems, but that's not what killed him. He had pancreatic cancer; that's what got him. That can get anybody. I think he was trying to make it. Richard Houston, who played for the New York Giants, died in a car crash. William Gaines, who was on our basketball team at the time, has died of cancer. So I am often reminded of our mortality and my good fortune. We were all part of integrating that school. I saw a lot of good stuff and a lot of bad stuff. It was a very interesting period.

My head coach was a guy named Ernest Hawkins. He talked with a real deep Southern drawl. One night they're playing a basketball game at our school before my senior year. I was watching the game in the Student Union. The only color TV on the campus was in the Student Union. I was sitting there, the only guy in the room. I was sitting there with my feet up on the table like this. One of the sportscasters is interviewing Coach Hawkins at halftime, asking him about prospects and bright spots for the next season. Coach Hawkins, in that deep Southern drawl, says, "We've got a big Negro boy from Dallas named Dwight White...." How are you supposed to take stuff like that? As I've said, it was a very interesting period. In Texas in those days, you were either black or white or a Mexican. That was it.

I grew up in Hampton, Virginia and now I have a daughter going to school there at Hampton University. It used to be called Hampton Institute when I was a kid. It was a school for black students. My father graduated from there and I was born on the campus. She's never seen some of the very bad things I experienced. I have reason to be a bitter person, but I'm not. I have always been proud to be an African-American; I never compromised on that. I have learned to be able to function in this world, imperfect as it and I may be. My daughter is 20 and she's part of the current sociology. There are some issues that I had that she doesn't have to deal with. She is interfacing with people on a different plane than I did at her age.

She went to school at the Learning Tree, the Falk School at Pitt, Shady Side Academy and Winchester-Thurston, all private schools, and she lived in a lily-white suburb. So she looks at things differently than I did. She's had a privileged life. She wanted to go to a black university. She corrects me on a lot of things. She sees things differently than I did, or I might. I'm still working at it. I'm definitely a work in progress. Her mother, on the other hand, is the vice president in charge of education programs at PBS or WQED. My wife used to be a teacher at CCAC on the North Side. She has her undergraduate and graduate degree and is working on a doctorate degree at Pitt. Her B.A is in education and her masters is in public administration and urban planning. I just completed my second three-year term on the board of directors at CCAC. Those people do a fine job serving a real need in this community.

I don't think anybody is the same person they were 25 years ago. I know some guys who have football on the brain. That's their entire persona. I got to play football on the highest level, but that's behind me now. Football is not the heart of my existence.

I used to tell Greg Lloyd to get involved here. He went home to some little town in Georgia every year. He built a huge house there, the biggest house in the area. I told him you're the biggest taxpayer in that part of Georgia. But I told him he should stay in Pittsburgh and find a place to work whenever his playing days were over. He was a popular player here. No matter how much money you make as a player, you have to plug in somewhere.

I told him, "This is not the real world." To my way of thinking, you've got to get up at seven and drive in traffic to your workplace. Get someone to take you by the hand and show you how to do something outside of football. You have to have a purpose in your life after you're done playing football.

"Three Rivers was our Yankee Stadium."

I went to the Steelers' last game at Three Rivers Stadium last year. I thought that was probably one of the most thrilling moments in Pittsburgh sports history. No. 1, of course, was when the Steelers won the first Super Bowl. But this was special, too, a reinforcement of self-esteem and pride. It conjured up all the great things that happened in that stadium. I have pictures in this room, and the stadium is the background in all of them. That was the stage where it all happened, or so much of it anyhow.

Heinz Field is gorgeous. I've been there several times. They did a real good job on that. But, for me, it's nothing like Three Rivers Stadium. That was like watching the Babe in Yankee Stadium, or Joe DiMaggio in Yankee Stadium. Three Rivers was our Yankee Stadium. You saw some great things happen there, with the Pirates and us. Roberto Clemente and Willie Stargell played there, too. Everybody on our team who returned to Three Rivers for the final game had a great time.

It reminded us of what it was like to play to that crowd. They gave us quite an ovation. It was good to hear them cheering for us again. Four times we won the Super Bowl. For a city that was viewed as the armpit of the country back then, with the local economy in turmoil after most of the steel mills had closed, that had to lift the spirits and self-esteem of everyone who lived here.

When they leveled the stadium it didn't bother me much. I watched it on TV. I had weaned myself away from that earlier. Back then, I played in the biggest office building in town. I realized the history of the place. Those were special moments in time. People who were there, the players and the fans, will always carry those special moments in time with them.

If you're a real competitor you will be a competitor in whatever you do. I'm still competing. I always wanted to be something. To come to Pittsburgh and achieve what I have achieved is still remarkable to me. I can't find the words to describe that feeling of success that I have.

The vast majority of guys who played on those teams have gone on to great success. One or two have fallen through the cracks.

"I think the money has diluted the desire."

Then you have the Rooneys. I think they're a well-respected family in the community, and deservedly so. They stayed through the lean years and that had to make the great years even more rewarding. They knew what it was like to come from the bottom, too. Now things are better. You learn something about people when you see them go through the complete cycle. Everybody has a story to tell. I think the Rooneys' story is one of a real strong commitment to values,

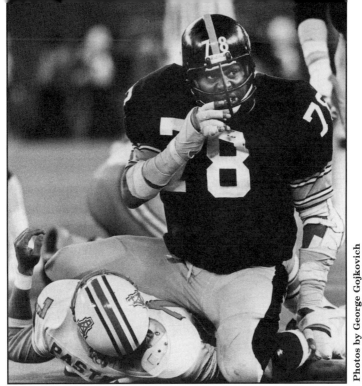

Photos by George Gojkovich

Dwight White got to the best quarterbacks in the business. White straddles a fallen Dan Pastorini of Houston Oilers and closes in, below, on Bob Griese of the Miami Dolphins.

religious values, family values. I think they've done a good job of adjusting their management style to the sports world you have today.

Their Mom & Pop organization — and I say that in a positive respect — is something they try to maintain. They still have the same community values and sensitivity and yet they run the business in a smart manner at the same time.

Chuck Noll now has a home in Williamsburg, Virginia. That's about 20 minutes from Hampton. I've run into him a few times. In fact, I owe him and Marianne a dinner. Chuck is enjoying retirement. Chuck is a lot more relaxed now and if you're around Chuck now you're a lot more relaxed, too. You have to keep this in mind. When I was in my 20s, guys like you and Chuck were old men to me. Now that I'm over 50 I feel closer to you.

When I signed with the Steelers in 1971, I made $16,000 that first year. My dad was making about $7,200 a year as a mailman in Dallas at the same time, to put it into perspective. So it was more important then, I think, to get into the playoffs and the Super Bowl. We made an extra $32,000 — double my first salary — when we won that first Super Bowl.

If you pay me $2.9 million a year for September, October, November and December and I can be home in time for Christmas, maybe I wouldn't care as much about winning the playoffs and Super Bowl. Maybe I wouldn't have the same drive. I don't know.

Whatever happened this year — and they can talk about injuries, coaching decisions, special teams, whatever — the bottom line is that they didn't do what they needed to do to go all the way.

It's all about where you ended up. This season when they got the home field advantage everyone was talking — including people with the team — like it was a done deal that they'd get to the Super Bowl. You have to act like you've been there before.

So they clinch first place and the home field advantage. Then they lose to the Cincinnati Bengals. You're supposed to run over a team like that at that point in the schedule. You should believe you're the best. But they let that game get away from them.

I think back to when I was playing. If we had two games to go in the season, we were going to stomp the hell out of whomever we played. I'm not in the huddle now, so I don't know what these guys are thinking, but I know we had an attitude about winning. We're gonna kick your butt because you're there. It's that simple. I've seen the Steelers blow chances in the playoffs before, so this isn't something new. Hey, if you can smell the playoffs then knock their ass down.

We always had a kick-ass attitude about us. It was always there.

I think the money has diluted the desire.

We weren't making that much money to begin with, so for many of us it wasn't about the money.

I get asked to come into to speak to some of the rookies each year right after the draft. John Mitchell, the defensive line coach, introduced L.C. and me and said we were two of the greatest defensive linemen in NFL history, and all that stuff, that we were part of the Steelers' rich tradition.

How do I know what these guys are thinking when we're talking to them? They weren't even born when I was playing. Their No. 1 draft choice was Casey Hampton, a nose tackle from the University of Texas.

I even said to him, "Casey, you're from Texas, home boy. Don't let me down."

They seemed attentive. Mitchell said something to them, asking them if they'd gotten anything from our message. "OK, guys, what do you think about what you just heard?"

And Casey, who looked like he was in a stupor, came back with "That was then and this is now." I didn't take it as a negative. Maybe he's right; I don't know. He'll make his own history.

Oh, well. So much for a pep talk from two old men. I also told them that if you win in Pittsburgh you couldn't play in a better place. I told them that if you lose here you could play in a better place.

It's simple. I own four Super Bowl rings that I have at home. You haven't done a thing if you don't have a ring.

Dwight White and I got together again, this time on Tuesday, April 2, 2002, for lunch at Atria's Restaurant & Tavern at PNC Park, on Federal Street on the North Side. It was 74 degrees and people were dining on the patio outside the restaurant. The Pirates had opened the 2002 season the previous day, losing to the Mets, 6-2 before a record Opening Day crowd of 53,734 at Shea Stadium. Pittsburghers were hoping the Pirates could improve on their record of the year before when they lost 100 games, but prospects remained dim. Atria's is midway between the statues of Roberto Clemente and Willie Stargell and that reminded White of his early days in Pittsburgh. "I was here for Clemente's last season," he said. "I wasn't much of a baseball fan when I was a kid, but I had a Roberto Clemente glove. And here I was in a city where Clemente was the baseball hero. It seemed to me that he became a bigger hero in Pittsburgh after his death. I think there were some racial issues before that. All of a sudden everyone was talking about him in glowing terms. There were days in the fall when we were sharing the stadium with the Pirates.

Willie Stargell used to come out and fool around with us. I remember head-butting him one day. He looked at me with wide eyes like he couldn't believe what I'd just done. Now he's a statue. I guess I'm getting old."

White was wearing a white warm-up suit with lime stripes on the jacket. He said he was going running at North Park that afternoon. He said he had a physical exam the week before and weighed in at 267 pounds, 12 pounds over his listed playing weight. His daughter Stacey called him on the cell phone once during lunch. He told her he'd call her later. "I like being Daddy," he said. "I tell her I will always be here for her. She calls me a minimum of two or three times a day."

We had a table along the wall on the second floor, overlooking the lower level. White held the banister as he went up the stairway, swinging his legs out wide like an old cowboy who'd ridden too many horses and was still wearing his chaps. He held the banister going back down those stairs later. He didn't mask his discomfort or the difficulty of the act. He went up and down those stairs like an 80-year-old man.

During a two-and-a-half hour conversation, he discussed many issues. He volunteered that he was never enamored with the likes of Dennis Rodman and Charles Barkley, two outspoken former NBA stars. "They say some stupid stuff," offered White. "They may be great players, but they leave a lot to be desired otherwise. With Rodman, I don't understand all those colors in his hair, the tattoos, all the body piercings. What's that all about?" On the other hand, White felt that Mike Tyson wasn't as bad as he was portrayed in the press and that the media was piling it on him when he was down. "I'm not defending Mike Tyson, mind you, but he is not capable of defending himself."

He said the autograph signing session in Chicago two weeks earlier had gone well. He enjoyed the reunion with Joe Greene, L.C. Greenwood and Ernie Holmes. "Only Ernie took sick, something about heart palpitations, and he had to be rushed to the hospital during our first day," said White. "He went home early, but he's OK now. With Ernie, you want to check in every day to see how he's doing. He's still carrying way too much weight."

I told Dwight how I had talked to Ernie's mother once and how she had said, "Some folks felt that cereal was a good breakfast. But I cooked steaks and eggs for Ernie. We raised cattle on our ranch, and Ernie ate well."

"I grew up in Texas and I know the way we ate back then," wailed White. "All those steaks for breakfasts are clogging ol' Ernie's arteries now, I'll bet. Poor guy."

He expressed some opinions about his relationship with Joe Greene, stressing they were good friends but how they had not always agreed on some topics during their time together with the Steelers. "Joe was the Steelers' man," said White. "They didn't have much else when he came here so they put the publicity mill behind him. He was a great player, mind you, but so was Ernie. Joe was just easier to market in more ways.

Dwight White checks out Johnny Angel and the Halos' Wall of Fame at Atria's Restaurant & Tavern at PNC Park.

White checks out old friend Willie Stargell's statue outside PNC Park, just across Federal Street from NorthSide Bank.

Two of the Steelers' greatest success stories in business world are White and former teammate Larry Brown, seen at United Way dinner paying tribute to team owner Dan Rooney at downtown hotel in December 1998.

"Too often Joe Greene's opinion was the only one that counted in the clubhouse. I went to Chuck Noll once and told him that Joe Greene wasn't speaking for me. I still feel that way. I could speak for myself."

And he did, indeed, while he picked away at a chicken Caesar salad and enjoyed several glasses of raspberry iced tea. "I watch what I eat," said White. "This Caesar dressing probably isn't doing me any good. But I didn't even eat any breakfast today."

Atria's is next to Seattle's Best Coffee at PNC Park. As we passed it, White said he was an investor in several Seattle's Best Coffee outlets, including several at the Pittsburgh International Airport. He smiled as he told me this. As we passed the statue of Willie Stargell, White leaped up and swung from Stargell's left arm. I was hoping it wouldn't break off under his weight. There was still a lot of mischief and a lot of kid in Dwight White.

Dwight White:

I had the benefit of two good parents, so being a husband and father is more than my obligation. It's a real responsibility. I tell Stacey, "As long as you're here you'll be mine." The one thing I'm proudest of is that I do know the difference between right and wrong. I don't think a lot of kids today really know that. You know that. You were brought up that way.

I don't have any use for the baggy pants and that grungy look. I know I had my Afro and platform elevated shoes when I was young, so I try to be more accepting. But I won't give on certain issues. I don't like the messages in the gangster rap music, and some of the garbage in movies. I know Stacey is going to see that stuff, but I tell her not to buy into it. That's not what the Whites are all about.

Sometimes I may be too honest for my own good.

Don't get me wrong, I like Joe Greene and give him a call now and then to check in with him. He was a great player, but there were some other players in the league who were just as good, like Wally Chambers of the Chicago Bears, but they didn't have as many good players around them as Joe did. Joe Greene was better because of the people who played with him. We all looked better because of that.

Joe was bigger than life. Ernie was never going to be like Joe. That hurt him. Ernie created a problem for himself and didn't do a very good job of damage control. People made fun of Ernie behind his back, but they patted him on the back and said what a good guy he was when he was around them. There was a lot of hypocrisy. If I had my choice of who to have in a foxhole with me, though, it would be Ernie and not Joe.

Ernie had personal issues that messed up his situation. I'm not saying Joe wasn't great, it's just that he got most of the attention and credit for our club's success. The media loved him. Hell, he went to the Pro Bowl one year when he had played only one game. He was hurt the rest of the season. But he was always there for them and he always had something to say. He was smart that way. He was like an ambassador. There was always a crowd around Joe after every game. He'd give them something to write about.

You take Lynn Swann, for instance. Swannie was a good salesman. He could sell himself better than John Stallworth. But who was the better receiver?

I look at Ernie the way I looked at Joe Gilliam. He was on skates to start with, and they just gave him a push. Joe and Terry used to put on quite a show at practice, throwing the ball all over the place. When Joe was on the team the black guys on our team were proud of him. He was one of the first black quarterbacks. He was not one of those black college quarterbacks who would be turned into a defensive back or receiver in the pros. He insisted on being a quarterback. He had come from a good family. His father was a college football coach. Joe had a lot of talent. He had everything you needed to succeed. The Steelers have their opinion about what happened to him, but I can document mine. Other players see it differently. You can get different variations of these stories. I know that Joe Greene always had a problem with Joe Gilliam.

In 1974, Joe Gilliam won the job fair and square. I'm not defending Joe at all, but he won the job. He did all the things you're told to do. He worked hard and he was prepared. Chuck Noll named Gilliam the starter the first few games. Bradshaw was stinking the joint out in the pre-season. The *Post-Gazette* came out with a ballot on the front page of the sports section, asking readers to vote for the quarterback they wanted to be the starter. They could pick from Bradshaw, Gilliam and Terry Hanratty. Guess who won? Bradshaw finished first and Hanratty was second. It seemed strange that the next week Chuck Noll benched Joe in favor of Bradshaw.

Joe was never the same after that. Instead of refocusing, he just tumbled into oblivion. Joe Gilliam and Ernie Holmes were roommates, which was not an inspired pairing. That wasn't good. One night after curfew, Joe leaves the hotel. He didn't make it back to the hotel for the pre-game meal. He shows up in the dressing room at 11 o'clock. We're dressed and ready to warm up. We let Joe know that this was not acceptable. Joe, you can't do that, we told him. He was with us for four years and then he was gone.

"If a man does his best, what else is there?"
— General George S. Patton

"I come from a better time."

So there were some things that happened that I didn't endorse. But that's not what my days with the Steelers were all about. My experience and what it's meant to me personally. None of this would have ever happened if the Pittsburgh Steelers hadn't drafted me.

A lot of people throw rocks at this town. Some will say it has a small-town mentality. I have this great relationship with this city. I've lived in Pittsburgh longer than any other place. I've been here just over 30 years. For me, for Dwight, Pittsburgh opened up the world to me, for me.

Coming out of the Texas '60s experience, Pittsburgh in a very rank and file way was an enlightening experience for me. Everybody has a story to tell. There are a lot of things I would not have been able to do if I hadn't come here. I came to Pittsburgh and became a Wall Street guy. I have relatives and brothers still in Texas. The dynamics are different. The ingredients are different. Pittsburgh is much different from Dallas.

If I had not played in Pittsburgh I never would have had the awakening I had. I'm not so great, but I think I'm on the plus side of the ledger. Here, I'm a family man and being part of the community means a great deal to me.

I don't play golf, but I go to all these golf outings and I talk to people. I was at a golf outing one day, and on the way home I'm listening to the radio and they're talking about Dave Parker and the problems he's having with the Pirates. He got into some bad drug scene and brought some bad guys into the Pirates' clubhouse. Now the Pirates were threatening not to pay him some deferred money that was in his contract. They were claiming he had breached his contract. Parker comes on this talk show and he's saying he was counting on that money so he could play golf every day when his playing days were done.

That struck me. Why would you want to spend the rest of your lifetime playing golf? I came here at 20 and I retired at 30. What was I going to do with the rest of my life? There's so much more to living than just playing football or baseball. I couldn't do what Joe Greene is doing. I wouldn't want to spend all my life in football. It's a strange life. I'm 52 now. I'm from the old school. I want to be something when I grow up.

My mother chopped and picked cotton. I used to drive my grandma out to the fields for her to pick cotton. I know what that's all about. Even so, I come from a better time. I had quality and not quantity. I'm not asking my daughter to be Madam Curie or Oprah Winfrey or Sophie Masloff; I just want her to be fulfilled and to be happy.

216

The word gratification comes to mind. My wife taught me that word. I used to do a lot of things for the right p.r. reasons. Now I have learned to do them for the right reasons. I've met people I helped in some way. There was this young woman that I hooked up with a job. I didn't think of it much at the time. But I've seen her since and she hugs me and tells me I changed her life. You can't believe the amount of gratification I get from that. That makes my day.

I went to the Elsie Awards dinner this year, the ones that Elsie Hillman gives out to achievers in the community. There were a lot of well-heeled people present, of course, as there always are at those kinds of dinners. Fred Rogers was one of the honorees. I call him Mr. Rogers. He says if you call me Mr. Rogers, I'll call you Mr. White. If you call me Fred, I'll call you Dwight."

He said something that night when he received the award that stays with me. He said something like this: "I'd like everybody to close your eyes and let's have a moment of silence. You think about the one person or persons that make a major difference in your life and contributed to your life."

When I do that I think about my family and I think about the Pittsburgh Steelers. We were talented people. They were all good guys in their own way. You can't win with rats. We had some characters, but we didn't have rats. They were all good decent people. They made a positive impact on my life. I was lucky to have come this way, to have met so many special people. I'm grateful. Things are OK with Dwight White.

Renaissance II didn't start with Mayor Richard Caliguiri. It started with the Steelers and the Pirates at a stadium on the North Side. All that's here now, this new ballpark and the new stadium and the convention center . . . that all started with the Steelers of the '70s. These are not because of the Steelers of recent seasons. They're still living on what we did. You don't have to be real smart to be the owner of the Steelers these days and to be successful. The same people still buy their tickets that came to see us play. When people in Pittsburgh think of the Steelers they still think of us. To them, we're still the Steelers.

> *"In the end, manners are about treating others as if they matter."*
> — Ellen Goodman
> Syndicated columnist, *The Boston Globe*

Rocky Bleier
Still fighting back

*"I'm 56 years old now,
but that kid is still there."*

I was excited and eager for the day to get underway Wednesday, March 27, 2002. I was going to the Pro Football Hall of Fame and I was going with Rocky Bleier. That's a special day.

Bleier, one of the best comeback stories in sports, owns a Purple Heart Medal from the Vietnam War and four Super Bowl rings from his days as a running back with the Steelers. He had been asked to speak at a ceremony in Canton, Ohio to open a new exhibit at the Hall of Fame called "Football and America: The NFL Responds During Times of National Crises."

Bleier obliged when I called him and asked him if I could go along for the ride. I met him at 8:30 a.m. at his beautiful gray stone home in the Virginia Manor section of Mt. Lebanon. Pat and Dan Rooney had a home nearby when they were raising their family of nine children, but had since moved into his parents' previous home on the North Side, just up the hill from Heinz Field.

Rocky's wife, Jan Bleier, greeted me at the door. She had Rosie, who's 3, in her arms. They were soon joined by Elly, who is 4. The former Jan Gyurina was an investment broker from West Mifflin when they met. I had met her on several occasions and always felt comfortable in her company.

The Bleiers have been married for six years. It's a second marriage for Rocky. They lived the first three years nearby in Scott Township and then moved to Mt. Lebanon when they adopted two adorable little girls from the Ukraine. Rosie and Elly were giving their Dad hugs and kisses as he was about to leave, and Rocky was smiling like he'd just scored another touchdown. Bleier looked great.

I wondered what those girls' lives would be like if they were still in an orphanage in the Ukraine. The Bleiers are just as lucky it appears. The girls were hugging Rocky around his legs, not wanting to let him go. They called him "Daddy" and you could tell how much they loved him.

Jan and I spoke to each other as Rocky finished getting ready for the trip. That never happened when I visited him when he was married to Aleta Jacobin and they lived in a handsome Tudor estate in Fox Chapel. Her father had been a highly respected physician at St. Francis Hospital in Bloomfield. Rocky introduced me to Aleta and she said hello and goodbye in the same motion. That was also the case when I came back for a second visit. They were married for 20 years and their breakup was a messy one, reported for weeks in detail in the local daily newspapers.

Rocky Bleier poses proudly at "Football and America" display at Pro Football Hall of Fame in March, 2002. He and wife Jan hold their daughters, Rosie, 3, and Elly, 4, whom they adopted from Ukraine.

Photos by Jim O'Brien

About 200 yards from his Mt. Lebanon home, we stopped at Starbucks Coffee. Rocky ordered a regular latte and I had a black decaf coffee with a cheese Danish. Dennis Colwell, the director of the River City Brass Band, was sitting, enjoying a cup of coffee and reading the newspaper. I introduced Colwell to Bleier. They are both Pittsburgh treasures. It was supposed to be a $2\frac{1}{2}$-hour drive to Canton, but Rocky missed the turnoff on the interstate highway and it took us three hours. He did the same thing on the way home. I didn't mind. We were so busy talking we weren't paying attention to the road signs. An extra hour with Rocky Bleier was a bonus.

Plus, we were riding in his 2001 black Mercedes-Benz sedan, a comfortable setting for an interview or a long drive. The car fit snugly in his garage, next to Jan's silver Honda van, complete with matching infant safety seats in the rear.

"They don't call him Rocky for nothing," cracked Craig Wolfley, a former Steelers' lineman who once blocked for Bleier, and now owns a martial arts studio in Bridgeville, when I told him about missing the turnoffs in our extended Hall of Fame odyssey.

The day started out gray, looking like it was going to rain or snow — it had done both the day before — but the sun came out and it warmed to nearly 40 degrees before the day was done. It said so on Rocky's instrument panel, which resembled that of a jet airplane.

Rocky looked resplendent in a brilliant silver-gray suit, a dark tie, and a white shirt with French cuffs. He had silver cufflinks. He wore the Super Bowl ring the Steelers were awarded for their fourth championship triumph on his right hand. It was the one with four diamonds in it. I saw it every time he nudged me in my left elbow to make a point, or to make sure he had my attention.

This was a great way to do an interview. I was reminded of a time when I went out to Long Island to meet Bill Bradley of the Knicks following a team practice at a high school gym in the early '70s. Bradley asked me for the keys to my car and said, "I'll drive and that way you can take notes while we're driving into the city." I've never forgotten that gesture. I should have known Bradley was smarter than most basketball players. He had been a Princeton grad and a Rhodes Scholar after all. He would become a U.S. Senator and if he had stayed in the race I was going to vote for him for President.

Bleier said he averages about 110 speaking engagements a year. He still attracts handsome fees. Following a brief stint as a sportscaster at WPXI-TV that didn't work out that well, Bleier has been making a living delivering motivational talks for nearly 20 years since retiring from pro football. He remains one of the most popular of the Steelers. His comeback after being wounded in Vietnam to star with the Steelers, to rush for 1,000 yards in a season alongside Franco Harris, is quite a tale. He makes a good living essentially telling his own story, and the events of September 11 only boosted the demand for his services.

He took training to improve his diction, his timing, and his theatrical manner. He doesn't sound like the same Rocky Bleier who came out of Appleton, Wisconsin to captain the football team at Notre Dame in his senior season, and put in 12 seasons with the Steelers. He's like Hal Holbrook playing the part of Robert "Rocky" Bleier.

He works with about 30 national booking agencies. He says he gets 80 per cent of his appearance requests from about 20 per cent of the top agencies. They get a commission from his speaker's fee. He has had the same administrative assistant, Gloria Ashcroft, for the past 14 years. She works out of her home in Shadyside, handling his calls and coordinating his speaking schedule. I first met her when she was working in an office at the Bleier home in Fox Chapel. She's always been pleasant and helpful.

He still frets about what he's going to say, and how he will be received. I understood where he was coming from. I do about 25 talks a year and go through the same pre-game anxiousness. You want to make a positive impression. I told him he'd be great if he was just himself. That the real Rocky Bleier would be all anyone could ask for. I felt like I was giving Rocky Bleier a motivational message. He said he was wondering what to say for openers.

As we were entering Canton, we both spotted a huge American flag fluttering over a car dealership alongside the highway. It was really big. I suggested to Rocky that he refer to that flag, and how big it was and how small he felt by comparison, when he delivered his introductory remarks. He was asked to represent all the NFL players who had served in the armed forces. The sight of that super-sized flag suddenly humbled him when he considered his assignment that day. I told him how I'd phrase that feeling.

He succeeded and then some at a luncheon program that preceded a ribbon-cutting ceremony. He opened with the opening I suggested, smiling at me as he said it. He mentioned that he and Jim O'Brien were coming into Canton earlier when they saw this huge flag! I suppose that was my credit line. I was glad I could help, considering his kindness to me in taking me there.

He made reference to a book he had read — one of my favorites, too — *Killer Angels*, a Pulitzer Prize-winning effort by Michael Shaara. He said one of the soldiers in it had said, "We all went to war. Some came home and some didn't. What happened in between is just the details." It was that way, he said, of his memories of playing in the NFL. "It's the memories that allow us not to forget. We need to tell their stories."

He spoke of those who served in the military as "boys who had a dream and wanted to do something." He added, "A hero is someone who does what needs to be done when it needs to be done and doesn't think about the consequences."

Bleier is featured in one of the display segments. It's an exhibit that was inspired by the events of September 11, the terrorist attack on America that sparked a renewed patriotic spirit in America. It's an impressive display showing NFL players' involvement in America's war and national crises. It was put together by the NFL and the Hall of Fame.

Ted Benson, the owner of the New Orleans Saints and a World War II veteran, had proposed such a display during Super Bowl Week in New Orleans. So far, they had been able to identify more than 1,200 known NFL personnel who were members of the armed forces during World War II, the Korean War and the Vietnam War.

One of the displays showed the New York Giants in full football gear marching with rifles over their shoulders, something they did for an hour each day at practice even before Pearl Harbor. Ironically, the Giants' training camp was located at Pearl River, New York. The publicity photo was taken on August 22, 1940. There's a listing of all NFL and pro football players who saw military service. It is compelling stuff.

"My dad used to tell me, "Son, someday you'll be in the Pro Football Hall of Fame,' " Bleier said for beginners, "and here I am, so to speak. I hope this counts, too."

"Welcome to the NFL."

When Bleier arrived at the Pro Football Hall of Fame, he was greeted by John Bankert, executive director of the Hall, and Pete Elliott, the previous executive director, along with Joe Horrigan, vice-president for communications and exhibits, who had done much of the research for the new display.

Two distinguished members of the Hall of Fame and its board of directors were present in Dave Robinson, a former defensive end at Penn State and with Vince Lombardi's famed Green Bay Packers, and Dante Lavelli, a former receiver from Ohio State and Paul Brown's Cleveland Browns. I usually see them every summer at the Hall of Fame induction ceremonies and they are both class acts. Dante Lavelli was always one of my favorite names in sports.

Rocky recalled in his remarks at the luncheon that as a rookie he played in an exhibition game in 1968 against the Green Bay Packers in Milwaukee. He said on the opening play he took a pitchout from Terry Bradshaw and ran right. He spotted a hole and cut back inside.

"That's when I saw Dave Robinson," said Bleier. "He hit me with a forearm shivver and I was ejected from that hole and sent reeling into our backfield. It was his way, I suppose, of saying, 'Welcome to the NFL.' Seeing him reminds me of that." The Steelers lost that game, 21-17.

Robinson said he recalled the game, but not that particular play. "I do remember that Rocky got a lot of play in the newspapers because he was a Notre Dame guy coming back home to Wisconsin to play against the team he followed and admired as a youngster," said Robinson. Still a formidable figure, Robinson faked a forearm shot into Bleier's chest to recreate their first meeting.

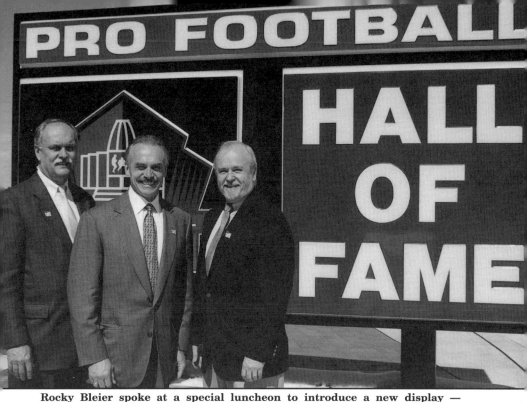

Rocky Bleier spoke at a special luncheon to introduce a new display — "Football and America" — at the Pro Football Hall of Fame in March, 2002. He is flanked by John Bankert, the HOF executive director, left, and Joe Horrigan, vice-president for communications. Rocky shares war stories with two familiar faces at Hall of Fame, former Cleveland Browns ace receiver Dante Lavelli, an Ohio State graduate, and former Green Bay Packers defensive end Dave Robinson, a Penn State graduate.

Photos by Jim O'Brien

In the lobby of the Hall of Fame, to the right of the huge statue of Jim Thorpe that serves as a centerpiece, there were illuminated plaques picturing the incoming Class of 2002. The first player pictured was John Stallworth, a star receiver for the powerhouse Pittsburgh Steelers' teams of the 1970s who scored the winning touchdown in Super Bowl XIV. He had been a teammate of Rocky, and had been voted into the Hall of Fame in his 10th year of eligibility. He had introduced teammate Lynn Swann at ceremonies the previous August. Next to Stallworth was Jim Kelly, who led the Buffalo Bills to four consecutive Super Bowl appearances. He was from East Brady, Pennsylvania, and I had relatives there who knew him as a kid. I asked Rocky if he remembered Kelly coming to the Steelers' offices at Three Rivers Stadium when he was a senior at the University of Miami. Rocky said he remembered. Kelly was a big fan of the Steelers, especially Terry Bradshaw, and even wore Bradshaw's No. 12.

In fact, Kelly had already contributed 17 items, including the No. 11 jersey he wore for the East Brady Bulldogs, to the Hall of Fame. He changed his number to Bradshaw's number when he played for the Hurricanes and Bills.

Kelly's is the second high school jersey from Western Pennsylvania to be included in the Pro Football Hall of Fame. The other is the jersey Joe Namath wore when he played at Beaver Falls High School.

Of the 18 modern-day quarterbacks inducted into the Hall of Fame, five are natives of Western Pennsylvania — Namath, Kelly, George Blanda, Johnny Unitas and Joe Montana. A sixth, Dan Marino, would be eligible in three years and he was a sure bet to be a first ballot selection. I hope to be in Canton when Marino is inducted.

I spotted the Steelers' display heralding what they had accomplished in the '70s. It included an enlarged and matted copy of the front page of The Pittsburgh Press of January 21, 1980. There were stories of the Steelers' 31-19 victory over the Los Angeles Rams in Super Bowl XIV in Pasadena, California. The bylines were those of Pat Livingston, now retired, John Clayton, now with ESPN, and Jim O'Brien. That display has been there for over 20 years. My dad never told me that someday I'd be in the Pro Football Hall of Fame, but, in a way, like Rocky, I was represented there, too. I could honestly boast that I was in the Pro Football Hall of Fame.

When I asked Bleier if he'd been to any of the induction ceremonies involving members of the Steelers' family, he said he had been there only for Dan Rooney's induction two years earlier. He also said he had never really taken a tour of the Hall of Fame. That's typical of most football players. When Jack Lambert was growing up in Mantua, Ohio he used to travel to Canton on his own and would check out the displays at the Hall of Fame. Now his bust is there right next to that of the immortal Jim Thorpe.

Stallworth and Kelly would be inducted into the Hall of Fame in ceremonies on Saturday, August 3 with the late George Allen, and

Dave Casper and Dan Hampton. The ceremonies that had traditionally taken place on the front steps of the Hall of Fame had been shifted to the nearby Fawcett Stadium. Hall of Fame officials said the induction ceremonies had simply outgrown the area available for fans. They could handle larger crowds at the stadium. They failed to add that they could also make money if they charged $10 for reserved seats in the stadium. Two years earlier, they had made another significant change, moving the annual pre-season football game from Saturday, following the induction, to Monday night. It stretched the Hall of Fame Week in Canton, but traditionalists were not in favor of the shift. They liked it better when you could see a doubleheader on Saturday — the induction and the game. L.C. Greenwood and Donnie Shell of the Steelers had both been among the finalists in the voting for the Pro Football Hall of Fame Class of 2002, but they didn't make it. They would have to wait for another year.

Rocky Bleier:

Some people criticized Franco for running out of bounds and avoiding collisions, or going down without fighting for more yardage if we didn't absolutely need it. Franco missed seven games in his career. So ultimately it was for the good of the team, not proving how tough you are. I might have done that myself, but I couldn't get that far. I was out of breath by the time I got near the sidelines. I wasn't fast enough to run out of bounds before I was tackled.

Along the way, we always see things from our own perspective. We worked out together, but sometimes you didn't get to see the other sides of people and get to know them as well. When you try to put into perspective life's accomplishments, you're always thinking how to make it better, more outstanding. People want to know why you did this or that. "Why were you successful?" they ask. At the time, you didn't know. Maybe now you know.

It's part of what I talk about. Before you become aware of what's happening, you have to reach a certain sense of security about yourself.

Will I know the plays? Are they going to holler at me?

That's more true of guys like Randy Grossman, Donnie Shell and me — they were free agents and I was a real late pick — than the majority of guys who make the team.

And your insecurities that you have — that you bring with you. Are you able to compete on that level? Certain insecurities can make you afraid to do things. When I think about it now, I know that I have experiences to fall back on.

Now I know I can do certain things and do them well. Because I've done it before. That doesn't mean you don't go over it in your mind, and worry about what you'll do, but you have your past experience to assure you that you'll get through it. The more you do, the more comfortable you become, just like playing football. Part of that is aging.

I always saw myself as the kid struggling to make the team. Part of that was a driving force. I wanted to excel. That driving force will always be there. I'm 56 years old now, but that kid is still there. That kid always resurfaces.

Yes, in a sense as you put it, I guess I am still fighting back, like in the title of my autobiography.

I feel a sense of renewal. It's hard to explain. I have a new family and I am finally living life the way it should be lived. I have the kind of relationships that I should have; that I'd never experienced before. The relationship I have with Jan and my surroundings, with my kids now, are so fulfilling. I feel alive again. I was married to Aleta for 20 years. Our daughter, from her first marriage, Samantha, is 28 now, and she has a travel agency in San Diego. Our son, Adri, who's 25, lives in San Diego, too. He is a car salesman. I keep in touch with them, yeah. My daughter is expecting her first child. I'll be a grandfather, believe it or not.

I was talking to my high school coach the other night. I had called him after learning that one of my high school teammates, a kid on our basketball team, had died. His name was Bobby Rammer. A classmate of mine in Appleton sent me the information by e-mail. He thought I would want to know, and I wanted to make sure Torchy knew. Bobby played on our basketball team. Torchy coached me in basketball and in football in high school.

Bobby Rammer died Saturday night. He had cancer. He was a year older than I was. Torchy had him from third grade through high school. He was a little rotund guy, a pretty good shooter from the corner.

Ultimately, Torchy and I got into a conversation about influences in our lives. He's 72 now and he teaches some classes at the University of Central Florida. He started the basketball program there when it was called Florida Tech, before it was Central Florida. He has a great recall for names and events from our days in Appleton. He remembers the players he coached. He was saying that sometimes he wondered whether he was too tough on certain people. One never knows. When he was talking about influences, he said he remembered asking me about that when I was at Notre Dame. He asked me who my greatest influence had been. He said, "In the back of my mind, I was thinking it was me." I told him he was certainly one of the biggest influences in my young life.

226

But I mentioned an event that had stuck in my mind that gave me great inspiration and resolve. Our family lived upstairs of my dad's bar and restaurant. From my bedroom, I could see St. Joe's Church, about a half block away on the left side of the street. On Sundays as I sat in my room, when I was 8 or 9, before or after we'd gone to church, I could see the people going to church. There was a football player who had played high school ball in Appleton. I happened to see him going to church. I knew he'd gone to the University of Wisconsin to play football. I remember wondering what he was doing home. He should have been at school playing ball. So I asked someone about that. I was told he had quit college and come home because he got homesick for his girlfriend. I thought to myself how stupid that was. I thought that if I had something like that I'd never give it up. I thought he blew it. At that moment in time it became clear to me that I'd never do something like that. You pick up stuff like that along the way.

One of the great things The Chief did, he always dropped the note or card. He took the time to show he cared about people.

The needs are simple. I picked them up in a management book. They're so important. One of the things that has been drilled into us — from coaches and teachers and parents — is that there's no "I" in TEAM. You have to work together as a unit. Do things for the good of the whole. But if you move the letters around a little in TEAM you can come up with ME. I've come to realize that there's always going to be some ME in what we do when we're on a team, whether it's in sports or in a work situation. You have to buy into opportunities.

There's six basic needs: 1) expectations; 2) you need materials to be able to do your job; 3) you need a chance to be the best you can be; 4) you need a pat on the back now and then to make you feel wanted and appreciated; 5) hopefully, you can find friendships within the team; 6) a sense that people are interested in you, that they will give you help when you need it.

I have a speaking engagement in Blacksburg, Virginia. I am going to be speaking to two groups that total 5,000 students — 6th through 12th grades — and then I'm speaking to 650 student-athletes and students at Virginia Tech. The theme is "Winning Choices." It's a program in character building. There's a state-mandated law that they have to teach character building as part of the school curricula. They started it last year. I've been thinking about it ever since I got the call. How do you relate to those students?

I was doing some rehab at Joey David's clinic in Mt. Lebanon. Nellie King was there. He was talking to me about how ballplayers are so different today. He said when he was playing ball the players used to talk to each other for hours during bus trips, that they even sang some songs. They talked to one another and they really got to know one another. He said that today the ballplayers put those earphones on as soon as they're on the bus or airplane, and they're listening to their CDs. Nobody talks to anybody anymore. They're all in their own little world. They want their own rooms on the road, even suites. Roommates used to be important people in your life. You loafed together, lunched together, went out together.

I've averaged about 110 talks a year over the last 15 years. It comes out to a couple a week.

You know you're getting older. How things are different now. All those things you hear about as a young man in your formative years are things you're telling others to do. You didn't put any relevance or importance to it at the time, but you were absorbing it. All the books, and things we read, the talks our parents gave us when we were kids. It might not come to the forefront till later on, but it's always there, providing you with a sound foundation for what you do and how you approach things.

I have empathy for players who are down on their luck. Some of them have encountered real difficulties. Things happen that put you in that situation. Some of them, though, are not doing what needs to be done. Sometimes you have to swallow your pride and just go out and get a job. It's harder the older you get to find a place in the job market

Doing motivational talks is my business. Other people do it as an adjunct to their regular jobs or business careers. They're not depending on it. This is my bread and butter.

"I wasn't really living what I was talking about."
— Rocky Bleier

After I got out of Notre Dame, I was selling insurance in the off-season in Chicago. I was doing what you do when you start out in the insurance business. You call family and friends to get going. I called a college teammate of mine. He was selling motivational tapes. I called and asked him if I could come and talk to him about his insurance needs. It was a difficult call. Selling was not a part of my personality.

Two things happened at that meeting. I sat in on a meeting my friend was conducting. Part of that meeting was a 20-minute motivational film. It was Rev. Bob Richards, the minister who was an Olympic pole-vaulter. Now I knew who Bob Richards was because he was pictured on the side of the Wheaties box that was on my breakfast table as a kid. In the early morning in grade school as I'd be eating my bowl of Wheaties I'd be reading about Rev. Bob Richards on the side of the box. That was before TVs were in the kitchen. As I watched the tape at my friend's office, I was mesmerized by the positive talk Rev. Richards gave. His body language and his voice inflection were great. He could really command your attention. I remember thinking that someday I'd like to do that. Then we talked about my friend's insurance needs. Ultimately, I ended up buying one of his motivational kits. It cost me $740. It proved to me that he was a better salesman than I was. I looked at the tapes and I remembered what I learned from them.

One of the points that were made was to be sure to pay yourself first. Don't wait till you've paid everyone else to set some aside for yourself, or you could end up with nothing. I was 23 years old and I had no reference to that kind of thinking. It wasn't that way with my parents. We always had enough to provide for our family's immediate needs. We didn't want for anything. But there was no money being set aside for the future, or for my parents' retirement. That was something I learned. Time goes so quickly; you'd better be prepared for tomorrow.

There was also something about making choices. The clearer the vision you have the better choices you can make. I can relate to that in my football life. But not in my personal life. To some degree, you lead your life the way you've been raised. My dad worked hard and had a business. My mother worked hard and she was always there for us kids. My father did the work and my mother paid the bills. She took care of the money. As you go along, those things kinda happen. You have an idea of how you want to live your life.

You make some choices. One of the things is that if you don't know an answer or where you want to go, you go with your gut instinct. Don't be talked out of something. You need to know what is happening in the world today. What do you want? How many children do you want? What are your feelings about alternative lifestyles? How do you feel about abortions? I think you have to talk those things through.

It's a thought process. How are you going to live your life? It's more difficult if you have no direction.

You are made up of three kinds of people: how others see you, how you see yourself and what you really are.

You have to be true to yourself. I found myself giving speeches about motivation, and I felt fraudulent, like I wasn't living my own life the way I wanted to. I was just reciting words. It sounded good. I wanted people to think well of me. But I wasn't really living what I was talking about.

When you confronted the truth, as I did, you say you have to do something about it. I had to admit I was living a lie. Ultimately, I came to that epiphany. What the hell am I doing? If I wanted to live the way I speak about I had to change my life. I had to be true to myself.

So I have lots of thoughts running through my mind right now. What am I thinking about as we're coming here today? You've been telling me about what L.C. Greenwood said and what Randy Grossman said and how good Dwight White was. Well, the competitor in me wants to be better than they were. I want to be more quotable than they were. I'm smiling as I say this, but I'm serious, too. I want to come off well in your book. How do I want people to perceive me? I want to be witty, charismatic, and insightful.

That's just part of my competitive nature.

"It's tough to say never."

I don't know whether the Steelers will ever repeat what we did in the '70s. It's tough to say never. I've been raised never to say never. I don't think so, though. The economic situation of the game has made it impossible to keep a team together like we did.

My take on this year's team was that they played their championship game when they played the Baltimore Ravens, and not in the AFC title game with the New England Patriots.

I'm not saying they weren't up for the game, and I'm not saying the coaching staff had not properly prepared them for the game. I'm not out to blame anybody. I just know you can't take anybody for granted. There are times when you're not at your emotional peak for the game. They still should have had the ability to win the game.

I don't understand playing Jerome Bettis in that game the way they did. I can understand having him in uniform and on the team, perhaps starting the first series. Maybe he deserved that. I don't think a healthy Jerome Bettis being out for six weeks is as effective as the guys who picked up the load during the time he was away. You have a rusty player coming back, no matter what he might say, no matter how much he might want to have his position back.

I thought that Fu and Zereoue had been doing a great job in the interim. You mess up the chemistry because of that. Then, too, the Patriots did a helluva job. The Pittsburgh fans don't think about this. New England was up to the test. Whether you thought they should have been there or not doesn't matter. They shut down our running game and they didn't make mistakes. And they made those big plays on special teams.

Four key members of the vaunted Steelers' offensive team of the '70s were, left to right, Mike Webster (52), Moon Mullins (72), Rocky Bleier (20) and Franco Harris (32).

Rocky Bleier runs outside on Steelers' sweep against Cincinnati Bengals.

New England did what they had to do to win three straight playoff games. You have to give them credit for that.

You have to give yourself a chance to win. The most important thing is not starting Jerome. It's winning the game. I think Bill Cowher got caught in a trap. I was sitting there like a fan. I could see on the first run that it wasn't the same Jerome Bettis. It was like he just ran into the line, not like he was going to hit an opening, or gain some yardage. Now it's second and ten and you're in a passing situation. I just thought Fu and Zereoue might have given them a quick opener. They're quick hitters. You get a few yards and then you can run or pass on second down. You keep them guessing.

I was talking to Torchy, my old high school coach. From a coaching perspective, he thought it was his job to put his team into position to win. That was his job. He took his basketball team at Central Florida up to New York to play St. John's. He stalled the whole game. They were booed. They eventually lost it, but the final score was close. If his team gets lucky at the end they have a chance to win it.

I'm a big fan of Jerome Bettis. Jerome is one of those surprising running backs. He runs with power. He runs straight ahead, yet it's tough to get a shot at him once he gets his momentum going. He has big legs and he's always pumping them. It's tough to wrap your arms around him. He's very effective and he can take a beating. Even when he was hurt he has been effective.

You can't compare him with Franco Harris. They have different running styles. The times are different, the offenses are different. Fu needs to have things develop for him. He has good size and speed. He hits that hole and nothing's there and he can move outside. Franco had great acceleration. Me, I hit the holes. I couldn't shift speeds. I was a one-speed guy.

I played with Dick Hoak my first year and then he was a coach when I came back to the team. Dick played the game on a pro level and that gained him a good deal of respect from the players. He's been in the league 40-some years now. As a runner, consistency was his strong point. He was reliable. He's very knowledgeable about the game. His goals are different from most assistant coaches. He's not there to move up; he's not there to rock the boat. He's an organization man.

He respects his players. He doesn't yell at you or scream at you. He corrects the mistakes. He teaches you what needs to be done. He complemented Chuck Noll very well, and I assume he does the same for Bill Cowher.

> *"Chuck Noll is a legend. He's brought tradition, he has brought pride to the city. And that's the thing I want to do also, in my own way. And I have no reservations about following Chuck Noll."*
> — Bill Cowher

There was a magic, indeed. The magic was created because of the continuity we had. And we had it for a long time. Teams can have magic for one year, but let's see what they can do over a long period of time. We had 22 players who won four Super Bowl rings. That's a strong nucleus. We had a lot of guys who had three and two Super Bowl rings. There are only 29 players in the history of the NFL who have four Super Bowl rings and 22 of them are from the Steelers. Five of them were with the 49ers, including Charles Haley who had five altogether. Matt Millen got four Super Bowl rings with three different teams, and Marv Fleming got them with two different teams. If there was one characteristic about our team it was that we were always ready to play. We came to play. I hope people remember that.

I go to most of the get-togethers involving our team. I see Andy Russell and Mike Wagner more often than most of them. I've been seeing more of Franco in recent years. We get caught up on each other's lives. This past fall Jan and I had three couples here for dinner at our home. Dwight White and Karen came, and Franco and Dana, and Andy and Cindy.

I always worked hard to make a good impression. It was a matter of wanting to be accepted and liked.

I have ten seats for the Steelers games at Heinz Field. My wife's family and some friends usually are there with us. Jan enjoys the games. I'm happy with Heinz Field; I guess it depends on where your seats are. I've got nice seats. I don't play on the field, so I don't worry about the field. I enjoy the games.

I'm happy to be in Pittsburgh. I could live elsewhere now and do what I do. Chicago might make more sense because I travel all over the country. But I like Pittsburgh. My fame and fortune are here. You get entrenched. If you marry a Pittsburgh girl you'll never leave.

Roots are important in Pittsburgh. People don't leave Pittsburgh. People who leave would like to come back. Jan has a close-knit family so I'm sure we'll stay here. We had 21 people for dinner at our place recently.

My mother, Ellen, will be 80 in September. My dad, Robert, died eight years ago. My mother and my two sisters, Pam and Pat, live near San Francisco. I have a brother Dan who lives in New York.

I've felt comfortable in Pittsburgh right from the beginning. I go back to the days when the Steelers hung out at Dante's in Brentwood. I remember the Wednesday night buffets there. Players don't do that anymore. I met people like Billy Conn and Joey Diven, real Pittsburgh characters and great guys. They were friends of Mr. Rooney. They liked Notre Dame, so they were good to me. We hit it off. So I know a little about the history of this city.

Paul Martha

He was "Star" to Mr. Rooney

"You remember your roommates."

Paul Martha and I were classmates at the University of Pittsburgh during a magic stretch from 1960 to 1964. We sweated in some of the same Spanish classes. As freshmen, we were both befriended by Beano Cook, the maverick sports information director at Pitt, and it changed our lives.

Cook promoted Martha from the start and was hugely responsible for Martha being named All-America as a senior running back on the 1963 Pitt football team. Cook introduced me to the best sports writing and best sports writers in the nation, and we started a lively tabloid called *Pittsburgh Weekly Sports* that same year. He also taught me to save money and how to buy stocks and bonds. He understood money more than he understood women.

I always admired Martha back in those school days. He was handsome and quite the all-around athlete and he knew how to deal with the media from Day One. He came from Wilkins Township, near Monroeville and Penn Hills, and starred in several sports at Shady Side Academy. He was a starter on the best freshman basketball team in Pitt's history. The other four starters would go on to play in the NCAA tournament as juniors and NIT as seniors. Martha was a slick infielder for the Panthers' baseball team, and played for Lawrenceville in the Greater Pittsburgh Baseball League.

He and Rick Leeson gave Pitt's football team a solid 1-2 running duo. They led the freshman team to a 6-0 record. The team posted a 9-1 record in their senior season, but did not go to a bowl game, still hard to believe. They lost only one game, to Roger Staubach and Navy.

A month after we arrived at Pitt, the Pirates were playing the New York Yankees of Mantle and Maris in a World Series a block away from the Student Union at Forbes Field. It would be one of the greatest World Series ever played and it would end with Bill Mazeroski hitting a lead-off home run in the bottom of the 9th inning. That came at 3:36 p.m. on Oct. 13, 1960. The ball sailed over the head of Yogi Berra, who was playing left field for the Yankees that day.

Another day that will live in infamy for us was the Friday afternoon of Nov. 22, 1963 — during our senior year — when we heard that President John F. Kennedy had been shot and killed by an assassin's bullets while riding in a motorcade in downtown Dallas. No one who experienced it will ever forget that afternoon, just like September 11 will stick in the minds of today's students.

I attended Martha's bachelor's party at a club on the North Side where Baldy Regan had arranged for the delivery of chocolate cream

Paul Martha pays visit to statue of old friend Art Rooney outside Heinz Field on April 7, 2002, and points out his No. 10 jersey in photo of Pitt's 1963 9-1 team that is on display at Atria's Restaurant & Tavern in Mt. Lebanon.

pies that everybody took turns pitching at each other. I attended Martha's wedding reception at the Pittsburgh Field Club. He married Bobbie Gott, the daughter of Edwin Gott, the president and CEO of U.S. Steel. Bobbie was a blonde cheerleader at rival Penn State, a smart young woman. They were quite the attractive couple. Paul had it all in those days.

He was the No. 1 draft choice of the Steelers in 1964. He stayed six seasons with the Steelers and played one more with the Denver Broncos as a defensive back and kick-return man. Art Rooney really liked him. Rooney often referred to Paul as "Star," and was responsible for getting him into Duquesne University's Law School.

"I remember the first day I met Paul," Art Rooney once told me. "He was that type of person. He was easy to know and easy to associate with, both physically and mentally. He's easy to be with. Like he's yours. Pittsburghers are like that. They have a special feeling for each other."

Martha remembers one of his early meetings with Mr. Rooney as well after he was drafted by the Steelers.

"My Dad and I visited Mr. Rooney a few days after I was drafted," recalled Martha. "We didn't have agents in those days. Mr. Rooney asked me what I would have done if they hadn't drafted me. I told him I was a pre-med student and was thinking about becoming a doctor. He told me to check that out. I did and I learned that I would be unable to attend medical school while playing for the Steelers because there was a time conflict with labs and practices. I went back and reported on what I had learned to Mr. Rooney. He asked me if I had ever thought about law school. I said I hadn't. He said I should. He told me he could set me up at Duquesne. A few days later, Dean Quinn called me. And that's how I became an attorney."

Martha became more than an attorney. He handled legal matters as a top executive for both the Pittsburgh Penguins and the San Francisco 49ers, both owned by the DeBartolo Family from Youngstown, Ohio. Martha teamed with Steelers' president Dan Rooney to help forge a critical labor settlement in the National Football League. They were the key players in the settlement of the NFL's 57-day player strike back in mid-November of 1982.

He was with the Penguins when they won back-to-back Stanley Cup championships in 1991 and 1992. He's the only man in Pittsburgh who can claim two Stanley Cup rings and four Super Bowl rings. Martha ran the front office of the Penguins during the days when Mario Lemieux was the team's star. He also ran the front office of the short-lived Pittsburgh Maulers, a project that caused ill feelings with the Rooneys. The Super Bowl rings came from the 49ers.

We shared a friend in Dave "Rooster" Fleming. I played on the same sandlot football team as Fleming as teenagers in Hazelwood. Our team was called the Hazelwood Steelers. Fleming had a tryout with the Steelers in Martha's second season with the team and they roomed together.

Fleming hadn't gone to college after his days at Gladstone High School. He should've made the Steelers, but he was cut. He was the star running back for the Pittsburgh Valley Ironmen in 1963, when I served as the team's publicity director. A year later, he went to Canada. He starred for ten seasons as a defensive back for the Hamilton Tiger-Cats of the Canadian Football League. He is in the CFL's Hall of Fame. "When you talk to people from Canada," recalled Martha, "they regard Rooster as a real legend up there. They can't believe you know him."

I remember Martha coming to a party in Hazelwood to honor Fleming at the Hibernian Club. One of Fleming's friends, named Tony Scalise, approached Martha and stood directly in front of him and poured a shot glass of whiskey on Martha's shoetops. That was Tony's way of saying hello and testing the outsider. Martha merely smiled at Tony. He knew better than to butt heads with the likes of Will Williams. When Tony Scalise, another of Fleming's flock, came to my going-away party when I was inducted into the U.S. Army, he stole the hubcaps off my Uncle Rich O'Brien's car. Funny guy that Tony.

Things aren't the same anymore. Paul Martha is no longer married to Bobbie Gott. They got divorced in 1994 after 33 years of marriage. He hasn't been involved with the Penguins since 1992. He's no longer involved with the 49ers.

He lives in San Diego now, sharing a home with his significant other, Roxanne Torquato, and he returns on a regular basis to Pittsburgh to check out progress with the Maglev project that operates from a historical landmark building near PNC Park. Martha is one of the officers in that government-sponsored project. That's a high-speed magnetic levitation transportation system that still hasn't gotten a green light in Pittsburgh. It's a controversial political football.

It's not a new story. When Martha first joined the Steelers in the mid-60s there was a skybus model by the Fair Grounds in South Park where the Steelers practiced. It never went anywhere, either.

While in San Diego, he had been doing some consultant work for the Padres when Larry Lucchino had been the team's president, but Lucchino, a former basketball player at Allderdice High School and Princeton, was now running the Red Sox in Boston. He is the brother of Frank Lucchino, an enduring Pittsburgh political official. He also hooked up with Pittsburgh-based agent Ralph Cindrich on representing athletes.

Martha always enjoyed the city, especially the North Side. He still frequented the James Street Tavern, where his late father, Al Martha, enjoyed the Pittsburgh Banjo Club night on the second floor on Wednesdays for years. It's a fun show and you can't be in that room and not be smiling and tapping your shoe. Joe Gordon and Dan McCann are frequent faces in the crowd. Martha likes to go there with his best friend, Pittsburgh attorney Steve Stepanian, who lives in the Gateway Apartments. I saw the two of them in the summer of 2001 at a reunion of the Penguins' Stanley Cup championship team at a golf outing at the Valley Brook Country Club in McMurray.

Martha seemed pleased to be back in the company of Penguins again, talking enthusiastically with general manager Craig Patrick, team owner and star Mario Lemieux, and some of the team's former players like Joe Mullin and Pierre Larouche.

I met Martha again in a planned get-together, on Sunday, April 7, 2002 at the Carnegie Science Center. He was there at a Maglev display that was part of a show to showcase some of Pittsburgh's high-tech projects. Also manning the Maglev display was another former Pitt classmate, Dave O'Loughlin. He was a star racquets player at Pitt. His family was one of the foremost tennis, squash and racquetball forces in the city for many years.

Martha and O'Loughlin were both optimistic that Maglev would be the answer to Pittsburgh's increasing transportation problems in the future. Martha and I took a walk across the street to Heinz Field and also checked out the statue of his old friend Art Rooney. They stirred up some pleasant memories.

I also took him for lunch to Atria's Retaurant & Tavern in Mt. Lebanon, as we had scheduled a meeting for an interview. There is a large team photo of the 1963 Pitt football team on the wall near the bar there. I thought Martha would enjoy seeing that he is still on a Wall of Fame in his hometown. No. 10 was still in the second row with that outstanding football team at his alma mater.

It's always great to see Martha, but he is not an easy interview. For one thing, I know too much about him. "You know all my stories," he said. Then, too, he'll tell me something I didn't know, and then he'll have second thoughts about it. "You'd better not use that," he'll say. "Let's not get into that. It's not worth it."

Paul Martha:

Rocky Bleier was my guy. Every veteran had a rookie to look after, and Rocky was my guy in 1968. That was before he went to Vietnam. He played with a great team when he returned. He played on one of the greatest teams in the history of the National Football League.

During his rehabilitation from his war injuries, he got bigger and faster, and he fit in perfectly with what the Steelers were trying to do. Everybody liked him and he had great enthusiasm. He was just what that team needed. They had so much football talent, but he gave them something special, an intangible, and the rest of the guys fed off that.

I wish I could have been part of that turnaround in Pittsburgh, but I was in Denver with the Broncos by that time. I played one year there and then came back to Pittsburgh and went to work. By the time I got to Denver, I was a lawyer and I had been admitted to the Pennsylvania Bar.

A lot of those guys meant a lot to me. I remember going to Ray Mansfield's funeral, and going to Froggy's afterward with a lot of the other players. That was tough. Everybody was feeling down in the dumps. Ray was one of the most popular guys in the history of the team.

I roomed with Ray when he was traded by the Eagles to the Steelers. He was a defensive lineman with the Eagles, but he became a center with the Steelers. He was my roommate for two years.

No one loved being with the Steelers more than Mansfield. He was a special guy. He played for the University of Washington, and they had a helluva team. We played them at Pitt Stadium and we beat them (13-6). But they kicked my ass. Jim Owens was their coach. We went 9-1 that year. We got beat (24-12) by a team, Navy, that wasn't that tough.

Bill Saul was another of my favorites. He came to us from the Baltimore Colts in my second year (1965). He was from Butler and we had some mutual friends. I roomed with him for five years.

Before Saul, I roomed for awhile with Sam Davis. It saddens me to think that Sam is in a nursing home in McKeesport. He was a great guy. Everyone on the team liked and respected him. Sam was really a nice guy. I've talked to his wife, Tamara. She's had a tough time with all his problems.

You remember your roommates.

The most important Steeler of the '70s was Terry Bradshaw. A lot of guys criticized Bradshaw for one reason or another, but for him they wouldn't have been champions four times. He had his critics, but when it came time to do it he did it.

Joe Greene was like that, too. He could do it. He was a player.

I would have liked to have stayed with the Steelers, but I saw the trade coming. We needed players. He needed offensive linemen at the time. I had a knee injury; I was hurt. Noll needed players. I think he got three offensive linemen for me. It's what he had to do. He was building a Super Bowl team.

Noll was well organized and he had good assistants. He was a good leader. I have no ill feelings toward him for trading me.

"I know how to do this stuff."

We've needed a new transportation system in this city for a long time. Pete Flaherty blew it when he was mayor. He could have had it up and running. We had a light rail system at

South Park when I first played for the Steelers. It ended up at Disney World in California. They also used it at West Virginia University and it made their campus. It's fabulous when it's used properly. Maglev is a different form of that light rail transit. They are now looking into using it at California (Pa.) University.

When J. Dennis O'Connor was the chancellor at Pitt, Corky Cost and I went to him with a proposal. We wanted the University of Pittsburgh to buy the Civic Arena. I was running the Civic Arena at the time and I knew it could be bought. We wanted the University of Pittsburgh to take it over, use it for their home basketball court, be a landlord for the Penguins, and complete the development around the Arena.

We wanted them to put a transit system in that would connect Oakland to downtown Pittsburgh, and possibly out to the airport as well. But it definitely would run from Carnegie Mellon University through the Pitt campus, past Carlow College and down to the Civic Arena — now Mellon Arena — and Duquesne and downtown. It would make so much sense.

The price would have been very reasonable. They could have connected the University of Pittsburgh to the City of Pittsburgh. It would have solved such a huge problem that Pitt had and still has.

O'Connor wouldn't go for the idea.

The Arena is still there. I don't think we need a new arena. There are too many problems with the economy in the National Hockey League. They have to be resolved before they can think about a new building here. Pittsburgh went ahead and built a new ballpark for the Pirates — and it's great — but they've got lots of problems that are unresolved. It's only in its second year and they're not drawing the way they did the first time around.

I'm not in love with Heinz Field, either. I returned punts for seven years in the National Football League, and I would not like to return punts at Heinz Field. The wind is definitely a factor, and with those rivers it's definitely tricky.

I dropped some, too; I didn't catch them all.

But the best of old stadiums and ballparks come and go. Look at what they're doing with Fenway Park in Boston. All the tradition and nostalgia — and I think that's important — will be gone when they build a new ballpark in Boston.

I loved Pitt Stadium, but Pitt Stadium was always a problem. There weren't any amenities that fans want these days. Access to Oakland was difficult. Right now Oakland is in constant gridlock. How do you get from Oakland to the city? It's impossible.

I saw three Steelers' games last year at Heinz Field, and one of them was the AFC championship game with New

England. I thought that New England could beat the Steelers, but I wouldn't bet on it. Bill Belichick came up with a defensive scheme that stopped the Steelers dead in their tracks. He changed football in one respect. When you have defensive linemen who can run like linebackers it gives you a real advantage. They shut down The Bus, and Kordell couldn't set up and throw. The line was so fast. That was the big difference in the game.

When you have a defensive line like that you can have six defensive backs instead of four. You have so much speed. That will be a big factor in pro football from now on. You'll see other clubs try to copy what they did.

Pittsburgh will always be my home, but I've been out in San Diego for two years, and it's hard to beat. I play tennis every other day. Marty Schottenheimer is out there now. He'll love the city, you'll see. He's the coach of the Chargers now. John Butler came from Buffalo to be the Chargers' general manager. I know both of those guys, so I'll be close to the Chargers, I'm sure.

I'll be coming back to Pittsburgh regularly, and I'm still hopeful we can get Maglev in place in Pittsburgh. We have no transportation system that works here. They are going to develop the area between Heinz Field and PNC Park. Now they have to find a way to get people there. We have to improve on that. When I come back to Pittsburgh now I love to go out to the Waterfront in Homestead. How'd they get that done? I'm happy to hear they're going to have the same people plan and develop the area around our new stadiums. They seem to know what they're doing.

I have four Super Bowl rings from my 49ers work, and I have two Stanley Cup rings from my days with the Penguins. I know how to do this stuff.

Jim O'Brien

Paul Martha, at right, and best friend and advisor Pittsburgh attorney Steven Stepanian show off Stanley Cup won by Penguins in 1991 and 1992 when Martha was front-office boss. They attended 10th anniversary reunion of 1991 team in summer of 2001 at Valley Brook Country Club in McMurray, Pennsylvania.

Remembering their roots...

Jim McCarl and Tony Dorsett are chairmen of annual Tony Dorsett McGuire Memorial Celebrity Golf Classic that attracts many former Steelers to play at Beaver Valley Country Club and Beaver Lakes Country Club. McCarl and his committee, including Dan Rains, a former teammate of Dorsett at Hopewell High School and a linebacker on Mike Ditka's Super Bowl champion Chicago Bears, have raised nearly $1.5 million for the children of McGuire Memorial.

Foge Fazio, the defensive coordinator of the Cleveland Browns and former head football coach at the University of Pittsburgh, joins Myron Cope each year at a golf tournament to raise funds for area autistic children at the Montour Heights Country Club. Here Fazio joins old friends Don DeBlasio, Mt. Lebanon restauranteur, and Jimmy Sacco, the Steelers' Director of Stadium Management, during post-golf party at DeBlasio's home in Nevillewood.

Photos by Jim O'Brien

Former Steeler linebackers Jack Ham and Andy Russell participate in many Pittsburgh-area charity fund-raising golf outings, including this appearance at the Mellon Mario Lemieux Celebrity Invitational at The Club at Nevillewood. Russell hosts his own golf outing there for local children's charities.

Dan Marino is in demand at celebrity golf outings across the country, but he always returns home to Pittsburgh to play in the Mellon Mario Lemeiux Celebrity Invitational. His caddy is Emil Boures, who blocked for Marino at the University of Pittsburgh and was later a valued versatile lineman for Chuck Noll's Steelers for five seasons (1982-1986). Boures is now a sales rep for Canon office equipment.

Ted Petersen
A great Dane

"I'm getting bolder as I get older."

Ted Petersen is in the picture in one of my most vivid memories of my years (1979-1983) of reporting on the Pittsburgh Steelers for *The Pittsburgh Press*. It came in the final minute of the American Football Conference championship at Three Rivers Stadium on January 7, 1980.

It is a picture that is framed in the game room of Rocky Bleier's home in Mt. Lebanon. Bleier scored a touchdown on a short burst off the left side of the line to clinch the victory against the Houston Oilers.

I was standing directly behind the right corner of the end zone that day as Bleier ran between left guard Sam Davis and left tackle Ted Petersen for that touchdown. The play was a 35-trap — the 3 back off the 5 hole, or left tackle slot. It was a four-yard run with only 54 seconds showing on the scoreboard clock and helped boost the Steelers' lead and the final score to 27-13. Davis and Petersen both pushed their opposing linemen aside and opened quite a hole. It happened about 20 yards away from where I was standing, right next to Joe Gordon, then the team's publicist.

My heart leaped and I had a tear or two in my eyes, I confess. The excitement of the moment had gotten to me. I had come back to Pittsburgh only ten months earlier, after working out of town as a sportswriter for ten years, and I realized I had made a smart decision in coming home.

The Steelers were going to the Super Bowl — for the fourth time in six years — and I wasn't going to miss out on it this time. I was going with them. I was happy. Those were happy tears. "What's wrong?" Gordon asked me. "Nothing," I said, smiling so he didn't think I'd lost a bet. Hey, sports writers want to work in championship environments as well as the players. I have had more than my share of my luck in that respect.

Two weeks later, I would be in Pasadena, California, in the press box high above the Rose Bowl and I'd see the Steelers rally to defeat the Los Angeles Rams, 31-19, before 103,985 fans and an international TV audience. It was the Steelers' fourth Super Bowl triumph in six years. Even my wife, Kathie, was an eyewitness. She was with the Steelers' party and she was able to share in this spectacular day in Pittsburgh sports history.

There were a lot of Steelers fans there that day. They were more evident and demonstrative, many wearing their own black and gold uniforms and waving their Terrible Towels, than the LA faithful.

Former Steelers lineman Ted Petersen, who helped coach the track & field team at Trinity High School in Washington, was at the WPIAL qualifiers at West Mifflin High School on May 7, 2002. Ted is flanked by his sons, Teddy, 21, at left, and Garrett, 18, at Glacial National Park in Montana on June 30, 2002.

Petersen wasn't in the starting lineup in Super Bowl XIV. He gave way to Jon Kolb, who had missed the previous nine games with a shoulder injury, including two playoff games.

Petersen was a reserve offensive lineman and, like most of the Steelers' linemen in those days, he was versatile enough to fill in just about anywhere on that line. In some short yardage situations, Petersen even played tight end, his position his first two varsity seasons at Eastern Illinois University. In Super Bowl XIV, he filled in for Larry Brown at both right tackle and at tight end. He was drafted on the fourth round in 1977 after being the first player in the history of Eastern Illinois to be named Division II All-America. He was co-captain as a senior and earned a bachelor's degree in health and physical education, as well as a teaching certificate. During his stay with the Steelers, he also picked up two Super Bowl rings.

He stood 6-5, and weighed 245 pounds. He was one of the lightest offensive tackles in the league. Most of the Steelers' linemen didn't weigh as much as most NFL linemen at their respective positions. But they were skilled, smart and athletic, swifter than many linemen, able to execute Noll's pet trap plays and end sweeps in which they had to pull out of the line to lead the blocking.

"I was never a big offensive lineman," Petersen said. "I was a suped-up tight end without the talent to play that position in the pros." In 1981 and 1982, Petersen played only nine games while rehabilitating from surgery to remove a benign tumor from his right hip. He was never quite the same after that operation.

The kid from Kankakee, Illinois was a blond Dane — they're rare in the NFL — and a handsome blue-eyed fellow who was well liked by his teammates. He was an easy traveler. His full name is Ted Hans Petersen III. He has been a physical education teacher in the Trinity School District in Washington, Pennsylvania, about 35 miles south of Pittsburgh. He was the head coach of the high school football team for five years, but surrendered the position when he didn't feel he was getting the sort of cooperation he needed to be successful. He was 47 years old.

Petersen played for the Steelers for eight seasons altogether, from 1977 through 1983, and then briefly in 1987. In 1984, he played ten games with the Cleveland Browns, and five more with the Indianapolis Colts. He sat out the 1985 and 1986 seasons, and came back to play three games with the Steelers when the veterans were on strike at the outset of the 1987 season. And three games count as a full season on the NFL players' retirement plan. It gave him nine NFL seasons to his credit. It was a real bonus for Petersen in several ways.

"I was doing construction work, and thinking all the while that I should still be playing pro football," recalled Petersen. "I thought I was in good condition. When the players were out on strike in '87, and the team was looking for players to fill the roster, I asked my friends on the team how they'd feel if I came back. I wouldn't have jeopardized my friendship for that. They urged me to do it; frankly, I could use the money as I was just scraping by at that time.

"I had more fun during those three weeks playing football than at any other time because there wasn't a lot of pressure. Other teams were putting makeshift teams on the field, too. But I was so banged up physically, and it was a real education. It underlined how important it is to be in proper condition to compete in pro sports. I thought I was in fairly good shape, but I wasn't. I never could have lasted 16 games. So it was nice to put those thoughts of continuing to play pro ball to rest for good."

Petersen started coaching in 1988, as an assistant to Bill Vosel at Canon-McMillan High School in Canonsburg. He had gotten to know Vosel in Bridgeville, where Petersen was living in the Hunting Ridge plan.

He did that for two seasons, and then assumed the head coaching position at Trinity High School.

Trinity High School sits on the crest of a hill high above College Field, where the Washington & Jefferson College football team plays its home games. I visited the school twice to interview Petersen. On the first occasion, I combined it with a visit to his friend and former teammate John Banazak, who was the head football coach at nearby W&J. Petersen was not in shape to do an interview or anything else that day in late February.

He had played basketball for the Steelers traveling team the night before, and was suffering from the outing. Tom O'Malley, the manager of the Steelers basketball team, had a hard time rounding up enough current players and, in desperation, called on some of the Steelers alumni to fill the void. Players like Edmund Nelson, Bryan Hinkle, Robin Cole and Louis Lipps had taken their game out of mothballs to answer the call.

Petersen looked jaundiced when I saw him coming down the hallway at Trinity High School. He was headed for the parking lot. He was going home to rest. He begged off the interview, asking me if I'd call him and reschedule it. I had to smile. He looked like one of Frank Perdue's yellow-tinted chickens.

I returned on Tuesday, April 9. I had a speaking engagement that day at an author's program sponsored by the Citizens Library of Washington, just across the street from Old Main on the W&J campus. It was raining en route from my home in Upper St. Clair all the way to Washington. I worried that no one would show up for the luncheon program, but there was a packed house of warm and friendly folks. It was an enjoyable and rewarding session.

So was my visit with Petersen. The rain had stopped, but the sky was still gray as I approached the main building at Trinity High School that day. The Trinity teams are called the Hillers, after the landscape where the school sits. It could pass for a small college campus.

I sat in a student desk in the gym while Petersen supervised a basketball doubleheader, one game for the guys, and one for the gals. Petersen said something to his charges on occasion, usually when somebody was getting too spirited or out of line.

There was a controversy raging in my community of Upper St. Clair at the time that was of interest to Petersen. Two of the head coaches at USC were under fire, with two members of the school board pushing for their removal. Jim Render, the head football coach, and Danny Holzer, the head basketball coach, were both coming off successful seasons. Render, in particular, had one of the most successful programs in the state over the past 20 or so seasons.

Petersen wasn't surprised. He'd been exposed to the politics of trying to coach a high school program in the area and had his own scars. His buddy, Banaszak, was also running into a difficult climate at W&J. His team was undefeated (10-0) during the regular season in NCAA Division III competition, and 1-1 in the playoffs, yet there was internal strife.

Petersen shook his head and smiled as we discussed what was going on at Upper St. Clair and at W&J. Those two schools shared more than black and red as school colors. Black and blue might have been more appropriate.

Petersen was wearing a light blue shirt with Trinity over the heart. The school colors at Trinity are like those at the University of North Carolina — Carolina blue and white. Petersen was in his 12th year of teaching in the Trinity School District, and 14th in the teaching and coaching profession.

He would be hired a few weeks later as the Athletic Director at Upper St. Clair High School and would begin his new duties for the 2002-2003 school year.

Petersen and his wife, Marian, live in a condo at Hunting Ridge in South Fayette. They would be celebrating their second wedding anniversary in May, 2002. His first wife, Linda, and their sons, Teddy, 21, and Garrett, 18, live nearby. "I wanted to be close to the boys, so I bought a place in the same plan," said Petersen. Ted and Linda were married for 17 years.

I visited with him again on Tuesday, May 7, at noon. He was getting ready to accompany the track and field team to a WPIAL qualifying meet at West Mifflin High School. He is an assistant track coach at Trinity, and helps with the weight throwers — discus, shot put and javelin — and as a strength coach. It was drizzling, much like it was the last time I went to Trinity High School. There had been some interesting developments since we last spoke. I traveled to West Mifflin that afternoon, and the rain eventually gave way to sunshine and a splendid track meet. I have always loved track & field meets. I caught up with Petersen who was helping officials conduct the shot put competition. We had a chance to talk again.

Ted Petersen:

I saw in the newspaper this morning that John Luckhardt has been hired to be the head football coach at California. I know John Banaszak had interviewed for that job as well, and Greg Gattuso. That job attracted some good candidates.

I've been looking into the athletic director's job at Upper St. Clair High School since I saw you the last time. Tunch Ilkin encouraged me to apply. I know Jim Render, their football coach, and I've met their basketball coach, Danny Holzer — he seems like a heckuva nice guy — and I'd enjoy working with people like that. I hear there's a teaching position open, too, so that could work out well for me.

I coached in the same conference in which Upper St. Clair competed, and I know a lot of those programs and the people running them. It's close to my home, so it has a lot going for it, from my standpoint.

I was with Tunch this past Saturday. I participated in the Light of Life Mission walk to raise money for their programs. Tunch heads their board and that's been his main community project since his playing days. Craig Wolfley and Steve Courson and I walked with Tunch. It was a 15-mile walk, and I went only halfway because I had something else to do.

It's always great to be with those guys. We've remained close through the years.

We were walking along, and we started talking about Mike Webster. I think I started it by asking, "Has anyone heard anything about Webby?"

We were comparing notes. Every so often we get calls asking us if we'd participate in a fund-raising banquet in honor of Mike Webster. The more you talk you realize they're not raising money for Mike. They're raising money because Mike owes somebody money. We know now they're not doing it for Webby. They're doing it to reclaim their losses.

I'm getting bolder as I get older by the way I approach these things now. I ask tough questions. I'm tired of enabling Mike to take advantage of people and to continue to lead a life of irresponsibility. He needs to get help to straighten out his life.

Tunch put him up at a Holiday Inn in Greentree for awhile a few years back. He was living off Tunch's credit card. And he ended up turning on Tunch, and doesn't talk to him anymore, either. That's what he does. It's a shame, really, and he was the last guy you thought would run into these kinds of problems.

The more I coached the more right on I realized Chuck Noll was about so many things. He was a great communicator. He said a lot with very few words. He spoke with authority because he knew what he was talking about.

While I was coaching here, I attended a clinic held by Joe Walton at Robert Morris. Noll was one of the main speakers. He went over football from A to Z. It wasn't a flashy thing. He mentioned that there are always new concepts, but it doesn't matter what you do it's how you do it. The execution is still the most important facet of football.

Chuck was so great of a teacher. He was the ultimate teacher. I always respected him for that. I learned a lot in one year from Dan Radakovich and from Rollie Dotsch for seven years. One year with Rad took two years off your life.

He never let us rest at practice. Other units would pull out players from time to time, but he never did. He had us walking even when we were supposed to be resting. With my physical stature, I'd never have played in the NFL if my techniques weren't the best. And you learned the right techniques from Rad; that's for sure. He's an absolute kook, a nut, a mad scientist, but you love to be around him and listen to him. At the time he was coaching with the Steelers, I hated him; I despised him. He used to say, "Do you want relief or do you want Super Bowls?"

We practiced so hard. It was a relief to go against some one else on Sunday. Those guys on our team came off the ball on every play and smashed you. They did head butts, everything. They even practiced hard on Fridays, which was a walk-through for most NFL teams.

The training camp doesn't last as long anymore. Things have been watered down. They don't hit as often.

It was no picnic having to go up against Joe Greene and Ernie Holmes and Steve Furness. Ernie was like a puppy eight or nine times and then he'd unload on you when you least expected it. One day I put a really good block on Ernie. He said, "OK, Petersen, so you want to play football?"

On the next time, Ernie was cranking up his forearm. He hit me so hard; he just crushed me. Chuck used to say that when Ernie wanted to play he was a beast out there. I only had to play against him for one year and then they traded him to Tampa Bay. The coaches were afraid of him, too. They didn't want to tell him what to do.

The games were easier, no doubt about it. There was a lot more mental pressure in the real games, but not physically. Going up against the Steelers was the toughest test of all.

They knew our plays. L.C. and Jack Ham would look in our backfield and call out the play. They could tell from the formation what we were going to do. They were always right. It was pretty impressive.

250

Steve lives out in the woods in the Laurel Highlands. Tunch Ilkin has a cabin nearby, so we always do a lot of things together. We try to get Jon Kolb involved when he can get away. We enjoy Jon's company.

"We always considered ourselves the whipping dogs of the team."

In our era, we were really a group of overachievers. We were good athletes, better than most at our positions. Through weight training, we worked hard to build ourselves up. We understood our roles well. We always considered ourselves the whipping dogs of the team.

When we didn't play well, Chuck (Noll) could always tear into the offensive line. To my knowledge, he never criticized the defense. Of course, they didn't have too many bad games. But if our offense wasn't working it was always the offensive line's fault. We weren't doing our job.

In our last championship season (1979), I started at right tackle in the last nine games of the season, including two playoff games. Jon Kolb had suffered a bad shoulder injury. But Jon was given the green light to play in the Super Bowl, and I understood the situation.

Jon went up against Fred Dwyer in that game. Moon Mullins was starting at right guard. Steve Courson had been playing there most of the season, but he severely hurt his ankle in practice that week, and was a scratch. When Davis got hurt in the game, Jon Kolb went to our line coach Rollie Dotsch and asked him to put me in there instead of the backup guard Thom Dornbrook. I think Jon felt badly that I didn't get to start because he was back. I hadn't played much guard, but I felt comfortable playing between Webby and Jon. I knew the plays and the calls.

I remember how emotional Rollie Dotsch was after that game. He was a very emotional man. He made every game seem like the Battle of the Bulge. He was so pleased that Jon had come to him with that special request, and that it worked out so well. That pleased him.

My job, my role, was to fill in wherever I was needed. I knew that. I made a significant contribution. I usually filled in behind Jon and Larry Brown. I was playing for a great team, and I obviously was a part of it. Now that I know more about coaching I have a better appreciation for my role as a player.

I have the utmost respect and admiration for Chuck Noll now. When Steve and I were out on the field when we were coaching the football team here at Trinity we'd be getting into

251

it and we'd shout out something to the players. Then we'd look at each other, realizing where that had come from. We were saying things that Chuck Noll used to say to us. We'd smile at each other.

When I first got into coaching I had a hard time teaching and articulating what I knew about football. Chuck had the ability to communicate volumes with just a few words, or even a look.

When we were playing we thought the offensive linemen were more like gentlemen. Steve Courson might have been a throwback in that respect, but the rest of us were mostly strong, silent types. Defensive linemen would be like more of a problem. The defensive linemen were more uncouth.

George Perles, who coached our defensive line, didn't like his linemen hanging around offensive linemen. He didn't want them picking up any of our personality traits, or our demeanor. He thought it could ruin them.

As an offensive lineman, you've got to have controlled fury. You have to keep your head about you. If you get too excited, or too angry, you can be aggressive to the point where it hurts your play. As an offensive lineman, you had to be more of a technician. Your form was more important. On defense, you could be more passionate in your play, and just let it all hang out.

When I see these kids at a track meet like this, and I see how each of them approaches the competition, and how they handle it, I learn a lot about what made us so good.

I think focus and intensity set you apart from the pack. Kids who take it seriously seem to have the most success. Of course, you have to have talent. I see a lot of athletes who pass the "look" test, but they don't perform to their best. Chuck stressed that focused intensity.

I thought I was focused in college, but I learned that I really wasn't once I came to the Steelers. Chuck and his coaches lifted my focus and intensity to a different level.

I used to go up against Dwight White a lot in practice. I also went up against Steve Furness and L.C. Greenwood and Robin Cole.

Of all those guys, I hated to go up against Robin Cole. He came hard every time. Some of those guys didn't go all out at practice.

Cole is still like that. Tom O'Malley called some of us former players when he was short on guys for the Steelers' basketball team earlier this year. We played a game at St. Vincent's College, and Cole was on our team. He was like a madman out there. He's all busted up physically, but he's still going all out.

Steelers' offensive linemen Ted Petersen (66), Steve Courson (77) and Mike Webster (52) worked out together in weight room during their stay with the Black & Gold. Below, Petersen paves the way for Rocky Bleier (20) against the Kansas City Chiefs.

Jack Lambert was like that in a game, but he was more like a student of the game in practice. L.C. wouldn't play extremely hard in practice; he waited until we were in the real games. Dwight played much harder in practice. Ernie Holmes didn't know the difference between practice and a game. He was out to kill the guy opposite him no matter the situation.

Sam Davis was such a great guy. He was such a likable guy. He had a great sense of humor. He was amazing. He weighed about 235 and he was playing against guys like Randy White of the Cowboys and completely neutralizing them. Sam owned him. You'd never hear White's name when Sam was playing against him.

I see the difficulties that Sam and Steve and Webby have gone through, and I recognize that, but for the grace of God, there goes I. And I say that with sincerity. I made some mistakes and it could have led to real problems, and I was lucky to have escaped pretty much unscathed by the experience.

"The Steeler coaches were against it."

I weighed about 245 pounds coming out of college. I played for the Steelers around 250 to 253 pounds. The most I ever weighed was 264 pounds.

I was talking to some of the guys on the team in about my fifth year, and I was trying to find ways to put on and keep my weight. I went to see a doctor to see what I could do about gaining weight.

There were drugs you could take to help, and they weren't illegal in the league at the time. To me, it was unethical, though. Those who took steroids now have more of a stigma than cocaine users, so I am sensitive to that. I played in that era, but I was never a user.

There are all sorts of problems involved with taking steroids and stuff like that. You become mentally dependent on them. If you're not taking them you don't think you can play as well. If you're not taking them your body shrinks, and that scares you, too.

As I tell my kids now, they're illegal and they're unethical.

I cite the case of Lyle Alzado, a former NFL player. He was on steroids for 20 years and he came down with a brain tumor and died. It's been established that there was a definite connection between his steroid use and his health problems.

The Steelers coaches were against it, I can tell you that. Chuck Noll was definitely against steroids. Jon Kolb was the strength coach late in my career with the Steelers. One day I had a particularly great day lifting weights. Chuck asked Jon,

"Is Pete on steroids?" And Jon told him I wasn't. Jon told me about Chuck coming to him and asking him after he saw the sheet on our weight lifting work that day.

If there was anybody who should have taken steroids it was me. I was the second smallest offensive tackle when I was playing. Mike Kenn of the Atlanta Falcons was the only one lighter at the position, and he was pretty good. They called him "The Thin Man." I used to look at Steve, and he was so strong. I'd think that if I were like him I'd have more success in the NFL.

But I didn't go there.

Dan Radakovich, our line coach, used to tell Steve, "You're going to die if you keep taking that stuff. You're going to kill yourself."

There was a time when we thought Rad was right on about that. But Steve has been fortunate. He fought his way back, in a sense. He did whatever he had to do — whatever it takes, I suppose — to get better. But he's still challenged. It's something he has to deal with every day the rest of his life.

"There was no one better than Chuck Noll."

The first thing I learned as a coach at Trinity High School was that you can't win solely by being enthusiastic. You need talent. With the proper attitude and great work ethic you can work to win. The best team I had went 6-4. The seniors on that team had been 1-5 or 1-6 as freshmen. We earned the first WPIAL Quad A playoff berth in school history. I had another team that went 9-0 as freshmen, and beat everybody in our conference. They ended up 3-7 as seniors. I left after their junior year.

The great thing I learned, and Steve Courson learned it, too, was that as far as knowledge of fundamentals and teaching philosophy there was no one better than Chuck Noll.

When people say he wasn't compassionate I don't buy that. When I had problems with my hip in my third and fourth year, he said, "I want you to know there will be a place here for you when you come back." He didn't have to do that, but it meant a lot to me.

When I was playing for the Steelers I thought I'd never want to coach. I'm a family guy and I didn't want to devote that amount of time to it. In high school, you devote a lot of time to it, but it's still possible to have a family life. I was married to Linda Kopperman for 17 years and I've been married to Marian Kail for the last two years, and I think I've been able to devote quality time to my boys during that time.

255

Getting into high school coaching was a real transition. I was making $150,000 my last year with the Steelers, and I made $18,500 my first year at Canon-McMillan. It's a good thing I saved my money. With the NFL pension plan, you can take an early retirement at age 45, and you can get your full pension at 55. You do better, of course, if you wait till you're 65 to take it. I'm 47 and I haven't drawn on it yet.

Bill Vosel helped me get started when he came back to coach at Canon-Mac. He was a good guy and I learned a lot from that experience. I wanted to lead my own team and use my own methods, so I jumped when Trinity was interested in me. I was a head coach there from 1990 to 1994. Two years before I came to Trinity, they won one game in two years. My records were 3-7, 6-4, 1-10, 6-4 and 6-4. We hit rock bottom my third year. We worked them harder the next year. The next guy came in and won four games in four years. I don't know that I'd have won any more during that span.

I hate to hear about what's going on with Jim Render at Upper St. Clair. In every school district, the parents get too involved.

I don't know that my parents ever spoke to a coach. It just wasn't done. I came home and said I was going out for football. And they said work hard and don't quit. That was it.

I hate when parents and board members tell a coach how he should be running his program. It's disheartening.

I've spent two years being the parent of a player, and all I've done is sit in the stands. Jeff Mattey was the head coach at South Fayette for my son, Garrett. I thought he did a great job with the kids. I learned something just from watching him.

Garrett played at 6-3, 170 pounds. He built up to 185 pounds, but he couldn't hold the weight.

I thought I was very objective with my kids. He wasn't the best player at his position. He didn't play that much. I remember how meaningful it was to me to see him get in at the end of the game. I'm going to learn from that. If the game is secure, I'm going to get those reserves in there.

That was an eye-opener for me. I could see what it meant, even if it was just two or three plays.

I think Jim Render had the best program in the past ten years that I ever saw, and he did a great job the ten years before that at Upper St. Clair. His record over that 20-some year stretch is the envy of every coach in the district.

In the second half, he'd substitute early. Then the next year they'd have experienced young players ready to move up. He built a program, not a new team each year. They were good. They improved as the season went on. They had a lot of good attributes that I saw. I can testify that there was no one whose teams were coached as fundamentally sound as

Render's teams. They reminded me of the Pittsburgh Steelers of the '70s. Everything they did was picture perfect. They had good techniques. He had great assistants. I think they had something like 150 years of coaching experience on his staff. Many of them were former head coaches at other schools. He coached them all in "football by Jim Render."

In high school, quick explosive kids are better than big kids. In college, you need both. In high school, you can get by with smart kids who know what they're doing, who understand what they're supposed to do on each play.

We have a great football coach here at Washington High School in Guy Montecalvo. There's another coach with a tremendous program. His program starts with the youth teams in the community. They're all on the same page. They have good coaches on every level. No one will outwork or outsmart Guy Montecalvo. He pays attention to every detail. I learned a lot coaching against him in the '90s.

I followed W&J under John Luckhardt and John Banaszak, and one of their assistants, Bob Johnson, who I replaced here. I met John Luckhardt after my first year here; he came up here on a scouting trip.

Ed Dalton is the coach here now, and he's doing a great job. He has the program going in the right direction. He's won wherever he's gone. He did a super job at Altoona. He's known for turning programs around. I don't know if it's harder to build a program or to maintain a good one. It seems to me that the more we won the more difficult it was for me to meet everyone's expectations.

I think having a good football team or basketball team, or athletic program, is great for school spirit on every level.

The main reason I gave it up was because I was moved from teaching at the high school to teaching at the elementary level. You can't run a high school football program when you're not in the school building all day. You have to make sure they show up for school, that they do their work, and that they're behaving. You have to keep your eye on them.

It's hard enough to win when the playing field is even, but you want to be in the same situation as the coaches you're competing against. There are no hard feelings. The administration has to decide what they want to accomplish.

I don't believe in whining or complaining so I walked away from it. I didn't have a lot of problems with parents, except for some instances. It wasn't a real problem and it's not the reason I gave up the job. Having been a player for those great Steelers teams meant more in the beginning. Maybe they thought I knew more than them. Maybe I was more intimidating in the beginning. My strongest point may be human relations. Everyone thinks their kid is an all-star, but I understand that better now, too.

Mike Wagner
He knew he could play in the NFL

*"Most people don't believe
I was ever a football player."*

M ike Wagner was so wonderful in the way he responded to my request for an interview for this book. He could not have been more cordial or cooperative, downright enthusiastic about getting together and talking about his Steelers' experience.

"When can we get together?" he asked. "What's convenient for you? I can meet you anywhere? Tell me what's best."

That's a far cry from Kordell Stewart scolding me when I approached him for an interview for one of my earlier books about the Steelers, rebuking me for not knowing about his rules relating to such matters, as in "I only do interviews on Wednesday."

Mike Wagner suggested we meet for lunch at noon at Bravo Italian Kitchen at The Pointe in North Fayette. He later moved the time back to 1 p.m. The restaurant is right across Summit Park Drive from Barnes & Noble Book Store, where I had done book signings in recent years. So I knew the territory.

It was a bright, sunny day, with temperatures in the high '60s, this Wednesday, April 10, 2002. Yes, it was Wednesday. I could have talked to Kordell Stewart this same day, come to think of it. But Wagner was such good company, why complain?

Wagner showed up looking sleek as ever in a pinstripe gray suit with a hint of light blue, the color of his eyes. He looked perfect and trimmer than he had appeared when he was wearing No. 23 in a black and gold uniform, a standout performer in the Steelers' defensive secondary. "Most people don't believe I was ever a football player when they meet me," Wagner said. Or they get him confused, he said, with Mike Webster or his old roommate Jack Ham.

He brought everything I asked him to bring. That's rare on the first visit. The restaurant was not far from where his office was located. He was back in the investment banking business, this time with old friends at Hefron-Tillotson, Inc. The company had just been named the best mid-size company to work for in the region, according to a survey by the *Pittsburgh Post-Gazette*. Their main office is on Seventh Avenue in downtown Pittsburgh, but Wagner was working out of their H.T. Capital Markets division in Building No. 3 at Penn Center West in Robinson Township. The previous year he had been working at a UPMC office near Mellon Arena. He was selling their health-care insurance to major corporations and businesses.

Mike Wagner with Becky Bolden at dinner on eve of Andy Russell's Celebrity Classic golf outing at The Club at Nevillewood, and with Russell in 1995 at card show in Greensburg.

The Robinson Township area, about 15-16 miles west of the city, had experienced tremendous growth in recent years. More development was on the planning boards. The Mall at Robinson Township, on the other side of the Parkway West from The Pointe complex, was expanding each week. Its developers were aiming to make it one of the largest malls in the East. It was already difficult to get into the parking lots because of the heavy traffic for too few roads. There was a similar growth going on at The Waterfront in Homestead, site of the old U.S. Steel Works. Continental Real Estate has since been hired to similarly develop the property between Heinz Field and PNC Park. The landscape of Pittsburgh and the surrounding area was changing dramatically. Neither the Steelers nor Pittsburgh was quite the same as in the '70s or in the '50s. Art Rooney was dead, Three Rivers Stadium and Pitt Stadium had been razed and had given way to new sports venues. The steel mills that once lined the rivers were gone or abandoned. It wasn't the Steel City or Smoky City anymore. It was seeking a new identity as an educational, medical and technology center, so it couldn't be as clearly labeled any more.

Wagner had given thought to what I told him I wanted him to talk about. He came prepared, the way Chuck Noll would have wanted, the way Wagner was when he played both safety positions in the Steelers' vaunted "Steel Curtain" defense of the '70s.

I arrived first and asked for a table away from the main dining area. There was a full house and it is a noisy restaurant. The food is great and so is the ambience, but I wanted to talk to Mike Wagner and wanted to be sure to hear what he had to say, so I could take notes. I was seated in a smaller room, off to the side, past the bar, and it was perfect. The sun slanted through the turned down blinds and there was a streak of sunlight across the white tablecloth at our table. Mike wanted to be sure he sat in a chair where the sun wasn't in his eyes.

Mike had Shrimp Diablo, a spicy linguini offering, and I had Pasta Woozie, fettucini with chicken and spinach. Mike started with a salad and I had a large cup of minestrone. He had regular iced tea and I had raspberry iced tea. We both drank lots of iced tea. We talked for three hours. Mike did most of the talking; he didn't need any prodding. I hardly had to ask any questions. He was ready and eager to provide insight into many subjects relating to his days with the Steelers. I enjoyed the session. For the record, Mike picked up the tab. He insisted. He said I now owed him a lunch. They were playing a CD by Andrea Bocelli over the stereo system at Bravo Italian Kitchen. When I told Wagner I had that same CD and how much I loved to listen to it, he mocked me in jest, saying "You're going to lose your membership in the sportswriters' club if I tell them you're into opera now. What's happening in the sports world?"

I'm really not into opera, but I love to listen to Andrea Bocelli sing, especially when he teams up with Sarah Brightman.

I had seen Mike at many dinners and different functions in recent years, so I was not surprised to see his neatly trimmed hair had gray in it. So did his mustache. He was still handsome as hell, distinguished, and well-spoken. There was much thought behind his reflections.

Wagner was born in Waukegan, Illinois on June 22, 1948, so he was nearing his 54th birthday. It was more than 30 years since he first reported to work in Pittsburgh.

Wagner had a bachelor's degree in accounting from Western Illinois University in 1971, the year he first came to the Steelers, and an MBA from the University of Pittsburgh, which he obtained in 1988, about eight years after he had retired as a player in the National Football League.

When I first knew him, he was living with his family in Upper St. Clair, and I'd see them together at high school football games. They also had a getaway place in Dillon, Colorado. Mike is an avid skier. His daughter, Heather, was 9 when I wrote about them in a story for *The Pittsburgh Press* back in October of 1979. When Mike told me Heather was now 32, I had to shake my head. That was tougher to accept than our gray hair. He also had a son, Farrell, who was 14, from his second marriage. He was now living with Becky Bolden at their home in McCandless Township. I had met her two years earlier when Mike was honored as a "Legend" by the Pittsburgh Chapter of the Italian-American Sports Hall of Fame at their annual dinner at the Hilton Hotel.

At our luncheon interview, Wagner was wearing the Super Bowl ring the Steelers won at the end of the 1979 season. It's the one with four diamonds to mark each Super Bowl victory. He wore it, even though he, and his best friend on the team, Jack Ham, had missed that game with an injury. Wagner had four Super Bowl rings in his collection. The other three were at his home in the North Hills of Pittsburgh. I never noticed that Wagner and Ham were both missing from the team photograph from Super Bowl XIV until Mike called it to my attention. The photo was taken during practice one day at a field near Newport Beach, California where they conducted practice the week of the game, and Wagner and Ham were both on the injured reserve list and did not dress for the game. I was there when they took the picture, and took some of my own.

Wagner was considered one of the best and smartest defensive backs in the NFL. He made a tremendous comeback in 1978 after fracturing three neck vertebrae in the third game of the 1977 season against the Cleveland Browns. He ranked high in all defensive categories and was a major factor in the Steelers winning their third Super Bowl. He was always a great clutch player and excelled in the post-season. He provided many of the intangibles championship teams need to win.

He told me how a similar neck injury ended the career of Eugene "Mercury" Morris, another NFL player he had spent time with in the Balkans during Super Bowl Weekend. Morris was an old friend of mine. We had teamed up on a series called "Diary of a Rookie" in 1969 when we were both rookies with the Miami Dolphins. Morris had lived as a child in the same North Side neighborhood where Three Rivers Stadium was built and played high school ball in Avonworth. He got involved with drugs and ended up doing hard time in prison.

Morris remembered Wagner well from the days when the Dolphins and Steelers were among the league's elite teams.

"All the hype our defense got through the years," said Wagner's buddy Ham, "I always thought Mike should have gotten more recognition. The line and linebackers got most of it. Mike was very valuable to us, and much underrated. He's made some big plays for us through the years."

Wagner was not overlooked, to be sure. He was selected to the Pro Bowl twice (1975 and 1976) and was elected to the Steelers' 50 Year Team. He tied Dick Anderson of the Miami Dolphins for the NFL lead in interceptions with eight in 1973. He was named All-Pro in 1976 by *UPI, AP, Pro Football Weekly* and *The Sporting News*. He intercepted 41 passes, including five in post-season games, during his career, and twice intercepted three passes in a game. He led the Steelers in interceptions in 1972, 1973 and 1980. He still ranks among the Steelers' leaders in interceptions, right up there with Mel Blount, Jack Butler, Donnie Shell, Rod Woodson and Dwayne Woodruff.

Not bad for an 11th-round draft pick out of Western Illinois in 1971. He started from the first game of his rookie season, and no one could bump him from the lineup until he decided it was time to walk away while he could still walk.

"Those old Steelers never forget the people." — Jack Giran, Athletic Director Steel Valley High School

Mike Wagner had been a guest speaker that same morning at a fundraising breakfast for the Boy Scouts at the Chartiers Country Club. He had spoken as a favor to his friend John Pippy, a state representative from the 44th district. "He's a former West Pointer and he's fun to be around," Wagner said of Pippy. Wagner spoke about the value and contribution by Americans around the world in peacekeeping missions. Wagner does that sort of thing on a regular basis. The month before he was a surprise visitor for a sports dinner to announce the players who would participate in the annual Foothills Classic out in Westmoreland County. This was held at John Ferrante's Lakeview Inn in Greensburg.

Rich Siniawski, the chairman of the event, shared this story with Norm Vargo, the sports editor of *The McKeesport Daily News*, and an old running buddy of mine when I was covering the Steelers for *The Pittsburgh Press* (1979-1983). Vargo wrote a column about it.

Siniawski said he received a phone call from "a guy" earlier in the afternoon on the day of the dinner, asking if it was OK for him to attend the dinner and accompany Steel Valley High's stellar running back Brandon Snyder. "I told him, 'Sure, you can come,' " said Siniawski.

And "the guy" showed up. It turned out to be Mike Wagner, the starting free safety on the Steelers' four Super Bowl winners.

"Yeah, was I shocked," Siniawski told Vargo. "I didn't have a clue to who he was. The guy comes over and shakes my hand and says, 'Hello, I'm Mike Wagner. Thank you for allowing me to come here to support Brandon Snyder. This is a big night in his young life.' I was stunned. I could never imagine Mike Wagner coming to a spaghetti dinner in Greensburg on a rainy night to stand up for a kid. That's really something. You don't expect that from a pro athlete ... even an older one.

"I asked Mike if he wanted to say a few words to the players. He declined because he said this affair was for the boys."

So why was Wagner there? It turns out that Wagner was there sort of as a big brother to Brandon Snyder. A friend of Mike knew Snyder and his situation. Young Snyder had lost both of his parents within a nine-month span. His mother died of cancer and his father succumbed to a heart attack. Snyder was living with relatives. Wagner just wanted to make this terrific high school player's night just a little more special.

Steel Valley athletic director Jack Giran was also amazed by what Wagner had done. "That's really something," Giran said. "That's a great story. I guess those old Steelers never forgot the people, the fans."

Vargo commented in his *Daily News* column that it wasn't unusual for the Steelers of the '70s to do something special in their adopted community.

Siniawski said he'd never forget what Wagner did. "Something like that makes it all worth it when you're trying to do something for the kids. Mike Wagner showed us he's somebody special."

Vargo ventured that "somewhere Art Rooney is smiling."

"Hey, you're Mike Wagner!"

On the day I spent the afternoon with Wagner I later went to a funeral in my hometown of Hazelwood. It was at the John D. O'Connor & Son Funeral Home operated by his youngest son, David. This was the O'Toole & O'Connor Funeral Home when I was a kid.

I went there for the funeral of John D. O'Connor. I was used to seeing him there, greeting and consoling the grieving family and friends of the deceased. He had died at age 86 after a long illness. He had been a good friend of my older brother, Dan, and they'd gone to a lot of sports events and outings in groups of local guys. O'Connor had been a big fan of the Steelers, and traveled out of town with the bus tours sponsored by Joe Chiodo's Bar & Restaurant in Homestead to see them play. He'd gone to Super Bowls to root for them. I remember seeing O'Connor and our good friend, Bob "Blue" Martin, at a Super Bowl in Miami.

I had never seen anyone laid out in brighter attire. O'Connor was wearing a white sports coat and a bright colored tie, with stripes of raspberry, teal and green, cuff links, his wedding band. He looked like he was going on an ocean cruise. He wore grays and blacks at the funeral home when he was in charge, but he always changed into bright attire away from the workplace. David knew that, and pre-pared his body the way his father requested for his final appearance in Hazelwood.

I bumped into some friends from my youth during my visit to pay my respects to David over the death of his father.

Sam Rende came by. He was into his 70s now, but showed me photos of his two youngest children, age 2½ and six months. That's correct. They were his children from a second marriage to a much younger woman. I have seen Sam at some of the biggest sports events in the area through the years. He's always been a hustler, a street guy, and some of his activities were questionable. For me, however, he was always one of my hometown heroes. He still looked good. He always dressed well, flamboyantly, like the old movie actor Errol Flynn. There was something about Sam that made him stick out from the crowd. In a day when people show up at funeral homes dressed to go to work in the mill it was reassuring to see Sam in a bronze sport coat with a beige golf shirt and dark slacks. He was debonair as usual. He was tanned. Sam has a tan in midwinter.

He was still working, tearing down houses in some government-sponsored housing project. Sam was always part of some scam. He's worked both sides of the street successfully. I was glad to see this was a government-sponsored scam.

He operated a second-hand store on Second Avenue for years. A priest at St. Stephen's was once asked about the nature of Sam's store, and he responded by saying, "All I know is that when it snows the snow doesn't stick on Sam's roof."

I remember my brother went to Sam's home in the Glen-Hazel housing project to play poker back in the '60s. Sam provided the set-ting, the beer and potato chips, and took a cut from every pot. Jimmy O'Connor, another good friend of my brother Dan, showed up at the funeral home to pay his respects to his uncle. Jimmy's sister, Carol O'Connor Vavro, was there. Her husband, Bob Vavro, who had been my boyhood barber, was not there. He was skiing in Colorado. He was 71 years old, and he made annual trips to Europe and Colorado for skiing. He was one of my hometown heroes, as well. I saw him in Tampa and New Orleans when I was on the Steelers' beat.

Pat Fitzhenry was also at the funeral home. I had played basketball with him and his kid brother Jack in our youth. Jack, who later played at Central Catholic High School, St. Francis of Loretto and Duquesne University, had died at age 56 the previous year.

I had walked past the Fitzhenry's old house a little earlier that afternoon. I had arrived about 20 minutes early for the 7 to 9 visitation period, so I took a walk around the old neighborhood. As a nine- and ten-year-old kid, I had delivered the *Post-Gazette* to the O'Connor residence, which was above the funeral home.

So I took a stroll down Second Avenue, heading east toward my old home on Sunnyside Street in Glenwood. I was walking along my old morning newspaper route. I saw a lot of familiar houses and I could still see the families who lived there when I called on them weekly for payment for the paper. I saw the homes of boyhood friends. Not too many of them looked too hot.

Hazelwood had gone downhill considerably since my days there. The kids called it Plywood because so many of the storefronts were boarded up. Just as many were missing altogether. There was an open space where the State Store was located when my mother worked there as a sales clerk when I was in grade school. Most of the restaurants and stores were gone from those days. I lived 22 of the first 24 years of my life there, leaving for a two-year military stint in my early 20s, and until age 24 when I married Kathleen Churchman at St. Stephen's Church, just across the street from the O'Connor Funeral Home. When I was in grade school, the funeral home gave the church its largest donation each week and always topped the bulletin page that reported on donations, marriage and death announcements and church activities.

I walked past the Pentagon Lounge, where I'd gone a few times with Dan to drink some Iron City beers with his buddies. A Greek fellow from Greenfield named Mike Turbovich owned that bar. Someone had painted the team logos of the Steelers and the Pirates on the gray stone walls that flanked the front door of the bar. The artwork wasn't bad.

At the funeral home, I also spoke to Bernie Cusick, who grew up in Hazelwood and now lived in Beechview. He was 66. He was there with his son, Joe, 38, a former member of City Council who'd gotten in trouble with drugs and alcohol and left office after serving one four-year term. He had cleaned up his act and looked terrific. I remembered seeing Joe, along with all the other members of City Council, Mayor Tom Murphy, and some other political leaders, in Phoenix in January of 1996. They were all there on an expense-paid junket as guests of the Steelers for Super Bowl XXX. Is it any wonder that Pittsburgh political officials rubber-stamp every issue involving the Steelers that crosses their desks? Bernie had retired after 35 years as a union iron worker, and was in his 10th year as a clerk in the prothonotary office in the City-County Building. So the Cusicks were still feeding from the public trough. It's amazing.

They were both big Steelers' fans. I mentioned that I had lunch with Mike Wagner earlier in the day.

"I met him at a fund-raiser at a restaurant in The Strip District for Mike Lamb, the prothonotary," said Bernie Cusick. "I was talking to him for awhile, but I had no idea who he was. He told me his name, but it didn't hit me for awhile. I think he's lost some weight from his playing days. I came back to him later on, and suddenly it hit me who he was. I said, 'Hey, you're Mike Wagner from the Steelers! You played for the Steelers.' He smiled and shook my hand again. He's a nice guy."

Mike Wagner:

"Some of the guys we had were once-in-a-lifetime players."

I went to Kosovo during Super Bowl Weekend early this year and we visited with our military troops who were stationed there. The majority of the troops I spoke to were reservists. I mention that in some of my talks around here. There have been Americans around the world doing this sort of thing even before 9/11. It refocused what our military does for us. The Balkans are just as deadly as the Mideast or what we are dealing with in Afghanistan. It's a dangerous area. That war there would be continuing if we weren't there with a United Nations peacekeeping force. I wouldn't have been able to play football and so many Americans wouldn't be able to enjoy the activities they have if it weren't for the peacekeeping troops that are stationed throughout the world.

I've been on other tours before to military bases. It's good to see how the rest of the world lives. The reservists I met were pretty gung-ho to be there. This is what they wanted to do. They'd rather be doing this than having monthly meetings or summer exercises. I flew into Macedonia, just below Kosovo, on a Friday, and we were flown in by helicopter on Sunday morning. We spent Super Bowl Sunday with the troops, and they got to watch the Super Bowl on large screens. I was there with nine former NFL players, including Mercury Morris and Napoleon McCallum. We were flown out on Monday and came home. So it was just a long weekend for us.

I had a chance to talk to Mercury Morris. He's quite a guy. I had heard him talk about ten years ago. He had come to Pittsburgh to speak. It was shortly after he'd gotten out of prison for offenses relating to drugs. He was quite a motivational speaker.

Mercury told me what ended his career was an injury he suffered at the hands of Mel Blount. He told me how Mel had picked him up and dumped him, spiking him into the turf. He had a nasty scar on the back of his neck from the encounter. He said he suffered some broken vertebrae in the encounter. So the terror of Mel Blount continues, I thought. Here I am in the Balkans and I'm bearing witness to the havoc he wrought on behalf of the Black & Gold. There were other reminders. I'm sitting in a military camp and a soldier walks up to me and shows me his Terrible Towel. He asked me if I would sign it. He told me he also had a Steelers' jacket back at his barracks. "If I bring it," he said, "will you sign that for me, too?" I said, "Yes, I can't believe you have it here." So he brought it to me. These guys were dragging all sorts of Steelers' stuff, and from other NFL teams, too, for us to see and sign.

It's typical for the young guys today to say we couldn't play today because it's a different day, a different game, and all that stuff. I don't buy that for a minute. You have to be careful being an ex-Steeler not to minimize what the players are doing today, either. They're pretty good.

If you look at Mel's career, he didn't really come into his own until our second championship season. It took him awhile to adjust to life in the NFL. Then they ended up changing the rules because of how good Mel became at bump-and-run pass coverage. When they changed the rules, however, it played right into his strength. It's like lengthening Augusta to tame Tiger Woods. It won't work. Mel could run with the little guys, like Billy "White Shoes" Johnson. He was always a great player, but Mel got better in the late '70s and early '80s. That's when he hit his prime. The young guys today don't realize what great athletic skills Mel had.

I'm so proud of our accomplishments, so I stick up for our guys. The players today are great athletes, but some of the guys we had were once-in-a-lifetime players.

I had breakfast at an NFL Alumni golf outing at Sewickley Heights with Chuck Noll last July and I asked him, "Chuck, did you ever in your wildest dreams imagine that you'd have eight players in the Hall of Fame?" I thought that was a good question. Did you ever ask him that? Of course, he didn't answer me. He said, "We have a couple more who should be in, and we have more to do to help them." It was a typical Chuck Noll response. He always had his own agenda. He never answered the question. You try to get a reaction from him, but he won't give it to you. After we won championships, he'd tell us we weren't finished yet, that we'd have to come back the next season and show we could do it again. We'd holler at him, "C'mon, Chuck, lighten up! Cut us a break. Let's celebrate this one."

Now the Steelers of the '70s will soon have nine players in the Hall of Fame. John Stallworth was voted in this year, so he'll follow Lynn Swann into the Hall of Fame. The year before that, Dan Rooney was honored. His dad is in the Hall of Fame and, of course, Chuck Noll is in there, too. They were all a part of our Team of the Decade.

Donnie Shell and L.C. Greenwood were among the finalists this year, too, so they still have a chance of making it. I have friends who want to wage a campaign to get me in there, too, but I tell them that's not how it's done. Rocky Bleier tells me people think he's in the Hall of Fame, too. That's the stature we've been elevated to. I don't deserve to be in the Hall of Fame, but I believe I contributed in a big way to our team's success in the '70s.

It's great to be an ex-player. You're not under the pressure you were under as a player. People aren't coming up to you in the street and saying you cost them $5 in a bet. People aren't blaming you for what's gone wrong.

Another good thing is that these current players are making millions of dollars and they're not interested in making appearances for a few hundred bucks or even a few thousand, so a lot of stuff falls into the laps of the former players. They want a Steeler and I guess we still fill the bill. We're still Steelers.

It's tough to compare players from different eras. I remember looking at Jack Butler when I first got here. He was really put together, but he was older and you wondered what he was like when he played the game. Guys look at me and they think, "He must have been a lot bigger."

No, I wasn't. But I greet the rookies in the fall and I see what they're like. I was around five or six of the defensive backs, and I'm bigger (at 6½, 200 pounds) than all of them. They don't know who I am, for the most part. Maybe one of them heard of me and knew I was a defensive back for the Steelers. Some of them weren't alive when I last played for the Steelers.

Our cornerbacks were bigger than our safeties. Some of these guys today are so huge, on both sides of the ball, but not the defensive secondary guys. Mel Blount is still the biggest guy around, but he cheats and wears cowboy boots. I tell Mel it's very unfair when I'm pictured in photographs with him because he's got his cowboy boots and his cowboy hat on and it makes him look much taller than everybody else.

I was with Mel and most of my teammates at the opening of Heinz Field. That's when they gave Lynn his Super Bowl ring at halftime ceremonies. People ask me, 'How could they tear down Three Rivers Stadium? I loved the place!" I can appreciate that. They have so many good feelings about that place. It was the fans' stadium.

268

MIKE WAGNER

Steelers' defensive stalwarts, from left to right, Jack Lambert (58), Jack Ham (59) and Mike Wagner (23) close in on Tampa Bay ballcarrier.

Five or six years from now, if the Steelers win a Super Bowl they'll have Heinz Field memories to light up their life. Baseball fans remember the World Series at Forbes Field and at Three Rivers Stadium. When they win a World Series they'll feel the same way about PNC Park.

I'm not surprised the wind is a factor at Heinz Field. The first time I walked down the field and saw that open-end facing the downtown skyline I knew it would be a problem. In the early '70s, before they closed off the openings on the third and fourth levels at Three Rivers Stadium the wind was a problem. The wind would swirl so much the ball would be knuckle-balling. I've seen spirals move 15 feet one way or the other when the wind came in off the rivers. Or, as Bubby Brister once said, "When the wind comes in off the lakes." It will be interesting to see what develops there. It's also a very soft field; it's sandy and that's a kicker's nightmare.

Noll would not worry about those things. He'd say both teams have to play in the same conditions. But I don't think Heinz Field will be a favorite place of the players.

"At the end of the day, he always won." — Wagner on Noll

Chuck Noll never wanted to take credit for what he did. He didn't like talking too much to reporters and he didn't like us talking too much to reporters. He didn't want any of the players talking about strategy or our plans for a particular opponent when we were interviewed.

We're remembered so fondly by the fans here. How the public treats players from the '70s is something the current players have to deal with. They love our guys. I don't know how appreciated Chuck feels.

If any of our guys left with an edge or a bad feeling about Chuck Noll maybe time heals that. You can always find fault about anything. We had some hard-headed players. And Chuck Noll could be stubborn about some things. You can find fault with how he handled Terry Bradshaw and the media. But at the end of the day, hey, he always won.

He'd be held at an even higher esteem if he'd been more personable with his players and the press, but that wasn't important to him. I never looked at him as a coach and said I wished I played for another team. He was a tough coach. But you can't say enough good about Chuck Noll.

He was kinda like a tough teacher. After you're out of school, you're grateful you had that teacher.

He didn't seek publicity. He wanted his players to get all the attention and the commercials and endorsements. There aren't many coaches like that.

He hired good assistants and he kept his staff together, for the most part. He lost Lionel Taylor, Bud Carson and Dan Radakovich when they went to the Rams, but he brought in other quality coaches. Those coaches are still highly regarded. They worked with Chuck and they picked up on his work ethic and plans and they delivered it to the players.

Bud Carson is considered one of the best defensive coordinators of all time. He was remarkable. On any given day I wanted to strangle him; he was so intense. He was upset with us one day after we beat the Cincinnati Bengals because Ken Anderson had completed 20 of 22 passes, or something like that. But it was for 150 yards. He was completing passes underneath our coverage. We kept them contained. The stats didn't look good, and he was upset. We screamed back at him, "We won!" Guys like Bad Rad would work on techniques with someone for 20 minutes after practice, and players benefited from that dedication to detail, but it could rub guys the wrong way at the time. At that time we were unruly, yet-to-be-molded animals out of the barn. We had to be directed.

"You know how to play the game."

We had all those once-in-a-lifetime players, those Hall of Famers, or what I always called our "A" players. But their success was dependent on the supporting cast.

I was part of that supporting cast, whether people today want to believe that or not. They see my Super Bowl ring, and people ask me, "Where'd you get that? Did your brother play?"

I asked Jack Ham if he ever gets mistaken for me, and he said he did. I told him that when someone mistakes me for him I swear at the guy and walk away from him so he goes away thinking Jack Ham is a real jerk. I'm just kidding, of course. I can live with it.

I went to a banquet once in Butler and the emcee read off Mike Webster's biographical sketch before he called on me. I had a blind date once and the woman thought she was going out with Mike Webster. She said, "I guess I didn't do my homework." Someone once hung up on me because they were trying to reach Mike Wagner of the Glenshaw Glass Company.

There were other guys like me who didn't look the part. You take someone like Randy Grossman. From Day One he was the longest shot for making it in the NFL. Yet he was a pivotal part of our offense. How's that happen? Randy just kept doing it.

271

I'll tell you a rookie story. I knew from Day One I could play in the NFL. It was a matter of staying healthy and getting a few breaks. After you're there for awhile, you realize it's all not just about size, speed, strength and that stuff. The more games you play you realize that you know how to play the game.

They always brought a lot of defensive backs to training camp every year. They wanted to be able to run the offense and they needed people to get all the quarterbacks enough work. They always had a lot of receivers and a lot of defensive backs. They'd be late round picks and free agents. They'd be lean and strong and they were timed at 4.4 in the 40. They could stop on a dime and accelerate in this or that direction. They'd see me and ask, "Who's this old guy? I can beat his ass!" After awhile, they'd realize I could hold my own. They'd say, "How's this guy doing this?" I'm sure when they walked out the door at camp for the final time they wondered what happened, and how I beat them out.

Maybe even Chuck Noll wondered. He'd get on me. He'd say I was guessing. He'd holler at me, "You don't do what I told you to do! You better do it right the next time!"

You can have all the great players, but you won't win if you have weak links. We didn't have any weak links.

Look at a guy like Gerry Mullins. He was a 235-pound guard and tackle. He had technique and heart and desire. He had such great footwork and he was so tough. He could get away with playing tackle because of his techniques. He was great on trap-blocking. He was picture-perfect and hit so hard. He was the kind of player Noll would salivate over.

And Bad Rad drove those offensive linemen crazy. Bad Rad would line up and go full speed against our linemen to make a point. We were concerned about his judgment from time to time. We had a great offensive line. And they were good for a long time; we had the same guys up there for eight to ten years. But they weren't big and they never got named to the Pro Bowl. We had so many guys going to the Pro Bowl and everybody couldn't go. Big guys like Anthony Munoz of the Bengals would get picked every year.

We had guys like Glen Edwards in our defensive secondary. He was one of the hardest hitting guys in the league, and he came up with a lot of big plays. Where'd he come from? He weighed about 175 pounds, and he signed as a free agent.

If you were a defensive back and you didn't knock yourself out a few times you weren't trying. Even Deion Sanders knocked himself out and there's a guy who didn't hit.

I've had a lot of concussions in my day so I don't remember everything about those days that well. I've heard that story from Dan Radakovich about how Jack Ham and I were supposed to have gone to him to save Joe Gilliam from getting released by Chuck Noll. I believe there's some truth to the story, but I think I just happened to be with Jack Ham when it came up. I was never concerned about it.

I'm one of Terry Bradshaw's strongest defenders. I played against some good quarterbacks in my day, but I went up against Terry Bradshaw every day in practice. He was a great quarterback. I saw something different in Terry and Joe. I know Bradshaw was the right choice as a starter.

People don't realize now how good Terry Bradshaw was. How many times did you see him throw a catchable ball in a clutch situation? There were certain quarterbacks I feared with four or five minutes left to play — like Roger Staubach and Joe Montana — and that's when the money guys came through. None was better than Bradshaw in that situation. That's how you become a championship-caliber ballplayer. That's something Kordell Stewart has to work on.

Joe was a smart guy with a lot of talent. Joe believed in his physical skills so much that he thought he could throw the ball in anywhere. There were times Terry was like that, too, but he also knew the best percentage throws.

There's an aspect of the Joe Gilliam story that always haunted me. Rocky's locker was next to mine, and then Joe's locker was the next one. When Rocky wasn't there I'd sit and talk to Joe from time to time. He had played some and had been benched this one time when we talked. Sometimes he'd just sit there and laugh and smoke cigarettes. This one time he showed me some of his mail. Most of the mail we got were requests for autographs or to sign cards. Joe's weren't like that. His would often be written in red or real large letters and there'd be mean racial messages, about leaving the country. He tried to laugh them off, but it had to hurt. He had been Mr. Tennessee in football and he had a lot of pride in his ability. So that stuff had to hurt him.

This other time, Terry was struggling and Joe was getting some playing time. Joe came in and he was really down. He said, "You're not going to believe what happened." He takes me outside where we parked our cars and shows me his car. He had a big Mercedes-Benz sedan and someone had dumped a gallon of paint on his car. He was living at the time in an apartment complex in Scott Township.

We all struggle as athletes to be better. Joe had to put up with so much. He showed me different letters from time to time and it was all ugly stuff. Joe was a glib guy. He was a party guy and he always had a line. "Let's go have fun," he'd say.

> *"This was the greatest football team that was ever put together."*
> — Dan Rooney

One of the things I'm proudest of Terry Bradshaw is how he handled all the criticism he got from the fans in his early days with the team. There was a dark side of surviving those bad days. Even the greatest athletes have been knocked around and abused. You hear all those thousands screaming at you. I'm so proud that Terry was able to get through all that. Joe fell victim to it. He went to drugs. There was a lot of temptation out there and he succumbed to it. I don't think the public ever realizes what they put us through. I was lucky because I didn't get much of that, but I got my share.

We do something we love to do, but people get upset because we get paid a lot to do it. Now it's even worse.

I retired when I did — I could have played a few more years — because I didn't want to have the fans get on me. I grew up watching the Chicago Cubs play, and one my heroes, Ernie Banks, stuck around too long. The fans started to get on him, saying he should retire. I thought then that if I ever had a chance to do this I wouldn't play that long. I never wanted to be in that situation. Ernie Banks is still a big hero of mine, but he should have quit sooner. The same thing happened with Willie Mays. One of my other sports heroes was Stan Mikita of the Chicago Blackhawks. They all stayed too long.

I've been lucky. Fans have been wonderful to me, for the most part. Getting back to my premise, I don't know how to deal with these people. Ninety-nine percent of the fans are great, but that one percent stays with you. Their criticism hurts. Some players bring it on themselves. It bothered Bradshaw, but he got through it. Joe sought relief in places he shouldn't have gone. It's not all glory. I've been on the sidelines for a lot of kids' soccer games and I can't get over how some of the coaches and the parents get on these kids.

I wish Terry would think more about the good things that happened to him and play down the disappointments. There was more good than bad. Good sportsmanship is an important topic to me. People have forgotten what good sportsmanship is all about. They need to be reminded. You can have ferocious competition on the field, but you still need to have a good time. Being an ex-athlete and one of the sports heroes in this town I think you have a responsibility to speak up about the need for good sportsmanship. You have to teach people how to win and how to lose. Many of us former Steelers are now a part of the Pittsburgh business community, and we care about what's going on here.

I went to that banquet for Brandon Snyder of Steel Valley because a friend of mine, Joe Wiesner, told me he was going. He told me about Brandon and about his parents dying. I didn't do this for publicity. I just said I'd like to go along to the banquet, and he got me a ticket. I thought it would be nice. I just tried to fill in the spots. I just wanted Brandon to know he was somebody special.

I know this about Rod Woodson and Kordell Stewart and Jerome Bettis and that's that they would play this game for a nickel. What's happened is that people are willing to pay them millions of dollars. There aren't many players who are just concerned about how much money they can make and how long they can stick around.

All these guys, and the ones I played with, loved to play the game. Not necessarily to practice, but to play the game. Who could have thunk this would all come to pass?

This is arrogance, coming from an 11th-round draft choice out of Western Illinois University, but I remember I was disappointed that I was coming to a losing program. When I told them I had an agent, I think they wanted to say, "Let's forget this kid." I got a $1500 signing bonus, and my first-year salary was $15,000. Then somehow my star got aligned with Chuck Noll and Dan Rooney and the Steelers and what a story it was. There's a lot of football lore.

Andy Russell tells the story about how when Chuck Noll first arrived as the coach he told the players that they weren't very good and that most of them wouldn't be around long. So he knew what kind of a ballteam he had to build to become a winner. I was part of that process.

I'd see someone like Ray Nitschke, who was so big to me when I was young, and saw how they behaved. Then reality set in. I was in the same league as Ray Nitschke. I was not as good, mind you, but I was in the same league. Hopefully, we're not legends in our own mind. One of these days, when I get out the old pictures, I can sit around and enjoy it then.

"We knew what they were going to do."

In the beginning the training camp was long and hot. We knocked the snot out of each other. We were just trying to get through camp without a major injury. We were trying to get to the season. In 1974, we had a pretty good team and we drafted a hot-shot named Lynn Swann. He was at the College All-Star Camp when we started up and were going through two-a-day practices. We were going to show Swann what Steelers' football was all about.

Noll liked to scrimmage a lot back then. And we really scrimmaged. It was like open season on wide receivers. We knew what they were going to do. Then there were times when a third-string quarterback threw up a soft pass. We wanted to see how tough the wide receivers were. When Swann came in he was hurt from the All-Star game. When he was able to practice, he went across the middle for a pass. I'm not sure if it was Mel Blount or who, but someone just crushed Swann.

Lynn held onto the ball, of course, but he just lay there for awhile. Noll came running in from the sideline. The blood was drained from his face. He thought we had killed little Lynn. Noll was upset with us. After that incident, we were no longer allowed to hit the receivers like that. So that play was one of my all-time favorite plays. Because that hitting took its toll on us, too. Lynn not only changed the NFL forever, he changed practices for the Steelers. Noll wanted his safeties playing deep. He didn't want to get beat for long passes. So Ham used to kid me because I wasn't always on the screen when they showed those overall views from above of our defense. He used to call me "Dr. Depth." He was calling me that once at the Pro Bowl practice. Then Jack Tatum came on the field. He was the defensive back from the Oakland Raiders and one of his nicknames was "Dr. Death." So Jack stopped calling me "Dr. Depth" because he didn't want Jack Tatum thinking he was making fun of him. You didn't want to upset Jack Tatum.

I personally hold Jack Lambert responsible for all the nonsense you see in pro football these days with guys taunting and pointing fingers and demonstrating after they do something. Make sure Jack knows I'm kidding. If Jack had just played football and forgot about screaming at people and pointing fingers he would have been a better football player. It's his fault. We'd have better behavior today if it wasn't for Jack Lambert. Then again that's one of the reasons the fans liked Lambert so much.

We had a lot of guys on our defensive unit who never stopped talking. They included Lambert, Dwight White, Glen Edwards, J.T. Thomas. They were always chattering about something. I was just trying to get my breath. Most of those guys played hurt. The difference between the best and worst players is sometimes their ability to play hurt. Many of our players played with injuries.

I had some hip problems in 1979 and it caused me to miss the Super Bowl. But there was a game before that when it was really hurting, and I was limping around. I made some kind of comment in the huddle that I thought I was hurting the team and I should go to the sideline. Joe Greene looked at me, and he said, "Mike, we want you to stay in the game." That meant a lot to me. These guys who are playing hurt do so because of the bond they have with their teammates. I remember "Bullet Bill" Dudley spoke to our alumni group once, and I was amazed by his combativeness and spirit. He really got into it when he spoke to us. He showed a little bit of the character and nature of the ballplayer he'd been. He still had a fierceness about him. His fists were clenched and he was really into it during a 15-minute talk. The way he was going you'd bet on him in a bar fight with Jack Lambert. You had to like his spirit.

I'll tell you one of our unsung heroes. That was our equipment manager Tony Parisi. He found these shoes in Canada. They made these clunky old football shoes with hiker's soles. They were sticky. They were great when the field was wet or icy. Three Rivers Stadium was always very slippery when it was wet, especially after they resurfaced it in the late '70s.

No one talked about it, but Tony was always saving us by coming up with special equipment that gave us an edge. It was little things like that that made us a winner. He used to give Franco a massage before games and loosen him up, stuff like that. The Dapper Dan ought to come up with a special award for Tony Parisi.

"We had a loaded team."

This town gets so excited about winning and it gets so down over losing. I know this sounds self-serving, but what happened to the Steelers this past season only serves as a reminder to all football fans about how hard it is to do what they did here in the '70s. It points up the greatness of Chuck Noll, the Rooneys, Bradshaw and all those great players, the Steelers' organization. We had a loaded team, not to be smug about it. We can be really cocky now. Dan was crushed by what happened last year. What you saw there was a New England team similar to the Steelers of the '70s. They hit hard. Their offense may not put a lot of points on the board, but they score enough to win. New England beat three different teams — it wasn't pretty — in winning it all. It was the kind of football the Pittsburgh Steelers won it with when we were playing. I like the Steelers' defensive backs. I think Chad Scott and Dewayne Washington are two cornerbacks who can handle their men one-on-one and they enable the Steelers to blitz as much as they do. You can't be a blitzing team without great corners.

> *"I played for Mike Ditka in Chicago.*
> *Like Bill, he grew up near Pittsburgh. There*
> *must be something about Western Pennsylvania*
> *that gives coaches dramatic facial expressions*
> *and mustaches, that makes them disciplinarians.*
> *But the way I look at it, I played for one coaching*
> *legend in Ditka. Then I played for an*
> *up-and-coming coaching legend."*
> — Mike Tomczak on Bill Cowher

Ralph Berlin
Liniment and cigars

*"I have no idea;
I'm just a plumber."*

Ralph Berlin had been to Bally Total Fitness, a health club on Oxford Drive in Bethel Park. Berlin has been going there three days a week to work out. He does 40 to 50 minutes on a treadmill, 20 to 30 minutes on a bike, and he does some exercises to strengthen his knees and upper body. He was walking fairly well when he entered the Food Court at South Hills Village, not bad for a 66-year-old man with his second set of knee replacements. He had also undergone triple bypass heart surgery in 1999, and also bounced back from that. He said he would be 67 in July.

For some reason, a lot of the people I remember who were responsible for the physical care of the Steelers and the Pitt sports teams in my student days — the doctors as well as the trainers — walked with a limp. They either had bum knees or bum hips. It was almost a job requirement.

Berlin was wearing a black ballcap with U.S. Marines insignia on the front of it, a black varsity jacket with "Pittsburgh Steelers" in gold script across his heart, and a gray T-shirt. He was wearing black sweat pants and white and blue sneakers. He looked the part of a retired trainer. It had been nearly nine years since he retired as the trainer for the Steelers. He started in the winter of 1968 when Bill Austin was in his last year as head coach, and continued for all 23 years when Chuck Noll was the head coach, and served Bill Cowher in his first year at the helm in 1992.

No one had known the Steelers any better than Berlin. He was the ubiquitous insider. Several of the players I had interviewed said that they thought Noll got most of his inside information about the players from Berlin and Tony Parisi, the equipment manager. Those two knew the needs, hurts and moods of the ballplayers better than the coaches and administrators, and certainly the sportswriters who covered the club. Berlin could work magic with a little liniment and lots of tape. He knew how to massage some massive egos and he knew the value of a pat on the back or the fanny. He also knew what stories stayed in the locker room.

Asked about Noll, Berlin surprised me by saying matter-of-factly, "I never felt close to him. We've talked more and easier since we both retired than we did when I was working for the Steelers. I have great admiration for the man and what he accomplished, and I was fortunate to be with him all those years."

Asked about Cowher, Berlin said, "He was always nice to me. A lot of people rap him, but I like the guy. He's done all right."

Veteran Steelers' trainer Ralph Berlin poses proudly with one of his favorites, Franco Harris, and consults with one of team physicians, Dr. Joseph Maroon, a highly respected neurological surgeon. That's Jackie Hart, the field equipment manager, visible behind Berlin in photo above.

He also talked about Austin in the interview that brisk afternoon, with temperatures dipping into the mid-40s following a welcomed warm spell. It was Monday, April 22, 2002.

We took a corner table near the window, close to Roxy's, a fine restaurant where Berlin and several other retired members of the Steelers' staff get together for lunch about every two months. Berlin had been to Roxy's for such a reunion the week before, sharing food and drink and catch-up news with Joe Gordon, the team's publicist during those glory days, and Mary Regan, a receptionist/secretary for the late Art Rooney and the Steelers most of her adult life. Mary brought along her sister Joan. Gordon lived with his wife, Babe, in a condo on Mt. Washington, and the Regans lived with their rather spry mother, Mary, in their home in Mt. Lebanon.

Tony Parisi, the team's equipment man, and Jim Boston, the team's business manager and contract negotiator during their heyday and the team ballboy way back when, were usually there, too, but they were away and missed this latest get-together. Parisi lived in Mt. Lebanon and Boston in Peters Township, further south on Rt. 19, out in Washington County.

One of the highlights of Berlin's long stay with the Steelers, he said, was the time he spent with Art Rooney, the team owner. They smoked cigars and read *The Racing Form* together, and shared some special moments. Berlin said he still missed Mr. Rooney.

Berlin called Bethel Park home during his long stay in Pittsburgh. It was about two miles, or a five-minute drive, from South Hills Village. He lived there with his wife of 42 years, Dee. They have two children. Beth Toth, 41, the mother of three children, lives in Allison Park, and Steven, 40, lives in Anderson, South Carolina.

Berlin didn't want anything to drink. I had two medium Diet Pepsis during our two hours together. Berlin was easy to be with. He enjoyed talking about those earlier days, and sharing his stories and memories.

I asked Berlin about his nickname "Plumber," which he came by during his stay with the Steelers. "One day one of the new assistant coaches asked me a question about how the Steelers had done something the previous year, and I answered him by saying, 'I don't know; I'm just a plumber.' Myron Cope was walking by and he heard that, and he started referring to me as 'Plumber' on his shows after that. The name stuck."

When I told Berlin I would be interviewing Andy Russell in another day or so, he said, "Tell Andy that I said that — even with my two knee replacements — I could still beat him in the 40-yard sprint." Berlin still liked to keep his boys smiling and on their heels.

> *"When we didn't win,*
> *some people didn't think we were smart*
> *enough to come in out of the rain."*
> — Art Rooney

Ralph Berlin:

The locker room was the players' home away from home. The only time you saw Chuck Noll in the locker room was on game day. Tony Parisi, the equipment man, and Rodgers Freyvogel, his assistant, would be there, along with Jackie Hart, the field manager, and me. Jackie went with the franchise; he'd been there so long. The best thing about Chuck Noll is that he let us do our job. He didn't interfere. We knew his expectations.

He never questioned what I was doing. If I told him during a game that so-and-so was unable to continue playing he just went to the next player. He never disputed what I told him, or tried to change my mind.

Noll was a very private person, a subdued individual. He wasn't a rah-rah guy. When we went to the first Super Bowl at the end of the 1974 season, he made a statement during the playoffs that was as close to a pep talk as I ever heard him deliver. We had beaten Buffalo (32-14) in our first playoff game, and we were playing the Raiders in Oakland.

Oakland had played Miami in the other AFC playoff game, and it was written up that the Oakland-Miami game was the real Super Bowl. John Madden, the Oakland coach, said as much. He said the two best teams were meeting in that game.

Noll got up at a team meeting a few days before that game at Oakland — he was mad — and he told our guys, "The best team in the National Football League is right in this room!" Yes, it was the closest thing to a pep talk Chuck Noll ever offered, and it really charged up our guys. We beat the Raiders (24-13) and then we beat the Minnesota Vikings (16-6) two weeks later in New Orleans to win our first Super Bowl.

There was no way we weren't going to beat the Vikings in that Super Bowl. We had their number before the game even started. You should've heard Glen ("Pine") Edwards hollering at them as we were about to come out of the tunnel and onto the field. The Vikings stood stoically outside a nearby tunnel and they ignored our guys. "Pine" was hollering at a guy he played with in college, but he wouldn't respond to him. That's when he told him, as only he could, that the Vikings better tighten their chinstraps because they were in for an asskicking.

Chuck Noll wanted people who were self-motivated. He didn't want to have to pump you up. Chuck called everybody together in a small room at Tulane Stadium before we took the field against the Vikings, and he went over the same aspects of the game that he had done for the first exhibition game that year. That was it.

281

He seemed cold at times back then. What you didn't realize then was what a very caring person he was. You learned that later on.

On the day he announced his retirement, Chuck Noll came back to my office — that was the first time he'd ever done that — and he told me he was retiring. He said he wanted to tell Tony Parisi and me about his plans before the press conference. I didn't expect it. I'm sure he had told Dan Rooney before what he planned to do, but nothing had leaked down our way.

When Noll came here, he set the tone when he drafted Joe Greene. Everyone knew Joe Greene was a good player; we didn't know he was a great player.

Noll treated people the way he felt they should be treated. He had a knack for judging talent when it came to cutting players.

We had the right chemistry. He had a oneness in mind. He only cared about the football team. He didn't care about commercials. He wanted that stuff to be for the players. He cared deeply about the ballplayers.

People say he was cold, but that wasn't true. He hated to break up that team and it may have been one of the things that brought on the team's decline. Some guys who could have made a contribution here were let go. Like when he held onto Dwight White for one more year and let Dwaine Board go. Then Board became a star on Super Bowl teams with the 49ers. Chuck cared, even though he didn't show it publicly.

He was a great leader; he was a great man. He let people do their job. He was fair. He did not play favorites.

Noll brought about several distinct changes from my first year here. When I got here, it seemed like football was a sideline for most of the guys. They weren't making a lot of money so they were always looking for ways to add to their income.

When we got off the field in these early days, they cleared out as quickly as possible. Sometimes when I got off the field, the only ones left in the locker room were Tony Parisi and Jackie Hart.

Bob Milie used to come in and help me on weekends. Parisi came in and helped me tape players on game day. We couldn't get them all taped. I told Chuck my problem, and Chuck said, "You're the trainer. You take care of it!" From then on, I never went to Chuck if I had a problem.

When we were taping the players, the quarterbacks had "cut" privileges. They could cut into the line. The rookies got taped first. The training room belonged to the veterans one hour prior to practice. If a rookie came in he didn't get taped. That was enforced by veteran players.

Assisting an injured Terry Bradshaw off the field are, from left to right, Mike Wagner (23), assistant trainer Bob Milie, head trainer Ralph Berlin and Rocky Bleier.

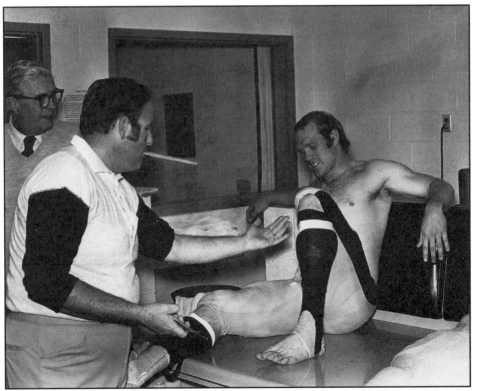

Dr. John Best, team physician, and Ralph Berlin, with unlit cigar in this mouth, tend to Terry Bradshaw on training table in locker room.

As far as treatment was concerned, we opened up early in the morning and tried to take care of everybody. During the season, I was usually in at 7 in the morning and I'd get home around 7 at night. At training camp, you were busy all day. You just worked and slept.

"Chuck Noll was Chuck Noll."

Dan Rooney hired me in the winter of 1968. Roger McGill had left as trainer to go back to Pitt. I knew that Bill Austin was skating on thin ice, and that it might be his last year. I asked Dan what it would mean if Austin would not stay on. He said, "You're working for the Pittsburgh Steelers. You do your job and you've got a job with us."

I came to the Steelers from Kentucky. I started with the Cardinals in St. Louis as an assistant trainer in the summer of 1963 and the summer of 1964. I started work as a trainer during my student days at Iowa State.

I came in during Austin's last year when the Steelers were still training at the Fair Grounds at South Park. I remember Dick Shiner and Ken Kortas and Fran O'Brien. We'd go to the Parkside Inn and South Park Inn. They had great fish sandwiches at the South Park Inn. Everyone ordered fish except Kortas. He'd order steak. He was drinking eight cans of Nutriment a day, trying to build himself up, trying to boost his weight.

Bill Austin made the mistake of trying to be Vince Lombardi, who'd been his boss in Green Bay. I talked to their trainer and he told me we were running the same drills in Pittsburgh that Lombardi had run in Green Bay. Austin was trying to do everything the same way. What Bill didn't realize is that we didn't have the same people, and that there was only one Vince Lombardi.

I ran into a similar situation when I was a trainer at the University of Kentucky before I came to Pittsburgh. Charlie Bradshaw was the football coach at Kentucky. He had played at Kentucky. He had played for Bear Bryant as a 155-pound center. He was tough as nails. He'd been in the Marines and went through the action in the Pacific. He'd been wounded in Saipan. He played football ten days after he'd had an appendectomy, and they had to cut you up pretty good in those days to do that procedure. He coached with Bear Bryant at Texas A&M, and followed him to Alabama. When Bradshaw became the head coach at Kentucky he tried to be Bear Bryant. But there was only one Bear Bryant.

That was one of Bill Austin's faults. There was only one Vince Lombardi. Chuck Noll was Chuck Noll. He wasn't Paul

284

Brown. He wasn't Sid Gillman. He wasn't Don Shula. That was a big part of his success. Plus, he had some pretty good draft picks.

When we were at training camp at St. Vincent's College in Latrobe, the players would go to the 19th Hole to relax after practice and drink beer. The only time Chuck would go out was when he'd take the whole staff to the Blue Angel Restaurant at the airport for dinner one night during camp. That was the only night he'd go out.

On the first night that everyone was in camp, the coaches would pair up the players for the Oklahoma Drill. I'd be at the meeting to make sure the guys that they were lining up for the drills were healthy and able to go.

The meeting went on. Finally, it would be about 11 o'clock. The meeting was over. Perles yells out, "Now where the hell is that fabulous pizza place?" They went to watering holes. Chuck never did. Obviously, nothing was written about it, but some of the players went out, too, legally and illegally.

They knew where the coaches went and the coaches knew where they went, and they stayed away from each other's spots. The sportswriters went where the coaches went, for the most part, except some of the younger sportswriters.

We had only one team doctor at the time and that was Dr. John Best. You didn't have big staffs like you do now. I think Dr. Best even thought he was a dentist. We called him "Big John" and he was in charge of all medical procedures. You didn't get in his way.

We had a good personnel department. Art Rooney Jr. had Dick Haley and Bill Nunn Jr. Nunn knew the people at all the black schools because he'd been the sports editor of *The Pittsburgh Courier*, and he had covered all those teams. He'd picked a black All-America team every year. He gave us an advantage over a lot of the other NFL teams who didn't scout those schools in those days. We made some other smart picks. If you'd seen Jack Lambert when he came here you wouldn't believe he was a football player. He was 6-4, 215, scrawny looking, legs like a stork. Mike Webster and Jon Kolb were both undersized to play up front in the NFL, but they built themselves up here.

One of the people who deserves more credit for what we achieved is Art Rooney Jr. He ran that personnel and scouting department and he deserves credit for assembling these teams as much as anybody. He got us players like Stallworth, Blount and Holmes. That had a lot to do with our success.

The only thing Chuck cared about was coaching. He didn't want to be the general manager. He just wanted to be the coach. I can remember when Woody Widenhofer and George Perles and that bunch were here.

George always worked out by the infield at Three Rivers Stadium. That was his end of the field for the defense. One day, George's group was done doing whatever they were supposed to be doing, and the defensive linemen were sitting down on the blocking dummies. Noll noted the inactivity, and hollered out from mid-field, "George, what the hell are you doing? Why are they sitting around? You should be teaching them something."

And George hollered back, "Chuck, what the hell am I going to teach these guys about playing football?"

Our biggest concern, at times, was not to get anyone hurt at practice. You had guys like Jon Kolb going up against Fats Holmes and Mike Webster going up against Joe Greene, and you didn't want them killing one another in practice.

I'm biased, I know, but we may have had the greatest collection of players in the National Football League, maybe in the League's history. Look at all the guys we have in the Hall of Fame. Even the great Green Bay Packers teams of Lombardi don't have as many guys in there.

"Joe Greene was the boss."

We played the last game of the regular season in 1975 at the Coliseum in Los Angeles. We had won 11 straight games going into that final game. We lost (10-3) to the Rams that day. Our dressing rooms were close to each other, and after the game, you could hear the Rams whooping it up in the locker room. They were chanting, "We want the Steelers! We want the Steelers!" Joe Greene got upset hearing that, and he hollered out to our guys, "They better watch what they want! They just might get what they want!"

The Steelers won the Super Bowl that year, their second in as many years, and they did so by defeating the Dallas Cowboys (21-17). The Rams didn't quite make it that far.

When Joe Greene retired (after the 1981 season), not only did you lose a great player, but you lost his leadership. Joe was the boss back then. When I had a problem in the locker room, I never went to Chuck. I went to Joe and he took care of it. In the beginning, I went to Chuck and he told me I was responsible for the locker room. He made it clear that he wasn't going to be policing the locker room for me. So I turned to Joe Greene instead for help.

They had those boom boxes in the locker room, and music would be playing loudly over them. On game day they were to be turned off at 11:30. So Parisi turned off the stereo at that

"This is something that likely will never take place again."
— Lynn Swann

time. Fats was in one of his moods, so he went over and turned the music back on. Joe Greene goes over and turns it off. Fats turns it back on. Joe goes over and tears the whole damn thing off the wall. There was no more music. There were only two guys Fats was afraid of. That was Lambert and Greene.

We were playing this game once, and Fats comes off the field and Furness goes in for him. Perles goes over to Fats and asks him why he's on the bench. Fats said Joe kicked him off the field. Fats was free-lancing instead of doing what he was supposed to be doing. He said, "Joe said, 'Get out!' " He wouldn't go back in until Joe said it was all right. So Joe comes to the sideline, and steam is coming off his head when he took his helmet off. He's standing there and Perles is patting him on the belly, trying to soothe him down. Fats is still sitting on the bench. Perles is asking Joe to let Fats get back on the field. It was unreal.

When Joe retired, it was not the beginning of the end. It had already stopped. But he was such a force, not only on the field, but what he meant to the Steelers' organization.

He himself had the ability to control what is basically a team game. He had the ability to disrupt and take control of the game. Also, in the locker room, he was feared. No question about that. You can't lead by fear alone. He also had respect, and he was respected throughout the league.

Problems that could have surfaced never surfaced because of his presence. I can't say enough about Joe Greene.

When Joe Greene came in the whole environment changed. We had some good players like Ben McGee, Chuck Hinton, Ray Mansfield, Paul Martha, Bruce Van Dyke, Sam Davis, Lloyd Voss and Andy Russell, but by 1974 we had an entirely new team.

Prior to Noll, weights were not stressed. Lou Recchi was the strength coach, but he came in part-time, at first. He'd be at training camp and he'd come in once in a while during the season.

The attitude in the locker room went from perpetual loser to complete confidence. In 1970 and 1971, we missed the playoffs. We had a history here that if something could go wrong it would go wrong. We had to overcome that.

We were playing Houston late in the 1972 season and we had to win to make the playoffs. Chuck opted to go for a first down on 4th and one at the Houston 40, and we didn't make it. As our defense started out on the field, one of our people said, "Here we go again." I know who it was, but I won't say who. Joe Greene turned and said, "No, we won't."

Greene sacked Dan Pastorini four straight plays. They started out at midfield and they ended up at the end of the game on their 13. We won the game (9-3) and got to the playoffs. From then on, the attitude of the team was one of great confidence, especially in 1974 when we won our first Super Bowl.

They were just confident we were going to win and that the Steelers were not going to be stopped. When we got the schedule, they would try to figure out who we'd be meeting in the playoffs. Our early teams here did not have a oneness and a closeness. Noll and Joe Greene changed that.

A bunch of us had this Tuesday poker game. Franco, Greene, L.C. and Moon Mullins. One year (1978) Jim Mandich played with us. We used to play at Franco's most of the time. Sam Davis played awhile, too, and we played at his house. There was a tightness. That same closeness permeated our team. Sam's nickname was "Tight Man" or "Tight," because the players thought he had it all together. It's a shame what happened to him.

"No one had a bigger heart."

So many of our guys have been successful. Look at how Larry Brown and J.T. Thomas are doing with all them Applebee's they're running. Larry Brown wouldn't say anything when he was here, now he has over 1,000 employees under him. I bump into Bill Hurley from time to time and he seems to be doing okay with his high school scouting service. Look at Dwight White and the success he's had. Dwight's mouth was always running when he was here, but no one had a bigger heart and he put his game on the line.

That first Super Bowl tells you all you need to know about Dwight White. Dwight had pneumonia when we were going down to New Orleans. He came to see me on the plane. He said he had a pain in his back. We checked in at this old hotel that was going out of business. I get a call that Dwight is in bad shape in his room. I go down to his room and here's Dwight on all fours. He can't get up and he can't get down. Joe Greene had called me to come and see him. Greene and Mel Blount roomed together in those days. We managed to get Dwight in a station wagon, and we asked the people at the hotel desk to direct us to the nearest hospital.

They sent us to Charity Hospital. That's exactly what it was, like a large clinic for poor people. It was in a bad part of town. Dwight's on all fours on a gurney, and these nurses are out in the hallways trying to get autographs from our guys. I got hold of the trainer from the Saints, and told him we needed to go to another hospital. He gave me directions to get to Methodist Hospital that the Saints used. So we get Dwight in there.

Dave Huber, one of our team doctors, comes down in the middle of the week, on the Thursday before the Super Bowl on Sunday. Dwight comes out of the hospital and tries to practice, but he can't. John Best, our old team doctor, is there, too.

On Sunday morning, Dwight calls me from the hospital and wants me to come and get him. He wants to come to the pre-game meal. The next thing you know he wants to dress for the game. Huber says no. Big John says to Dave, "Let him dress. You don't know if we'll ever get back to a game this big again. It can't hurt to let him dress."

So Dwight warms up, and Huber says he shouldn't be exerting himself, that he has pneumonia. Huber says he's too hurt to play. Big John says, "Let him do what he wants to do. How long can he play? He'll fall out after the first series."

So Dwight plays and he goes all the way, and he scored the first points, touching Fran Tarkenton when he slipped and fell in the end zone for a two-point touchback.

We get him back to Pittsburgh, and Dwight was in Divine Providence Hospital for two weeks. Dwight, for all his mouth, was tough.

We had a lot of tough guys. One time Mike Wagner cracked vertebrae in his neck (in the third game of the 1977 season), and Doc Steele was our doctor then, and told Chuck what he thought had happened. We didn't have X-ray machines at the stadium then. While Doc Steele is telling Chuck about it, Wagner has gone back on the field. Noll spots him on the field. "What's he doing out there?" Noll asks Doc Steele. Before they could get him out, Mike made another tackle. He was out the rest of the season. That injury nearly ended his career.

Glen Edwards was a tough guy. It was tough to keep him off the field. Mike Webster dislocated three fingers. He put them back in place in the huddle. He tore a cartilage in his knee; it locked on him, but he wouldn't come out. I remember all the physical problems Rocky Bleier had when he came back from Vietnam. In the movie about him, they had Terry Hanratty rubbing his toes, but I was the one who did that. It used to bring tears to his eyes. And The Chief was the only reason Rocky was still with the team. He told them to put him on injured reserve; they carried him until he was physically able to resume playing. Joe Greene had a bad shoulder, but you couldn't get him out of the lineup. L.C. hated to practice, but he went out on Friday so he could play. He couldn't practice again on Monday.

Lambert pulled me aside at half time of a game and told me I was the worst trainer in the world. I had taped his ankle before the game and he said his ankle was bothering him. He

289

wanted me to re-tape him. So I took the tape off and his ankle just ballooned. He'd broken it. He still wanted me to tape it up again so he could go out for the second half. He ended up having his career cut short by turf toe. Everything you do you do off your big toe and that was a painful injury. It had to be to sideline Lambert.

Franco, in his own way, was tough. Franco would work out on his own for an hour and a half after practice every day. He took care of his body. That's why he lasted so long. Every time he took a handoff in practice he'd run 50 yards with the ball and then jog back upfield. He'd slow down practice, but he had his own workout rituals. He wanted to get used to running 50 yards.

We had some tough guys when Austin was the coach, too. Dick Hoak was always quiet, but very tough. Bill Saul was tough. He broke both wrists once and just had us tape them up and he continued to play.

In the old days, you could always tell when we were playing Cleveland, Houston or Oakland. Our guys put on extra pads, extra everything. Those games were special. Some was for protection, some was for a weapon.

As Chuck used to say, "You can't play this game for money."

I remember what "The Chief" used to say. He said, "You can't pay the Bradshaws and Swanns and Francos and Stallworths enough money. They're worth it. Where you get in trouble is when you pay people a lot of money who can't play."

I remember another incident. I'm on my way out of the locker room one day at Three Rivers Stadium and I see Fats Holmes sitting in front of his locker. This was not long after he'd been arrested for shooting a rifle at a police helicopter in Ohio. The Steelers had him on a budget at the time, and would dole out just enough money for him to get by on. They were trying to keep him from getting into trouble.

I go out on the field and Perles asks me, "You seen Fats?"

I told him he was in the locker room. "Go in and tell him to get his ass out here!" Perles tells me.

So I go in and I say, "Fats, you better get out there. George wants you now!"

Fats said he wasn't practicing. He's in one of his dark moods. I don't know what happened. Maybe he'd gone down to the front office and tried to get some more money from them or something. So I go back out on the field.

George sent me back in to get Fats. He looked at me this time, and if looks could kill I'd have been dead. Fats looked right through me. I went back on the field. George gets on me. I said, "George, I've already gone in there twice. If you want him, you go back in there!"

He never came out. The next day Fats was fine and he practiced with the team. It was episodes like that one that kept my job interesting.

"We'd just sit there together."

When I think of Art Rooney I can smell the cigars. He smoked good cigars, and he told me I could stop in his office any time and help myself to one. I had carte blanche to his cigars. I didn't abuse the privilege. He liked people who enjoyed a good cigar.

I liked that man. He meant more to me than my father. I never knew my father, so Mr. Rooney filled a void. For a lot of people, I guess. The Chief was such a presence in the Steelers' offices at Three Rivers. When he died there was a void created that no one could fill.

By the time Chuck came to the Steelers Dan Rooney was really in charge of the operation. But The Chief was still in charge of Dan. He was still his father, and Dan had so much respect for him and his thinking on everything.

The Chief took an interest in everyone. It didn't matter whether you were the president of U.S. Steel or somebody at the 222 Bar on the North Side. He treated you the same. He was some man.

I'd go into his office and sit down and smoke a cigar. He'd be smoking one cigar and chewing another. I used to cut up his cigars for him so he could chew a bit of them as he pleased. Sometimes he'd be reading *The Racing Form* while I was there. We didn't even talk sometimes. We'd just sit there together.

Once, I went into Divine Providence for a knee operation. He came to see me every day for 10 days. He'd eat all the candy that had been sent to me. He loved sweets. One day it was dark out by the time he was ready to leave. Divine Providence was about two miles from his home. He said he was going to walk home.

There are a lot of characters in West Park at night. It wouldn't be safe for some of the Steelers to stroll through there at night. I told The Chief I'd call him a cab. He protested. I told him this wasn't the same neighborhood it was 30 years ago. He said he'd be fine. And he left my room. I called down to the front desk. There were some cops in the lobby who'd just brought in a drunk who'd split his head. They said they'd take Mr. Rooney home. They told him, "Mr. Rooney, we don't go in there with a patrol car at night. We're taking you home."

I remember he was a patient at Mercy Hospital once. It was a non-smoking hospital. But he had his own suite. I'd stop and see him twice a day. They were doing something to adjust his pacemaker. He was having some problems. I always had a pocketful of cigars wherever I traveled. He asked me if I had a cigar and I lied and said no. He said, "When you come back tonight, bring some." That night we were both smoking in his room. Dr. (Noel) Gillette came in to see him. Dr. Gillette said, "Mr. Rooney, why don't you quit smoking those cigars? It would be good for you." And Mr. Rooney said, "How much time I got left?" Dr. Gillette said, "We got your pacemaker straightened out now. You've got about six to seven years if you'd quit smoking those cigars, maybe three to five if you don't." Mr. Rooney blew out some smoke, and said, "Doc, I'll give you the extra years. I enjoy these cigars."

One time I was driving Mrs. Rooney somewhere with Art. I'd bought a new Plymouth. She was up front with me, and Mr. Rooney was in the back seat. He was chewing a cigar. That way he could spit out the window without hitting anyone.

Mrs. Rooney asked me how I liked the Plymouth. "We have a Buick," she said. "We've always had Buicks. If I had the money, we'd have a Mercedes-Benz, if it were up to me." And Mr. Rooney said, "She wants to put on the dog for the neighbors."

Imagine that. They had the money, but they just didn't live on the level they could have. Dan and Art Jr. still live a low-key existence, but I think the other three brothers live a different lifestyle in Florida.

Mr. Rooney's gone and it's not the same at the Steelers' offices anymore. So many of the people I knew are gone. With Mary Regan gone, hardly anyone there knows me either. I took Dwight White over to see the new facilities a few months back. He'd never seen it. Dwight and I were close when he was on the team. I've only been on the second floor where the offices are on two occasions. That's when I went to see Dan. Now that "Dirt" Dawson's gone, I don't know any of the players. I picked up Jerome Bettis one day and took him where he was going. I like him. But he's the only one I know a little bit now. I don't feel at ease there anymore. I was with them from 1968 to 1993, and it was a great ride.

When I first came on board we'd go to training camp on July 6 and we couldn't come back until after Labor Day. The Fair Grounds at South Park weren't available to us until after the Fair that ended the summer. When we practiced there if it rained we'd go inside the stables and practice there. That was something. Training camp gets shorter than ever each year. If they ever build a hotel near their facility on the South Side they wouldn't have to go anywhere else to train. I can see that coming.

292

Roy Mansfield (signature)

"I was part of the greatest team that ever played."

In looking back on what happened here, at the time I don't think any of us realized what we were doing. I just happened to be on the fringe of it. As I look back on it now it's just a phenomenal feeling. Even in a small way, I was part of the greatest team that ever played, or at least one of them.

When all those guys you worked with went into the Hall of Fame it was a great feeling. We had quite a run. When it ended it came crashing down.

Mansfield's funeral had special significance for all of us. It was the first time in a long time that many of us from that era were together. And it was a reminder that we weren't immortal. It was tough for me. I'd looked after Mansfield for most of his pro career.

When Ray died, it was like the beginning of the end. Since then we've lost Steve Furness and Joe Gilliam, Tyrone McGriff and Dan Turk. And we just lost one of the originals, Byron "Whizzer" White, the Supreme Court Justice. Now he was way before our time (1938 season), but he was a special Steeler in the team's history. It was like losing someone from the family.

Jim O'Brien

Two key contributors to keeping the Steelers' house orderly were equipment managers Rodgers Freyvogel and Tony Parisi.

Andy Russell
He's climbed many mountains

"I love this city and sell it wherever I travel."

A ndy Russell has quite a view from his spacious and neatly decorated office high above Dominion Tower in the heart of the city's Cultural District. From his desk, depending on which way he looks, he can see Pittsburgh's present, its past and perhaps its future.

"It's a great city," he observed, as he stood looking out one of the two nine-foot high windows. "I'm not a native, but I love this city and sell it wherever I travel. I'm always bragging about it."

Russell, the former All-Pro linebacker for the Steelers in the '60s and '70s, is managing partner of Laurel Mountain Partners, merchant bankers, and is associated with several other high-finance ventures. He is one of the real success stories of the Steelers.

He had turned 60 the year before, and his two children had given him five grandchildren. It was hard to believe that Andy Russell was a 61-year-old grandfather. My, how time flies in the fast lane. He was wearing his gray hair short to the scalp. His smile and enthusiasm were arresting and made one instantly comfortable.

He was nearing 50 when I last interviewed Russell at length for my book *Doing It Right*, and I wrote at the time that I couldn't believe he was almost 50. Of course, I was almost 50 at that time. That helps put my wonderment in its proper perspective. I can't believe I will be 60 by the time this book is printed. There's a part of me that keeps telling me I'm 14. That part of me is telling a lie.

The window-blinds were pulled up to the top, allowing lots of natural light to fill Russell's office on the 31st and next-to-the-penthouse floor of the Dominion Tower. There was enough room in his office to play racquetball, always one of his favorite releases, but he didn't have far to go whenever he needed a workout. Everything he required was at the doorstep of Dominion Tower, except a golf course.

It was a Wednesday, April 24, 2002, when temperatures in Pittsburgh had risen from an overnight low of 30 degrees — threatening the white blossoms on the fruit trees that line Liberty Avenue in the front of the building — to an afternoon high of 64 degrees. The weather had been a little crazy in its extremes the past week or so.

The Pirates were winning, but the fans weren't coming to PNC Park, which was clearly visible just across the Allegheny River. The Bucs had gotten off to a great 12-6 start, far beyond what anybody anticipated, and they were in first place in the National League Central. From his window, Russell could actually watch the next day's afternoon game between the Bucs and Dodgers without leaving his

Andy Russell displays photo of his former linebacker mates Jack Ham and Jack Lambert on the wall of his office high above Dominion Tower.

Photos by Jim O'Brien

Andy Russell and Cindy Ellis team up to boost price for signed Terry Bradshaw jersey in auction at Andy's Celebrity Classic golf outing at The Club at Nevillewood in May of 2002.

desk. He might not be able to see the right fielder and center fielder, but other than that he could see the rest of the field. The scene was striking.

There was road construction wherever one went in the city, topped by the closing of the outbound lanes of the Fort Pitt Tunnel. I had to get through three construction sites near my home in Upper St. Clair before I even approached the Fort Pitt Tunnel. The road woes weren't helping the Pirates pull in fans either. Anybody who didn't have to go into the city was avoiding the hassle.

I went to the Pirates-Dodgers game that same evening at PNC Park with my pal Alex Pociask. We dined in the Gunner's Lounge, which memorializes Bob "The Gunner" Prince, the "voice of the Pirates for 28 years," and sat in the club seats of USFilter high above first base. It was a pleasant night to watch a baseball game, but there were only about 12,000 fans in the stands. Had the allure of the new ballpark worn off this quickly? If so, the Pirates were in trouble.

I glanced over several times at the Pittsburgh skyline and saw the setting sun reflecting off the shiny surface of Dominion Tower. A stranger in the seat next to mine remarked at how bright that light was. The light was glancing off the area around the windows of Andy Russell's office at the top of the building. It was blinding at times. It was like a star in the East. After all I had learned about Russell earlier that day, it seemed ___ ing.

"There's more to be done here."

If Russell looked down river to the left, he could see Heinz Field, where the Steelers play. Across the Allegheny River, he could see the relatively new Alcoa headquarters building, the Roberto Clemente Bridge, and Allegheny General Hospital. To the far right, the David L. Lawrence Convention Center was nearing completion.

As we spoke, my wife Kathie, who works at AGH as a social worker in the oncology unit, was having her right wrist checked out over there, following surgery two weeks earlier. It was the third procedure she'd undergone on that wrist since she broke it a year earlier when she fell while playing tennis. I was thinking about her when I saw AGH high on the hill. The hospital had recently been named No. 21 — Clemente's number — among the nation's hospitals in a poll of doctors across the country. The high rating was a point of pride to all associated with the hospital.

I pointed out the Renaissance Hotel just below us. "We tried to put a Ritz in that area down there," Russell remarked, pointing to the right of the Renaissance. "We weren't able to buy the buildings we needed for the space. There's more to be done here."

The Dominion Tower is in a great location. It's flanked by Heinz Hall and the Benedum Center. It's within short walking distance of the Duquesne Club on Sixth Avenue, where Russell was scheduled to have lunch at noon with one of his partners, Jeff Kendall. Morton's of Chicago — The Steakhouse is in the lobby of the Dominion Tower.

Kendall and Don Ray are partners with Russell and, to hear him speak, they are teammates of the same fiber, intensity and dedication as Jack Ham, Jack Lambert and Russell, another trio that left its mark in Pittsburgh. Before visiting Russell, I had spoken with Julie Buscher, the concierge at Dominion Tower, and Art Cipriani, an executive with Dominion, the city's energy company which was in the midst of shifting its headquarters from Pittsburgh to Richmond. Cipriani would soon be working out of an office in Clarksburg, West Virginia as well as other satellite offices.

Getting through lobby security was as difficult as maneuvering through the construction sites near my home that morning. One of the three-guard phalanx had to call Russell's receptionist, a lovely woman named Farrell Manuel, to see if it was OK to let me come up. Russell was busy on the telephone when I arrived for our scheduled 9:30 a.m. meeting, so Farrell got me some steaming hot coffee. She couldn't have been a better host, and she was always helpful when I called Andy after my initial visit to check on facts. There were copies of *The New York Times* and *Wall Street Journal* on end tables in the waiting area. There was marble tile on the floor and walls. It was impressive. PNC Ventures was sharing the 31st floor at the time, but was in the midst of moving elsewhere.

There are lots of framed photographs and Steelers mementos displayed in Russell's office. Many of the photos are of his family.

His daughter, Amy Russell Zemper, 32, was living in Columbus, Ohio with her husband, Dave, and their three children, Molly, Jaclyn and Derek. I told Andy that my younger daughter, Rebecca, who would be 25 in another three weeks, had been living in Columbus the past two years. His son, Andy Keith Russell, 35, and his wife, Brigitte, who is from Germany, have sons, Carsten and Finn. Young Andy works for Nike and lives in Portland, Oregon. He speaks fluent German and often deals with German bankers in their own language. He previously worked for a German Venture Capital Group in Frankfurt, which is where he met his wife. His father spent two years in the U.S. Army stationed in Germany in 1964 and 1965 after his rookie season with the Steelers. So it's in the genes. His grandfather, William Russell, graduated from the Harvard Business School and ran Monsanto Chemical Company's European operation while living in Brussels.

"My father made me promise not to play pro football," the former Steeler recalls. "He said, 'I want a son who's serious about life.'"

So Russell played pro football anyhow, but made sure he was serious about sideline pursuits that became career pursuits.

"What lives in us lives in our heart — our heritage, our traditions, our culture . . . but more importantly our faith."
— Bishop Donald Wuerl,
July 7, 2002

"The Hall of Fame would be nice."

There were pictures on the walls and shelves, showing Russell with Ray Mansfield, his best friend from his days with the Steelers, who had died at age 55 in November of 1996. There was another framed and signed photo of Russell with Ham and Lambert when they formed one of the most formidable line-backing trios in National Football League history. Ham and Lambert are both in the Pro Football Hall of Fame. When Andy appeared the week before at a sports banquet at the Thompson Club in West Mifflin, where we shared a spot on the dais, several speakers said he also belonged in the Pro Football Hall of Fame. During his 12-year career with the Steelers, Russell had played in the Pro Bowl seven times. By comparison, Lynn Swann and John Stallworth, who got into the Hall of Fame in consecutive years, both played in three Pro Bowls. Then, too, Russell got into some of those Pro Bowls when the Steelers weren't very good, but every NFL team had to be represented.

When I cited those numbers to Russell, he smiled and said, "I don't think I should have to campaign for the Hall of Fame. It's unlikely it will ever happen, but maybe. Look how long it took for Dave Wilcox of the 49ers to get in. I bumped into Frank Gifford at some event this past year, and he introduced me by saying I should be in the Hall of Fame. He also said that it would be tough for three linebackers from the same team to get in."

Then Russell showed me a letter he had received soliciting an endorsement from him on behalf of Randy Gradishar, a former stand-out linebacker for the Denver Broncos. Some friends of Gradishar were putting together a strong case to support his candidacy for the Pro Football Hall of Fame. "I think more of this sort of thing is being done these days," related Russell.

"The Hall of Fame would be nice, but I don't know that my life can be any more fulfilling than it has been."

When I was talking about my wife's problems with her wrist, I told Russell what a difficult year she had experienced. Her mother and father had died within a six-month span in the second half of 2001 while they were at Asbury Heights, an assisted-care facility in Mt. Lebanon. "I know exactly what that's about," remarked Russell. "I went through the same thing in late 1996 and early 1997."

I knew that his dad, William, and his mother, Esther, had died in that order over a similar span while in residence at Friendship Village, a senior care facility in Upper St. Clair. Andy and I had both spoken at seminars at Friendship Village and I had been introduced to his parents.

I nearly bought a home in Upper St. Clair where Andy and his wife, Nancy, had lived before he moved to Fox Chapel in 1979. He and Nancy were divorced in 1998 after 36 years of marriage. He was 20 years old and a student at the University of Missouri when they were married. He was now living with Cindy Ellis, his "significant other" as

Eddie Johnston of Penguins and Chuck Noll of Steelers get together at charity golf outings hosted by Mario Lemieux and Andy Russell, respectively. Former defensive backs Dwayne Woodruff, now an attorney with offices downtown and Shadyside, and J.T. Thomas, a partner in Applebee's Neighborhood Grill & Bar, meet at Steelers' alumni golf outing at Diamond Run.

Photos by Jim O'Brien

he put it. He was aware that many of his teammates had gotten divorced in recent years and had new mates. He didn't offer any explanation. "I know we're old-fashioned and from a school that stayed together," he said, "but things change."

I had an opportunity to meet Cindy Ellis at the 26th Anniversary Andy Russell Classic for Children, a fund-raising golf event at The Club at Nevillewood on May 16-17, 2002. It was impressive to see that Russell still had the ability to bring some of the best football players of all time to participate in his highly-successful event.

Russell was also elbowing his way into my business. His first book, *A Steeler Odyssey* had been well-received two years earlier, and he had just finished writing a sequel, *An Odd Steelers Journey*. He said it would be published in the coming summer months. I asked him if it was about an odd Steeler, or an odd journey. Writing, he said, was one of his most enjoyable hobbies.

Business was his main business. He had a Masters' Degree in Business (MBA) from the University of Missouri. I know something about savings and investments, but Russell is involved in high-finance ventures that are beyond my comprehension. The numbers are too big and mind-boggling.

Laurel Mountain Partners is a merchant bank that was formed in 1996. They have acquired controlling interest in numerous companies. Andy is vice-president/secretary of Liberty Waste Services, which has acquired over 45 companies since 1996. He is founder and chairman of one of the country's largest regional municipal bond firms. Russell, Rea, Zappala and Gomulka Holdings, Inc. Rocky Bleier was once part of that consortium when I first came back to Pittsburgh to cover the Steelers for *The Pittsburgh Press* in 1979. Back then, their offices were in the old Roosevelt Hotel, once headquarters for the Steelers as well. Bleier got out of the financial services business to go into sports broadcasting. At the time, Russell told him he was crazy. Russell concedes that things have worked out fine for Rocky

"We've done over $30 billion in bond underwriting," related Russell. Russell is chairman of National Waste Industries, Inc., a co-venturer in one of the country's largest waste-to-energy plants ($300 million). He is president of Russell Investments, Inc., a real estate syndication firm that has placed more than $100 million equity into various real estate, oil and gas drilling programs, and corporate investments. Keep in mind, a smiling Chuck Noll noted, that Andy's firm doesn't get to keep all that money.

Russell was drafted on the 16th round of the 1963 college draft. There were only 12 teams in the National Football League at the time. He explained to me that today, with 32 teams in the NFL, he would have been a 5th round pick if taken in the same order.

He and Bleier were both 16th round picks, and they are easily the best late-round picks in Pittsburgh Steelers history. Russell was the only NFL linebacker to play in six consecutive Pro Bowls between 1971 and 1976.

He was the captain of the Steelers for 10 years. He won the Byron "Whizzer" White Award in 1970 when he was the team's Most Valuable Player. He was the Defensive MVP in 1968. He played for two Super Bowl championship teams, in 1974 and 1975.

He's been inducted into the Pennsylvania Sports Hall of Fame and the University of Missouri Hall of Fame.

He's long been active in many community efforts. He has served on the board or as chairman for fund-raising events for the following charities: Vietnam Veterans Leadership Program, Dapper Dan Charities, Juvenile Diabetes Association, Sudden Infant Death Syndrome, Cerebral Palsy, The Leukemia Society and the NFL Alumni Players Association. He was the 1989 Big Brothers & Sisters Man of the Year.

He was chairman in 2002 for the American Heart Association Heart Ball. He was a Press Old Newsboy for 19 years and raised over $2.5 million for Children's Hospital and UPMC children's charities with his annual golf tournament.

He assembled the first and only NFL Alumni USO Tour to U.S. Navy Fleet in the Mediterranean. He was a consultant to international companies on eight consecutive round-the-world trips, including a Westinghouse-sponsored trip to Korea, Sony-sponsored trip to Japan, Kuwait Oil Company trip to Kuwait, Aramco to Saudi Arabia, and McDermott to Singapore.

Russell's resume is most impressive. So were his reflections on his experience with the Steelers and Pittsburgh, offered during a generous 2½-hour meeting:

Andy Russell:

When I retired I said I'd never go to another Super Bowl. And now I've been there every year. Some company is always calling asking me to attend some associated event there on their behalf. I see a lot of my teammates there. Franco Harris has a charity golf tournament at the Super Bowl site each year, and I'll see Rocky Bleier, Lynn Swann, Jack Ham and Mike Wagner, guys like that. Old Super Bowl players are still in demand.

Franco, interestingly enough, is probably the best Steeler at making sure we get together from time to time. Franco is always looking for opportunities to get together. We seldom talk about football. We're always talking about business. That's what those guys want to talk about. They're always asking how we do this and that, when it comes to getting venture capital and financing business projects. My partner Don Ray was in New Orleans with me, and they were asking him all kinds of business questions. They were totally business.

301

If I were one of the current players I'd get sick of hearing stories about the Steelers of the '70s. So I tell them stories about the Steelers of the '60s. I came to the team in 1963. We had some fabulous characters, from the coach, Buddy Parker, down to the players. There was never a tougher Steeler than Ernie Stautner. I missed Bobby Layne as a player, but he was there as an assistant coach, helping Parker that first year. I made some great friends among that bunch.

It was much more difficult to be good on a bad team than it was to be good on a great team.

I remember one time how Ernie Stautner dislocated some fingers on his hand in this game. He just shoved them back into place, and had them taped. I couldn't believe it. I tried it once myself when it happened to me. And I passed out.

Talk about having a passion to play. Stautner comes into the huddle and his thumb is broken back against his wrist. There's a tear near the break and his bone is sticking out. He has a compound fracture of the thumb. He takes his thumb in his hand and he wrenches it down into his fist.

He doesn't show it to anybody. He doesn't say anything. He looks up and says, "What's the defense?" And I thought to myself, I'm not in the right business. This guy has a compound fracture of his thumb and he's not even going to leave the game.

So he stayed in for the rest of the series and then we came off the field, and I'm watching him because I think I'm the only guy who saw that he had a compound fracture. I saw the bone. So I'm figuring he's going to ask for the doctor, and may leave to go to the hospital because this thing could get infected. And he says, "Give me some tape!" So they throw him some tape and he just starts wrapping tape around this big fist.

Then we go back in. He played the entire game. He never misses a down. I'm just astounded and he's using this hand which is broken as a club. He's beating people with it. After the game, we go into the locker room and he says, "Hey, Doc, I think I got a problem," and I'm thinking this is just unbelievable. That is passion for what you do. That guy wasn't making that much money. He just loved to play. What a commitment.

Another classic is Rocky Bleier. He is the only player to go to Vietnam and be wounded in combat and come back and play in the NFL. When he came back, he had a bullet wound in his thigh and shrapnel in his foot, and he was about 178 pounds. The Rooneys were very nice to him, but no one expected him to really play again.

He got a call from Chuck Noll in the off-season, saying, "Rocky, you should really not come back to camp. You should seek your life's work." Noll liked to say that. Instead of doing

302

Steelers' Alumni gathering includes, left to right, Larry Brown, Andy Russell, J.T. Thomas, John Banaszak, Rocky Bleier and Franco Harris.

Soon after Bill Cowher was hired as head coach early in 1992, he hosted a get-together of former Steelers at Three Rivers Stadium. Mike Wagner and Ray Mansfield hold forth in front. Taking a knee behind them, left to right, are Pete Rostosky, Bill Hurley, equipment men Tony Parisi and Frank Sciulli, and J.T. Thomas. Standing, left to right, are Steve Furness, Ted Petersen, Craig Wolfley, Emil Boures, Robin Cole, Craig Bingham, John Banaszak, Cowher, Jack Lambert, equipment man Rodgers Freyvogel, Rocky Bleier, Moon Mullins and Andy Russell.

that, Rocky chose to hire a physical trainer. When he was a rookie before he went to Vietnam, he was 5-8, 185 pounds and he ran a 4.84. He made the team on guts and effort. He's just that kind of guy. He came back after Vietnam decimated by the wounds, but then he built himself up to 230 through weightlifting, and he ran a 4.5. And he worked himself up to the starting halfback position where, eventually, he was primarily a blocker for Franco Harris. Franco moved the ball well when Rocky was in there. Then one year (1976), Rocky had a 1,000-yard rushing year, right behind Franco. That's a phenomenal story.

The guys on my team, in the '60s, weren't making that much money, so they had to find other ways to make money, and not just in the off-season. In 1968, I started my own business, syndicating real estate. That was the first year I made more money on the outside than the Steelers were paying me.

I went to see "The Chief" — Art Rooney — and I said, "How can I justify to my family that I continue to play football when I make more money on the side?"

And Mr. Rooney said, "You don't have to justify anything. If you want to retire go ahead and retire."

That stopped me short. They were tough when it came to business. Then he looked at me and said, "The truth is, Russell, you'd pay me to play this game." He smiled at me after he said it.

I knew he was right.

The Steelers said I did three things no one else ever did. I made more money in the off-season than I did playing for them. That record is never going to be broken, not with the money these guys make today. I asked for stocks or warrants as part of my compensation package one year. And I told them they should cut my salary one season. They said no one else ever did those three things.

I went to the Pro Bowl after the 1968 season. There were some great linebackers there like Sam Huff and Ray Nitschke. They were all making three times what I was making. I was making about $25,000 at the time.

I had started out in 1963 at $12,000, with a $3,000 signing bonus. And you know what? It was the richest I ever felt in my life. When I came back after serving two years in the military service, Fran Fogarty, the business manager — he was tough — wanted to cut my pay because they thought I'd be rusty after a two-year layoff. I was getting my MBA at Missouri at the time. They upped me instead to $14,000. Then I got up to $18,000. By 1968, I was up to $25,000.

I asked Dan Rooney, "Do you think I deserved to be in the Pro Bowl?" He said, "Yes, you should have been in it last year."

304

Then I told him the Pro Bowl linebackers were making $50,000 to $75,000. He said, "They're winning. We're losing and we're losing money. We can't justify paying you that kind of money." So they gave me a 40 percent bump, not the 300 percent bump I was looking for to get me on the same level as those other linebackers.

Then Chuck Noll comes in and we go 1-13. It's kind of hard to make the Pro Bowl on a 1-13 team. I tore cartilage in my knee that year, and I broke my thumb, and I didn't play well. I didn't make the Pro Bowl. So this time I go in to negotiate my next contract, and I said, "I want a pay cut. We had a deal, and I didn't make the Pro Bowl this time."

Dan wondered what was going on. "Do you have a press conference lined up outside?" he said. "Are you trying some scheme to make us look bad? I'll give you a ten percent raise. Now get the hell outta here."

The next year (1971) I'm the Steelers' MVP and I make the Pro Bowl for the second year in a row and my third time altogether. This time Dan Rooney says, "I don't want to know what you want to get now. Look, we're still losing." I asked him if they could give me some stock in the team, or some warrants as part of my compensation. He said, "You mean you'll take paper?" I said I would. I had my MBA by then, and I figured I should put some of what I learned into my negotiations. They didn't give me any stock or warrants. That would have been a great deal for me. Look at what that franchise is worth today. Look at what they're paying these guys. It's just a different world today.

"What could we do to replace football?"

When Ray Mansfield died it was really devastating for me. We had become the best of friends. We shared some special times together. It hurt not to have him around any more.

A lot of players have a real issue with replacing football in their lives. I had the least problem because I had been working when I was playing. I had been working 20 hours a day seven days a week. When I retired, I doubled my income the first year out in the financial services field. So I wasn't hurting in that respect.

Even so, some of our friends were always razzing Ray and me about being old jocks, about being washed up, and about having no way to replace the thrill in our lives that we had experienced as pro football players. This business I'm in now is much different from football. Here, everything happens real slowly. In football, you grade out every day. You get instant feedback on your performance. We were reminded by our friends that we would never again perform in front of 200 million people in a Super Bowl. So we were washed-up jocks.

Ray and I started talking about this after we retired following the 1976 season. How can you possibly replace football?

We agreed that there was a sublime kind of feeling following a football game. That you were worn out, that the fatigue had taken everything out of you. It was a euphoric kind of feeling. We thought we might be able to replace that by running marathons. Then we realized that our knees were too bad, and wouldn't take the pounding of running that much. So marathons were out. We were 35 or 36 years old and feeling pretty strong.

So we found this demanding test that took place up in northern Minnesota near the Canadian border. It was a 165-mile non-stop canoe race. It was called the Boundary Waters Canoe Area. It was a real challenge, where you had to travel across 48 lakes and some land in between some of them — it was an old French trappers' trail — and we managed to do it in 63 hours and 47 minutes.

That was a great test. We were up in the wilderness of Minnesota and Canada, running through the woods in the darkness carrying a canoe on our heads. Ray was about 270 pounds then, and had never been in a canoe before. I was about 185 pounds and I was in the back of the canoe. Sometimes I'd dip my oar to row and I didn't hit the water because the back of the canoe was sitting up so high. Ray and I didn't balance the canoe very well, with him up front and me in the back. So we struggled at times.

It was our first year out of football. We began it on the same day that training camp opened for the Steelers that year. It was very symbolic to us. After we finished, we were standing in a cabin in the woods, completely wiped out, and Ray said this was as good as winning a Super Bowl. Now maybe if we had thought about it for awhile we wouldn't have felt that way.

It really wasn't as big a thrill as winning the Super Bowl. For one thing the course record was 48 hours, set by two young bucks, so we didn't do such a great job. Just surviving it was an achievement for us.

For one thing, no one really paid any attention to this event. Most people said, "Why would you do that?" There was no real crowd. There was no TV. No one wrote about it at the time. No one really cared.

But we did something like that every year. Some long hike, climbing mountains. We even climbed mountains in Nepal with Mel Blount. It kept us in shape. We had to work out in preparation for these events. Just like we used to get ready for training camp. We had to work out or we couldn't have done the things we did.

It was an annual gut-test. I wrote about this in my first book, *A Steeler Odyssey*.

One of our favorite places was the Grand Canyon. We both loved to take hikes through the Grand Canyon. We'd gone on a dozen different Grand Canyon hikes. It's so beautiful. It's a symbolic place to do a three-day backpacking hike. To do that, we had to be in good shape. Those backpacks weigh about 50 pounds and they feel heavier the longer you're hiking.

He called me to do it one more time in November of 1996. I couldn't do it. I had a business commitment. So he went with his son Jim and a friend of Jim's. I was out looking at a factory we wanted to buy in Arizona, so I met him at the airplane gate in Phoenix when they arrived there. He was surprised to see me. I told him I wanted to see him before he went on this hike without me. It's eerie that I saw him just before he left for that last hike.

He didn't seem sure that he wanted to do it. I think he was concerned about what shape he was in, and he'd been having some health issues. He was trying to find ways not to do it. Something was wrong. His body was telling him something. But he was a play-hurt kind of guy, so he went. His death on that hike was devastating to me. We had become much closer friends after football. He was like a brother to me.

We had gone round the world giving speeches together. I was his straight man. They were serendipitous experiences.

"We thought it was a good way to get out and meet people."

The current Steelers have a certain attitude about what they'll do in the community. The more money they make the less willing they are to make appearances for free, or for a few thousand dollars. They don't need to do it, or at least they don't think they do. Being invited to speak at a charity-related fund-raiser becomes an onerous deal.

When I was playing our thinking was different. It was a good way to get out and sell yourself, and to do some good in the community at the same time. We thought it was a good way to meet people So if somebody offered us a free dinner we'd go out.

You learned how to express yourself. Some guys go out and take the money but they don't think about what they're going to say, or they're not dressed properly and they get up and say, "I don't know what to say." Yet they're looking for a payday.

We viewed it as a good business opportunity. Plus, the Pittsburgh Steelers wanted us to be ambassadors for the organization, and to be a catalyst for getting things accomplished in the community. It was important to put your best face forward. I did it all through the '60s and then started doing it on a world-wide basis in the '70s. I went to Tokyo, Japan for the Sony Corporation. I remember signing autographs with Lynn Swann in Tokyo, and people were standing in a long line, out in the rain. You couldn't see the end of the line. It was like nothing we'd ever experienced here.

I did some things in Europe, too, and I remember telling Dan Rooney that the NFL ought to have some exhibition games over in Europe. I thought there was great interest there in what we were doing. Dan thought I was nuts.

Now they have NFL Europe. The Steelers have played exhibition games in Barcelona and Dublin, as well as Mexico City. I enjoy my work. I hope to work till I die. It's fun. There's a teamwork here, too, and a real sense of camaraderie. There's a wonderful sense of accomplishment. Life's been pretty good. I've been very fortunate. I have great partners and wonderful opportunities.

I'm glad I grew up in the National Football League when I did. Most of my teammates were fortunate to go out and reach their potential in other ways. I played until I was 35, and not too many guys are that lucky. I never missed a game in high school, college, the Army, or in pro ball. The Steelers had connections to keep me out of a two-year stint in the Army, and I could have gotten a deal with a reserve unit. But I was in ROTC at school and felt I should serve. I'm proud of that.

There's a part of me that doesn't want to live in the past. I'm trying to wean myself of the devil ego. But I still know right from wrong, and I still have my standards for how to do things right. I have some thoughts that I think would help these young guys, if they'd take the time to listen.

Today the players don't feel the urgency to create careers for themselves beyond football. They make so much money that if they handle their money properly they may never have to work again in their lives. I'm not sure that is such a good thing.

You find yourself 35, or usually younger than that, and you have all the money you need for the rest of your life. You might find yourself playing too much golf, and not having enough to amuse yourself. Some people think you should recreate yourself every ten years anyhow.

Today's athletes have another sort of challenge. It's hard to feel sorry for anyone retiring at age 30 with all the money they'll ever need, but I can see the negative side of it, too. You

Photos by Jim O'Brien

Former placekicker Matt Bahr, a Penn State grad, remains in Mt. Lebanon. He is a partner in Radio WBUS in State College, and does volunteer work in a national educational program for Health South.

Robin Cole, a former Steelers' linebacker, lives in 84, Pennsylvania. He conducts programs for middle school students on behalf of Body Masters Sports Industries, Inc. He is president of the Pittsburgh chapter of the NFL Players' Association.

Craig Bingham, former Steelers' linebacker, has served several terms as president of the Pittsburgh chapter of the NFL Alumni. He lives in the South Hills and owns and operates Federal Enterprises Freight Lines, Inc. Bingham, Cole and Bahr all participated in Andy Russell's 26th Anniversary Celebrity Classic at The Club at Nevillewood.

John Brown, a tackle in the late '60s, is a retired PNC Bank executive living in Pittsburgh's North Hills. He remains an officer of the Allegheny Club and has resumed taking piano lessons at the African-American Music Institute in Homewood.

need to have meaning in your life, a sense of purpose, and other mountains to climb.

They used to have me come in and talk to the players about their "life's work" and about money. John Brown, who was an executive with PNC Bank, would come in and tell them how to open bank accounts and how to budget themselves. I'd talk about investments and about getting involved with the corporate community while you were playing.

I was lecturing them, and scolding them somewhat. I told them there were too many fancy cars in the parking circle outside the Steelers' offices at Three Rivers Stadium. I told them they didn't need fancy cars and fancy clothes. I said, "Don't buy any restaurants." I told them to go back to school and do whatever they had to do to get their degrees. I told them to meet people and get another career started while they were playing. After awhile, they didn't want to hear that, or to hear from me. I was going over like a pregnant pole-vaulter.

So they don't call on me to do that anymore.

"This is a guy I want to play for. He understands."

I've always been an admirer of Chuck Noll, even when I was playing for him. And I look at how he's handling his retirement. You don't see his name popping up when coaching jobs come open. That's behind him now. He has other interests. He's still doing things here to help where he can with community projects.

To see how he turned it around, to see how he handled it in 1969 when the Steelers went 1-13 in his first season. He kept it together. He kept his cool. I remember how respectful he was. I had huge respect for him when I was playing for him, and I have even more for him now.

I remember a game where I made a mistake and it cost us a touchdown. I was the first person in the Stadium who knew it was a mistake. I gave up a touchdown. I came off the field and I was waiting to get hollered at. I went over to the end of the sideline as far from him as I could get. He took his time and he came down and stood next to me. In a quiet voice, he asked me, "Andy, on that play, what was your thought process?"

I said, "Chuck, they've run that formation only ten times in the last five years, and they've run off it a total of nine times, and they threw a pass once. Why would they run the play and pass first before they'd run the ball and set it up for the pass?"

He looked at me, and smiled at me. He said, "Maybe they know how you think."

Then he walked away. I told myself, "This is a guy I want to play for. He understands."

Chuck was very leery of the media. He was always cautioning us to be careful about what we said to reporters. He didn't want us discussing strategy or our plans for an upcoming opponent. He didn't want us to say anything that would aid the enemy. In 1976, we may have had our best team, but Franco Harris and Rocky Bleier were both hurt and unable to play when we met the Oakland Raiders in the AFC championship game at Oakland. We'd been using a two-back offense all year and we went with a one-back offense in that game, using Frenchy Fuqua and Reggie Harrison as that one-back. Al Davis had managed to get someone into the Allegheny Club who watched us practice all that week. They knew what we were doing on every call. Ray Mansfield said they were calling out our plays before the ball was snapped. We were trying to win three Super Bowls in a row, but we lost that game (24-7). It's one of the reasons Noll has never been a big fan of Al Davis.

Chuck Noll's greatest legacy is that he taught us how to be a team without ego. There was no locker room politics, no jealousies. We'd stay after practice to help young players work on their technique. It was a wonderful environment. Players could definitely have an input into game plan. We were involved strategically.

We were totally committed to the game plan. Once we did it, Noll told us not to change it, or go in a different direction. Once we decided how we were going to attack another team, offensively and defensively, we were going to do it the best way.

Sometimes practice films showed I was wrong, sometimes they showed that I was right. Sometimes the game films showed we were all wrong. I tried to take those old-school values I learned from my family and teachers and with the Steelers into the business world. I think they work in both places.

I spend money these days on experiences. Some day when we're lying on our death bed we're not going to think about how much money we made. We're going to think about what we did and with whom we did it. And how we did it. I think it's a good idea along the way to make sure you invest in friends.

You have to find the right people and surround yourself with them to be successful in whatever you do. That's what the Steelers did. They did it the right way and, as Noll said, we did whatever it takes to be winners.

Jim O'Brien

Merril Hoge
Still a Big Sky guy

"Everybody loves Merril."
— Jimmy Krenn, WDVE

Merril Hoge looked like he'd just come back from elk hunting. He hadn't shaved his face in a few days, and his dark brown hair with the gold highlights didn't seem quite right. He looked disheveled. He had called and pushed back our luncheon meeting by an hour to 1 p.m. and then showed up at 1:35 p.m. with an apologetic greeting. "Just be glad," I said, almost sternly, "I'm not Chuck Noll."

"I wouldn't be having lunch like this with Chuck Noll," he said, flashing a crooked smile, as he slipped into our booth table at Atria's Restaurant & Tavern on Rt. 19 in Wexford. This was Thursday, April 25, 2002. It was sunny and bright, with temperatures in the mid-50s.

"You're right, though," he added. "If I had a meeting with Chuck Noll I would not be late." He stressed the "not" in that sentence.

I was originally planning on watching the Pirates play a matinee game that afternoon, but I didn't get to PNC Park until the last inning of their 3-1 victory over the Dodgers. Everybody was in a good mood by the time I arrived.

Hoge did say that he had killed two black bears on a hunting trip in British Columbia a week earlier. One of them was 6-8, the other 7-2, according to Hoge, so they were big black bears. It's legal to kill more than one bear, as long as you have proper tags, in British Columbia. He also does some elk hunting. He'd have been a natural to have been on with Curt Gowdy when he had the "American Sportsman" show on ABC-TV in the '70s.

Hoge had a meeting the same day we met with Noll's successor, Bill Cowher, at the Steelers' offices at the UPMC Sports Complex on the city's South Side. The Steelers were starting a three-day rookie orientation the following day and Hoge wanted to talk to Cowher about his first-year class, the state of the Steelers, and to see what Cowher thought about other NFL doings.

Hoge is happy he can have such conversations with Bill Cowher. He calls on him frequently. Hoge does his homework, which is one of his great strengths as a football analyst. He works hard at getting inside information.

"I get to go to a lot of NFL facilities these days, and none of them is as nice as the Steelers' facilities," said Hoge. "They're at the top of the class now; that's for sure. It's phenomenal."

Hoge had on a Steelers' windbreaker, black with gold sleeves, and "Steelers" in gold in the center of his chest, just above a Nike swoosh logo. Hoge reports on the NFL at large for ESPN, among other outlets, but his heart still belongs to the Steelers.

Photos by Jim O'Brien

Toni and Merril Hoge were hosts for Caring Foundation golf outing at Southpointe in May, 2002. Bill Hillgrove, 'the Voice of the Steelers,' was among the celebrities who answered the call from, left to right, Mark Bruener, Hoge and Hines Ward.

Only the week before, during a draft day show on ESPN, sidekick Ron Jaworksi had kidded Hoge about his insider status with the Steelers. During an interview with Cowher, who was speaking from Steelers' headquarters via satellite transmission, Jaworski asked Cowher if it were true that he had Hoge present at all Steelers' team meetings. "We game plan every Wednesday with Merril," came back Cowher with his ear-to-ear grin, going along with the roasting. "We go over our draft picks with him, too."

That exchange threw off Hoge's concentration, he later admitted, and he forgot what he wanted to ask Cowher. The question that begged to be asked was this: "Why did the Steelers select Antwaan Randle El over Antonio Bryant with their second pick?"

There had to be some rationale for why the Steelers selected a 5-9$\frac{1}{2}$ quarterback with speed and agility from Indiana over a 6-1 proven pass-catcher from Pittsburgh to join their receiver corps.

Hoge had a chance to ask Cowher that question this time around, when the two were talking at Steelers' headquarters. Hoge thinks the Steelers did the right thing. "They already have two head cases at wide receiver in Plaxico Burress and Troy Edwards, and they didn't want a third at the same position," said Hoge. "They'd feed off each other. If you lose your locker room you lose your team. Everyone has a problem child or two, but you can't have a bunch." Cowher knew that Bryant was a problem better than anybody, said Hoge, because the Steelers share practice fields and facilities with the University of Pittsburgh football team. "He knows that Bryant was often late for practice and drills," said Hoge. "When he interviewed him at the combine in Indianapolis, Bryant talked to Bill like Bill wasn't aware of his background. Bill knows better. El Randle is going to give them some great flexibility. He might be something special."

Hoge and Jaworski watch game tapes of pro action several days a week, and they watched tapes of college action as well in preparation for their NFL draft coverage. Jaworski, who came out of Youngstown State to quarterback the Philadelphia Eagles, is famous for his dedication to watching game tapes. He knows his stuff.

Merril gets very analytical when he discusses NFL teams such as the Steelers. He knows the numbers, the statistics, the plays, the tendencies, you name it. "I'd be a much smarter football player today," he said.

Hoge was one of the best running backs in Steelers' history. A fullback, he ranked eighth in total offensive yards (5,169), just ahead of Rocky Bleier (5,159) in the team's record book. Hoge was tenth in rushing yards (3,115), seventh in pass receptions (241), ninth in rushing touchdowns (27), and 16th in scoring (204 points). He scored three touchdowns in a game twice, against the Los Angeles Rams and Miami Dolphins.

Hoge was working with Jaworski and Suzy Kolber as an analyst for Edge NFL Matchup, which airs on ESPN and ESPN2, and for The NFL on ESPN Radio, which airs 11 a.m.-7 p.m. Sundays throughout the season. Hoge also provides reports for Sunday NFL Countdown and serves as an on-site reporter for that two-hour pre-game show. Additionally, he provides game analysis for ESPN's coverage of the Arena Football League. Hoge joined ESPN in 1996, working as game analyst and sideline reporter for ESPN2's college football coverage.

He continues to check in Monday mornings with Jimmy Krenn and Randy Baumann on WDVE Radio in Pittsburgh. Hoge has been doing that since his second season with the Steelers. "We like him," commented Krenn when I talked to him about Hoge two days later when I saw him at a book-signing at Waldenbooks at Ross Park Mall. "He tells some funny stories. He can crack you up. Once in awhile, we talk about football, too. Everybody loves Merril."

Hoge maintains a residence in Sewickley, a suburb north of Pittsburgh, and joins his family each week at a home in Fort Thomas, Kentucky. He also keeps a home in his native Idaho, on an island called Island Park. He has a lot of frequent flyer miles on his airline accounts. "I tried to file taxes using USAirways and Delta Airlines as my home," he said. "I'm on those planes all the time."

An eight-year NFL veteran, Hoge spent 1987-1993 with the Pittsburgh Steelers, playing for both Noll and Cowher in his career and was the Steelers' starting fullback for five of those seasons. He was with Noll for three seasons, then two with Cowher. Hoge set the team record for most receptions by a running back, totaling 50 in 1988. He concluded his career with the Chicago Bears after the 1994 season because of suffering too many concussions in his playing career.

"I'm the poster boy for concussion stories in the NFL," said Hoge.

A 1987 Idaho State graduate with a degree in education, Hoge set 11 school records, including career rushing attempts, career rushing yards, career all-purpose yards, season rushing attempts, season rushing yards and season all-purpose yards. He also scored 44 touchdowns, a Big Sky Conference record.

Hoge came to the Steelers as a starry-eyed small town boy. It remains part of his charm. "The Steelers asked me to speak at a midget football league banquet," he said to an audience at St. Agatha's Church in Bridgeville way back then, "and I went there fully expecting to find midgets to hear me speak. I'd never heard about midget football before." Hoge still says it took some time before he got used to Eastern ways.

He used to run successful summer football camps, but he turned those over to Jerome Bettis and Mark Bruener, current members of the Steelers.

He has been married to Toni for nearly ten years, and they have two children, daughter Kori, 9, and son, Beau, 5. His younger brother, Marty, 36, was with him at Atria's. He's two inches taller than Merril, and much more muscular. He was wearing a black leather jacket with lots of chains, and I could see some tattoos on his upper torso. Marty Hoge looks like a biker who lifts weights. He runs a car rental agency back in Idaho.

Merril remains busy in the Pittsburgh community. He is chairman of the board for Caring Foundation, which is affiliated with Blue Cross & Blue Shield. He sponsors a golf tournament at Southpointe to raise funds for it. He used to host it along with Kordell Stewart, but does it now with Bruener and Hines Ward. Beginning with his third year with the Steelers, the Caring Foundation has been his primary project.

Two former running backs of the Steelers died, coincidentally, the week before my meeting with Hoge. Their names appear on some of the same pages as Hoge in the Steelers' media guide. Joe Geri, a tailback when the Steelers used the single-wing offense, and was third in the NFL in passing and rushing in 1950, died at age 78 in Milledgeville, Georgia after a lengthy illness. Geri came to the Steelers from the University of Georgia in 1949 and played three seasons. The Steelers went to a T-formation offense with Jim Finks as the quarterback, and Geri went on to play one more season in the NFL with the Chicago Cardinals.

Sam Francis, a former fullback with the Steelers, died two days before my meeting with Hoge, at age 83 at his home in Springfield, Missouri. Francis was an All-American as a senior at the University of Nebraska in 1936, when he was runner-up for the Heisman Trophy to Yale's Larry Kelley. Francis was named to the College Hall of Fame in 1977. He also placed fourth in the shotput at the 1936 Olympic Games.

He played for the Steelers in 1939, sandwiched in between stints with the Chicago Cardinals and Brooklyn Dodgers.

Hoge enjoys learning more about Steelers' history. It makes him even prouder of his participation with the Pittsburgh franchise. The Steelers had their ups and downs in the '80s, but they turned out more than their share of TV and radio analysts in Hoge, Terry Bradshaw, Mark Malone, Jack Ham, Tunch Ilkin, Craig Wolfley and Edmund Nelson.

Merril Hoge:

I am often asked to compare Chuck Noll with Bill Cowher, my coaches during my days with the Steelers. That's easy. Chuck is like playing for your dad that you respect, and Bill is like playing for your big brother that you admire. They are both completely different men, completely different coaches. Chuck is a teacher and Bill is more of a motivator. They've both been successful, so there's no one way to be a winner.

Now that I see Bill today I realize that, as a coach, he was definitely a work in progress when he first came to Pittsburgh. I respect him for adjusting things that he thought were the word of God in the beginning. He made a rule on our team that you would never lose your spot because of an injury.

Neil O'Donnell was hurt for four weeks in Bill's first year (1992), and had given way to Bubby Brister at quarterback. We went 11-5. Bill started Neil in the playoff game with Buffalo. We lost that game (24-3) and the Bills never should have beaten us. To this day, Bill will admit that was a mistake. From now on, he said he was going to make the decision in the best interest of the team, not by any rules.

Some people might think he made the same mistake when he brought Jerome Bettis back this past year after he had missed six games and started him in the AFC championship game against the New England Patriots. I'm not one of them. He thought Bettis was his best back, his best chance to win. I know he's been criticized by the fans and media for doing that.

I don't think that was the problem. People don't realize that Amos Zereoue had more carries for less yards in the first quarter than Bettis did. I don't know if anybody could have gained any yardage that day the way the Patriots were playing their defense. Even so, if you throw one play away — a punt return on special teams — and the Steelers win the game. In talking to the New England people, they had a key — and they wouldn't tell me what it was — and they knew what the Steelers were doing. New England had the right game plan and it wouldn't have mattered if Walter Payton was running the ball against them.

That was one of the better defensive coordinating schemes I've seen at work. They had the right scheme and, more important, the performance. You had about 16 guys who had to learn that scheme and execute it properly. That's not easy to do in three days. They knew what the Steelers were going to run. They had it all figured out.

The guys at ESPN wanted me to shave my head after the Steelers lost that game. I had said at Week Ten that I would shave my head if they didn't win the Super Bowl. I thought they were the best team in the NFL. How could a team that was so dominant, especially in the running game, get stopped like that? I don't know a team that was more balanced in the league. They ran 51 per cent of their plays to the right, and 49 per cent of their plays to the left. They ran 51 per cent of their plays to the strong side — where your tight end is lined up —

and 49 per cent to the weak side. How's that for balance? They were like that in everything you can imagine. The New York Giants were 70 to 30 in those same categories.

There's no doubt in my mind the Steelers would have destroyed the Rams in the Super Bowl. I think they have a great chance this year. They were drafting for depth. They have their team ready to go.

When I watched the tape of that game I could see what they were doing. I knew what the tendencies were from different formations. I knew that when I was playing, too. But I'm much smarter now. I have the luxury of being able to call coaches like Jeff Fisher at Tennessee and Bill Cowher in Pittsburgh and Brian Billick in Baltimore, and many others, and I get to explore with them. I get all this massive information from some of the great minds. I think some of those guys would love to have those same kinds of conversations with other coaches. Bill Cowher and Brian Billick would like to tap into each other's thinking.

I learned a lot from Chuck Noll in my early NFL days. I tried to emulate him, and do what he wanted done. He spoke about striking a rising blow, and how first contact wins, and same foot same shoulder, stuff like that, and it stays with you. They were all teaching components.

If you remember and practice what he told you, you'll win.

Chuck Noll came up to me once at camp and said something to me that stays with me till this very day. I had led the team in rushing and receiving the year before, and no one trained harder. In fact, if anything, I trained too hard.

I had a sore hamstring that I pulled before I came to camp. I had bruised my shoulder and cracked a rib at camp. I was a wreck. I was having a difficult time doing what I was supposed to do. I was warming up the quarterbacks this day, and he came up to me and stood next to me. He said, "They said you were just a flash in the pan, and I defended you. But I guess they were right." I wanted to wring his neck. How dare he say that to me. I was fuming. He got the best of me that day. It stayed with me all year. We turned it around that year and went to the playoffs. We almost went to the Super Bowl.

That year (1989) was amazing. He was testing my character when he made those remarks to me that day at camp. It was like a 500-pound wrecking ball came out of the sky and took me out.

The year before that, he called me the stupidest football player in the world. That's when I called out some numbers we previously used to call out punt blocking assignments. I didn't block my man and he blocked the punt. I called the wrong numbers twice, and we got away with it once. I also dropped a pass — I thought it should have been an incomplete pass — and Robin Cole, whom we had dealt to the New York Jets, picked it up and ran it in for a touchdown. It cost us the game (24-20). Chuck's going crazy. He came after me and screamed, "You have to be the stupidest football player I've ever seen in my life." I did this in New York. After the game, I had media guys eight deep at my locker. It was like I was the Super Bowl MVP.

I was the last guy to shower that day. And when I went in the shower there was only one guy left in there and that was Chuck Noll. He had soap in his hair and on his body, but he ran out of there because he did not want to share a shower room with me. I was in a hurry to get out of his way, too.

When I left the stadium, I got in the first bus. There were two seats open by the door. I sat down in one of them. I forgot that the first bus is always the coach's bus, that the first seat is the coach's seat. He got on the bus and went and stood in the back of the bus all the way to the airport. That day was my worst nightmare. But you know what? He made me the team captain the following year.

That's probably why Terry Bradshaw didn't like him. He didn't praise you and cater to you all the time. That man taught me more than any teacher or coach I had in my life.

I remember another incident with Noll. We lost at Denver (24-23) in one of the best playoff games ever. That was at the end of the 1989 season. We get to the airport in Denver and we find out our flight is going to be delayed. Tim Worley is playing some jazz music in the back of the airplane. Noll comes back in the plane and all of us were a little nervous, not knowing what he was going to say or do. He talked to us for about 45 minutes about jazz and wine. Nobody would believe that. Some coaches might have blown up when they heard someone listening to music after such a tough loss. Not Noll. He was telling us some places in Pittsburgh to go for good jazz, and telling us about good wines. He was talking to us like nothing else happened that day. We'd just lost the most important game of the year by one point. People wouldn't believe it.

That was the year we got beat 51-0 in the home opener against the Cleveland Browns, and 41-10 in the second game at Cincinnati. We bounced back from that to go 9-7, and we beat Houston (26-23) in the wild-card playoff, and we should have beaten Denver, too. Noll really turned things around that year. It showed the kind of coach he really was.

I've read a lot about General George Patton, especially about him during the 1940-1945 period. When I read about him the only guy who went through my mind was Chuck Noll. The way he handles people, how he handles things. Sometimes he knocks you down and leaves you in the mud, but he helps you to survive. He pats you on the back when you need that, too.

Dick Hoak was a great backfield coach. Dick could get across a teaching point in fewer words than any coach I can remember. If you were having trouble with your timing, he'd say, "Take an open step before you go into the line. That'll take care of it." And it did. He didn't go into any dissertations, and he didn't flare up at you. He was always calm when he talked to you.

He was great at halftime. He knew what was up, and what we needed to do. He was always right on target. I love Hoakie.

"You win with character guys."

When Bill Cowher was at the Senior Bowl (after the 2001 season), he was checking out Ian Gold, who ended up with the Denver Broncos. He said he couldn't take his eye off Kendrell Bell at the workouts and in the game itself. Someone told Cowher that Kendrell Bell couldn't play in the league. Cowher felt otherwise; he thought he could be a great player.

He was right. I've never seen a guy with as much explosive power as Kendrell Bell. I was walking by the linebackers at training camp last year and I stopped and watched him. He was doing some dynamic stuff. They had signed Mike Jones from the Rams to take the place of Levon Kirkland, but this guy was going after that opening himself.

They say Ray Lewis is the best inside linebacker in the game today. I'm telling you Kendrell Bell will be the best linebacker; he'll set the standard. Maybe of all the Steelers' linebackers in the team's history, he'll be regarded as the best. No one else will ever surpass Jack Lambert for toughness and game-day nastiness, but Kendrell Bell will be talked about with the great ones.

He ran over the center in the first game with Jacksonville. Jeff Fisher of the Titans said he'd never seen anything like it in ten years. Against Kansas City, he ran over the guard, and knocked the guard into the quarterback, Trent Green, who banged into the running back. It was like dominoes falling down in row. He did something like that against Cleveland. He hit a back so hard you couldn't believe it.

I played against Mike Singletary and Lawrence Taylor. Kendrell Bell has more power than both of those guys. He's a team guy. He has some special qualities. When all is said and done, he'll be the standard.

> *"I don't care who he is; I care what he is."*
> — Toni Hoge, talking about her
> husband Merril Hoge

I think they have a great running back in Jerome Bettis. No one is more physical, and runs harder, yet he fumbles once or twice year. He really takes care of the ball. Earl Campbell, by now, was done. Jerome has the same mindset as Earl Campbell, but he continues on, at age 30, and he's still running strong.

I like Kordell Stewart, too. I think he's a scary player. I know people are still reserved in their judgment about him because they want him to get them to the Super Bowl. They want him to win the close games. He'll close the door this time.

After what he's been through, a lot of people would have folded. I think Mike Mularkey has been a savior for him. What Mike has done is cater all the plays to the strength of Kordell Stewart. Kevin Gilbride was a philosophy guy, like Joe Walton. Here's the way we're gonna do this. It still blows me away that some offensive coordinators think their system is the only way to win. You have to work with what you have to work with. That goes for college coaches, too. You have go with your strengths and hide your weaknesses. But they don't want to leave the comfort zone of what they believe in.

I look at the game a lot differently these days. That's why I can appreciate a player like Mark Bruener. He does so much that doesn't show up in the stats. The Steelers don't throw to him much, but he has a tremendous effect on their passing game as well as their running game.

I've tabbed him as being the best blocking tight end in the game today. Most teams want to put a defensive end on a tight end, but you can't create a mismatch you want with Mark out there. You will need help from a linebacker or defensive back to neutralize him. When you do that you're more vulnerable in the secondary. You end up with single coverage on somebody like Plaxico Burress or Hines Ward, and they have a chance to win the battle for the ball.

It's less coverage for Kordell to read. With less people in the secondary it limits what they can do, and how many coverages they can show. The passing game doesn't have to be complicated. When they played the Jets, Kordell completed something like 22 of 31 passes, and about 15 of those completions came on plays where Kordell was reading just one guy. Bruener is an MVP person as well as an MVP player. Your book won't be long enough to write about him as a person. It permeates the way he practices. He is a character guy. You win with character guys.

I don't think people will consider him a star, but he makes a major contribution to that club, and they're not the same without him. He would have been a factor if he hadn't hurt his shoulder and missed the playoffs.

"Little things like saying grace before dinner are important. I want to instill the same values I was taught."
— Mark Bruener

I think they got a great second round pick this year, too, when they took Antwaan Randle El of Indiana instead of Antonio Bryant of Pitt. Cowher interviewed them at Indianapolis at the pro combine. They'll see at the end that Cowher made the right choice. The fans will be split about the selection, thinking they should or shouldn't have taken Bryant. They'll see what Randle El brings to the game. They did the right thing for the team. They need a guy like this. He's like Hines Ward. He's not selfish.

Hines Ward, to me, is the epitome of a rough and tough football player. Forget about his receiving skills. I've never seen a receiver physically dominate a game like he did against the Baltimore Ravens. On the first three plays, he went up and looked up Rod Woodson and Jamie Sharpe. He nailed both of them. Ward deserves credit for the 80-yard touchdown pass to Bobby Shaw in that game. Ward ran a little post and Woodson wanted to get him back for what he'd done to him earlier. Woodson left an area where he should've been and it put Shaw in a situation where he could make a great catch. Stewart threw an unbelievable pass, too, but it was Ward who made it work. Woody wanted to get Ward. I don't know a receiver in the game who brings the kind of physical play to the game as Hines Ward.

For the purist, it was great to see a team become the best and stay up there for awhile. They did it through the draft. That was awesome in its time. You had the Steelers and the 49ers, the Cowboys and the Raiders. They all had their day. With this new generation, there's hope for everybody. A team like the Rams or the Patriots can come up from nowhere to win it all. They used to be pitiful. With free agency and the salary cap, every city has a chance. That's not the case in baseball. The odds are so stacked against a small-market franchise like the Pirates.

With the Steelers of the '70s, that was the epitome of football. You had the total concept. Chuck used to break down the game into three elements — offense, defense and special teams — and that, even on your good days, you're probably going to lose one of those. But if you win two of three you should win.

Players today are bigger, stronger and faster but, still to this day, if you gave me the 11 best defensive players in the game today at all the positions, I don't know if they'd be as good as the Steelers' starting defense during the glory days of the '70s. I don't know if you could exceed the quality of that group. They were just remarkable. And it'll never happen again. You can't keep a group like that together anymore.

Edge NFL Matchup on ESPN has expert panel consisting of, left to right, Merril Hoge, Ron Jaworski and Suzy Kolber. They kid Hoge about his loyalty to Steelers and his close relationship with Coach Bill Cowher.

Jim O'Brien

Merril Hoge is joined by Tony Ferraro, executive sales director at Pittsburgh Brewing Co., and Pittsburgh restaurateur Don DeBlasio at Atria's Restaurant & Tavern in Wexford.

I'm not surprised if they were flat for the Patriots. I was an honorary captain and on the sideline for the game with Baltimore the week before. Joey Porter almost got into a fight with Sam Adams. Then Earl Holmes almost got into it with Shannon Sharpe over something Sharpe had said during the week. They were talking about respect. Maybe they spent all their emotional energy in that game. That was their championship game.

"That's the team I grew up loving."

I saw the four Lombardi Trophies in the hallway when I walked into the Steelers' offices at Three Rivers Stadium for the first time. It was impressive. Winning four Super Bowls in six seasons was a hard act to follow.

In the '80s, when I first got here, I'd go into the huddle and I'd be seeing John Stallworth and Mike Webster, and I knew I was in great company. These were the Steelers who'd been on all those great teams!

The first guy I had to block in practice was Donnie Shell. He hit me harder than anybody had ever hit me.

No, I never felt it was a bad shadow. I grew up loving that shadow. That's the team I grew up loving. It was no big deal to me that we were measured against those teams. Thirty years down the road that shadow will still be there. I don't know if it's as dark or as long.

That's the standard; that's the way I see it. You have to go back to the top man to have that kind of cornerstone. It goes from The Chief to Dan Rooney to young Art. Contrast that to the Tampa Bay ownership, which has always been screwed up. Look at William Snyder now in Washington; he has no clue as to what this is all about.

That's why the Redskins will always be the laughing stock of the league. This is not a rotisserie league. He's not a good football person. He's a fan with a lot of money. The Rooneys respect the game too much to talk the way he does about their players and their prospects. They hire the coach and let him coach the team.

I still do stuff for the Steelers and I'll always have a place in Pittsburgh. I love Pittsburgh. I like the people here. There's no better city in America.

We were trying to rebuild when I got here. The Steelers were trying to get back to where they were in the '70s. We struggled. We were not very good for awhile, but we became very good in 1989. We had the right personnel. Defensively, we were strong. We needed another wide receiver on offense.

I still blame Tom Moore (in jest) for ruining my career. He was our offensive coordinator, but he went to Minnesota because he thought he had a better chance to become a head coach if he went there. He left after the 1989 season when we had gotten to the playoffs. Joe Walton came in as the offensive coordinator for the 1990 season. Our personnel simply didn't fit Walton's philosophy. We really rebelled against what he wanted us to do. We resented all the changes he made. We were as close as an offense to saying we're not playing as you could come. Noll laid down the law with us, and got us back on the job.

I loved Joe Walton as a person, but I was as confused as anybody by what he wanted us to do. People say Bubby Brister wasn't smart enough to run Joe's complicated offensive schemes, but Bubby knew it better than anybody else on the team. Bubby had a better command of it than we did.

We were playing at New Orleans late that season, in mid-December, I believe. It was like a heavyweight fight. That's when New Orleans had a great defense. We're trailing 6-3 late in the fourth quarter. We're at the New Orleans 45-yard line. Its third-and-ten. Bubby called the play in the huddle and no one knew what to do. I'd been playing football for 24 years and I didn't know what to do. I started panicking. Bubby started swearing at everybody. That was his answer to all problems.

He put me in the right position, but I still didn't know what I was supposed to do. Tim Worley says, "What's it on?" Bubby starts swearing again. He's calling us stupid this and that. He repeats that it's on a 2-count. When Bubby turned around, Worley flips him off with a hand gesture. Louie Lipps ran some route downfield and I went out in the flat. Bubby throws me the ball and I go down the sideline nearly all the way. It was a first down on the one-yard line, and we ended up scoring to win the game (9-6). Walton was furious, even though we got a first down. We hadn't run the right play. We all ran the wrong way.

It was that way for two years. We were always a game away from getting into the playoffs. He had us doing things we weren't good at doing. We didn't make the playoffs either year, and we were good enough to make it. He had me running sweeps, for instance, and I wasn't any good at that. They were pitching me the ball, but I didn't have the speed to get outside.

When Bill Cowher came in he assessed our strengths and weaknesses, and he straightened us out. He geared his philosophy to fit our personnel. He came in and created our own identity. Walton was always talking about how the Redskins or the Jets did this and that, and players hate that. They want to hear about the Steelers.

325

One of the big things Cowher did was cut Huey Richardson. He was the Steelers' No. 1 pick in 1991. He was a linebacker from Florida. He was the worst football player of all the 80 players we had in camp in 1992. It was Cowher's first year, and Richardson's second year.

That sent a message. That said something. Everyone gravitated toward Cowher after that. They knew he was going to keep the best players.

Another thing he did was to call a fake punt against Houston, and we ended up scoring. They were the Central champs but we beat them twice in Cowher's first year. That helped win the players over, too.

We had two quarterbacks who couldn't have been more different personality-wise and yet they were both winners. I'm talking, of course, about Bubby Brister and Neil O'Donnell. Bubby was a gun-slinging, old-fashioned western star like John Wayne, and Neil was soft-spoken, quiet...it's hard to find somebody who was like him. They were complete opposites. They didn't know how to manage Bubby's enthusiasm and excitement. Bubby would come to the sideline to get a play from the coach and he'd be spittin' and swearin' and wanting to get back out there. Neil was more cerebral, more patient. I'm sure he was smarter.

If it was third and ten, Bubby didn't want to punt. He wanted to go for a first down. Neil was not like that. He might have wanted to go for the first down, too, but he also knew the percentages. He'd say, "OK, Coach, give me something."

This was Bill's first year (1992) as a head coach. When you come in that first year you don't know what you're doing. I was talking to Jimmy Johnson during the draft and he said that in his first year in Dallas he had no clue about what he was supposed to be doing. He said he made it up as he went along. You can't fault those guys if they made some mistakes the first time around.

 Bill made the decision to go with Neil over Bubby, and you can't fault him for that. Both guys had their pros and cons about them. It's a shame they lost Neil when they did, just when he was beginning to blossom. It was Neil who took them to the Super Bowl (in 1995 season). If they don't have Neil they don't go to the Super Bowl. There's no two ways about that.

The interceptions cost them in that Super Bowl, but they weren't necessarily all Neil's fault. There was some miscommunication with the wide receivers. They weren't on the same page, as Noll liked to say. The fans turned against Neil. He had a chance to go back to New York, his home area, and make some big money. It's hard to fault him for that.

Players have options these days. It's not a one-way street. So Neil went home to New York. He grew up in New Jersey, and he has family there. Playing at home, though, is not so grandiose as it might appear to be. I'm sure he didn't like playing for Bill Parcells with the Jets. Parcells didn't like him. And he didn't like Parcells. Now's he got a great situation with the Tennessee Titans. He loves Jeff Fisher and Jeff Fisher loves him. He's the backup there, but he's played a lot and he's making big money. It should extend his career. He knows what he's doing.

"Hey, this is cool."

It was doing that show with the guys at WDVE that sparked my interest in the broadcasting business. When I was a rookie, I did an appearance on B94, and I was asked to call in each week. I did that for most of the season. The guys at WDVE heard me and liked what I was doing. Scott Paulsen and Jim Krenn called me. They wanted to know if I wanted to do a show with them each Monday morning after our games. I did the show at B94 for free — hey, I was a rookie — and now I was getting paid to do this. They wanted me to be in the studio. I said it was on my way to work, and I could do that. The first time I was in the studio I said, "Hey, this is cool." We talked about football maybe 30 percent of the time, and I'd tell stories about my elk hunting, and my high school days. I'd tell them about being in the huddle with Bubby. That's one of the funniest things I did. You never knew what was going to happen. They'd be talking about different subjects when I'd come in, and they'd ask me what I thought about something. And we'd be rolling. Something would spark some stories. I enjoyed that. I still do.

I had to give up football because I suffered too many concussions. One of my nicknames is "Brickhead," but I hardly rate that name. If my head were harder I might still be playing. I had six concussions in my football career, counting elementary school.

A lot of stuff I've found out about the lingering effects from concussions came too late for me to do anything about it. My vision is not the same. Sometimes my eyes go black, and sometimes one of my eyes is an inch higher than the other one. The doctors relate it back to my concussions.

I had three in the NFL. The last two came within five weeks of each other. I suffered head trauma in a Monday night game with Kansas City. For about ten to twelve hours, I didn't know who I was, or where I was. I shouldn't have been playing the next week, but I was. I ran the risk of suffering a fatal injury to the head.

I received more treatment for a blister on my foot than I did for my concussions.

Jim O'Brien

Hines Ward
The good son

"It's an honor to be in the NFL."

Hines Ward was playing for the Pittsburgh Steelers traveling basketball team on a Friday evening, April 26, against a team of local police officers at Bethel Park High School. Paul Zolak, the athletic director at Bethel Park, assisted me with credentials and was looking after me. Zolak was Joe Montana's backfield coach at Ringgold High School, where he also served a long tenure as athletic director, and he was the father of former NFL quarterback Scott Zolak.

Ward was on the same level as Scott Zolak when it came to being a class act and a personable young man who made you immediately comfortable in his company.

I liked Ward because of the way he played football, a clutch receiver who could block with the best of them, and a young man who always seemed to be enjoying himself. There was a sunshine about him.

He and Deshea Townsend kept taking turns attempting three-point shots and they both jumped up and pumped their fists toward the rafters when one of their long shots hit the nets. They had a little bet going on as to who would hit the most three-pointers. Ward was playful with everyone on the court. Ward wanted to win, of course, but he wasn't taking the game or himself too seriously. He joined his teammates in signing autographs for all the young fans at halftime.

He was most cooperative when I introduced myself and mentioned our mutual friend Dick Bestwick as an ice-breaker.

I first became aware of Ward when the Steelers drafted him out of the University of Georgia as their third round pick in 1998. Soon after, I received a scouting report from an old friend, Dick Bestwick, who served as an assistant athletic director in support services at Georgia. I first met Bestwick, who was from Grove City, when he was an assistant coach on Dave Hart's first staff at the University of Pittsburgh in 1966. He was later an assistant at Georgia Tech and the head football coach at the University of Virginia. He couldn't say enough good about Ward. He predicted that he would be a first-class performer for the Steelers on and off the field.

He said they had created a special award at Georgia to give to Ward to recognize his all-around scholar-athlete qualities. He was the first African-American athlete in the football or basketball programs to graduate with a 3.0 grade point average or better (3.1 GPA, to be exact) at Georgia. He made the All-Academic team in the SEC.

He played several positions for the Bulldogs. He played flanker, tailback, quarterback, tailback and quarterback in that order. Finally,

George Gojkovich

the coaches kept him at wide receiver. He finished his career ranked second in school history with 144 receptions and third in receiving yards with 1,965.

Ward finished his fourth season with the Steelers as the eighth-best pass-receiver in the National Football League with 94 catches to his credit good for 1,003 yards and a 10.7 yards-per-catch average. He was an alternate to the Pro Bowl and got to play when injuries forced others out of the game.

One of Ward's qualities is patience. Ward waits his turn. He outperformed two flashier, but seldom as consistent No. 1 draft choices at the wide receiver position in Pittsburgh, namely Troy Edwards and Plaxico Burress. Neither of those individuals performed as well as Ward, and they were problem children whereas Ward was a model citizen. Everybody liked Hines Ward.

People in Pittsburgh were pushing for him to change his name to Heinz Ward, so he would fit in even better at the Steelers' new playpen on Pittsburgh's North Shore. Then again, if he gets any better they might want to change the name of the home facility to Hines Field.

Ward, a 6-foot, 200-pound receiver, led the team in receiving in 2000 and 2001, tying Edwards with 61 catches and then topping Burress as the team's best. He became the starter at the flanker position, and left Burress and Edwards to battle for the starting wide receiver position.

"I'm not sure he's looking for the limelight," said Mike Mularkey, the Steelers' offensive coordinator in 2001. "He loves what he's doing and it shows."

Ward understood what his situation was and felt it best not to make waves. That wasn't his style. "They invested so much in Troy and Plaxico, so those guys were going to get all the attention," said Ward. "I'm pretty sure all eyes are going to be on those guys. And that's fine with me."

In truth, though, Steelers' fans felt more enamored with Ward right from the start, and appreciated his blue-collar work ethic, modest manner and marvelous demeanor. He was their kind of guy. He excelled his rookie year primarily as a hard-nosed tackler and blocker on special teams. He came into his own in his second season.

"He just quietly does his job in the run game and pass game," added Mularkey. "He makes plays over and over. Quarterbacks trust that. Your backs trust he's going to be in there blowing somebody up."

This is a guy who had the anterior cruciate ligament removed from his left knee because of a bicycle accident in fourth grade. Ward wants you to know he knows what's behind his success. "It's heart," he said. "You have to fight through it, fight through all that stuff that I've been through and keep producing on the field."

He gives much credit for his success to his mother, Young Ward, who was born in South Korea. Hines Ward Sr. met her when he was stationed with the U.S. Army in Seoul, South Korea. She was then called Kim Young He, and was a clerk in Seoul. They were married, Hines Jr. was born, and the family moved to the United States.

The marriage didn't last, though, and young Hines was sent to live with his father in Monroe, Louisiana. His father had been a good football player there in his youth. His mother worked at several jobs, saved her money and learned the English language. When Hines was 8, his mother was awarded custody of him by the courts. He was able to move in with his mother in Forest Park, just east of Atlanta's Hartsfield International Airport. There was still a language barrier.

He was a latchkey child from a broken, biracial home. He knew of no other family. There were no uncles, aunts or cousins. There was no father except for an occasional telephone call. His mother used to tell him, "I live every day of my life for you," and, in time, he realized how fortunate he was to have such a caring mother.

He spent much of his $150,000-plus rookie salary to improve her position in life. He signed a new $9.5 million contract in September, 2001 and upgraded her car from a Toyota Avalon to a Lexus. He had bought her a new home in suburban Stockbridge that first year as well.

"At first, it was kinda hard because I couldn't understand what she was telling me," he recalled. "I was a little kid. I wasn't used to being around her. I was pretty cruel. I deserved a whipping more than once."

The kids in the neighborhood made fun of him for having an Asian mother. "I remember ducking when she took me to school," he said. "I was kind of ashamed."

That's all changed as he learned to appreciate his mother and the impact she had on his development. "She is my inspiration," he said.

Hines Ward:

My mother raised me to be the way I am now. She never wanted people to look down upon us. Her name is Young Ward and she told me to treat people the way I wanted to be treated. It's that simple; it's the old golden rule. There was just the two of us, her and me. I was an only child. It was more of a team thing. She had to work two or three jobs, and she wasn't around as much as she'd have liked. So she wanted to make sure I didn't get into any trouble.

My mother still treats me like I'm a teenager.

She preached that I should respect everyone. She especially wanted me to respect my teachers. She said you may disagree with what they say, but you should always be respectful.

I was living by myself from an early age, and I had to learn responsibility. She would go to work early in the morning before I was up. She would make me breakfast and leave it out for me. I had to get up myself and fix breakfast, and get on the bus to go to school. My mother wasn't walking me to school.

When I came home at midday my lunch would be on the table. She was off to another job. She'd come home and make me dinner and, more often than not, she was off to another job. She usually left my dinner for me in the microwave. She cleaned dishes at a Marriott hotel. She was cashier at a convenience store at night, and sometimes she cleaned hotel rooms.

In my rookie season with the Steelers, my whole first paycheck went to her. It wasn't about me. I wanted to be able to repay my mother. I saw my mom sacrifice so much. She's the reason why I go out there and play.

We live in Stockbridge, Georgia and she's been up about three or four times. She didn't like being in the stands at the game. People say stuff about guys on the team, and she didn't like that. People are talking bad about other players she's heard me talk about. She'd rather watch it on TV.

I was a baseball player before I was a football player. I played baseball in eighth and ninth grade. I was drafted in baseball as a high school player and, for awhile, I thought my professional career was going to be in baseball.

I was small in high school. I was six feet tall and weighed only about 165 pounds. I built myself up to 200 pounds in college.

My first awareness of my prospects as a pro football player came during my junior year. That's when I first thought I had a chance to make it. In my freshman and sophomore years, I was just glad to be a part of the football program. It was a dream come true just to be playing football for Georgia.

One thing I'm especially proud of at Georgia was that I was the first African-American football player to have a 3.0 or better Grade Point Average. I had a 3.1 GPA, and I completed my requirements for my bachelor's degree in 3½ years. I majored in economics and minored in real estate.

I actually enjoyed going to classes. It was a chance to interact with other students. I didn't want my life to revolve around my teammates all the time.

I enjoy playing pro football. My teammates ask me why I'm always smiling. But I'm also smart enough to know that it's more like a business than any football I played before I signed with the Steelers. I see players come and go. I know teams have to pick up players and get rid of them to stay under the salary cap from year to year.

I'm not complaining about that. A lot of guys my age would love to be in the position we're in. Doing what we love to do on the highest level.

We get paid so much more than they used to get paid. I had an opportunity this winter to play basketball with some of the former Steelers, guys like Louis Lipps and Edmund Nelson. It's great to get respect from guys like that who can appreciate what it's all about.

I met Lynn Swann a few times when I was in college. He came in with ABC to do some of our games. I had no idea then that I'd be playing the same position he did with the Pittsburgh Steelers.

I hope I have a good reputation on and off the field. My approach to the game is go out and do whatever it takes to get the job done, and to make the best possible contribution. I'll sacrifice my body to block for our backs and other receivers. I hope they'll do the same for me.

I like to put hits on those defensive backs because if I go across the middle for a pass they'll try to take my head off.

I got a lot of attention for the blocking I did on Rod Woodson in the playoff game with the Baltimore Ravens. Hey, a lot was at stake in that game. Rod was a great player around here, and the fans still love Rod. But not when he's going up against the Steelers. I like Rod. I have a lot of respect for him, and I hope I'll earn his respect. I don't take it personally. I wasn't out to get Rod Woodson per se. He was just the man I had to take out.

"I just love playing football."

There's a lot of interest in the Steelers here, and you can see it everywhere you go. I live in Shadyside and I like living in the city. Other guys live in the suburbs. I go to their places, too. I think the guys like playing in Pittsburgh.

They want to play here. We've got great facilities. We've got a grass field. We played in Three Rivers Stadium and we know how hard that surface was. So we know what those great teams had to go through every day at practice, playing on that hard surface.

The Steelers have one of the better fan bases here. They love their Steelers. I go down to Atlanta and they don't care about the Falcons. They don't rally behind the team the way Pittsburgh does. Pro football isn't as important there as it is here.

I know what the Steelers did here in the '70s. They won four Super Bowls in six years. That's a hard act to follow.

333

Hines Ward holds ball firmly after making catch against New York Jets.

Steelers' star-crossed receiver Plaxico Burress beams after getting praise from quarterback Kordell Stewart. Fans wish Burress was as well behaved and as consistent a ball-catcher and blocker as Ward. Former players believe Burress has tremendous potential and can mature and improve game as Stewart has done.

Every player wants to go to the big dance. We wanted to go to the Super Bowl last year and we would have wanted to win it. But we never quite made it.

Now we want to prove something. I don't know if winning four Super Bowls is doable, but it's not unheard of, of course. We want to win one for starters.

I think we have the team chemistry to do it.

When I first came here they put me on the back burner. I was a third round pick and nobody gave me a chance of getting into the Steelers' starting lineup. But here I am.

When you see No. 86 on the field, he's going to bust his butt every way possible, blocking, catching, just the little things, special teams if I have to. Sometimes I get frustrated, but when I strap on the pads I love the excitement of football. I love playing, and I think it shows on the field. I'm always smiling. I just love playing. There's nothing I would rather do. Troy and Plaxico got all the attention when they came. Nobody talked about me. I went out and was the best ballplayer I could be. When I was drafted, I was just hoping I could stick here.

Now, after making 94 catches and playing in the Pro Bowl, there will be big expectations for me. That's fine. When I was practicing for the Pro Bowl in Hawaii, Tim Brown, the great receiver for the Raiders, told me that the best way to get recognized and appreciated is to be consistent.

Just to be out there with people like Troy Brown and Marvin Harrison and Tim Brown was so great. Just to be associated with Tim Brown is a big thing. Those guys tell me the little things and it should help me get better.

I was calling him "Mr. Brown," because that's the kind of respect I have for someone like him. He's been playing this position a lot longer than me. I want to last long in this league, like Jerry Rice.

If I do, I'll still be smiling. Why be sad? Thanks to my mother I had the opportunity to do something special. There are not too many 26-year-old people making the kind of money we get paid. Everyone else would love to be doing what I'm doing.

So I'm going to keep working and try to get better and, of course, more consistent.

I watch what someone like Jerome Bettis does. He's a true professional. He has a great attitude. He knows how to present himself to the public. He's a great people person.

I see Jerome Bettis and I want to be like that. Football is not going to be forever. I have to have people skills. I'll have a nine-to-five job someday, and I have to be able to deal with people.

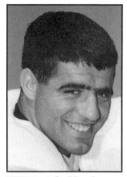

Dick Hoak
Still a hometown hero

*"I was just a skinny kid
who played for the fun of it."*

Dick Hoak was in his hometown of Jeannette, Pennsylvania and it appeared to agree with him. He looked more relaxed than usual, more bright-eyed, his forehead less furrowed. He was much more casual in conversation than when he is in the Steelers' offices at their South Side complex, or as I remembered him at Three Rivers Stadium. When he's at work, Hoak tends to blend in with the black and gold décor. Hoak is a quiet guy who shuns the spotlight and he has never been regarded as an easy interview. The less said the better. He is known as an organization man, fiercely loyal to the Rooneys. But he was talking easily and expansively, smiling often as he told stories from his high school, college and pro days. He was terrific. He arched his dark caterpillar eyebrows as he expressed himself. The transformation was amazing from the fellow who always seems to be staring at his shoe-tops when he is walking through the halls at the Steelers' offices.

He is as square as his shoulders, an old-fashioned fellow who can still fit in with younger fellows, but holds onto the values his family fostered in his youth. There was nothing fancy about his running style. He still runs straight ahead as hard as he can. He's financially fixed and doesn't have to run anymore, but he likes his life and plans to continue coaching as long as the Steelers want him.

This is a man who considers himself blessed to have turned a childhood play activity in Jeannette's hardscrabble south side in the 1940s and 1950s into a life-long career. He talked about his days at Jeannette High School, Penn State University and the Steelers. He praised his parents, Regina and William Hoak, who laid the foundation. He used to play pool with his pals at Punzo's Confectionary Store, a favorite hangout for young people, but he knew when to leave and get home and take care of his schoolwork. It was a haven for smokers and sports enthusiasts, but Hoak held true to his family's behavior standards and knew how to sidestep trouble.

Hoak, age 62, was sitting at a table alongside a wall-length window in the main dining room at DeNunzio's Restaurant at the corner of Lowry Avenue and Locust Street, about a quarter-mile from Hoak's modest two-story boyhood home on Wylie Avenue. "Just like the street in the Hill District," he said, pointing up the hill where his home still stands. "I can get there from here in five minutes. I don't know the people who live there now, but I've often thought about stopping and telling them I grew up there." So Hoak is a grandfather and proud of it.

Jim O'Brien

Dick Hoak is at home in Jeannette to discuss his days with Steelers.

Tony DeNunzio

Dick Hoak celebrates holidays with his family at DeNunzio's Restaurant in his hometown of Jeannette. With him, from left to right, are daughter-in-law Andrea Hoak, son Rich Jr., son-in-law Kevin McMillen, daughter Katie Hoak McMillen, wife Lynn and Dick, daughter Kelly Hoak Shuster with her husband Michael, and their son, Bob.

He was sipping on Diet Coke and I had iced tea. Lisa McCallen, the waitress, kept pouring fresh drinks from a pitcher and we kept drinking and talking. Hoak has said his stories "were something to talk about over a beer," but it was about four o'clock, a little too early for beer. It had been raining most of the afternoon, quite hard at times, and the skies were still gray. Even so, natural light illuminated his face and salt-and-pepper hair as he reflected on his life and his long stay with the Steelers. It was Tuesday afternoon, April 30, 2002, with temperatures in the high 50s. It was a windy, dank day and it seemed colder. Hoak arrived at 3:45 p.m., right on schedule. He'd come directly from the Steelers' practice facility on the South Side of Pittsburgh, a 75- or 85-minute drive. He leaves for work at 6:15 a.m. to get there before 8 a.m.

Hoak was warmed by old friends who stopped by to say hello. One of them was an elderly gentleman named Joseph Capretto. He is the father of a local orthodontist, Dr. Robert Capretto, a good friend of Hoak who followed him as a football star at Jeannette High School and Penn State. Mr. Capretto hugged Hoak and patted him on his back. His old friend, Tony DeNunzio, a former banking executive in Jeannette, greeted him with great gusto. Tony has long been one of Hoak's biggest boosters. Tony helps his son, Ron DeNunzio, who has owned and operated the restaurant since 1977, as well as one in Monroeville. Ron is a close friend of Frankie Gustine Jr., a former Pitt athlete whose father owned a similar popular restaurant on the University of Pittsburgh campus for more than 30 years.

Jeannette is a community about 30 miles from downtown Pittsburgh, along Rt. 30, sandwiched between Irwin and Greensburg. There are a lot of Italians who live in Jeannette, and Hoak is proud of his heritage. Once upon a time Jeannette was known for its glass factories, but they've long been closed down. It remains a proud community. It always looks so great during the Christmas holidays. Coming out from Pittsburgh, one turns left at the Park Classic Diner and PNC Bank to get to DeNunzio's, just past the McKee Elementary School and McKee Stadium, where the Jeannette Jayhawks still play their football games.

The Steelers had a practice and light scrimmage there last season, and the local citizens paid tribute once again to Hoak, still the hometown hero. For years, when Hoak was playing, the Steelers held a full-scale scrimmage there during their summer stay at training camp at St. Vincent's College in nearby Latrobe. The event was coordinated and promoted by Tony DeNunzio and his late friend Aldo Paulone, and it was a big deal in the community.

Later that evening, I would see Joe Mucci, who coached the Jayhawks to several WPIAL titles, including one in 1983 when he sent Dante Wiley and Mark Brasco to Pitt when Foge Fazio was coaching the Panthers. I remember accompanying Fazio to a banquet in Greensburg to pay tribute to that team. Mucci was now retired.

The Jeannette Police Benefit Assn. held a Man of the Year dinner in Hoak's honor in 1996 at the Four Points Hotel in

Greensburg. It was a big-time affair. Bishop Anthony G. Bosco of Greensburg offered the invocation and benediction. Bill Hillgrove was the emcee, Joe Paterno of Penn State was the main speaker, and Myron Cope and Merril Hoge — he flew in from Phoenix for the event — provided some lively banter. "Hoak was a cool guy," recalled Hoge. "He never lost it. He'd tell you what adjustments needed to be made, and he'd do it with a few words."

Hoak quarterbacked Jeannette to a WPIAL championship in his senior year. He was known for his unflappable demeanor. He had the ability to quiet a huddle and tend to business. He was a man for all seasons then, running track and playing basketball for the Jayhawks. He led the section in scoring in basketball as a senior, and scored 39 points in a game, the school record at the time. Then he moved on to Penn State, where he was a standout running back and quarterback from 1958 through 1960. He was named the team's MVP as a senior and graduated in 1961 with a degree in social studies. He was the MVP in the Liberty Bowl as Penn State ripped Oregon, 41-12. In that game, Hoak threw two touchdown passes, scored two touchdowns and intercepted two passes. Not bad for an afternoon's work.

Dick Hoak was the Steelers' seventh-round draft choice in 1961.

"Hoak was the most perfect player in my time." — Bobby Layne

Hoak's No. 42 black Steelers' helmet is on display atop the backbar in DeNunzio's Restaurant. His picture appears in a dozen places on the Wall of Fame, right up with two other local favorites, golfer Arnold Palmer of Latrobe and Pirates' hero Bill Mazeroski of Greensburg. Hoak and his wife, Lynn, have lived in neighboring Greensburg ever since he became a coach with the Steelers in 1972. They have three children, Kelly Hoak Shuster, Katie and Richard. They have two grandchildren and a third was expected in September.

Hoak stops by DeNunzio's for fish dinners most Fridays. Mazeroski is a frequent visitor as well, and Palmer has been there about six times. I had seen Mazeroski there in December, just after he had shed 60 pounds following his induction into the Baseball Hall of Fame in Cooperstown. Ron DeNunzio, who plays golf to an eight-hand-icap, is proud to have played with Palmer at Turnbury in Scotland. Their scorecard is laminated on a plaque by the bar. Ron has also played with Palmer on several occasions at his Latrobe Country Club. There was a signed photo of Hoak and Maz at a local golf tourney.

Hoak is second in seniority with the Steelers to club president Dan Rooney. He was a solid halfback for the Black and Gold for ten seasons (1961-1970), and joined Chuck Noll's coaching staff two years after his retirement as a player and has been there ever since. In the one year in between, Hoak was the head coach at Wheeling Central

Catholic High School. He blushed when I reminded him that his team posted an 0-11 mark in his debut as a coach. Things have been better since then.

He served Noll for 20 seasons and Bill Cowher for 10 seasons as offensive backfield coach. He was the only coach Cowher retained from Noll's staff. Hoak worked and helped develop such running backs as Franco Harris, Rocky Bleier, Frank Pollard, Walter Abercrombie, Merril Hoge, Barry Foster, Bam Morris and Jerome Bettis.

He owns five Super Bowl rings, four from Noll's tenure, and one from Cowher's reign, a runner-up ring from the 1995 Super Bowl. He is the longest-tenured coach in club history. I first met Hoak when I was a student at the University of Pittsburgh and the Steelers played the 1963 season at Forbes Field and the 1964 season at Pitt Stadium.

Hoak and Andy Russell share the distinction of being the only Steelers to have played for the team at Forbes Field, Pitt Stadium and Three Rivers Stadium. All three of those sports facilities have fallen to the wrecker's ball. Now the Steelers and Panthers play their home games at Heinz Field on the city's North Shore. And Hoak is one of the few who can say he went to work at all four facilities. There are sportswriters and ushers who can make the same boast.

Hoak's name still shows up in several places in the Steelers' record book. It's there along with Hall of Fame running backs like Franco Harris and John Henry Johnson and future Hall of Famer Jerome Bettis. Hoak led the Steelers in rushing three times, played in one Pro Bowl and was the NFL's fourth-leading rusher in 1968 with 858 yards in 14 games. He averaged 4.9 yards per carry that season, still the fourth best mark in club history. Going into the 2002 season, he ranked fifth in career yards rushing (3,965). He is second in most rushing attempts (1,132) to Harris (2,881). He is sixth in rushing touchdowns (25), 11th in career touchdowns (33). He is 20th in receiving with 146 catches. He is sixth in total yardage (5,417), right behind Lynn Swann.

Legendary quarterback Bobby Layne once hailed Hoak as "the most perfect player in my time."

The Pittsburgh Maulers of the USFL twice tried to lure him away from the Steelers to be the head coach of their team, but he turned them down out of loyalty to the Rooneys. In 1996, he turned down an offer to become offensive coordinator on Tony Dungy's staff with the Tampa Bay Buccaneers. He was comfortable with his situation the way it was.

He also disclosed that he was offered a job as an assistant at Pitt at the same time he was offered a job to join Noll's staff in 1972. He considers himself "lucky."

"It's not just the rings or what we've done," continued Hoak. "How many coaches can say they have lived in the same house through their entire pro coaching career?"

As Hoak was leaving to go home, he paused to talk to Tony DeNunzio. As he was looking up the hill toward his boyhood home, Hoak had a memory flash through his mind.

"I remember when I was a kid," said Hoak, "that a welder electrocuted himself right down there. His entire body was burned badly and he died."

"Yeah," said Tony DeNunzio. "That was Tito Cataldo!"

I was the speaker that evening at the Judge John J. Driscoll Scholar Athlete Dinner just up Rt. 30 at the Lakeview Lounge in Greensburg. At the 46th annual dinner, there were 38 boys and girls from 19 high schools in Westmoreland County who were being recognized for their achievements in athletics and academics. It was an impressive gathering. I spoke to them about "Hometown Heroes."

At one of the schools, Hempfield Area High School, a tragedy that rocked the community had occurred only a week earlier. A student killed his brother with the aid of another student, bludgeoning him with a sledgehammer. A third student was arrested after a teacher discovered a "hit list" on his desk at school. The student identified two adults and two students he wanted to kill. Judge Driscoll was to hear the case in juvenile court.

Grieving students had gathered the week before at the Evangelical Lutheran Church of the Holy Trinity in Jeannette to pay their respects to their deceased classmate. A photograph of the students embracing each other with tears in their eyes at the service dominated the front page of the *Pittsburgh Post-Gazette* the next day. "That's the dark side of this," Judge Driscoll confided to me. "Coming here tonight and seeing these kids is always a tonic for me. There are still a lot of great kids out there. We ought to give them attention, too."

Dick Hoak:

My days with the Steelers have been great. When I started playing football, at age 9, with Father Boniface and the Sacred Heart Midgets, I was just a skinny kid who played for the fun of it. I just enjoyed football. Then I went to Jeannette High School, and I was fortunate to get a scholarship to Penn State.

To get drafted by the Steelers and to come here, and be in my home area, it was just great.

When I was drafted it wasn't the big deal it is today. I didn't know they were scouting me when I was at Penn State. I found out I was drafted when I was playing in an all-star game at Phoenix. The draft was in December in those days. The all-star team took a bus from Phoenix to Las Vegas — that was part of the promotion — and when we got off the bus I was greeted by Harry Gilmer, who was an assistant coach with the Pittsburgh Steelers. He used to wear these cowboy hats. He said, "We drafted you."

And I said, "Who's we?"

He answered, "The Pittsburgh Steelers."

That's how I found out they drafted me. There were five or six guys who'd been drafted by the Steelers who were on that all-star team. Gilmer got us in a hotel and tried to sign all of us right there. I think some of the guys signed because they wanted some money to go gambling. I wasn't sure what I wanted to do, so I didn't sign there. I hadn't thought much about it.

Pappy Lewis, the old West Virginia coach, also worked for the Steelers. He came to my home in Jeannette when I got back. I needed six credits to graduate from Penn State. I figured I'd get some kind of signing bonus from the Steelers and I'd at least have the money to get my degree. I still didn't know if I was good enough to stick with the Steelers.

My father, William, had worked in a foundry in Jeannette. It was the Semler Company. That had been a big company. They made all kinds of metal things for the war effort. They made grenades there. He was a foreman there. But he lost his job there. They went out of business in the mid-to-late '50s. So he was working part-time at any job he could get. He was bouncing around.

It was tough at home. My dad didn't make much money in those days. If it weren't for getting a scholarship for football I wouldn't have gone to college. In those days, most guys came out of high school and went to work in the mills.

I was a quarterback on the freshman team at Penn State. The next year they had three pretty good quarterbacks coming back, in Richie Lucas, Al Jacks and Bob Scrabis. They told me they were going to red-shirt me. Then some guys got hurt, and we're opening at Nebraska and I'm the second string halfback. I returned kickoffs in that game. Then a fellow named Dave Kasperian got hurt, and I was the starting halfback in the next game against Penn.

I played there for two years. They switched me back to quarterback as a senior because by then we had only one veteran quarterback, Galen Hall. We both played the same amount of time because we played both ways in those days, and you had two units that split time. I played safety on defense. They wanted two equal teams. You were allowed to substitute only two or three players. It was strange.

Rip Engle was the head coach and Joe Paterno was one of his assistants. I enjoyed my time at Penn State. I wish I could go back and do it again. It was one of the best times in my life. If I had to do it over again I'd pick the same school.

As you can see, I've always been around good coaches, some of the best in the business. I'm sure that's one of the reasons I am a coach today.

The guy I played for in high school was great, too. His name was Markley Barnes, and he coached at Jeannette forever. He won a championship there in 1939; that's how far back he went. When I used to think about what I wanted to do someday I thought I'd like to be a coach like him. I admired Barnes so much that I decided I wanted to be a coach. I was never a ballplayer. I was always a coach in my dreams.

It was Coach Barnes who told me that football would make college possible. And it did.

When anyone asked me what I wanted to do when I was in school I said that I wanted to coach and teach in a high school. I saw what Coach Barnes did, and I had a lot of respect for him. Then I was associated with Joe and Rip at Penn State, and they were special. It made me realize this is what I wanted to do. I was sure of it.

I didn't win in my first year as a coach at Wheeling Central, but I enjoyed the kids. It was the other parts of the job, dealing with the parents, and disciplining the kids for stuff they did in someone else's class, that I didn't care for. The nuns used to report to me what my boys were doing wrong in their classes, and I was expected to do something about. But I enjoyed the experience overall. One year of losing like that (0-11) was enough for anyone, but I was prepared to come back the next year.

I got a call at school one day and it was from Carl DePasqua. He was the head coach at Pitt. He had been an assistant with the Steelers (1968) before he went to Pitt, and he knew me pretty well. He asked me if I would be interested in coaching in college. He said he had an opening. I said I was interested, and we agreed to get together. A few days later I get a call, and I think it's Carl calling me back. This time it's Chuck Noll. Max Coley was going to Denver to be the offensive coordinator, and Chuck needed a backfield coach. He asked me if I was interested in coming back to the Steelers to coach. As it turned out, I had the interviews scheduled on the same day: Chuck in the morning, and Carl in the afternoon. Chuck Noll offered me the job. I was going to the Steelers, and I was staying here. I called Carl and told him what happened. He said, "I understand. You've got to take that job." And 30 years later, I'm still with them.

The first thing I found out when I went back to the Steelers was how little I knew. I thought I knew a lot as a player. You know your position. You know what you're supposed to do. Chuck Noll coached you the way he wanted you to coach the players. He taught you the game all over again and he taught you how to coach it.

Most of our guys came from within the organization. He didn't trade for anybody, for the most part. He didn't bring in other people's cuts. He'd bring in somebody he cut from our team earlier. He wanted people we had coached. He wanted them doing things the way he wanted them done. He didn't want to have to teach them his way from scratch. That's why he brought back people like Tunch Ilkin who'd been cut earlier at training camp.

"I was happy to be in Pittsburgh."

Buddy Parker was my coach when I first came to the Steelers in 1961. We weren't too bad the first few years (6-8, 9-5 and 7-4-3). Buddy, to me, was an excellent offensive coach. He had a great offensive mind. Last year, we ran one of his trick plays. It's called the "What's the matter?" play. Kordell walks away from the center like there's something the matter and the ball is snapped directly to Jerome. We ran that against Minnesota. Then we ran a reverse off it against Baltimore in the playoffs. People thought it was so innovative. We ran that same play 40 years ago with Buddy Parker.

We were sitting around one day last year talking about trick plays, and I said we ran this particular play when I was playing for the Steelers, and Mike Mularkey liked it. So we put it in the game plan.

My next coach with the Steelers was Bill Austin. He had been an offensive line coach for Vince Lombardi's great Green Bay Packers teams. Bill tried to be something he was not. He tried to be Vince Lombardi. I think that happened to a lot of those coaches. He should have been himself. He should have been Bill Austin.

I can't be too hard on Bill Austin, though. He gave me the best opportunity of playing. He put in the I-formation, and he put me in there as the deep back. They tried some other backs like Don Shy for the first three or four games, and then he put me in as a starter. I gained 800-and-some yards that year, and I ended up playing in the Pro Bowl. So I always had a soft spot for him. Of course, if he had started me the first few games I might have gained a thousand yards. He was OK. I think Bill was an excellent assistant coach.

Everybody strives to be a head coach. It didn't kill me that I never became a head coach in the NFL. With some guys it consumes their lives. If it doesn't happen they're miserable. I was happy to be in Pittsburgh. I enjoyed being around here. My kids went through the same school system from start to finish. I didn't have to uproot them.

When you have to move and uproot your kids every few years they have to make new friends and get to know new people. Maybe some people don't mind it, but I think it's tough on a ten-year-old kid to have to find his way in a new school, or when he's a sophomore in high school and to have to start all over again.

344

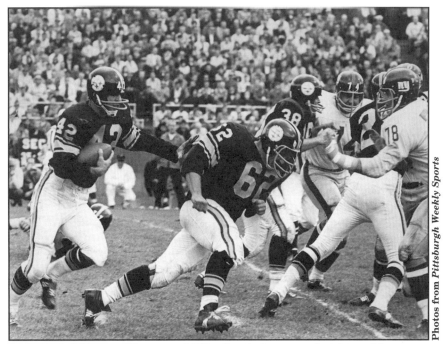

Photos from *Pittsburgh Weekly Sports*

Dick Hoak follows pulling guard Mike Sandusky around right end for seven yards in game against New York Giants at Pitt Stadium in October of 1965.

Hoak crashes off right guard for touchdown against New York Giants at Pitt Stadium. Steelers lost the game, 23-13, in October of 1965. That's Paul Martha (20) at upper left side in stint as receiver.

It's crazy moving around, to become a coordinator, to get experience under different coaches, different systems. Of course, you have to do it if you get fired. The Steelers like stability and I was lucky to serve two head coaches who wanted to be here, too.

Tony Dungy wanted me to come down to Tampa Bay and be the offensive coordinator. But I didn't want to leave. Another time the Philadelphia Eagles expressed some interest when Marion Campbell was their coach. I was offered the job with the Pittsburgh Maulers twice if I wanted it. I talked to Ed DeBartolo and he offered me the job and a three-year contract. It was for more money than I was making with the Steelers.

I came home and I talked to my wife about it. I couldn't see myself leaving the Rooneys and competing against them at the gate in Pittsburgh with another team. The Maulers changed coaches later on, and they came back with another offer. I said no once again.

There's been a loyalty both ways with the Steelers. They did some things for me when I was a player that I remembered.

When we moved to Three Rivers Stadium, I used to love to go back in the kitchen area and listen to Mr. Rooney telling stories about the old days.

In my last year as a player, I got hit in the head and suffered a concussion. I was in Divine Providence Hospital on the North Side for a week, and Mr. Rooney came every morning and every evening to see me.

He told me he was praying for me next door at St. Peter's Church. That was his family's church. He'd bring me the newspaper, and whatever else I needed. He'd say, "Just tell me what you want me to bring."

In 1968, we played at New Orleans in the last game of the season and I separated my shoulder halfway through the game. When the season was over, I had to go to the Steelers' offices at the Roosevelt Hotel to get paid. We went there every two weeks to get paid. I checked in with Fran Fogarty, our business manager. He told me Mr. Rooney wanted to see me. I go to see him, and he says to me, "We didn't have a very good year (2-11-1 record), but you had a good year." With that, he hands me an envelope. "Here's a check for $10,000," he says. "You deserve this."

A little later, I have to go see Dr. (John) Best, our team doctor, about my shoulder. His offices were across the street from the Roosevelt Hotel. When I was there, I thought I'd stop over to the Steelers' offices since I was so close, and just say hello. I go in there, and Fran Fogarty says to me, "Dan wants to see you." Then Fogarty hands me an envelope and says, "Dan wanted me to give this to you." I open it, and there's another check for me for $10,000. I figure this has to be a mistake; I'd already gotten $10,000 from his dad. So I go to see Dan Rooney in his office. I said, "Your dad gave me a check about three weeks ago." And Dan said, "No, this is no mistake. We want you to have this, too."

They didn't have to do that. I had a contract for that year and they met all their obligations. I always felt they didn't have to do that.

So maybe when those jobs came up to go elsewhere I figured I owed them something. These people were good to me.

I've worked with two head coaches there, Chuck Noll and Bill Cowher. They're different. It proves there are different ways to do the job, or different ways to skin a cat. If you do your job, and do what's expected of you, and if you know what you're doing, you won't have any problems with Chuck or Bill. If you don't understand, you could have a problem. If you do your work, and you put in your hours, everything's fine. A lot of people who left here left for better jobs. Guys like Dom Capers, Dick LeBeau and Jim Haslett have all become head coaches in the NFL.

I can remember times when we were putting together game plans with Chuck Noll and we'd have shouting matches. The same thing is true with Bill Cowher. You put ten guys together who think they know something about football, and you'll have some heated discussions. Someone has to have the final say.

Bill's done a good job. He's been here ten years and we've been in the playoffs seven years out of ten. I'd say that's pretty good.

I think there was a long shadow cast on the team by the team of the '70s, but I think that was more true in the mid-to-late '80s till 1990. It was true then, but I don't think it's true anymore. Some of these guys weren't even born then.

They ask me what those guys were like. They enjoy hearing stories about some of the guys from the '70s. Kenny Jackson, our receivers' coach, has a daughter who's about nine or ten years old. They were looking at some old Steelers pictures and she saw Terry Bradshaw. She said, "Look, Dad, there's the guy who does all those funny commercials on TV." That's how she sees Terry Bradshaw today.

"I know the bankers."

My wife is from Greensburg and she likes living there. We've been in the same home for thirty years. If I want to go to a dentist I go to someone I know. I like knowing my doctor. If I want a new furnace and air-conditioning unit I'll call a friend.

347

I don't want to go to Sears. If I want a new roof, I know who to call. I know the bankers if I want to get a loan to do something. I'm comfortable here. It takes me an hour to get to and from work, maybe a little more, depending on traffic.

I think one of the reasons that Arnold Palmer and Bill Mazeroski are so popular is that they're hometown people. I can remember when Arnie first started winning all those big tournaments and he got a jet. He'd finish play on Sunday and fly back to Latrobe that night. There'd be a traffic jam at the Latrobe Airport — now they call it the Arnold Palmer Airport — because his fans would go there just to see him get off the airplane and get into his car to drive home.

He was as big a name as you can talk about in sports, and he never left his hometown.

Maz grew up in Ohio, not far from Wheeling, but he's been living in Greensburg since he was playing for the Pirates. He's such a big hero from hitting that home run in the '60 World Series, but he's a very humble person. He never did anything bad, he never hurt anybody, and he never said anything bad about anybody. He's easy to be around.

People appreciate that.

"That's what you call good timing."

My first year of coaching with the Steelers coincided with Franco Harris coming to the team. That's what you call good timing. If you're going to be the offensive backfield coach, it helps to start off with backs like Franco Harris and Rocky Bleier.

Franco came to camp about two weeks late because he had played in the College All-Star Game in Chicago.

He didn't impress anyone at training camp. You'd give the ball to Franco and he didn't look that good. He was a great cutback runner, and it didn't show up in practice when guys are going half-speed. Franco would run a play that was designed for him to go into the eight-hole, which is wide right. And he'd end up going into the five-hole, on the left side.

In practice, he didn't look good. You'd think, "Oh, boy, what's going on here?" He'd run a 4.6 in the 40, but he never ran the full 40 full blast. He'd coast the last five yards. I'd ask him, "Why don't you run through and get your best time?" He'd say, "I don't want to pull anything."

We go to Atlanta for an exhibition game, and he's not starting. But he goes in on the second or third play of the game, and he runs a certain play to the left. It's all blocked up, so he comes back and goes to the right side and he's outrunning all these little defensive backs. He goes 80 yards

Tony DeNunzio

for a touchdown. That's when you realized he's something special.

He worked hard in practice. He was going full speed, from the start. From the first day, he ran out every play, going upfield 40 to 50 yards. I never had to tell him to do that. I tell guys now that Franco Harris is in the Hall of Fame, and he did that every play. He ran every play for a touchdown. Some guys do it on their own; some you have to stay after. Jerome Bettis does it.

Franco took good care of himself. He'd be in the trainer's room after practice every day, icing his knees, icing his ankles. He took care of his body. I know he had a reputation for running out of bounds rather than getting hit or tackled on sideline runs. But see what the game was; see what the score was; see what the down situation was. If we were ahead, 28-7, late in the game, yes, he'd go out of bounds. If the ballgame was tight, if we needed a first down, he never ran out of bounds. His way worked. That's why he lasted so long.

My only problem when he came to the team was not to overcoach him. Franco's greatest asset was his vision. He could see the whole field; he could see everything. He didn't run the plays the way they were drawn up on the board. He looked for daylight. He was patient, and could vary his running speed. He had a burst when he saw an opening, and could get through it.

And we had Rocky. He was a good guy. I knew him from when I was playing, before he went to Vietnam. When he was a rookie we were teammates.

Rocky studied hard and knew what we wanted to do. He knew what he was supposed to do, and what the other guys were supposed to do. That's why you say if this guy had this guy's mind and this guy's heart maybe he'd be a great ballplayer. Few of them have all the ingredients you're looking for. The guys who aren't as talented realize they have to study and find an edge.

Rocky was very smart. He knew his limitations. He knew Franco was the guy. He blocked for Franco. He did whatever he had to do. He was the last guy to make a mistake. After his rehabilitation from the wounds he suffered in Vietnam, I think he was bigger, stronger and faster than when he first came to us out of Notre Dame. But even in his rookie year he was smart, and knew what everybody was doing.

We were playing Atlanta in a Monday Night game and we ran Rocky at fullback. We had worked him at both spots. Rocky tells the story like we did this at the last minute, but we gave him plenty of warning about what we were going to do. It's a better story the way he tells it. Normally, Rocky was the halfback and Franco was the fullback, and the fullback was the main runner in our offensive system.

Rocky didn't have the vision that Franco had. Rocky ran into whatever hole was drawn up on the board. The blockers knew this; they knew he was going to be on their hip. They say they had to hold their blocks longer for Franco because they didn't always know where he was.

Bruce Van Dyke, one of our guards, used to get after me when I was the running back. He'd say, "I got through that hole. Why didn't you?" I said, "Because I had the ball; that makes a difference."

Franco might have had a problem if he'd been with the wrong team, the wrong staff. I've talked to Merril Hoge, and he's told me about coaches who won't put up with running backs not running the ball the way it's drawn up on the board. Hoge says these guys want you to run in the hole that's called for, no ifs, ands or buts. Franco would never survive in a system like that. We gave Franco the freedom to find a hole.

I still see Franco at certain gatherings, and we always end up talking about Penn State. There's a special bond. We teamed up my first year of coaching, his first year of playing. He's the greatest player I ever coached. Jerome Bettis is a great player, too.

They're completely different guys, different runners. The one thing they have in common is that they both work hard. Jerome has a good work ethic, and he tries to take care of himself. This guy comes to work every day. He's like Franco was; he's not up one day and down the next. He's not a moody guy. He enjoys football, coming here, sitting in meetings. He's the same every day. He enjoys playing.

I don't want to tell Jerome where he ranks while he's still playing. It might go to his head or it might tick him off. But he's one of the great backs in Steelers' history, there's no question about that. I don't know where he's going to end up ranking among them. You had a lot of great backs here.

You had Bill Dudley, John Henry, Franco . . . You had a lot of backs, Barry Foster, Bam Morris . . . but they didn't maintain it, for one reason or another. Barry did it one year and never did it again. He got off to a great start the next year, had an injury and I don't know what happened to him after that. Barry had a lot of ability, no doubt about that. But Jerome is a lot like John Henry and Franco in that he's sustained it. It hasn't been a one-or two-year thing. He's done it over a number of years.

Jerome and Franco are from different eras. Franco played in a two-back system, and often shared the carries with Rocky. They both ran for more than 1,000 yards one year (1976). That's the only time in Steelers' history that happened. Foster and Bettis have played in a one-back offense and gotten more chances.

It's hard to compare people. Franco and Jerome were both willing to work with the young kids, to help them along. I can tell someone the right way to do something, but it carries a little more weight when Jerome shows them what I'm talking about. Most of the good ones are good guys.

I never had a problem with anybody. I can say that honestly.

When it comes to handling players, I haven't had any problem. I always felt a respect.

"We've had some tough players."

I played with some interesting guys when I first joined the Steelers.

Bobby Layne was a real character. When I got to Pittsburgh, he was at the end of his career. I can't remember whom we were playing, but a halfback missed a blitz and the guy got Bobby real good. Bobby grabbed the back — I don't want to tell you who it was — by his jersey and pulled him to the sideline. When they got there, Bobby told Buddy Parker, "If you ever let this S.O.B. in the game again . . . " That guy was gone the next week.

He liked to have a good time. He took me under his wing. He liked me. You had to sing all those songs for him, and he had all these games he liked to play. Some of them were drinking games like "Buzz." If you lost, you either had to down a shot of whiskey, or you had to set up the rest of the guys. He could be intimidating. One of the reasons he intimidated people was he always had Ernie Stautner at his side.

I just saw Ernie recently. He came over to see the Steelers' complex. He had a lot of people with him. I asked him what he was doing in town, and he couldn't tell me. One of the fellows told me he was in to do a signing at a card show. I've heard Ernie has Alzheimer's Disease. That's a shame.

He was a great player and a great coach and a great guy. They had him back last season for one of the ceremonies at Heinz Field. They had him over to the office. He was with Joe Walton and Dan Radakovich.

I've seen a lot of football players in my life. I've been around. But mentally and physically, Ernie was the toughest guy I was ever around. No one was lifting weights when he played, but he was strong. I saw him black and blue from his hip to his ankle and he'd go out and play. He wasn't that big, but he was tough. We've had some tough players like Joe Greene and Ernie Holmes, but Stautner was as tough as anybody.

Ernie Stautner

John Henry Johnson

John Henry Johnson was here when I broke in, too. He was tough, too. I remember in a game against the Rams he got into a fight with some players on the sideline and when they came after him he picked up one of the yard markers and used it like a spear to fend off his attackers. He was swinging it wildly at them. He was a great runner, and as good a blocker as a fullback as there was in the league. Not so much for run blocking, but for pass blocking, or punt blocking. I saw him unload on some guys. He'd really pop them. He'd annihilate people. Pro football was like that then. You'd have great players and great characters like Bobby Layne, Ernie Stautner and John Henry Johnson. They were different. But they're all in the Hall of Fame.

Pro football was like that in those days. You had a lot of characters on all the teams. Those great Green Bay Packer teams of Vince Lombardi had lots of characters, like Paul Hornung, Max McGee, Fuzzy Thurston and Ray Nitschke. They had more characters than anybody.

Layne and Stautner and several other Steelers used to hang out at Dante's Restaurant in Whitehall. I was never in on that. I went to Dante's maybe two or three times in my life.

I remember when we practiced at the South Park Fair Grounds that we'd go to lunch at the Parkside Inn or the South Park Inn. They'd have fish sandwiches and some of the guys would have a few beers. Some guys would have as many as four or five beers at lunch. We'd go back in the afternoon and watch game film. They had these big projectors with 16mm film. A lot of the guys would fall asleep in the dark room. I remember walking by the defensive unit's room one day and you could hear the film going flop, flop, flop. It had run out. Everyone in the room was fast asleep, including the coaches.

We had our beers, and some guys drank hard stuff at night. But you never even heard about drugs. I saw some guys take pick-me-up pills to get ready to play, but that was about it.

We had a big offensive tackle named Charlie Bradshaw, who was from Texas. He'd report late because he was in law school. One time we were training at West Liberty. Jim "Buff" Boston ran the equipment room. Bobby and Ernie always took Buff with them when they'd go drinking. When they had a good time Buff was always with them. So when practice was over, Buff locked up the equipment room and went with Bobby and Ernie. Well, Charlie Bradshaw got locked in. He had to crawl out a window to go home and he hurt his back doing that. He was a big guy.

When we were on the road, everyone had to show up for a buffet. You had to wait until Buddy Parker came in before you could do anything. If we lost, Buddy would have a few drinks before he showed up. He was jumping all over people as he was prone to do after a loss. He had a habit of cutting players or trading players after losses. He'd go crazy. He had this little guy named "Boots" Lewis, who was supposed to be his good luck charm. This one night, Buddy is so upset he even shouts at Boots, "Your luck's running out, too."

He got on Buff. "All you think of is that big belly," Buddy screamed at him. "You hurt one of my players!" He spared no one. He was swearing up a storm.

When I was at Penn State, you weren't allowed to swear on the field or in the locker room. "My first game with the Steelers, we're playing the Colts in Roanoke, Virginia, and late in the game Bobby Layne and John Henry Johnson and Buddy Parker were all calling the referees every name in the book after they made a bad call.

I thought to myself, "What in the world did I get myself into?" These guys were different from what I was accustomed to. I wasn't used to anything like that. But I blended in.

That's probably because of the way I was brought up. You respect people, you respect your elders. That's what I learned.

I think that's the biggest factor in what I find in the young guys today. It depends on the way they were raised, the home environment. When I was in high school, my father didn't have a steady job. Things were tough at home. I learned how to survive.

I have two brothers. Both of them went into the military service. They both worked at General Tire out here. Then one of them became a mailman. They're both retired now.

I saw an opportunity by what I did to go to college. I didn't want to work at General Tire. Not that that's bad. I just wanted to be a teacher. And, of course, a coach.

My first year with the Steelers they trained at Slippery Rock College. I saw all the players and what they could do, and I wondered what I was doing there. They drafted Brady Keys from Colorado and he was a running back in the beginning, before he became a defensive back.

They had Tom "The Bomb" Tracy. Talk about characters. I was the last-string halfback. We had a weekend off and I came home. I didn't have a car, so I had to beg a ride to Jeannette. I told my dad I wasn't going back. My two brothers came over to the house and talked to me. I told them I can't make the team; I'm the last- string back. They talked me into going back. They said I had nothing to lose.

I was supposed to be back to camp by 7 o'clock. I got back around 9 and I told Parker that we got a flat tire on the way back. We played the Colts in Roanoke. Tom Tracy starts. After that game, I was the second back to go in the game. I felt like I belonged. I'm glad I went back. I'm grateful to my brothers, Don and Charles, for getting me to go back.

I was the baby of the family. I had two sisters, Frances and Betty, so they looked after me pretty good.

Walter Abercrombie got criticized, but he wasn't that bad. I went back and checked the guys who were drafted in the first round that year, and only about three guys had better careers than Abercrombie, and one of them was Marcus Allen. Walter was a pretty good ballplayer for us. He was not a complete flop like some of those other guys you mentioned (Bob Ferguson, Dick Leftridge, Bob Campbell, Greg Hawthorne, Tim Worley).

Worley was all right in his rookie year. He gained 700 and some yards (770). He fumbled the ball too much. He had small hands and he often held the ball way out here. But he couldn't handle the life in pro ball; that's what ruined his career. He didn't know what to do with all the money. He had to have the biggest car, the best clothes, and other things. He could have been a good back.

Ferguson was a first round draft pick from Ohio State (in 1962). He looked pretty good in camp and during the exhibition season. We opened in Detroit against the Lions and one of their linebackers (Carl Brettschneider) clothes-lined him with a forearm to his Adam's apple, and Fergy was never the same after that. He stayed one more year and was let go.

Penn State coaches Joe Paterno and Rip Engle were major influences on Hoak's career decision.

Penn State sports information service

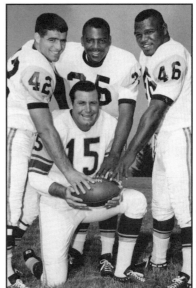

Steelers' 1963 backfield included backs Dick Hoak, John Henry Johnson and Bob Ferguson with quarterback Ed Brown.

Pittsburgh Steelers

Lynn Swann
His finest hour is complete

*"I always thought I could
have done better."*

L ynn Swann was recognized as one of the great pass receivers in the history of the Pittsburgh Steelers and National Football League when he was inducted into the Pro Football Hall of Fame in ceremonies at Canton,Ohio on August 4, 2001. Swann, who was 49 years old at the time of his induction, had performed admirably for nine seasons (1974-1982) for the Steelers. His credentials included winning four Super Bowl rings and being named a Super Bowl MVP and to the Super Bowl Silver Anniversary team.

He was the first-round draft pick of the Steelers in 1974, the 21st player picked from the college ranks. In the NFL, he was a slight 5-11, 180-pound acrobatic athlete known for making spectacular catches and many of those in clutch situations. He ended his career with 336 receptions, 5,462 yards and 51 TDs. He performed in three Pro Bowl games and, at the time of his retirement, held Steelers' records for receptions, yards, touchdowns and punt returns.

Dan Rooney, Chuck Noll and Joe Gordon lobbied on his behalf, writing to the Hall of Fame voters with their thoughts about why he was deserving. "He not only played super in the Super Bowls," noted Rooney, "but he did so much in the regular season and the playoffs to get us to the Super Bowls."

"Nobody played better in big games, and that's the mark of a great player," said Noll. "If we threw the ball a lot more, he could easily have as many catches as other players who are in the Hall of Fame."

He was used primarily on punt returns as a rookie. He saw limited action as a wide receiver in the late season and his TD catch against Oakland in the AFC championship proved to be the game-winner. He became a regular wide receiver his second season and responded with 49 catches for 781 yards and a league-high 11 touchdowns. He finished the season by winning MVP honors in Super Bowl X with 161 yards on four receptions, including a 64-yard game-winning touchdown.

Mel Blount, a Hall of Famer himself, said of Swann, "Without him, we would not have had four Super Bowl rings. If there is such a thing as a Hall of Fame receiver, Lynn Swann is it."

At a press conference in Tampa the day before Super Bowl XXXV was played there, I was in attendance at the announcement of the Pro Football Hall of Fame Class of 2001. When he arrived, Swann said,

Jim O'Brien

Lynn Swann stands with four other members of 2000 Class of Pro Football Hall of Fame who were present for announcement at Super Bowl XXXV in Tampa, Florida, from left to right, Marv Levy, Jackie Slater, Jack Youngblood and Nick Buoniconti.

Pittsburgh Steelers

Lynn Swann has first face-to-face meeting with Chuck Noll when he reported to Three Rivers Stadium after being drafted on first round from Southern Cal in early 1974. Check out their respective hairstyles from that era.

"When I was on Monday Night Football and we covered the Hall of Fame game, I would see these guys at the podium, and I had the pleasure of introducing Franco Harris for induction into the Hall of Fame, and the guys are up there crying, and I said, 'Oh, no, that's not going to be me.' I cried all the way over here (from his hotel to the press conference several blocks away).

"My being here, it's obviously not just me. It's Dan Rooney. It's all my teammates. I'm here because I played on a football team of great people, not just great athletes. I appreciate the fact that while it may have taken 14 consecutive years as a finalist before getting elected, that while it was difficult, maybe it will make me appreciate more the honor of being elected to the Hall of Fame."

Dan Rooney was present at the announcement. "I couldn't be more pleased," related the Steelers' owner. "Now, it's all great that he's in. I really was concerned that I didn't want to be in here in place of him. Now, it's complete. It was more emotional than I was for myself. I thought this one should have been a lock. I felt he belonged when he was first eligible."

Lynn Curtis Swann was born March 7, 1952 in Alcoa, Tennessee. There was a satellite of Pittsburgh-based Alcoa there, and it might have been a sign that someday he would be with the Steelers. He moved to California as a child and attended Serra High School in Foster City. He has been with ABC-TV Sports since 1983. So it would make sense for him to live in New York City or in Beverly Hills, but he has chosen to stay in Pittsburgh and be a part of the community.

Swann is a mover and shaker on the social scene in Pittsburgh. He has a home with his wife, Charena, in Sewickley, where his neighbor is another Hall of Famer, Jack Ham. Swann's name is often seen in the "Seen" society column in the *Pittsburgh Post-Gazette*, attending charity-related balls and parties at hotels and clubs around town.

In March, he was among a celebrity cast of local sports and media stars who participated in "The Poetry of Sport" program produced by the International Poetry Forum at Pittsburgh's Carnegie Hall. Other former Steelers who read poetry relating to sports were Andy Russell and Craig Wolfley. In May, he was honored at the 10th Annual History Makers Award Dinner. Others similarly honored were Mellon Bank punjab Marty McGuinn, Bill Block Jr. of the *Pittsburgh Post-Gazette*, and Director of Homeland Security Tom Ridge, the former governor of Pennsylvania.

On June 20, 2002, he was named the Chairman of the President's Council on Physical Fitness & Sports. "It's a lot of work," Swann told us, "but that's what you get when you volunteer." On July 6, Swann rounded up former Steeler Hall of Famers for a celebration that drew 3,500 fans to Heinz Field.

In early May, 2002, he was the keynote speaker at the Pittsburgh chapter of the National Association for the Advancement of Colored People (NAACP) 48th annual Human Rights dinner at the Pittsburgh Hilton and Towers. Swann's career fit the theme for the dinner: "Breaking the Mold — Achieving the Dream."

He was introduced, sort of, in a roast-like manner, by former teammate L.C. Greenwood. "I have no idea where Lynn lives," gushed Greenwood. "He asked me to drive him home after one of those celebrity golf outings, and I drove into these dark woods, and he told me to stop, and leave him out on the road. He's my best friend — ha, ha — but I've never been in his home."

One of my hometown heroes, Herbert Douglas Jr., who won a bronze medal in the long jump in the 1948 Olympic Games in London and launched a successful business career and became an active member of Pitt's Board of Directors, was recognized with the Homer S. Brown Award at the same NCAACP affair.

Swann has been the national spokesman for the Big Brothers and Big Sisters mentoring program since 1980. He has also served on the board of trustees of the Pittsburgh Ballet Theater, where he has created a youth scholarship. He also worked with Project HOPE, an organization that teaches entrepreneurial skills to fifth- and sixth-graders.

Swann was named the 1981 NFL Man of the Year, a prestigious award determined on the basis of an NFL player's contributions to his community as well as for his playing excellence. He also was voted to the All-NFL team of the decade for the '70s.

Lynn Swann:

When I was inducted into the Pro Football Hall of Fame, I was told it was my finest hour. In my acceptance speech, I was serious when I said that it was my finest half-hour, and the other half-hour would be when John Stallworth was similarly honored. I am looking forward to sitting back there behind the inductees at the Hall of Fame in Canton this summer and seeing John get his just due. We both deserved to be in the Hall of Fame.

I'm sure I will feel somewhat the way Dan Rooney felt when I got in. Mr. Rooney said he felt a sense of relief that I was in and that he hadn't kept me out when he was inducted a year ahead of me. There was a sense of relief that he didn't take my spot. John was up for consideration at the same time I was, and many saw it as a pick-em as to which one of us would get in first, that we wouldn't get in at the same time. I'm glad John is getting in. That makes it three years in a row that someone from the Steelers is being enshrined. I kept the door open, so to speak, for John the way Mr. Rooney kept the door open for me. Hopefully, the door is still open for Donnie Shell and L.C. Greenwood to get in as well.

I wanted John to be my presenter at the Hall of Fame so that everyone would see us together, the way we played together for the Steelers, as a reminder that he, too, is deserving. I wanted him to share the spotlight with me. I wanted him to be next. He's having his son introduce him and that's good, too.

Seeing him get in will be the rest of my hour. This makes me feel so much more comfortable that John's now in. Now the door is open for another Steeler to get in. The door is not closed.

There are so many Steelers in the Hall of Fame now, so many from our teams of the '70s when we won the four Super Bowls, but there are others just as deserving. Some of them will never get in.

It hasn't really changed my life. I don't do any more commercials or endorsements. Maybe for some other guys it makes a difference. I still do the same things I've done before. I'm still involved in the same things. I still do a college football game every weekend. I just have a sense of capping off my professional football career, that's all. It's simply being in a place I should have been in for some time. It hasn't done more than that for me.

It's great to be there. It's that final piece of a career. But I realistically don't view it individually. I got there on the backs and shoulders of a lot of people who will never get there. People like Larry Brown, Jon Kolb, Gerry Mullins, Sam Davis and so many others. The reason we have so many people in the Hall of Fame is because of the success of the team. We were always coached that the team came first. Chuck Noll always spoke about synergism — that the whole was greater than the sum of its parts.

The largest part of our success was the willingness of everyone to make the sacrifice, to do what was best for the team, to do what would help us win.

I think I appreciate our approach more now than I might have back then. When you're distanced from the events you come to appreciate them more. You have a better appreciation for what you accomplished. I think every athlete is in that category. Every athlete who has his head screwed on straight would recognize that. You don't appreciate the successes you have until it's all over.

You see certain other teams get to the Super Bowl and not win it the way we did all four times. You think about the Buffalo Bills going to four straight Super Bowls and what a great accomplishment that was. There were 30 teams at the start of the season with the same goal in mind, and the Bills were one of only two teams that made it there in four straight years. But they lost all four. Marv Levy and Jim Kelly are both in the Hall of Fame now, but they may not look at it the way I do. But it was an accomplishment to have been there. They probably don't look at is as an accomplishment, but it was. The same was true earlier for Fran Tarkenton and the Minnesota Vikings.

We always talked about team goals. It must start with team goals. We wanted to win the league championship every year. The goals were simple and they were always short-term goals. We always took the old one-game-at-a-time approach. You'd have goals for the season. And when the season was over you'd start preparing and focusing on the next season. You start wondering where you fit in and what your role will be.

Individual accomplishments are nice, but there's none as good as team accomplishments. Winning four Super Bowls was the best. I probably don't think of Chuck Noll any differently now than I did when I was playing. Chuck is still the same. There were some things that we thought were issues when we were playing, decisions he made personnel-wise or whether we were a passing or a rushing team, but when you bring it up to Chuck now he doesn't even remember. They're not that important to him. It was something he did at the time because it made sense to him. He just wanted to do whatever we needed to do to win. As far as he's concerned, whatever it was that might have annoyed or disappointed us, we should get over it.

Sure, I'm still a Steeler. Number one, I never played for another team. So my heart is still with Pittsburgh. In college, I'll always be a Trojan from USC. And I'm happy with that.

That's a question for a guy like Rod Woodson. He played for San Francisco and he won a Super Bowl with Baltimore. So is he still a Steeler, a 49er or a Raven? Or, that's a question for Deion Sanders. Is he a Falcon, a Cowboy or a Redskin? He might just say he's a National Football League player. Or even a Major League Baseball player. You have to ask them where their heart is.

You take a guy like Mike Haynes. He's in the Hall of Fame. He played as a defensive back for seven years with the New England Patriots and he played for seven years with the Oakland Raiders. Is he a Raider or a Patriot? He had Howard Slusher, who was our agent, introduce him at the Hall of Fame. So he went with a neutral alliance.

For us, and for people like Sam Davis, Jon Kolb, Larry Brown, Randy Grossman and Rocky Bleier and all of us who won four Super Bowls and stayed here, we are Pittsburgh Steelers and we will always be Pittsburgh Steelers. Franco's little blip in Seattle doesn't even count. He's still a Steeler, too. It's a no-brainer. We are, as you say, all Pittsburgh Steelers forever.

"He's The Chief and he's there."

When you first come in as a young man and meet Dan and Art Rooney you thought Dan was running the team. Art Rooney was there. He's the Chief and he's there. But he's not the guy running the club anymore. At the league meetings, Dan is sitting up front with the other owners and his dad is in the back of the room, just taking it all in, talking to everyone who approaches him. Just a grand old man of the game. I talked to Pete Rozelle, the NFL commissioner, years later and he told me how important Art Rooney remained in the league. All the other owners didn't care much for Al Davis, and didn't talk to him unless they had to. Davis is giving the league problems. Art Rooney is still talking to him, though. They got along great even though Art Rooney didn't agree with everything Al Davis was doing. He kept the communication line open. So Dan's dad was still a major influence and involved with owners, and his opinion was still respected by everyone. So first appearances were deceiving. What I thought were the roles of Dan Rooney and his dad were facades about what was really happening. Dan still discussed everything with his dad. He was in charge and he was making the hard decisions, but his dad was aware of what was going on. The Chief looked like everybody's grandfather by then, but business-wise he was still a tough cuss. He was generous with a lot of people, but the Steelers were still tough in contract negotiations. He didn't let them give away the store. I've stated before why I love Pittsburgh and why I stayed here. The fans are really behind you here. Football is a little more important in Pittsburgh than some places. That makes it enjoyable. I feel comfortable here.

I don't like to get into my private life. I've had many requests through the years to do interviews at my home, but I have always declined. I don't want to get into my personal life and my personal business. It's not a part of my being that I want to get into. I don't want to put it out there. It's not about you. It's not about trusting you. We've always had a good relationship. I just don't want to put that part of my life out there. One of the things I learned in my journalism class at USC was that celebrities have a choice about what they want to open up to the public.

> *"We are a big part of the history of Pittsburgh, not just because of our success, but because of our era. When I first came up, Pittsburgh was still known as a steel town, a dirty town, and the Steelers weren't very good. But during the '70s, we became known as one of the greatest dynasties ever, and Pittsburgh made the transition to the most livable city. So we are part of it."*
> — John Stallworth, Hall of Fame celebration at Heinz Field in Pittsburgh, July 6, 2002

"He didn't care about his own pain."

I had some great catches and great games, but one of my most cherished memories is seeing a photograph of Joe Greene carrying me off the field at Three Rivers after I had been knocked unconscious by a brutal hit by George Atkinson of the Raiders.

Of all the things that happened in my career, that incident still stands out most in my mind. Here I was knocked cold, lying out there on the field and Joe Greene runs out and picks me up. Now you must understand that Joe Greene was nursing a badly pinched shoulder. It was a bitterly cold day, and Joe was in terrible pain. But he still picked me up and I was like a rag doll in his hands.

A picture of the scene hangs in my home in Pittsburgh. I look at it as symbolizing the spirit of those Steeler championship teams. It showed that Joe Greene's biggest concern at that moment was for a fallen teammate. Nothing else. He didn't care about his own pain. The guys on those teams genuinely cared for one another and that's one reason we won so often.

That hit pinpointed a problem we had in pro football at the time. There was too much violence, too many flagrant hits like that, aimed at hurting people. I spoke out against that. I didn't sit in a corner and let what I considered a cheap shot go by without saying something about it. I testified at the trial. I gave my version.

George Atkinson lost the lawsuit and the league the next season passed the so-called George Atkinson rule. That's when a player can be suspended, or fined for committing a flagrant foul. I think football today is cleaner because of it. I hope I'm remembered for my contributions in this area.

I guess I'm what you would call a goal-oriented person. I always have tried to be the best in everything I can do. I'm never satisfied with myself. In my own mind, I never thought I played my best football game. I always thought I could have done better.

How do I want to be remembered? I guess as a person who played his best games under pressure. When the games meant the most and we had our backs against the walls, my teammates could count on me to come through. It seems like the big events always brought out the best in me. Maybe it was a fear of failure that made me play better in such circumstances.

Embarrassment is a great motivator. There are some people who play very, very well just so they don't get embarrassed in front of their friends and a national TV audience.

The guy behind you keeps you going, too. Competition is a good thing for everyone. There's nothing like competition to keep you going. That's one secret we had on the Steelers. Everybody on the squad was so good you had to keep playing your best just to stay on the field.

I always knew where I was on the field and that enabled me to make some sideline catches that caught people's eye. At any part of the field, I knew where I was.

I'd like to be remembered as one of several people who played on possibly the greatest football team ever assembled. It comes down to one thing. A winner is someone who simply won't take anything less. He has to be the best. I'd like to be remembered as a person who contributed to the community and to his friends and gave a little bit more beyond his football skills.

I've always thought that professional sports is a great part-time job. It allows you to work at something you enjoy doing, it gives you the opportunity to make a substantial income and it gives you a great deal of time in the off-season to prepare for a career. All too often — especially with the kind of money they're making today — I see athletes who aren't prepared to make that transition and don't leave football when it's time to. They decide to linger on, and I never wanted to be one of those people. If I chose to, I could have played for some time. I think it was my time to quit playing.

I promised myself I wouldn't play for more than five years. Then six came, then seven, then eight and nine. I never thought of myself as really being a football player. I went to dancing school as a kid because my mother thought it would be good for me. Gene Kelly should have been a football player and I should have been a dancer. Playing football was a fluke from the start. I only played because my brother played and I continued playing because my mother told me not to come home crying if I got hurt, and I wanted to show her I was tougher than that.

I played at USC because I had a scholarship and couldn't afford college without it and I played pro football because I was a first-round draft choice.

"Hey, I knew I could do it!"

I went to public elementary school with the kids from my black neighborhood. I always played football and because smaller kids like myself were always receivers, I just naturally learned to catch the ball. Nobody ever taught me which way to hold your hands or that sort of thing. I grew up knowing always to catch it with my hands, not against the body.

One of Lynn Swann's "most treasured possessions" is this picture showing teammate Joe Greene carrying him off the field after he was knocked unconscious by a savage hit by George Atkinson of the Oakland Raiders.

Lynn Swann skies high for another acrobatic catch against Los Angeles Rams in Steelers' 31-21 victory in Super Bowl XIV in Pasadena, California in January, 1980. Swann was one of Steelers' stars in their fourth Super Bowl triumph in six seasons.

Sometimes with Bradshaw, who threw a real hard ball, you had to catch it with your arms or body if it was a wet or very cold day. Sometimes it came at you like a rifle shot, or like it was coming from a .44 magnum gun.

Anyway, I got a scholarship to Junipero Serra, an all-white boys Catholic high school, though I was a Baptist. I got my leaping ability from playing basketball. I was able to dunk the ball when I was a junior in high school and I was only 5-10 then. I was the state long-jump champion, too, at San Mateo High School and I'd like to think I could have made the Olympics if I had stayed with it.

I long-jumped 25 feet, four-and-a-half inches in high school. I high-jumped 6-2, I pole-vaulted 13 and a half feet. I ran the high hurdles in 14.9 and I ran the 100-yard dash in 9.7. But leaping is a matter of timing. And timing is something that's inside of you and you just work at it.

Discipline is an important part of being a successful receiver. Having physical ability is great, but if you don't have the discipline to do what's necessary then all that ability goes to waste. Concentration can be learned. It's easy to be distracted. You have to shut out all distractions and just go for the ball. I think that most good ballplayers see themselves as heroes, making great catches and great runs. Then when it happens you say, "Hey, I knew I could do it!" I'd been wanting to do something super for a long time.

"Breaking the Mold"

I was asked to be the keynote speaker at the NAACP Pittsburgh Branch's 48th annual Human Rights Dinner. "Breaking the Mold, Achieving the Dream" was the theme for the evening.

My life is a wonderful history. I'm happy. Many great things have happened. (If you are an African-American or a person of color), you might say, "That's great for you. You're Lynn Swann. You haven't had to go through what we've gone through. You don't have the same sort of difficulties. That's not true.

Back in high school, I was one of four African-Americans at a Catholic school with over 900 students. The kids I grew up with in my community decided when I went to that private all-boys school that I was no longer a member of their community. And I certainly wasn't a member of the school community.

I lived in a home when I grew up that was different from the homes of most of the kids at school. We were Baptists, to begin with. My parents didn't understand what I was going through. I felt terribly alone. I was the only one in my family going through this.

I got into one fight at school my first year. A guy called me "a shoeshine boy." He didn't use the n-word. I was a freshman and he was a junior. I beat him up. I'm not proud of that incident, but no one messed with me the rest of the four years. It was the only fight I had. I wasn't into that sort of thing. That wasn't me.

My mother felt the school was the best foundation for me. She wanted me to stay there. I wanted to run away from home.

Then I got interested in all kinds of sports activity. I got a number of athletic achievements. In my senior year, I achieved great things. I thought I was one of the most popular students at the school. I ran for student body judge in a school election. You know I was gonna win, right? I ran unopposed. Then the other guy ran on the day of the election and I lost. I'm trying to figure this out. I realized that a lot of the kids in the school were putting on a good show. When it came time for me to step up, to get a position of importance in the student government, it wasn't a place for me.

When I went to USC, I knew what to expect. I knew what color is. People can get a nose job, or get some hair transplants, or change their appearance, but if you are a person of color that's how you are seen and that's how you are perceived. Every time someone of color walks down the street that's the first thing people see — your color.

When I first came to Pittsburgh, there was another perspective of Lynn Swann. After I was drafted in the first round by the Pittsburgh Steelers, I went out with my brothers and celebrated in San Francisco. We were stopped, falsely arrested, and put in jail. People in Pittsburgh saw that in the news and they're saying this Lynn Swann gets drafted, gets drunk and what do we have here?

People thought of me as being part of the criminal element.

Some times when you break the mold you have to do it from both sides. Sometimes you have to lead the way. After it's broken and shattered, you've redesigned certain things. You have to act like you've been there before, that you'll be back, and that you have other things yet to accomplish. And you're confident you can do it.

The Steelers helped to break that mold. Now I came from USC, which was a nationally recognized major school. But L.C. Greenwood came from Arkansas AM&N. He's probably the best football player that school ever turned out. I'm sure of that. L.C. is sure of that.

There was a time when if someone just like him was available from Michigan they'd take the guy from Michigan.

Except for a guy named Bill Nunn — yeah, you know him — was working in the personnel department of the Steelers. He'd been a sports columnist for *The Pittsburgh Courier*, an important black newspaper. He knew about guys like L.C. and Dwight White. He said, "These guys can play the game." He knew about Sam Davis and Donnie Shell and John Stallworth, too. He went back to the boss, Art Rooney and Dan Rooney, and he said, "If you want to win a championship, you better start drafting some players."

And they did. And we were making some progress. Then you have to act like you've been there before. I marvel at athletes who celebrate everything they do on the field. They're getting paid $3 million a year, with a $1 million signing bonus, and they go four yards for a touchdown, and he's going around celebrating. What is he getting paid for? You're not acting like you've been there before.

Act like you're going to do it again. The satisfaction has to be in your heart; that's good enough. You know what you've done. The fans know what you've done without you calling attention to yourself with all that celebrating.

You can't say, "I've arrived." You have to say, "Now where do I go?"

I achieved every dream I had in my first year with the Pittsburgh Steelers. With the money I was paid, I bought a new car, I owned a condo. I had money in my pocket. I had money in the bank. I was golden. I had my degree. I played one year for the Steelers and we won a Super Bowl championship.

I'm full of myself. The next year we win the Super Bowl championship again and I'm the MVP. I bought another car. I traded in the first one. I went to Europe. This is great, I thought. Now what do I do?

I've broken the mold. I'm the first one in my family to go to college and get a degree. I've had all sorts of success in several sports.

The third year was the worst year of my life. I was depressed. I had nothing to do. I had achieved all my dreams.

Dreams need to change when you're having success. You have to keep lifting the bar like I did as a high jumper in track & field.

We all have to keep moving forward. Yes, the goal was to win a championship. You wanted to do that every year.

In life, goals must change. We have to make those strides. We have to work beyond our earlier goals.

To achieve what we need to achieve as African-Americans, we need all of our talent to have the opportunity to succeed and flourish. Our nation has been hit by a big crisis this past year. We were changed by the events of September 11. It will never be quite the same again.

We need to do this together, as one nation. So the community and the nation can't let one individual with talent go to waste. I've spent 22 years with the Big Brothers and Big Sisters Program. That organization has mentored over 5 million kids. So I see it every day, every year. We reach out to the community for mentors. We stress the importance of one person's life.

A mentor can do so much to change the life of one young person. I've seen it happen again and again. We've got some great success stories.

We had a kid whose parents had given up on him. He had emotional and mental problems. His family could not handle him. In the end, with the work of a Big Brother, he became a real success. It turned out he was a genius. One man took the time to help one child. That's what it's all about.

The NAACP has been around a long time and has helped a lot of people. If one person can help a child so much, just think what an organization like the NAACP can accomplish. We, as an organization, should be able to have that kind of impact.

Who Selects New Hall of Fame Members?

Charged with the vital task of continuing to be certain that new enshrinees are the finest the game has produced is the Pro Football Hall of Fame's 38-member Selection Committee.

The Selection Committee consists of one media representative from each geographical area with a current NFL franchise. If a geographical area has more than one franchise (such as New York City) there shall be a selector for each franchise. A 32-member board has a representative of the Pro Football Writers of America and there are six at-large delegates.

The Selection Committee meets annually at the time of the Super Bowl to elect new members to the Hall of Fame.

"I don't think I could be in the Hall of Fame unless there was a John Stallworth. The competition between John and me, the things that we made each other do in terms of working and getting ready, I knew I always had to be ready."
— Lynn Swann

Louis Lipps
Glad to be back

"Pittsburgh seems like home now."

Louis Lipps felt like Louis Lipps again. His name was on the banner of a first-rate event, the 17th annual Charitable Golf Outing & Barbecue at the Pittsburgh Field Club. Lipps was the lead man among 136 golfers in raising nearly $100,000 for Variety — The Children's Charity.

He was playing with a foursome that included board president Dr. Ken Melani and Dennis White, vice-president of event sponsor GlaxoSmithKline and John Cushard of Highmark. As Lipps looked over the scene from the veranda at the Field Club he had to smile. The scene at one of the area's most beautiful country clubs on this brisk Monday, May 20, 2002 and the company he was keeping assured him that he had made the right move a year earlier when he returned to Pittsburgh.

He had been back home in Reserve, Louisiana the previous five years, following an outstanding eight-year (1984-1991) stint as a wide receiver and punt-return man for the Steelers. He had left Pittsburgh to return home to be with his mother and sister and her children, but began to believe it was time to get back to Pittsburgh where his money-making opportunities would be improved.

Louis Lipps is still a sports star in Pittsburgh. At age 39, he even resumed playing with the Steelers' basketball team in a half dozen of their games at area gyms last winter. He still has his shooting touch. He was always quite the athlete. He gained more fame for his baseball playing than his football performances during his high school days in Louisiana.

The previous Friday, he was among the former Steelers who filled the celebrity lineup for the Andy Russell Celebrity Classic at The Club at Nevillewood. He mixed with former teammates such as Robin Cole, Mark Malone, Mike Merriweather, Edmund Nelson, Dwayne Woodruff, Craig Wolfley, Rick Strom, Mike Mularkey and Emil Boures.

His name is secure in the Steelers' record books. He is second in career receiving only to John Stallworth, who was about to enter the Pro Football Hall of Fame for what he did during 14 seasons with the Steelers. Stallworth snared 537 passes in that span. Lipps is second with 358, just ahead of Lynn Swann, with 336, who was inducted into the Pro Football Hall of Fame in August of 2001.

Lipps is second to Stallworth as well in receiving yardage — 6,018 to 8,723. Lipps' per-catch yard average of 16.8 is superior to Stallworth's 16.2 and Swann's 16.3. Only four receivers had a better per-catch yard average during their stay with the Steelers: Buddy

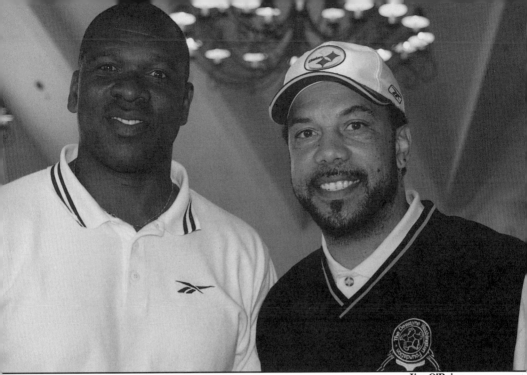

Jim O'Brien

Former teammates Mike Meriweather and Louis Lipps were in lineup at Andy Russell's 26th Celebrity Classic outing at The Club at Nevillewood.

Ron Fees

Louis Lipps was the headliner for 17th annual Charitable Golf Outing and Barbeque at the Pittsburgh Field Club on May 20, 2002. His foursome included, left to right, Dr. Kenneth Melani, board president for Variety Club; Lipps, Dennis White, vice-president of sponsor GlaxoSmithKline and John Cushard of Highmark.

Dial (20.6), Gary Ballman (19.2), Roy Jefferson (18.4) and Ron Shanklin (18.4).

Of Lipps' 39 touchdown catches, one of them — good for an 89-yard touchdown — is better than Stallworth's best (74 yards) or Swann's best (68 yards). Lipps was 9th in scoring going into the 2002 season with 276 points, but Jerome Bettis was breathing down his neck with 252 points to his credit. Stallworth has the most 100-yard games among Steelers' receivers with 25. Lipps is second with 16 and Swann and Yancey Thigpen are tied for third with 10.

As for the most touchdown-catches in a career, it's Stallworth 63, Swann 51, Buddy Dial 42 and Lipps 39. Lipps and Buddy Dial hold the Steelers' record for touchdown catches (12) in a season. Lipps did that in 1985, after scoring 11 TDs as a rookie the year before, two of those on end-around plays.

He tied running back Merril Hoge for receptions with 50 to pace the Steelers in 1988, and then led the team in receiving the next three seasons, with 50 on two more occasions and 55 in 1991. It was odd that Lipps caught 50 passes three years in a row.

Lipps played in two Pro Bowls, one less than Stallworth and Swann. In short, the statistics bear out that Lipps, at 5-10, 187 pounds, was one of the leading receivers and scorers in Steelers' history. It's a shame he didn't stick around longer; it could have been better. He signed as a free agent with the New Orleans Saints for the 1992 season and they released him at mid-season. He had talked with the Jets and Chiefs before deciding to sign with the Saints. After he was released, he sat out the rest of the season.

He called Dan Rooney to see if he could return to the Steelers. He signed and went with the team to Barcelona to start the 1993 exhibition season. Bill Cowher cut him from the squad during the last week of training camp. Lipps was sidelined by a pulled muscle at the time. He filed a grievance with the league and the Steelers were directed to pay him for a half season. So he is credited with ten seasons toward his NFL pension program. He stayed in Pittsburgh for several years before returning home to Louisiana.

Born as Louis Adam Lipps Jr. in New Orleans on August 9, 1962, there was a time when he was leading the pack in more than golfing foursomes. He was the Steelers' No. 1 draft pick out of Southern Mississippi in 1984. He was the league's consensus rookie of the year and played in the Pro Bowl. He set an NFL rookie record with 656 yards on punt returns and led all rookies with 1,587 all-purpose yards and 11 touchdowns. He also paced all AFC rookies with 45 receptions for 860 yards.

As a rookie in 1984, he established a team record by returning 53 punts. He is third, behind only Rod Woodson and Theo Bell, in career punt-return yardage with 1,212. Lipps returned punts 76 and 71 yards for touchdowns in 1984 and 1985, respectively, and shares the team record with Ray Mathews with three touchdowns on punt returns. He ranks fourth in career total yards from scrimmage behind

Franco Harris, John Stallworth and Jerome Bettis. It's not in the Steelers' record book, but Lipps probably is the leader in all-purpose yards, combining his pass catches, punt returns and end-around scampers. Woodson would be right up there among the leaders as well, mostly on kickoff returns and interception returns.

Lipps was twice named the Steelers' MVP in a voting of the team's players, in 1985 and again in 1989. He was regarded as one of the league's premier big-play receivers. He was a triple threat as a receiver, runner on end-around plays and punt-return duties. He scored touchdowns all three ways and even threw a touchdown pass.

During his stay with the Steelers, Lipps was one of their most popular players and served on many local charities and service agencies. He was the honorary chairman for Children's Miracle Network Telethon benefiting the Rehabilitation Institute, and was active with Big Brothers/Big Sisters as bowlathon chairman. In the off-season, he addressed high school students for Blue Cross of Western Pennsyvania Drug & Alcohol Education Program. He was involved with Variety.

Lipps could light up a room with that smile framed by a mustache and goatee. It appeared that the world was Louis Lipps' oyster in those days. His wife Toni Seawright had been Miss Mississippi in 1987. But she, along with much of his money, was now gone. He married Toni in June of 1989, and the marriage lasted one year and a half. He said he was financially well off these days, but conceded that "it was a wicked divorce. It could have been worse." He was single and did not have any children.

He was working as a marketing manager and loan officer at 1st Federated Mortage Inc., with second floor offices on West Liberty Avenue in Dormont. He was doing radio commercials for the company. That also sparked renewed interest in Lipps around town. We met in April and again in May for lunch at Atria's Restaurant & Tavern in nearby Mt. Lebanon, about a half-mile from his office. A young man who parked his car called out, "Hey, aren't you Louie Lipps?" Lipps smiled in reply and waved to him. "It's been like that ever since I've been back," allowed Lipps. "It gives you a good feeling to know they remember you. Pittsburgh seems like home now."

One of the proprietors at Atria's, Jay Dabat, told Lipps that he got an autograph from him once at a special day at White Swan Park which used to be out near the old Pittsburgh International Airport. "White Swan Park . . . " repeated Lipps. "I remember that. Gosh, that was 20 years ago."

"I remember when Bill Cowher came in to replace Chuck Noll, and I was thinking, 'Man, I'm glad I'm not in his shoes.' But he did an amazing job. He built an attitude that continues to this day. And that's taking nothing away from Chuck Noll. But what Coach Cowher has done is extraordinary."
— Merril Hoge

Louis Lipps:

The best time for me was my first three seasons with the Steelers. I had so much success. Then I got married in 1989 to the prettiest girl in town. That was great, too. Over time, unfortunately, it just went sour.

Coming back to Pittsburgh was one of the best moves I've made in my life. When I got here, it was like I had never left. The people and friends I met back then were still here when I got back. I definitely made the right decision.

It was good to get hooked up with the Variety Club again. I was involved in their first golf tournament in 1984. I was co-chairman for that event. We've already set a date for next year — GlaxoSmithKline is coming back as the lead sponsor — and I agreed to lend my name to it once again. That's a real honor. They already have pledges for support in place for the next outing.

We had quite a turnout and we were playing on the same day as Merril Hoge, Mark Bruener and Hines Ward were having their tournament, and Joe Walton was holding his tournament.

I handle lots of p.r. stuff and promotions where I'm working, at 1st Federated Mortgage, Inc. I've been rekindling as many friendships and contacts as I can. This is the town that made me what I am.

I met Jay Berger, the president of the agency, when I was a rookie and we've kept in touch ever since. We've been close friends since I first met him. He talked me into coming back.

I went home because I wanted to make sure everything was OK with my mother — she's up there in age. I came back when it was time for me to move on solo. My father died, at age 67, back in 1982. I've been taking care of my mother and my sister since he passed. My mother's name is Melva. My sister is Sybil. She's 41, and she has three kids. She has two boys and a girl. She's a single parent, and she lives with my mother.

My work at the mortgage company has been good. It's been steady and I've been busy. I live in Aspinwall and I like my life right now.

When I played basketball this year, I got some good cheers wherever we went. These people will never forget you. If there was ever a city where you wanted to play sports this was it. They don't forget.

374

"Get your butt back up here to Pittsburgh."
— Mel Blount

When I first came to Pittsburgh it was like a dream come true, like a fairy tale. In my first year, we went all the way to the AFC championship game (before losing 45-28 at Miami). We were one game away from the Super Bowl. I was the AFC Rookie of the Year, and I got to go to the Pro Bowl. The following year I went back to the Pro Bowl and my teammates named me the Steelers' MVP. It doesn't get much better than that.

Things were just happening. There was a lot of personal and team success. I was getting a chance to meet a lot of people and I couldn't have felt better about myself and my situation.

Mel Blount and I are real good friends and he's been advising me for a long time. He said, "Go home and do what you have to do, but get your butt back up here to Pittsburgh." He said he did the same thing. He said every year after the season he'd go home to Georgia. He did that for the most part during the 14 years he played. He said he missed out on making stronger connections in the corporate community. He says he should have stayed here more. He said, "Don't make that mistake. It's still good, but it could have been better."

I remember Mel Blount was into a business venture with cell phones. He was signing up people to use them. They were huge and heavy in the beginning. He got me a cell phone and he gave me pep talks. He'd say, "You keep doing what you're doing and you'll end up in the Hall of Fame."

Mel looks like he could still play. When I see how big he is, I imagine what it must have been like to go up against him.

"Learn your routes."
— John Stallworth

Stallworth was still with the Steelers when I came here. That was great for me. It was amazing to me to be able to work out with him, and watch him at practice. First of all, it seems like that was yesterday. One day I'm watching the Steelers on TV, and the next day I'm practicing with them. Calvin Sweeney, Weegie Thompson, Gregg Garrity and Greg Hawthorne were all on the team. They wanted me to succeed. They helped me any way they could. They helped me in every way.

One day Stallworth's doing a rep, and I remember the way he shielded the defensive back from the ball when he caught it. He told me, "You can look at that play all day long in the playbook, and you can practice that play out of the book and put it on the field. You've got to see how it will work. It may not come out exactly the way it was drawn up. Just make sure you're all by yourself when the ball gets there and catch it." The stuff I picked up from him was invaluable to my growth as a wide receiver in the NFL.

John Stallworth and I hit it off right off the bat. I can't put my finger on it. We were roommates for four years, and at training camp for three years. I'll be there this August when John gets inducted into the Pro Football Hall of Fame in Canton, Ohio.

I was always hanging with Bennie Cunningham, John Stallworth, Donnie Shell and Calvin Sweeney. I'd go out to dinner with them. When they weren't on the field they were showing me something else to help me learn the ways of being a pro player. I got along with all the guys on the team, but those were the ones I was with the most.

We went to chapel the morning of the game. The same guys were always there. Calvin Sweeney, Donnie Shell, Jon Kolb, John Stallworth.

The playbook was so thick it resembled a phone book. I was flipping the pages one day, and John says, "How's it coming over there?" I must have rolled my eyes like I was lost. He said, "Man, I'm going to tell you something. A hook route is always going to be a hook route. A square-out is always going to be a square-out. A square-in is always going to be a square-in. Learn your routes and learn the defensive schemes and you're going to be in the league a long time."

He told me how to simplify what I needed to know from the playbook. What did I learn from him? I learned patience. I learned awareness. I learned how to recognize coverages. I learned the importance of just getting open. He was just as generous a person as can be. Even when I was in Louisiana, I'd talk to him once a month. He was always a caring person.

"Maybe I can play this game."

I remember when I came here I saw Swann and Chuck Noll standing in the hallway, just talking. When I walked by Swann, I realized I was just as big as he was. When you looked at him on TV, he looked larger than life. I thought, "Maybe I can play this game."

When you look back there were games you wish you had played better. We knew we should have done better. Why didn't we? It's hard for players to dissect that. Us, as a

John Stallworth, who went into the Pro Football Hall of Fame this August, was with Steelers when Louis Lipps joined the team. Stallworth became a mentor to Lipps, and helped guide him in many ways, on and off the field.

Louis Lipps reported to Three Rivers Stadium on second day of NFL draft and could see his name on listing card in media room. He was the Steelers' No. 1 draft pick in 1984, the 23rd pick overall.

receiving corps, we always stuck together. Noll told us, to a man, just do your job.

We worked with different quarterbacks. First, it was David Woodley and Mark Malone. Then it was Bubby Brister and Neil O'Donnell.

Privately, guys had their favorites. But the guys kept that information to themselves. We were always showing our respect for Coach Noll and his decisions, whatever it was. One thing as players, we never tried to point the finger. Noll said, "Don't you ever point the finger at anybody, unless you can back it up."

They do a lot of finger-pointing now, even during the games, right out there in public. They get a lot of that from what they see on TV. There's a different breed of ballplayer today. They grew up differently. They're not taught proper respect or proper behavior in all cases. Noll didn't want us showboating when we scored a touchdown. He told us, "Look like you've been there before."

I think celebrating a touchdown is great. But there's a certain degree between what's acceptable and what's out of line. When it comes to someone like Plaxico Burress, I don't think Chuck Noll would have accepted some of the stuff he does.

These guys today have so much ability. Sometimes, it seems to me, they don't know how good they can be. I was fortunate to play with guys like Larry Brown and Jack Lambert. They weren't going out there to bullshit around. They took care of business. I was fortunate to play with guys like that.

The thing I liked about Lambert is that if you were playing good he'd let you know. If you weren't, he wouldn't say anything to you. In my first game, against Kansas City, I caught three passes. Lambert said, "Thatta way, Louie, kick their ass." That made me feel so good. I wanted to keep doing it. You wanted Lambert to like you.

These fans here are unbelievable. They were great at training camp and at Three Rivers Stadium.

I went up to training camp last year and I couldn't get over the difference. There weren't as many fans there. It was all roped off like Fort Knox. Merril Hoge, Craig Wolfley and I did a football clinic for women at the camp. We had a hard time getting around. We kept getting stopped and asked to show our media badges, or guest badges, whatever they issued us. And that was before September 11.

Some teams treat their alumni better than other teams. It's hard to get tickets here for a game. The Cleveland Browns have an executive box where they let former players sit. You can buy two tickets to a Steelers' game, but you need to reserve them in advance. Those tickets are in the nosebleed section. It's tough to get around. That reminds you that you're a former player. I miss people like Joe Gordon. Joe always took good care of me. He would try to help me if I had a special request. He remembered how I would do things at the last minute if he asked me to go somewhere. It works both ways. I always appreciated everything he did for me.

I did a lot of stuff for free, but I always got paid in one way or another. The fans were great to me.

"He'd be swearing at everybody."

You never had two quarterbacks as different as Bubby Brister and Neil O'Donnell. Bubby was something. A lot of people don't realize because of his actions and expletives that the boy was a competitor. He didn't like to lose. No kind of contest.

You hear a lot of stuff about what he was like in the huddle. We didn't mind him being so pumped up before the game even got underway. But we told him, "You're running the show. You need to be calm. Just call the play, whatever it is." Sometimes he was too excited. He'd be swearing at everybody. You'd have to call time out; there was not enough time to call the play. He was definitely a competitor and the boy had some real talent. He could throw the rock.

Neil O'Donnell was pretty much like night and day compared to Bubby Brister, and the way they approached the game. Neil was more of a calm and cool kind of guy. He was more at ease. He was keying on getting the job done. He had a very good touch on the ball. He was a big quarterback. He had good size and good strength. Where Bubby was always "mothering" everybody, Neil was calmer.

Bubby threw harder. Neil had a quick release. If you were open the ball was gone! Noll had to deal with them differently. I was here only a brief time with Coach Cowher, so I can't make the comparison with how he dealt with them.

As far as Chuck is concerned, what can you say about him? He's the only coach I ever played for in the NFL. He's the only coach who could look at his team and knew if it was tired or ready to play. His outlook and his knowledge of the game were remarkable. He always talked to us. He talked about priorities. He'd go all around the field, getting in with different groups, and saying "Try this" and "Try that" as he walked about.

> *"Bill Cowher always promised us as players that he would take care of us. 'If you give me every thing you've got, I'll take care of you.' Cowher is not only a great coach, he's a great friend. He's been able to toe that line. He does it from the heart. You can see how it works."*
> — Merril Hoge

"You don't realize the impact you have on people."

When I was out in Shadyside, I met a pest control guy there when I was playing for the Steelers. I was throwing some garbage out when I spotted him. He hollered out, "Louis Lipps, it's a pleasure to meet you!" I waved to him. Then he got nearer and he said, "I don't want to bother you, but if you want to make a kid's day, my son is having a birthday party this weekend. What would it take to get you to come?"

He gave me his phone number and asked me to call if I was interested in coming. I called him back and told him I could make it. It was out in Penn Hills. I went and I had more fun than the kids. I would do stuff like that from time to time. Hey, they couldn't have treated me any better. It was an open date on my schedule.

When I came back to town last year, they had a pep rally at Market Square and I showed up along with Mark Bruener, Jerry Olsavsky and Edmund Nelson, and this guy is pulling at my pants' leg. He kept putting this picture up for me to see. It showed me shooting pool in his basement. I talked to him, and it turned out that he was the pest control guy whose son's birthday party I had attended. He said his son was married now, and had a little baby. So sometimes you don't realize the impact you have on people. They don't forget. He's telling me his wife wants to cook dinner for me once again.

So I went, and there were four people who were there when I was at their home 17 years earlier. It was quite a reunion.

I used to spend my off-season here. Joe Gordon would get me so many appearances I was always busy, and making some extra money. I might get $1,000 for being some place for two hours, signing autographs. I played on the Steelers' basketball team. Every night we were playing at a different court. It was fun. You couldn't get enough of it. Now this year I was back on the circuit, even if on a part-time basis.

Everywhere I go, people tell me I have better stats than Lynn Swann, and he's in the Hall of Fame. They let you know that. But he's got something I don't have. He's got a Super Bowl ring. He's got four of them. If I had the same quarterback, I'd have gone to more Pro Bowls. I feel this. Hey, we went with what we had, and we did the best we could.

I have no regrets. I would have done the same thing all over again.

> *"When I played high school football I didn't really think about college. I just thought about doing the best I could in high school. When I got to college I didn't think about pro football. I never considered playing pro ball. I just kept going to those different levels, and I loved it."*
> — Andy Russell

"He was the same way as my dad."

Reserve, Louisiana is a small town. It's in the middle of the state, between Baton Rouge and New Orleans. There's maybe 8,000 to 10,000 people there. It's the kind of town where everybody knows everybody. My old high school buddies are still there, and lots of relatives. I got involved with some horses there, and doing some trail riding. I rode horses in the Mardi Gras parades in New Orleans. I have a friend taking care of my horses now. That was something Mel Blount and I bonded about. He has horses out on his ranch in Taylorstown. He looks more like a cowboy. He wears those big hats and he's so tall. He looks the part. My dad, Louis Sr., was a custodian and delivered documents for a local bank. He died during my sophomore year in college. My mother, Melva, was a seamstress, and she sewed for friends at our home. My parents were very strict. So I had to toe the line when I was growing up.

When I was a kid, I was a huge, huge baseball player. If you go back to Reserve now they'd tell you how good a baseball player I was. They think if I hadn't gone to the National Football League I could have made it in Major League Baseball. I started out at third base but ended up in center field, and I pitched when I was playing both positions.

My dad was a big baseball fan and he coached me. He wasn't really a coach, but he coached me. He would always talk about what I didn't do well. I could be pitching and strike out ten and go three for four, and he'd talk about a hit I gave up or an at-bat when I didn't get a hit.

He thought you should practice what you didn't do well. Chuck Noll was the same way. He said people tend to do what they do well, over and over again. It feels good to them. That's why I fitted in so well with Coach Noll. He was the same way as my dad. They had the same kind of work ethic.

Tom Moore was my position coach. He was the offensive coordinator, quarterback and receivers coach. He was good. He's with Tony Dungy now at Indianapolis. You might be having a bad day, and might be cussing yourself or you have the long mouth. He would come up to me after I dropped a few passes in practice, and he'd say, "You know the only person who never dropped a pass. God, that's who! He was the only one who never dropped one because he never had one thrown to him." He let you know it happens, and you have to get over it. Noll was a big help in other ways. He let you know that football was not forever. Most of the guys I played with aren't around anymore. I see Rich Erenburg once in a while. I see Dwayne Woodruff and Edmund Nelson. I see the guys from the '70s. A lot of them are still around. People think I played with them, so I've always felt comfortable in their company.

Jim Sweeney
A Pittsburgh guy

"I root for my friends."

It had been five years since Jim Sweeney and I last met for lunch, but he had not forgotten the occasion. "We'll meet at King's again," he said. "And this time it's my turn to pick up the check."

So on Monday, May 13, 2002, the day after Mother's Day, we had a reunion at King's Family Restaurant on McMurray Road in Upper St. Clair. He was driving a new champagne colored Lincoln Navigator, a sports utility vehicle built along similar lines to Sweeney's.

Sweeney was sitting in a booth in the back of the biggest room, arriving a few minutes ahead of schedule. He was still a powerful looking figure. He played at 6-4, 295 pounds. He could play guard, tackle, center and even tight end in short yardage situations. He knew his responsibilities at whatever position he was asked to play. He could bench press 500 pounds and he had worked with martial arts to help quicken his hand speed. He was down to 280 pounds when we met this time, but didn't appear to be dieting.

When the waitress came to take our order, Sweeney said, "I'll have two hamburgers, a bowl of vegetable soup, some fries and let me have a chocolate milk shake, made with vanilla ice cream."

I had to smile, at both the size of the order and that he liked his milk shakes the same way I do when I dare to order one these days. Sweeney is not the guy you want to eat with if you want to lose weight. I was also glad he was picking up the tab. "You still trying to keep your weight up?" I asked in jest.

"No, I'm just hungry," he said. "I didn't have much of a breakfast." Hartley King would have enjoyed seeing Jim Sweeney so at home in one his restaurants.

There had been a bad storm over the weekend that knocked out the electrical power in several pockets of Western Pennsylvania, including the South Hills where Sweeney resided. It caused some inconvenience at his home. "I had to wash the dishes this morning because we couldn't use the dishwasher over the weekend," he said, "but that was OK." Sweeney seemed happy to have been useful, as always.

He had grown up in Beechview, and gone to St. Catherine's Grade School, Seton-LaSalle High School and the University of Pittsburgh. He was living in Venetia, or Peters Township. "No one knows where Venetia is," said Sweeney in that throaty voice of his. His wife, Heather, was from Brookline. They had three children, Shannon, 8, Liam Richard, 5, and Aislinn Neev, 18 months. They are all Gaelic names. He said he would be 40 years old in August and that Heather was 31.

Mike Fabus/Pittsburgh Steelers

He said Shannon had received her First Holy Communion the day before and the kids were wearing their Communion outfits at another Mass that morning. Heather had accompanied her to the ceremony while Jim remained at home to care of the baby. "That's where I'm coming from," he said. "I love being able to do that."

"I was always a Steelers' fan."

Sweeney and I were old friends from our days together at Pitt. He was a student when I went to work there in 1982 as the assistant athletic director for sports information. He weighed 205 when he first showed up at the Oakland campus. He often credited Pitt's strength coach Buddy Morris for his physical development. No one worked harder in the weight room than Sweeney. No one had to worry about Jim Sweeney getting into trouble. He'd been an altar boy at St. Catherine's and he still served Mass on occasion. At Pitt, just prior to my arrival, he had been one of the terrific offensive linemen that protected quarterback Danny Marino. They included Jimbo Covert, Ron Sams, Emil Boures, Bill Fralic, Paul Dunn, Rob Fada and Bill Fralic. They were Joe Moore's boys and they would all play pro ball.

Sweeney had worked out for the Steelers in his senior year of 1984. He knew they were interested in him. He'd been a Steelers' fan for a long time. He grew up idolizing the likes of Ray Mansfield, Mike Webster and Jim Clack. He was drafted by the New York Jets on the second round before the Steelers could select him.

He played 11 seasons with the Jets, one with the Seattle Seahawks and signed as a free agent with the Steelers in 1996. He was reunited with Tom Donahoe, then the football operations director of the Steelers. Donahoe had coached him at Seton-LaSalle. It took Jim 21 seasons to realize his boyhood dream of playing for the Steelers. He liked playing for Bill Cowher, who had spent the first eight years of his life in Beechview.

They were soul brothers, so to speak. Beechview was their bond.

Sweeney stayed four seasons and made a solid contribution on the field and in the locker room. He was the best kind of teammate. He had hoped to play 15 seasons in the NFL, and he ended up playing 16 seasons. "I enjoyed that bonus year a great deal," said Sweeney.

When Sweeney was selected by the Jets, he received a congratulatory letter that was hand-written by Art Rooney, the owner of the Steelers. It's still on display in Sweeney's home office. It reads: "Dear Jim, I'm a friend of your grandfather. He was a fine man and a top athlete. I hope you will be a superstar. I'm sorry you're not with our team. You will find Leon Hess and Jim Kensil of the Jets good men. I'll be rooting for you. I met your brother Mike at the Stadium. Good luck. Art Rooney."

After Mr. Rooney died in 1988, Sweeney wore the initials AJR on the back of his helmet while playing for the Jets. The Steelers had special shoulder patches with AJR (Arthur Joseph Rooney) stitched on them that they wore that season. "I figured I owed him something," said Sweeney at the time.

Sweeney said he had remained a Steelers' fan, during all his years in New York and his one-year stay in Seattle.

"My dad used to keep me informed on what was going on up here when I was away, telling me how they did, how they played," said Sweeney. "I was always a Steelers fan, except the few times we played them. You can take the kid out of Pittsburgh, but you can't take the Pittsburgh out of the kid.

"I'm a Pittsburgher, not a New Yorker. I'd say you have to be born in New York to enjoy it. If you spend a few days there it's OK, but if you spend more than a week there, you're crazy."

While with the Jets, he befriended Doug Miller, the team's assistant public relations man, who grew up in my neighborhood in Upper St. Clair and was one of my proteges. They attended each other's weddings in Pittsburgh. Sweeney's was held on the weekend of a record snowstorm, so he had a history of dealing with the worst weather Pittsburgh had to offer. With his bull neck and determined approach, Sweeney could handle all challenges. I often saw Sweeney and his family strolling through South Hills Village, or dining at King's Restaurant and Eat'n Park Restaurant.

He even delivered photos of his family to my home when I requested them, saying he knew the neighborhood because he had been to Doug Miller's home. I told him I'd be glad to meet him somewhere, but he said that wasn't necessary.

When Sweeney retired after the 1999 season, he started helping out as an assistant coach for his old high school teammate, Greg Gattuso, who was coaching the football team at Duquesne University. Gattuso had played his college ball at Penn State.

Sweeney is a sentimental guy. We talked for nearly two hours at King's, and toward the end of the conversation, when Sweeney was talking about his dad, who had died in late December, he got wet-eyed. When I saw Sweeney wipe away a tear or two from his cheek with those big paws of his I knew it had been a good interview.

As always, he had given it an honest effort. He had put his heart into it and, toward the end, that heart grew a little heavy for him.

Jim Sweeney:

I get treated like a former Steeler around here, and I still get recognized in New York. So maybe I'm bilingual when it comes to my identification as a football player. I remember when I was playing with the Jets, I met Buddy Morris and Jerry Olsavsky for lunch at Billy's Black & Gold Bar in Sharon. Jerry was a rookie with the Steelers and he was getting lots of

attention from the folks at the restaurant I was in my fifth or sixth year with the Jets, but they could have cared less. "That doesn't count," one of them said. "You're not a Steeler." If I didn't play for the Steelers, they didn't care. And I wasn't in Seattle long enough to connect. That was a long commute, and I was happy to be able to come home again. If I was to go to Billy's now I think they'd regard me as a Steeler.

Growing up, I always wanted to play here. I still rooted for the Black and Gold, except when we played them. My dad kept me abreast of what was going on. I root for Pittsburgh people.

I like the Miami Dolphins because Dave Wannstedt, their coach, comes from Baldwin and Pitt. I like the Cleveland Browns because Foge Fazio and Buddy Morris are there. I was happy for the New England Patriots last season when they won the Super Bowl because two of my former Steeler teammates, Mike Vrabel and C.J. (Charles Johnson) were playing for the Patriots. I root for my friends.

You can't shortchange New England for what they did. I really admired them for being introduced as a team at the Super Bowl. Maybe that's a lesson to be learned. I know that means a lot to a player. You want to be a part of it. They stressed the importance of the team. They were saying we believe it, we preach it and we show it.

If the Steelers played New England nine more times they might win all nine times, but they didn't win it that day. It was New England's time to win. There was something underlying there.

Pro football might still be a business, but you don't have to view it as a business all the time. I'm still a fan in a lot of ways. I used to just love being in the locker room. Believe me, 99 percent of the guys are good guys. I hated people who viewed it as a business. There are some like that on every team.

I don't like free agency. It doesn't benefit everybody. It's hard to keep a team together. And there's a big discrepancy between what guys are making. It's difficult when the guy next to you is making ten times as much money for playing the same position. That's especially tough on the offensive line where you have to work together more to be able to execute plays properly. Free agency is going to ruin the game, if it hasn't already done so.

The ones I know that are still there in the Steelers locker room are not just great athletes. They're great people. Mark Bruener is as good as they get. Earl Holmes was one of my friends, and I think they're gonna miss him. I know they miss Levon Kirkland and Dermonti Dawson. You won't find a better person that Dermonti. I was lucky to have known him and

Mike Webster, two of the greatest centers ever to play the game. Any father looking for a role model for their kids could do no better than Dermonti Dawson or Mark Bruener.

Hines Ward, Deshea Townsend, Will Blackwell, Mike Tomczak, Roger Duffy and Josh Miller were some of my favorites. I hate mentioning names because I'm going to forget some good guys. Someone like Will Blackwell will say, "Mr. Sweeney, how are you?"

There are other people who make the dressing room a pleasant place. John Norwig, the trainer, and Chet Fuhrman, the strength and conditioning coach, and Rogers Freyvogel and Paul Gallagher, the equipment manager and his assistant, and Rich Baker, the field manager. Frank Sciulli still helps out in the locker room. He was a good guy, too. You had the gals in the front office. Seeing their faces every morning, hearing them saying "Hi" and "Hello" was all a part of it. It starts from the top, with Dan Rooney and his son, Art. It works its way down the ladder. My wife had a surprise retirement party for me and some special people showed up at Tambellini's on Rt. 51 for the occasion. Dan Rooney signed a picture for me with a nice message that I treasure. It'll be up there with the one his dad sent me at the beginning.

"My dad was my heart and soul."

We always had a Mass for the Catholic players when we were on the road, but we didn't have one at home for games here. They didn't think they could get anybody to do it. I knew Father Dave Bonnar and I asked him if he'd want to do it.

Father Dave and I had gone to school together at Seton-LaSalle and we'd kept in touch. When he came to St. Thomas More I started to attend his Mass with my family. I knew he was a big fan of the Steelers. There are Steelers' fans who are priests in every city where we play. Father Dave was just appointed pastor of St. Bartholomew's parish in Penn Hills.

So Father Dave started saying Mass for the Steelers at the Hilton before our pre-game meal. We had the usual turnout. Mark Bruener would be there. Roger Duffy. Mike Tomczak. Kevin Gilbride. Mr. and Mrs. Rooney would be there. Sometimes young Art and his family. Chet Fuhrman. John Norwig. My wife and kids. It was good. The Steelers take Father Dave on one road trip with the team each season.

Father Dave's mother passed away last year, and I know that was a real loss for him and his family. When he found out my father was dying, he called me. That meant a lot to me. He came to see my father. He asked me if I wanted him to give my father the last rites. We hugged and held each other.

I love football, but I don't want to do it for a livelihood anymore.

I'm sure my dad's death has played a part in my outlook. I saw him December 1 when our Duquesne football team played Sacred Heart in a bowl game at Rooney Field. Two weeks later, December 13, my dad was diagnosed with cancer. He had suspected for a few months, he told my mother and me, that something was wrong. He died at the end of December, just 15 days after he was told he had cancer. He knew. We had some good talks about it.

He was my heart and soul. He's the reason I played. I wanted him to watch me. I knew how much he enjoyed it. My dad — his name was Jim, too — was 72 when he died. My mom, Shirley, is still at home. Since my dad died, I don't know if I'll watch football on TV the way I used to. We used to watch the games together. I think my best day was the day I was drafted into the NFL. My family was so happy for me. It was a dream come true.

My dad used to drive up to New York to see me play. He didn't like it when they had back-to-back home games or four o'clock starts. It made it tough to get up for work the next morning after driving home late Sunday night from New York.

He'd come up and we'd go to Mass together on Saturday night. He'd spend time with me in my room until bed check, and I'd see him after the game. He'd still coach me. He'd still recognize what I was doing, or what I was supposed to be doing. He didn't hesitate to tell me.

My father taught me so much. He and my mom told me to treat people the same way you wanted them to treat you. We never knew prejudice in our house and my kids don't know it, either. There's not just race prejudice; there's all kinds of prejudice. My dad didn't care who you were. If you were on his good side he'd give you the shirt off his back.

He had big strong hands. I miss them the most.

"How can you live with yourself?"

Offensive linemen are used to getting all the blame and none of the credit. I wanted to be part of a team, one team for life. I wasn't playing for the money. You see a situation like the Pirates were in with Derek Bell and Pat Meares. They had to pay them millions no matter what. How can you live with yourself? Any man with self worth would feel guilty taking the money. That's just the way I am.

Right now, I am not ready to take on a full-time job. I'm into my third year of coaching the offensive line at Duquesne, and I've been doing some work relating to air-cleaning units in homes. We learned about that while looking for something to help our baby with her asthma. I was really impressed with what we discovered. The company is called Your Environment, and it's out of Glassport. They produce these air-purification devices.

Until our youngest gets into school, I plan to continue to stay home with the children. It's great I can be home with them. These are their biggest growing years. I want to build the proper character in my children. I like being with my wife. She's my best friend. I put her on a pedestal and I keep her there. You know how pretty she is. With her, people might say he's out-kicked his coverage. I don't want to blow it. I enjoy being around the family.

It's hard during the football season because we don't start at Duquesne until 4:30 and we don't stop till 7:30 or 8 at night. It's easier for me to get the baby to sleep than it is for Heather. My belly is bigger since I retired and the baby just lies on my belly and falls asleep. I missed the other two at this same stage. When I went to Seattle, I missed the first six weeks of Shannon's life. She wasn't too sure about me, or who I was, when she first got to see me.

The oldest two children are Momma's kids. With the baby, I am Da Da, and I like being home and being that. I play softball with Shannon and hockey with Liam, and I practice different things with them, and help them do their homework. I like that.

I haven't played much golf in the last two years. The golf courses aren't going anywhere, but my kids are. We have a pool in the backyard. I like being there with the kids. I'm their lifeguard.

"I was no angel."

My dad always said you don't want to ruin your family name. You don't want to do anything wrong that will bring shame on your family, or ruin the family name. We had great pride in our family name. It went back to my grandfather. We took pride in being Sweeneys.

We knew what was right and we know what was wrong. I was no angel. I tried to pull off some things.

My dad used to whistle when he wanted our attention, or he wanted us to come home. I could pick up my dad's whistle out of 80,000 fans in the stands in Buffalo when we played there.

We couldn't get away with any mischief in our neighborhood. My grandmother used to listen to the police radio dispatcher. I was with some guys who were throwing rocks at a neighbor's tool shed. One went right through the side. It must have been soft or thin wood. Somebody called the police about it. My grandmother called my Dad, and said, "What are your boys doing?" Then she told him he better get his boys home before they got into trouble.

He came out and whistled. That meant for us to get home. When I was a kid, no matter how far from home you were, you could hear his whistle and no matter where you were you better come running.

One of the reasons I was glad I came back here was my dad was able to come to training camp and to watch our practices. He didn't have that far to travel. We have a picture of him with Coach Cowher. He really treasured that and having the opportunity to go out on the field and talk to him. That was a big deal with my dad. Coach Cowher was good with my dad.

My dad and my mom and I used to go up to training camp when I was a kid and watch the Steelers practice. Greene, Ham and Lambert were there. It was really special to see them walk by. It was even more special to be on the other side of the fence and have fans asking me for my autograph when I was with the Steelers.

When I signed with the Steelers, Tom Donahoe said I should have been in that uniform from my first day in the NFL.

There were great fans in New York. There were more Giants fans than Jets fans, but the Jets fans were pretty loyal. They were good to me.

It was upsetting to see what happened there on September 11. I have a friend who is a fireman in New York. One of his buddies in the fire department, whom I had met briefly, was killed while fighting the fire in one of the World Trade Center towers. My friend went there during the cleanup and took some photographs that he sent me. I can show you them. That was rough.

"Grimm's great for the young players."

I thought Jeff Hartings did a good job at center last season. It's not easy to make the transition from guard to center; not everyone can do it. I think Alan Fanaca had a great year at guard. Alan is sorta a throwback. I think the Steelers did so well on the front line because Russ Grimm got the attention of the players. Grimm's great for the young players.

Russ knows what it takes to win in this league. He was a player for 12 years, and he played every position. He was known as one of the best. He can relate to every experience.

Jim Sweeney and his son, Liam Richard, say goodbye to Three Rivers Stadium.

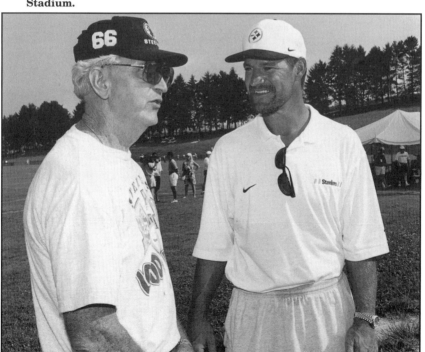

Jim Sweeney, the father of Steelers' lineman Jim Sweeney, enjoyed opportunity to meet and talk with Coach Bill Cowher on sideline at St. Vincent College following practice session. "That meant a lot to my dad," said his son.

Plus, he knows when you're trying to pull the wool over a coach's eyes.

I think they drafted a good prospect for the front line with their first pick, Kendall Simmons, a big lineman from Auburn. He has great leg strength, from what I've seen on tapes. They have to straighten him out on a few things. He has a tendency of pulling defenders in towards him. You want him pushing them away. He needs to push. They can fix that easily enough. That was just an observation of mine.

No, I don't want to follow in Russ Grimm's footsteps and become a pro line coach. You have to put in too many hours. I'll do something else, eventually.

Heather is certified in personal training now and that's something we could do together. I know how to train athletes. Maybe it's something we might get into in the future. We might like to have a get-away place somewhere like Deep Creek, Maryland. I've checked that out and we like it there. Yeah, I heard that Art Rooney Jr. has a place down there.

That's why I was lucky to be able to finish up in my hometown and make a name for myself here. I didn't have to pick up and travel. My dad only had to drive four miles to see me play instead of 400 miles to see me play in New York. I am a Pittsburgher; I like being in this city.

There's not a better place in America. This is home. My wife is from here. Her family is here. You watch. I'll bet Tom Donahoe comes back here when he's finished working in Buffalo. That's the kind of people I grew up watching. I was lucky to be influenced by people like Art and Dan Rooney, Tom Donahoe and Bill Cowher. Along with my mother and father, those were my major influences.

Cowher is from Beechview originally, so we had a bond of sorts. I think the secret to his success is he knows how to motivate people. He makes sure you stay on the straight and narrow.

I think one of the keys regarding the team's chances for the coming season is that they didn't lose any coaches this year and that's important. They should not miss a beat. They should be better. I hope they don't rest on their laurels. I hope they stay hungry. Buffalo and Cleveland will be better this year.

When you think about the Steelers you think about them winning Super Bowls. The first thing you think about are the Steelers of the '70s. But even before that, back in the '50s and the '60s, from what my father told me, they always had some tough guys and they played hard.

Back in the days of Sam Huff and Ray Nitschke and Johnny Unitas, the Steelers had one of the toughest bunch of guys in the league. They had shortcomings then, but not in the heart department. We might not have had the best teams, but we had some of the toughest people. So there's quite a legacy associated with the Steelers.

"What were they thinking?"

I'm hoping Greg Gattuso gets things straightened away at Duquesne. That really hurt him when those kids killed that other kid in a drug-related deal this year. Greg had gone to bat for one of them earlier when he'd gotten into some skirmishes at school. He got him reinstated to the team after he had been suspended. Both of those kids came from good families in Mt. Lebanon. They were always respectful of the coaches. It's hard to figure.

Why would they kill someone? How did they think they could get away with something like that? What were they thinking to get involved with that stuff in the first place?

It was a shock. I was talking to a fireman friend of mine from New York, when I saw on TV about these two kids from Mt. Lebanon being arrested in a murder case. My first thought was about Greg. Never in a million years did I think these kids were capable of doing something like that. When they saw me, it was always "Yes, Sir," and "No, Sir," when I spoke to them. You don't know anyone's personal life; I only knew them from the football team at school. They sure did a good job of hurting their family's name. How could they kill someone over drugs or money?

Maybe they see some of that stuff on HBO and figure they can get away with it. I think a lot of this stuff is imitating television and the movies. They were trying to be thugs and they weren't thugs.

Greg has addressed this situation with the rest of the team. He's very good at handling situations. He spoke to them and told him how he felt about everything, and warned them to stay away from the wrong people, and situations that can lead to trouble. He told them what was expected of them as football players and students at Duquesne.

You feel bad for all the families involved in this senseless death. These kids' lives are over. They're 20 years old and they could spend the rest of their lives behind bars. I liked these kids and I feel sorry for them and their families. I feel sorry for the kid who was killed and dumped in the river.

After September 11, I didn't think anything could shock me again, but this did. This reminds you that you have to always be vigilant and on the lookout. You have to keep reminding young people of the right way to do things. You can't take anything for granted.

Kendrell Bell and Rodney Bailey
Brawn and Brains

"We were both a big part of the
team's success last season."

They are an odd couple, but they seem good for each other. Kendrell Bell and Rodney Bailey have traveled different roads in their lives, but they both ended up in Pittsburgh as rookies with the Steelers in 2001.

Bell was the Steelers' second selection in the college draft, right behind Casey Hampton, a nose-tackle from Texas. Bell was a 6-1, 250-pound linebacker from Georgia. Bailey was a 6-3, 292-pound defensive lineman from Ohio State.

Both stuck with the Steelers. Bell was a blast, a newcomer so good that he was named the National Football League's Rookie of the Year. Bailey added depth to the defensive line.

They shared an apartment on the South Side of Pittsburgh. Their pad is high on a hill, up on Pius Street where there were still signs about the annual passion play "Veronica's Veil" that has been staged at St. Michael's since I was in grade school, and that was 46 years ago.

Their apartment is in a building that was once St. Michael's High School. The South Side was once full of such parish schools, but most of the churches and the schools were closed down years ago. There was once a Catholic Class B basketball league consisting of such schools. It was a feeder program for nearby Duquesne University, just across the Monongahela River.

Their apartment is within a few miles of the University of Pittsburgh Sports Performance Complex where the Steelers and Panthers had their office complexes and practice fields. "We can get there in ten minutes," said Bailey during a visit to their apartment on Monday, April 13, 2002. One of their teammates, Clark Haggans, was in the apartment when I arrived, but he cut out soon after.

Bailey and Bell take turns feeding the tropical fish in a large tank that's in the middle of their kitchenette/lounge area.

The view from the deck of their apartment was impressive. The skyscrapers downtown were to the left, and off to the right, on the distant horizon, one could see the Cathedral of Learning, the centerpiece of the campus of the University of Pittsburgh. Off to the far right, I could see familiar landscape leading up the Mon to my hometown of Hazelwood. I couldn't help but point out and identify what was out there to the two newcomers to the city.

I had spoken to both earlier at a Steelers' basketball game in my current neighborhood of Upper St. Clair. I had spoken on the same program as Bailey at a Pittsburgh Club dinner at Columbus. His

Rodney Bailey and Kendrell Bell share an apartment on Pittsburgh's South Side near St. Michael's Church.

Photos by Jim O'Brien

Edmund Nelson checks out Rodney Bailey's biceps and tattoos during timeout for Steelers' basketball team.

fiancée, Ann Dannemiller, a junior at Ohio State who hails from Arlington, Texas, was with him that evening. They were an impressive young couple. They are both attractive and smart. Bailey had gained a bachelor's degree in communications in 3½ years at Ohio State, a school that gained some negative publicity during his stay there because of the poor classroom performances of several of the Buckeyes ballplayers. He was encouraging Bell to go back to school and do whatever was necessary to complete work for a bachelor's degree in child and family development. "I'm bigger than he is," said Bailey, the more boisterous and talkative of the two, "but I'm the brain and he's the brawn." Bell has been taking home-study classes and is determined to get his degree at Georgia.

Bailey is as bubbly as Jerome Bettis in conversation, while Bell is more laid-back. He seems more serious. He, too, is a friendly young fellow. He liked what he saw when he came to see Bailey's apartment, and he just moved in. They were getting along just fine.

Bailey told me he had recently gone to Columbus and given Ann an engagement ring. "She was real excited," he reported. He surprised himself by finding a spot for himself with the Steelers. He was even in the starting lineup for their second game at Buffalo, filling in for the injured Kimo von Oelhoffen.

Bell was assured of staying with the team, and Bailey was working hard to do whatever he could do to stay with the Steelers. Corey Hampton is now a fixture on the defensive line as well. So the Steelers really shored up their defense with an infusion of rookie talent. These three, along with Chris Hoke, teamed up this past year to lend their support to fund-raising efforts by Every Child, Inc., an East Liberty-based program that provides aid to 700 children with special needs.

Bell quickly found his niche in a linebacking unit that featured menacing pass rushers Joey Porter and Jason Gildon at the outside spots, plus reliable inside linebacker Earl Holmes. Bell had a big uniform to fill within the Steelers' 3-4 defense because the team had cut salary by releasing inside linebacker Levon Kirkland, who had played nine seasons with the Steelers. Bell was the Steelers' first rookie starting linebacker since Jack Lambert in 1974. At 6-1, 236, he is about 30 pounds lighter than Kirkland, but Bell more than makes up for that by being faster. He played defensive end at mini-camp this spring.

"He is both extremely aggressive and explosive," said Steelers' linebacker coach Mike Archer. "He has the sudden burst to get to places very quickly."

Kendrell Bell:

I've learned about what the Steelers of the '70s did. I've seen those four Lombardi trophies they won at those four Super Bowls. We all know about that. They definitely set the standard for the organization. You need to have a standard

Jim O'Brien

Kendrell Bell comes off practice field at UPMC Sports Performance Complex on South Side, about ten minutes from his apartment.

"Freshly-cut grass, to me, reminds me of training camp. It reminds me when the ground crew is keeping the grounds fresh for you because you are going through two-a-days, and they got to keep wetting the grass four to five times a week. Just the smell of freshly-cut grass, to me, sends a chill through my body because I know it's time to go back to work. It's summer time and training camp is coming up and it's time to start my back-to-work training. I really start to get psyched up."

— Lee Flowers

when you're playing anything. It's our job to fulfill that standard.

A lot of people say we're going to be another Steel Curtain. I hope we have the players to rate that kind of comparison. Everybody on the squad now knows what we are capable of doing. We were a big part of the team's success last season.

I'd like to win a Super Bowl so we have one for the thumb. Life will be easier in Pittsburgh for everybody on the team

I try to be a low-key leader. I try to lead by what I do on the field.

They didn't draft me to worship anybody. They drafted me to play. I think I filled some big shoes. There are big expectations for me now. I have certain ambitions. I worked hard in the off-season to give myself the best opportunity to play. I've always been like that.

I knew about Greg Lloyd. He stood out among the linebackers. I'd see the way he hit people. He wasn't a bad guy off the field. I'm a nice guy off the field. On the field I'm a different person.

It's a fight or flight situation. Some guy is pounding on you or spitting on you. It's live every day. It's almost like a fistfight. I've met some of the old Steelers. I met L.C. Greenwood, Dwight White, Louie Lipps and some others. They take care of themselves. I respect them.

A lot of kids today don't have proper respect. I do respect them. It's great to meet them. I try to keep it in perspective. A lot of other players don't have the words to say to show them how they feel. A young guy came up to me at an autograph signing and said something I wasn't thrilled about. But I don't think he meant any harm. He just didn't give much thought to what he said, I figure. A lot of kids today don't know how to express themselves properly.

I'm from Augusta, Georgia and that's my home. But I like Pittsburgh. There are a lot of good people here, and that makes me enjoy everything about Pittsburgh. People take pride in their Pittsburgh Steelers, and you hear so many of them talking about the team.

If I'm out with Rodney, we attract some attention because he's so big. They figure we must be football players. The kids will ask us who we are. They don't know us that well yet.

I worked hard to prepare myself for training camp last year. I continued to do what got me selected as high as I was. I felt there was no reason to change my routine. I kept going to school. I kept taking classes. I'm taking classes now. I have six more credits after the six credits I'm taking in order to get my diploma. I want that real badly. I've got my discipline to do it.

Whatever I do, I do it all out. I try to give it everything I've got. I forget we get paid. I'm in it to win. If somebody pancakes me I'm going to get up and go after someone. I get a kick out of running to the other side of the field and tackling someone, like I did with Curtis Martin of the Jets.

It took me awhile before I got real interested in sports. I didn't really like playing football until my junior year at Georgia. I ran track all my life. I started playing football in high school mainly because I was bigger than most of the kids.

My grandfather pushed me to play. One day I quit the team because I wasn't enjoying it. But I had a coach who coaxed me back and supported me. He told me I could develop into a fine football player.

I remember I used to hear about Greg Lloyd of the Steelers because he grew up and lived in Georgia. The only other team I ever really heard about was the Tampa Bay Buccaneers. For some reason, I didn't follow the Atlanta Falcons.

I was really disappointed last year when we didn't go to the Super Bowl. I think I took it as hard as anybody did. I never really won anything in football. I never got a ring for anything. When I heard we'd be getting rings if we won, I damn near went crazy. I knew we were going to win.

It was especially upsetting because two of my teammates at Georgia, Richard Seymour and Patrick Pass, were playing for the Patriots. Richard Seymour, who's a defensive lineman, won an award I should have won my senior year. So that was very upsetting.

I was hysterical before the game, but I didn't think everybody was up for the battle. I was going around asking people, "What's wrong?" I don't know. I felt like we were missing the edge.

Everybody we played we hated them for one reason or another. Something they said about somebody or someone on our team. Like Ty Law made some critical comments about our receivers. Somebody always had a comment. We didn't have enough to work with against New England. If we could have hooked onto something, maybe we would have won.

We have good people here, and we have kind of a brotherly love. It doesn't matter whether they're black or white. There's no trouble. I can speak to any of our guys. Jason Gildon is our leader. He doesn't say much, but when he says something you feel it. Chad Scott speaks up, and Lee Flowers isn't afraid to speak his piece. He's one of the guys who just gives his all. Kordell and Jerome are the leaders of the offensive team.

Rodney Bailey:

When you play for the Pittsburgh Steelers, you are as much a part of the city of Pittsburgh as anyone who's grown up here. Being a player here is different. You go into stores, whether it's on Carson Street, or in the suburban shopping malls, and people might or might not recognize you. I like it. People here really care about football and their Steelers.

I'm from Cleveland and there are a lot more hills here than you have in Cleveland. Ohio is flat country. Pittsburgh is more compact; Cleveland is more spread out. I'm glad the Steelers wanted me.

I didn't know how much interest there was in me before the draft. I didn't know if I was on anybody's list. So I didn't have expectations of playing. That was like a lofty dream.

I wanted the opportunity. Now that I've gotten it, I'm working hard to improve on my play. I've come to a great team and I want to stay here. I like working out year round. It's a chance to be with my teammates all the time.

I've laid down my plans and now I want to act on it. I get in early during the off-season and get my workout in, and I have the rest of the day to do what I want to do. Some people don't like the weight room, but I do. I've always been a big fan of it. Kendrell is quite the weight lifter. He's unbelievable the weight he can lift.

I was always good in school and I'd like to go back and get my master's degree. I know how it will feel to me to accomplish that. It would be something hard to do, but that's part of the satisfaction and reward.

From the time I signed my letter of intent to go to Ohio State I knew I would get my degree. My mother said to me, "No matter what you do, you're graduating." I always liked school. I was known as the kid who liked school. I had good friends in school and I enjoyed being with them.

I always wanted to go to class. There are some people who can get the syllabus the first day and never come back except for the tests. They do the reading and preparation on their own. You have a lot of time on your hands in college, and I thought it was better to go to class.

I grew up as a Browns' fan. I had an opportunity to go to some of their games. When I was ten years old, I got in the Dawg Pound twice. The stadium is right down the street, but I'd rather watch the games from the warmth and comfort of my home. When I was a junior in high school, I got to go back to the Dawg Pound. I got tickets for volunteering to go down

**Rodney Bailey, left, and
Kendrell Bell
were rookies
who made a difference
for Bill Cowher's ballclub.**

Photos by Jim O'Brien

there on Saturday and stuff two to three thousand bags with toys for distribution to the needy during the holiday season.

I was very aware of the Browns' players. I can still see them coming out of the Indians' dugout and out onto the playing field. And I'm aware of the Browns-Steelers' rivalry. But now I play for the Pittsburgh Steelers.

I had family and friends at my apartment in Columbus to watch the draft on TV. From the moment I was drafted by the Pittsburgh Steelers everyone in my family became a Steelers' fan.

I like to look at the history of the Browns. I was a big fan of Michael Dean Perry. I knew Sam Clancy, the defensive end who came from Pittsburgh. I was a high school classmate of his son, Sam, who's now playing in the NBA. I know Sam made the Browns as a free agent. I remember Clay Matthews.

"I talk about guys from the old days."

You're sitting with two guys who could have made Steelers' history last season. Kendrell caught Tim Couch and sacked him in the fourth quarter to equal the team record for sacks. If I had sacked him on the first play of the game we would have had 56 sacks. Even so, 55 was the high for any team in the league last year.

We gave up a touchdown on a short run late in the game. All I had to do was tackle him. I dove and tried to take him out. We could have limited the opposition to four touchdowns rushing. But even five was the lowest in the league. But we could have made history. We fell two plays short of establishing new club records. Those are the kind of things you play for. We'll have to strive to do better this year. We'd like to win a Super Bowl ring.

I see it as incentive to become the best.

There's a great tradition here. They've had so many guys go into the Pro Football Hall of Fame. The guys laugh at me because I talk about guys from the old days. I know about players like Lyle Alzado.

I've been to Canton three times to see the Hall of Fame busts. I had a chance to meet all four linemen from the Steel Curtain. I met them at an autograph show in Chicago.

I saw Ernie Holmes in a Wrestlemania show, along with "Refrigerator" Perry and Bill Fralic. You've got some tough guys there.

All the players on our team want to establish some history here.

We lost the last game we played and that's left a sour taste in our stomachs. I know how we felt after the game. We look at it differently now. We're looking ahead, and hope to build on what we did.

402

We had a great year. The veterans were respectful and helpful. Maybe you were a little timid, a little nervous, at the beginning of the year, but now that you have a year under your belt you remember what you needed to do in order to be successful. Now it's time to get better to work hard and to go all the way. It's something I really feel. It's time for it to happen. You've got to get it done. You could have done better. You've got to give it all you've got.

George Gojkovich

Kendrell Bell was named the NFL's Defensive Rookie of the Year in 2001

Chuck Noll
Into his life's work

"Now I'm a fund-raiser"

I was driving on US 79 across a bridge over Neville Island and the Ohio River, and Louis "Satchmo" Armstrong was singing "What a Wonderful World" on WSSH Radio. He was singing about skies of blue and clouds of white and that's exactly what I was seeing above the rolling hills ahead of me.

It was about 9 o'clock on a Wednesday morning, May 15, 2002, and the song was perfect for my mood and the change of weather in Pittsburgh. It had rained, sometimes quite hard, the previous three days. They had been gray, dank days. There had been exasperating long rain delays at the Pirates games at PNC Park. There had been gusty winds, destructive winds, especially in Westmoreland County, and trees had fallen on electric lines, across roads and on automobiles. There had been lots of damage and blackouts.

So this was a pleasant change. It was about 60 degrees at that time, and temperatures would rise to 65 that afternoon. The sunlight made it seem even warmer.

I was on my way, about midway through a half-hour drive from my home in Upper St. Clair to Sewickley, to pay a visit to Chuck Noll and his wife, Marianne, at their stylish apartment. They also have a home in Williamsburg, Virginia. They used to have a home in Hilton Head, South Carolina, but the frequent commute to Pittsburgh was too taxing, so they got a home that wasn't quite as far away.

When Noll was coaching the Steelers over a 23-year span, he lived the entire time in a home that club owner Dan Rooney found for him in Upper St. Clair. It was a half-mile from South Hills Village and exactly 1.1 miles from the home I would buy 10 years later. I have now lived in that home for 23 years. Rooney also found him a friend, former Duquesne University basketball coach John "Red" Manning, whose wife, Pat, became a close friend of Marianne Noll. Some people thought they looked like sisters. The Mannings had remained friends of the Nolls. Pat had died two years earlier of cancer. In fact, later that day, when I mentioned that I had bumped into Red Manning at PNC Bank and Giant Eagle, the Nolls informed me that Red had visited them in their home in Williamsburg only the week before. I related that Red found some consolation in that he had grandchildren near his home in Bethel Park.

That's when Marianne volunteered that she and Chuck were determined to make quarterly visits to Farmington, Connecticut, to see their son, Chris, and his wife, Linda, and their two children, Kate, 8, and Connor, 3. Chris is a teacher at a private school there. His parents had just been to Connecticut earlier in the month.

Bill Amatucci

Chuck Noll is introduced for induction into the Pro Football Hall of Fame by Steelers' owner and president Dan Rooney at 1993 ceremonies in Canton, Ohio.

Jim O'Brien

Former Steelers' publicist Joe Gordon enjoyed a 23-year run with Marianne and Chuck Noll. "He was a class act from Day One," Gordon said of the Steelers' head coach. They both came to the club in 1969.

As I drove to Sewickley on a bright morning that demanded sunglasses, I felt like I did the day ten years earlier when I drove to Ohio to visit two members of the Pirates' 1960 World Series champions, Harvey Haddix in Springfield and Rocky Nelson in Portsmouth.

I remember telling Chuck Noll about that trip once, and he said, "You were in Oh-hi-oh to see Haddix and in Oh-hi-ah to visit Nelson. My wife is from near Portsmouth. That's at the southern tip of Oh-hi-ah, right by Kentucky. Down there, it's called Oh-hi-ah."

Noll has always been full of such interesting information — on many subjects. I thought of how many Steelers fans and friends of mine would love to spend the morning going one-on-one with The Emperor.

I was excited because I was going to be interviewing a coach I had gotten to know during the four years (1979-1982) I covered the Steelers for *The Pittsburgh Press*, and in subsequent years while writing books. I was going to be interviewing one of the greatest football coaches in the history of pro football. He won four Super Bowls in as many tries over a six-year span. He's enshrined in the Pro Football Hall of Fame. I was going to be interviewing a good man.

He had always been reluctant to reflect on his success while he was still coaching, but he had retired after the 1991 season. He had been in retirement for more than 10 years, and had marked his 70th birthday on January 5, 2002. He was a grandfather. Twice. I figured the time was right for him to share his stories and insights.

When I telephoned him in Williamsburg to seek an interview and a date the next time he was in Pittsburgh, he said, "Why don't you just come to our place." I considered that a good sign, and a tribute to the relationship we had developed through the years. For whatever reasons, I was never able to get that close to Bill Cowher. Cowher told me he didn't want to get too close to any members of the media in Pittsburgh, believing it was the best way to go. I've covered clubs that were coached or managed by some of the best in the business and I appreciated their willingness to work with me, to understand that I had a job to do, too. You couldn't keep them happy all the time, but that was the nature of the business. I preferred them to be pleasant and always appreciated a smile and a kind word in passing.

The directions Noll provided were short and sweet, and I got to the four-story apartment building near Rt. 65 in Sewickley without any difficulty. The Nolls have a penthouse apartment. He was waiting for me when I got off the elevator and we went into a large party room.

It had been 11 years since I visited the Nolls in their home in Upper St. Clair for an interview for my book *Doing It Right*. When I asked him to autograph a photo of himself from his coaching days with the Steelers, he looked at it and said, "Who's that skinny guy?"

He was gracious enough to sit and discuss his days with the Steelers and his retirement activities during a 2½ hour conversation.

Noll was always fond of saying, "The only thing that's constant is change." I remember that Cowher once said, "You have to get up the next morning and move on."

406

I thought about that at breakfast as I read the front page of the morning's *Post-Gazette*. The three stories above the fold on the front page were about a treaty agreed upon by the U.S. and Russia to reduce their stockpile of nuclear weapons; about a meeting in Havana between Fidel Castro, the dictator leader of Cuba, and Jimmy Carter, former President of the U.S., as Carter advanced our desire to bring democracy to the neighboring country; and a story about a priest in Baltimore being shot by a man who said he had been abused by the priest. I knew Noll would be upset by the growing sex-abuse scandal involving priests in the Catholic church. Noll took great pride in his faith, and had attended Catholic schools all his life, and still attended Mass regularly.

"The newspapers prefer stories about man's downfall rather than about man's successes," he said at our meeting. "But there are obviously problems out there and, yes, it concerns me."

Noll's 39-year football career included seven seasons as a guard-linebacker for Paul Brown's Cleveland Browns, nine as an assistant coach, and 23 as a head coach. He began as a 21st round draft choice of the Cleveland Browns out of Dayton University in 1953. He played for the Browns through 1959 and retired as a player at age 27. He became an assistant coach in 1960 to Sid Gillman with the Los Angeles Chargers in the first year of the American Football League. In 1966, Noll joined Don Shula's Baltimore Colts for a three-year stint. His last game with the Colts was in their Super Bowl III upset loss to the New York Jets. The following year, he came to Pittsburgh. His record with the Steelers was 193-148, a .566 winning percentage.

"Who wants to be respectable?"

Charles Henry Noll was born in Cleveland, Ohio on January 5, 1932. He attended Holy Trinity Grade School and Benedictine High School prior to enrolling at Dayton University, another Catholic school, where he studied education and was captain of the football team. He is a charter member of the school's athletic Hall of Fame.

Noll graduated from Dayton in 1953 with a bachelor of science degree in education, and in 1980 was presented a Distinguished Alumni Award. He also has two honorary degrees, receiving one for humanitarian service from Duquesne University in 1980 and one in commercial science from Robert Morris in 1990.

I have a great deal of respect for Chuck Noll. He was never an easy interview, but he was honest and had integrity. I admire the man. He is a decent individual. He reminds me in those respects of another Hall of Fame coach, Red Holzman, who coached the New York Knickerbockers of the NBA in their glory days. Noll would always stop and say hello, and he would exchange family information a lot more casually than football information. That was my experience, anyhow.

Often when a player was cut, Noll would not offer any reasons. "He didn't fit into our plans," he'd say, or he might say, "He isn't here. He's gone. And I don't want to discuss somebody who isn't here."

He did the same thing when there was a holdout at camp. He isn't in camp," Noll would say, curtly. "I'll talk about anybody who is here, but not about somebody who is not in camp."

Once, when that holdout was Franco Harris, Noll tried to inject a touch of levity in his non-reply. He said, with an impish smile, "Franco Who?" That caused him some problems. People saw it as a putdown. That's the way the newspapers played it. That was not Noll's intent.

He could be stern and stubborn for a sportswriter on the Steelers' beat back in the late '70s and early '80s, but he was always available and fair. At his press conferences, I could tell you in advance how he would answer most questions, and when he wouldn't even attempt an answer. A smile or an arched eyebrow over those steely blue eyes would suffice.

Asked about his concerns regarding the media, Noll said, "When you're talking to the press you're sharing information with your opponents. That's why we had a lot of people who didn't talk much. Some who did gave out a lot of misinformation."

At his first press conference, upon being introduced as the new Steelers' head coach in 1969, he was asked what he was striving for in his first year. Respectability?

Noll repeated the last part of the question. "Respectability?" he responded. "Who wants to be respectable? That's spoken like a true loser. We're aiming for a championship now. We're not aiming for respectability or any other such words. The only true respectability in this game is winning the championship."

He may have been humbled a bit by his first year record of 1-13, winning the first game against Detroit and losing the rest of the games, but he was not deterred.

"We aren't going to build this team by picking up players who can't make somebody else's roster," he said before his first draft. "If you start bringing quality athletes in here, you'll start winning games. What we have to do is get the best player on the board tomorrow and build around him."

The Steelers selected Joe Greene of North Texas State — or "Joe Who?" as he was referred to in the next day's daily newspaper — with that first pick, and the next year they used the first pick to get Terry Bradshaw of Louisiana Tech. Noll and the Steelers were on their way to becoming the best football team in the National Football League. They had the building blocks to build a championship team. Maybe the best team in the history of the league.

Jim Kriek, a fine storyteller who covered the club in those days for the *Connellsville Courier*, had great respect for Noll. Kriek wrote a column in which he expressed some disenchantment with the media regarding their treatment of Noll.

"It was always a personal feeling of resentment in this corner," wrote Kriek, "that despite all of the coaching honors he earned, that Noll was never named Coach of the Year. If it means criticizing some members of my profession, then so be it, but this slighting of Noll only bears out the charge made before in this corner that personalities often decide how some writers vote. Unlike some coaches, Noll was never a 'hail fellow have a drink with the guys' sort of coach, he never buttered up the media, nor did he give them anything controversial to jump onto. He didn't publicly run down another coach or player, and that wasn't what some writers wanted. They wanted Noll to tear into another player or coach, which he refused to do."

Kriek liked to chew tobacco, but never did so around Noll, because he knew Noll disapproved. In time, Kriek kicked the bad habit altogether. I asked Noll during my visit if he was struck by the frequency of divorces among his players. He looked uncomfortable with the subject. "I don't want to read into that," he said. "It's a two-way street. You don't know what's going on. You don't know who's at fault. But, yes, we've noticed." He nodded toward Marianne when he said that.

Noll is now an ambassador for the Steelers, still on their payroll as Dan Rooney's way of saying "thank you" for elevating the franchise to another level. He was back in Pittsburgh to participate in three charity-related celebrity golf outings, hosted by, respectively, Andy Russell for local children's charities, Mark Bruener, Merril Hoge and Hines Ward for the Western Pennsylvania Caring Foundation for Children and Mario Lemieux for cancer research.

Noll would be reunited with Andy Russell and many of his other former players the following night at a dinner and auction at The Club at Nevillewood, and he would be playing golf with a foursome there on Friday. It was like being on the pro golf tour. He looked forward to such gatherings with great relish these days. His players, almost to a man, admired him more than ever, appreciating his contribution more with the passing years, and they preferred the lighter mood of their meetings now. The tension was gone. "He's more relaxed and I'm more relaxed with him," said Dwight White.

When Noll saw me snapping photos of the Steelers at a dinner at The Club at Nevillewood on the eve of the Andy Russell Celebrity Golf Tournament, he scolded me for using a conventional Nike 35-mm camera. "Why aren't you into digital?" asked Noll. "It's so much easier. You know exactly what picture you're getting, and it's so simple to print your photos. I used to have a dark room in my home, and I did my own printing. This is so much easier."

I replied, "Chuck, I know you're right. But new stuff is always coming along. You used to say 'if it ain't broke don't fix it.' That's my philosophy. I still get what I need for my books doing it this way. Maybe someday I'll get up to date."

Noll also served as chairman of the board of directors for Pittsburgh Vision Services that helped visually impaired people. It was a merger of the Greater Pittsburgh Guild for the Blind and

---

"I get as much satisfaction that they're doing well in life."
— Chuck Noll

Pittsburgh Blind Association. He had been the chairman for six years, and on the board for ten years altogether. "I have found my life's work," he said. "It's fund-raising. That's what I do now."

"I thought you were Arnold Palmer."

While in Sewickley, I stopped at Quaker Valley High School to pay a visit to Zeb Jansante, the principal, who is the son of Val Jansante, a star end for the Steelers in the '40s. We had become friends after I had interviewed his father for a chapter in *The Chief — Art Rooney and His Pittsburgh Steelers.*

Zeb Jansante told me he frequently saw Franco Harris and Lynn Swann at the Sewickley Café. I stopped there, hoping I might get lucky and catch them having lunch, but they were nowhere to be seen in the village of Sewickley. It's a neat community and when I saw FOR SALE signs in front of some lovely homes near the business community I was tempted to inquire about them. Sewickley reminds me a lot of Shadyside in the inner-city of Pittsburgh.

When I was a student at the University of Pittsburgh, I remembered landing a date with a young woman who wrote for the student newspaper at Duquesne University. I was excited when she told me she was from Sewickley. I thought I was moving up in the world. I thought everyone in Sewickley was wealthy. That may be true of Sewickley Heights, but not Sewickley. My date lived in a rather modest home on the other side of the tracks in Sewickley.

Chuck Knox, who coached the Los Angeles Rams and Seattle Seahawks, grew up in Sewickley. His family lived over a saloon and his mother waitressed there. Chuck Noll was often confused with Chuck Knox during his heyday in the NFL. Noll's name was often misspelled.

A book that just came out in the spring of 2002 called *Passion in Sports* refers to the Steelers' coach repeatedly as "Chuck Knoll."

Noll has gotten used to this. It keeps him humble. "I remember checking in once at the Greater Pittsburgh Airport, and a redcap asked me if he could have my autograph," recalled Noll. "I signed it for him and handed it to him. He looked at it, and looked at me, and said, 'I thought you were Arnold Palmer.' That brings you down a little."

Noll has never reminded anyone of Arnold Palmer when he's playing golf, much to his chagrin, but he enjoys the outings. He even has some good golf stories to share:

Chuck Noll:

I played in a celebrity golf outing at Disney World hosted by "Deacon" Jones, the Hall of Fame defensive end from the Los Angeles Rams. At lunch, I sat down at a table with these guys who were in the rock band that was providing the entertainment. I had been told they were from Cleveland. One of them looks at me and says, "They don't like you in Cleveland."

And I smiled and said, "You got that wrong. I grew up in Cleveland and I played for the Cleveland Browns. My mother was the oldest of 13 children and my father was in the middle of eight children. I've got more relatives in Cleveland than come to the games. My grandfather built the house where we went to live." I told him where we lived on the Lower East Side of Cleveland, and described the neighborhood.

Finally, this fellow turns to his band members and says with great zest, "He's from the 'hood!" So I was OK with them after that.

I went to Canton once to play in a celebrity golf tournament to raise funds for the Pro Football Hall of Fame. They put me with four guys from Sewickley Heights Country Club. It was a scramble. I learned a whole lot that day.

We came in at 22 under par and won the event going away. They eagled every par 5. I say "they" because I had little to do with it. I always believed that you drove for show and putted for dough, but that day I came to realize that if you can drive for show then you can putt for dough. These guys were really hitting their drive shots way down the fairway. I think one of them used to be a pro.

I played with one of them later on at a golf tournament put on by Joe Walton, the coach out at Robert Morris who was my offensive coordinator for two years. I usually play in that, but I have a conflict this year. You learn on the golf course, too, that you need talent to win. The best players make up the best foursomes.

I have a tendency to remember the players I played with and coached the way they were when they were in their prime. One time I was playing in this golf tournament, and Otto Graham was playing on the tee on a level just below us in the next fairway. Otto was not only a great quarterback, but he'd also been a top-notch basketball player at Northwestern. I remembered him as a 1-handicap golfer.

I told the guys with me, "Hey, watch this. This guy can play the game!" I forgot he was 78 years old and he wasn't quite as good as I remembered him. He didn't look so hot hitting the ball. Those guys must have wondered where I was coming from. But you have a way of remembering people as they were.

When I think of the players on our team, I tend to think of them as they looked when they first showed up at St. Vincent College at our summer training camp.

When you're able to interact with them now, as a group, the sparks start to fly. Everybody is excited to see one another. It's a great feeling. It's like a school reunion. It's an exciting time. I have a tendency to remember them as they were.

"It's not about the nice things people do."

Marianne and I talk about everything that's in the news. You can't escape some of the bad things that are going on in this country, and in this area. It comes back to the same thing. These are the stories the media chooses to put forward. It's not about the nice things people do.

They get more into the negative part of human beings. It's considered more newsworthy. It sells papers. I don't think it makes for molding a great society. We're educating people on how to do bad things. That's the stuff that's in the papers. You have imitation crimes that are caused by what people read about, or see on television or in the movies. You've got a copycat aspect of society.

I'm trying to get computer education. I'm struggling to get there. I'm not doing too well. I have to call my son, who teaches about computers, when I run into a snag. He knows what happens. I'm trying to learn how to send and receive photos. We'd like to keep track of what's going on with our grandchildren.

I haven't read as many books as I'd like lately, because of my computer activity. The best book I've read lately is the one by David McCullough — *John Adams*. I also read his book *Truman*. I've always liked historical stuff.

That's something I have learned about retirement. You think you're gonna have time to do all this stuff for yourself. But you can't find the time to do the kinds of things you think you'd like to do. There's a good definition of retirement: "When you wake up in the morning you have nothing to do, and when you go to bed at night you have half of it done."

Professional football is a part-time endeavor and you have to get ready for your life's work. I'm into my life's work now. It's fund-raising. I never thought I'd enjoy fund-raising, but the people you meet are just super. There are a lot of people out there who want to help other people. People are

412

George Gojkovich

Chuck Noll and Terry Bradshaw both appear vexed after sideline exchange.

trying to help. Meeting these people can be rewarding. The response is so great. They want to help.

Meeting the public from this position has not changed my view of Pittsburgh at all. It's such an open, outgoing city that wants to accept everybody who comes in. That hasn't changed at all from my first impression over 30 years ago.

It's not one of those places that if your family wasn't here for 900 years you won't be accepted, or you won't fit in. Every area has a different feeling. I spent a lot of time in California, for instance, and that's a place where there are very few natives. Everyone is from someplace else. The first question they ask you is "Where are you from?" They want an attachment.

There are a lot of cities like that in the South, in places like Atlanta. They're just growing like crazy and they're coming there from all over the country. In Pittsburgh, people tend to have grown up here and stayed here. They have an attachment. There's a real different feeling. If you go into a store on the East Coast, and somebody is waiting on you, they usually give you the impression they're doing you a favor. As opposed to Pittsburgh, where they ask, "What can I do for you?" or "Can I help you?"

"We tried to get good athletes and good people."

I didn't like to reflect on what we'd done for good reasons. I was reluctant to do it because we tried to live in the present.

One of the things we did that paid off for us was that we tried to get good athletes and good people. If you get someone who is not a good person, the selfishness comes in, and it can be disruptive. Our emphasis was always in getting good people.

When Dan (Rooney) brought in everybody for the 25th anniversary of our first Super Bowl team, everybody had to get up and tell what he was doing. I sat in the back and listened to these guys who've been very successful after football and it was great to hear how they were doing. We tried to get bright guys who were interested in a challenge.

You take a guy like Stallworth. He was back home in Alabama and running an aerodynamics company that employed a lot of people. It went on and on like that. There were very few into coaching. Many of them were in the media.

We tried to get grade transcripts on these guys when we were checking them out in college. We wanted to see who was taking basket weaving and who was taking real college courses that demanded some concentration and studying.

After a while, the schools stopped providing those transcripts for us. We wanted to learn more about these guys.

We also put a lot of stock in the personal interviews we had with them. There are different kinds of intelligence. There's physical intelligence. There's the ability to read and write. That's kind of a different thing. There is an emotional intelligence. Can you control yourself? Will you be smart enough to stay out of trouble?

When you accomplish something you didn't think you could do there is always a special exhilaration. You get a lot of young football players and they come on the field for the first time and they put themselves in danger. When they can master a technique to be successful in that kind of environment it is reassuring.

I'll never forget a situation that shows that kind of breakthrough. I took the coaches' kids to Florida, back when I was flying. I taught them how to snorkel in the hotel pool, and we were going to the ocean for them to do some snorkeling there. The movie "Jaws" was out at the time, and just about everyone had seen it. In their imagination, these kids were sure they were going to run into "Jaws." You could have heard a pin drop as we were traveling to the beach. They were so quiet. I took them to a reef that was well protected and where I knew they'd be safe.

They went under the water and they started seeing all this ocean life. It is spectacular. They overcame their fear in a hurry. Coming back from the beach they were so excited. They were jabbering like magpies. They were so exhilarated. That happens to a lot of football players.

"Nobody likes to be told what to do."

I was always interested in the technical side of the game. When it came time to make a decision about what I was going to do after I was finished playing football I felt it was something I should try. The great thing about playing football is that you can investigate all kinds of careers before you have to make a commitment.

During my last years of playing with the Browns I went to law school at night. It was a four-year program and I went for two years. I was getting married and I needed to make some money. I thought that the one thing I knew a lot about was football. That was 1960 and they had just formed the American Football League. I called Sid Gillman, the coach of the Los Angeles Chargers, and expressed an interest in becoming a coach. Fortunately, he hired me. Now here I was a guy with no coaching experience at all, but he was willing to give me a chance.

I was 28 years old and I thought I knew everything about the game. All new coaches do. It was great. You worked like hell to be successful and you got paid for doing something you liked to do.

There's a what-to-do and a how-to-do aspect of coaching. Anybody can tell you what to do, but if you can help with the how-to part you are helping them to become successful. And that should be the goal of every coach, to help the players become successful.

That's what coaching is all about. A lot of people think coaching is all about yelling and screaming at players. Sometimes people have to overcome a lot of things to be successful. We thought we had good people to work with. There were exceptions, of course. If the majority of your players are good people you can be successful. You can't have too many bad apples in the barrel, though, or everything will spoil. That's a truism.

Nobody likes to be told what to do. They like to make their own decisions. The key is can they accept your instruction and work with it?

You like people who want to play the game. If somebody is in it for the money and they don't really like the game they'll get hurt, or fail. That's one of the things that stood out about Joe Greene. Joe Greene liked to play the game.

No. 1, you have to believe you can do it. We had a lot of good people. One of the problems today is that they win it (the Super Bowl) and they forget what they did to get there. There aren't too many teams that repeat as champions anymore.

You have a very long season when you go through the regular schedule and go deep into the playoffs. There's not much off-season anymore. You're still celebrating and training camp is ready to start again. It's a new season, a new beginning for everybody.

You never start off where you left off. You have to start over.

"The game is different now."

Now you have third parties involved. You've got the agents and the advisors and the union. Used to be you had guys who wanted to be the best. Now they want to be the best paid.

The game is different now. You have salary caps. I used to have to make personnel decisions based on merit. Now you have accountants making those kinds of decisions.

416

It was a necessary thing to cut some players who were on the downside of their playing ability, but it was not a fun thing. Sometimes we kept a few players too long. They had done so much for you, you trusted them, and it was tough to give up on them.

We had to make decisions about them when they were at the end of the line in their careers. Now you have to make those kind of decisions when they might be at their peak. The agents and the union have driven a wedge between the coach and the player.

I testified at a trial once in Minneapolis regarding free agency in the NFL. The union was suing for free agency. They had figures to show that a special teams player for the Detroit Lions was superior to a special teams player for the Minnesota Vikings who was making more money. The jury bought it. That, to me, is the old 16-year-old mentality.

When my son was 16, he came to me and said he wanted a motorcycle. I told him, "No, I don't want you to kill yourself." He said, "But Johnny's dad got him one." I didn't care. You have to make decisions based on your own circumstances, not what someone else is doing. They have a salary cap so they don't drive each other out of business.

It puts more emphasis on the monetary reward of playing football. It's much tougher to get a player's attention and dedication these days. It's tougher for them to focus on football.

You get a lot of people who come into pro football who are not ready to play on that level. They have a lot to learn. You work with them on technique so they can play. By the time they're ready to perform at a first-rate NFL level they're gone. They not only leave, but they're playing against you. So, in a sense, you're coaching the other team.

I didn't want other people's cuts, or players who were at the end of the trail and were just looking for paychecks. I preferred to build from within, and we were able to keep the core of our team intact in those days.

It's different now.

"You're influenced by everybody."

I had a notebook for every game. They're stored in boxes at my home in Williamsburg. They carried a review of the game. They had to do with where we were, and where we wanted to go and what we had to do to get there.

I guess I picked that up from Paul Brown. You're influenced by everybody, not just by the coaches, but by players as well. You may have a thought about getting something done, but it doesn't work with a particular player. He can't do it. You may have to change something you once thought was sacred.

I had a coach in high school, an assistant coach named Ab Strosnider, a good German name. I was successful in high school because of the technique he taught me. He helped me to be successful.

Paul Brown was very well organized, probably more so than the other coaches at the time. He left no stone unturned. He had good assistants. He was one of the first head coaches to have full-time assistant coaches.

Paul Brown was one of the first coaches who believed in teaching football in a classroom environment. We all had to come to those meetings with our notebook. He had a philosophy that he wanted to dictate to you. They'd check your notebooks every so often to make sure you were getting it right. His emphasis on teaching, and on tests, forced you to learn your assignments. He had a team that didn't make many mistakes.

I really didn't know Sid Gillman before he hired me in Los Angeles. Dayton had played against Cincinnati when he was the coach at Cincinnati. Si Burick — did you know him? — was a sports editor and columnist for the newspaper in Dayton. He knew Gillman and he put in a good recommendation for me. So you know Burick had a good reputation and a lot of people respected him. He was a good guy.

Sid's whole thing was offense. That was his only concern. He let his defensive coaches go it on their own. We had to find a way to get it done. I started out coaching the defensive line. Jack Faulkner and I were working together. He had the linebackers and backs. He left to become the head coach in Denver, and I got his job. Walt Hackett came in and took my job. When I came to Pittsburgh, I had Hackett on my first staff.

Don Shula had played for the Browns, so he adopted a lot of Paul Brown's philosophy about football. He was like Paul in some respects. That was his background and mindset, so that worked out well for me. I was familiar with that philosophy. Don brought his own assets to the job as well.

So Jack Ham thought I learned a lot from that loss we suffered in my last game with the Colts, against Joe Namath and the New York Jets in Super Bowl III. Well, it was a helluva learning experience. We went into that game with nobody giving the Jets a chance. We got to Miami a week early and you talked to sports writers and they'd say, "What makes you guys so great?" We started believing it. It was a death knell by the end of the week.

418

I was fortunate to be associated with a lot of outstanding coaches before I became a head coach. I took a little from each of them, but I didn't try to be any one of them. You have to be yourself. You can't be somebody else. If you try you'll be a poor imitation.

You learn from everybody, but in the end it has to be your own thinking. Dan Rooney was a good fit for me, oh yes. Dan gave you an assignment and let you do it. He backed you every way he could. You can't ask for more than that.

If the players tell you I taught them more than football that's good, I guess. Football is life. It very much parallels it. The things that will be done on a football field — such as the team concept — are the kinds of things you do in life. It has to carry over into life.

It wasn't a consensus thing. This is what you have to do.

"You have to create your own image."

We never had a race problem on our team. I grew up in a neighborhood where you had all kinds of kids from different backgrounds, different colors, ethnic mixes, and I played ball with those kids in grade school and high school. It was never a big deal.

Paul Brown had black players on his Ohio State and Cleveland teams. Bill Willis and Marion Motley were among the pioneers in that respect in pro football. We had so many great players. There was an environment where everyone who did their share was respected. We were all Browns.

People are people. I grew up respecting a lot of people. There are some people you don't respect. People's actions are what speak loudest about them. Their moral fiber is evident. These are things you can pick up quickly.

Character counts. Being able to handle success as well as failure. That's become a big part of it. Sometimes it's easier to recover from failure. You lose a game and next week you really go after it. You have to be able to handle success. Sometimes people win and then they don't put the same effort into it the next time out.

Our personnel department, with Art Rooney Jr. running it at the time, did a good job of finding good athletes and good people. Bill Nunn was a big part of it. Besides his scouting work and signing people, he was also the training camp manager. He was a guy who had the ear of a lot of our players. He was someone they could go to when they needed help. And he did help them.

He scouted a lot of good players for us, Swann as well as Stallworth. He brought us quality people, not just football players.

Some players have something special going for them. I was with John Unitas in Baltimore for three years. I didn't have a lot of interaction with him because I was working on the defensive side. He had a presence on the team. He wasn't one of the flamboyant "me" guys you run into a lot with quarterbacks. He did his job. The team reflected his approach to the game, and getting it done. We had Earl Morrall at quarterback, too. He was also a quality guy. Both of them had been with the Steelers earlier. They should have kept them. They were the best kind of guys.

You asked me why Terry Bradshaw seems to have some issues about his stay in Pittsburgh, and his relationship with me. I have never quite understood Terry's complaint. I have positive feelings about Terry. As far as what he's said since he left, that's Terry being Terry. He'll tell you what you want to hear. I have the highest regard for Terry Bradshaw and what he meant to this club. He had a presence about him, too, and the team reflected that.

The kind of people we have brought into Pittsburgh has benefited the city. A lot of them have stayed here. They have businesses here and they have raised families here.

You say we cast a long shadow over this team. There are different ways of looking at that. When I first came here, you remember I had to hear about S.O.S. — the Same Old Steelers. That was a big thing. When we didn't get off to a good start, that stuff reared its head again. Same Old Steelers.

What was done in the past was in the past. You can't let an image hold you back, or hold you down. You have to make your own image.

I think that's important. Whether you come off a losing situation or a winning situation, you start fresh every season. It's a new year. You never pick up where you left off the previous season. It doesn't work that way. Football takes on a life of its own.

Three Rivers Stadium was a big, big thing for us. Now it's gone. It's been imploded. So that's a part of the past. Now you have Heinz Field. The Steelers can start something new there. They got off to a great start in their first season there.

It was a pleasure working with the kind of guys we were able to bring in, the people who were part of the organization. Not just the players. But the support people who handled the equipment, the training room, the administrative staff, the secretarial staff, everyone. It was a great time, a fun time. It started at the top with Mr. Rooney and his son Dan. They created an environment that helped us be successful.

420

Certain values have always been important to them. We clicked right away.

You asked me how difficult it's been for me to see some of my players like Ray Mansfield, Steve Furness and Joe Gilliam and some of the other guys — Dan Turk and Tyrone McGriff — pass away. It's life, no doubt about that. There are going to be these passings. I still think of them as young men, so it's difficult to deal with these losses.

That's why I always enjoy these get-togethers so much. It's great to see them now in a different light, and to learn about what's going on in their lives today. It's always good to see them.

Pittsburgh Steelers

Chuck Noll had some strong picks early in the 1970 NFL draft.

"When people say that it seems like it happened yesterday, I can understand it because it seems that way to me. That was a special time for all of us. It was a special time and there was a special bond between the fans and the team. I get excited every time I get together with these guys because it brings back so many memories."
— Chuck Noll
   Hall of Fame reunion at Heinz Field,
   July 6, 2002

Terry Hanratty
Still hometown hero in Butler

"I'm the first Terry."

Terry Hanratty had been back home to Butler the night before. He sees friends like Mike Kelly, a former Butler High School and Notre Dame teammate who owns a highly successful Chevrolet dealership in their hometown. Terry returns there for funerals, when someone is kind enough to inform him of the passing, and special occasions. "Mike and I go around and check out the old neighborhood," he said. "You should see how they've fixed up Pullman Park where we used to play baseball. We end up in the Butler Hot Dog Shop seeing some familiar faces."

Hanratty is the other Terry — "the first Terry," as he puts it — the one who comes back frequently, and doesn't have to be coaxed to do so. Hanratty was in the men's locker room at The Club at Nevillewood, getting ready to play in Andy Russell's 26th Anniversary Classic for Children. It's a scramble with four local golfers playing with one of the sports celebrities Russell continues to attract in a well-coordinated effort to raise money for Pittsburgh area children's programs. This was on a cold and wet Friday afternoon, May 17, 2002, and Hanratty's group had to give up the grind after 11 holes.

He still has those glistening coal-dark eyes and eyebrows but the hairline has receded, and the hair has more gray in it than one remembers from the last meeting. He still has that prominent beak and big smile. He looks, I'm told by Butler sports broadcaster Jim Lokhaiser, just like his late father.

Hanratty and I would be joined for lunch by the likes of another Notre Dame hero, Rocky Bleier, and other former Steelers such as L.C. Greenwood, Gordon Gravelle, Bob Adams, Emil Boures and former Rams center Tom Mack, a Hall of Famer who played in nine Pro Bowls. Another former Notre Dame and Steeler performer, Myron Pottios of Charleroi, was somewhere in the banquet room. Russell stopped by to make sure everything was OK for everybody.

I have a history with Hanratty. "He knows all my stories," Terry told a friend who accompanied him. Indeed, I traveled to Butler when I was 26, and he was 21, about to start his senior season at South Bend, to interview him for a story for *Sport* magazine. We drank our share of Iron City beer that night, played pool and Terry smoked a few cigarettes. Ed Vargo, the National League umpire from Butler, came into Natali's Restaurant when Terry and I were talking at the bar, and Terry pushed his ashtray with a glowing cigarette over in front of me. "I don't want him seeing me smoking," said Terry. "I've gotta protect my reputation."

Photos by Pittsburgh Steelers

The Steelers had three talented quarterbacks in the '70s, left to right, Joe Gilliam, Terry Hanratty and Terry Bradshaw.

Hanratty says he was always there to lend his thoughts to the mix when Bradshaw was playing quarterback, but he says Bradshaw was brooding on the bench whenever he wasn't in the lineup.

"What about my reputation?" I complained to Terry.

He's always been a likable guy, fun company. He's been in the investment business with offices in Manhattan for years. He was still with Sanford C. Bernstein as an equity sales trader for institutional funds. Terry and his wife of ten years, Kelly, live in New Caanan, Connecticut. It is his second marriage. They have two children, Conor, 8, and Erin, 4. He has three children from his first marriage of ten years' duration, Kelly, 32, and twins, J.J. and Becky, who would be turning 31 in August. Hanratty bounced back from a real lowpoint in his life caused by a bout with alcoholism. "I was lucky to have friends who steered me straight," he recalled in an earlier conversation. "I needed help." He stopped drinking alcoholic beverages in 1985. Scotch and soda stock went into a tailspin on the stock exchange the next day, he likes to tell people. His father was referred to as "a pleasant drunk" by people who knew him in Butler. So it was in the genes.

Hanratty was one of the most popular players on the Steelers after they selected him in the second round of the college draft in 1969, right behind Joe Greene. He was the second player picked under Chuck Noll's regime. Local fans were more excited about getting him than they were about getting Greene. "JOE WHO?" read the headline in the *Post-Gazette* the next day.

Terry Bradshaw was the No. 1 choice the next season. Joe Gilliam was grabbed on the 11th round from Tennessee State in 1972. They were some trifecta. Each had his own supporters. For awhile, Noll used them all, and had a difficult time settling on which one would be the starter. The *Post-Gazette* even polled its readers early in the 1974 season to see whom they wanted as their quarterback. Bradshaw, Hanratty and Gilliam finished in that order.

"I don't remember how it came out, honestly," said Hanratty. "I don't have a clue. Shows you how important that was. You know I took out an ad of my own in the same paper a few days later. I asked the readers to pick their favorite Pittsburgh sportswriter. Linda Lovelace (of "Deep Throat" fame) won that poll on a write-in vote.

"The best part of that is that Dan Rooney reimbursed me for the ad. It cost me $230 to run that ad, and that was chunk of change in those days. Dan said he enjoyed it so much he wanted to pay for it. That was a nice gesture on his part." Bradshaw became a big TV star. Gilliam got into trouble with drugs and died in 2000, shortly after coming back to Pittsburgh to join former teammates in a parade on the field to close down Three Rivers Stadium. Bradshaw has frequently voiced his unhappiness with Chuck Noll and with fans in Pittsburgh for the way he was treated. Hanratty has no complaints in either respect. His complaint is with Bradshaw's complaints.

> *"The more successful we were the more people wanted our players to be associated with their programs. We encouraged our guys to get out and meet the people."*
> — Steelers' publicist Joe Gordon

Terry Hanratty:

Joe Gilliam had a marvelous arm, but he didn't have the concept of the total game. He just wanted to rear back and throw the ball. The first series in the game was always set up in the game plan. After that, in those days, the quarterback made 90 per cent of the calls.

That first series would be the only one that Joe would work in the running game. After that, Franco and Rocky would be blocking backs.

You look at most teams that are successful in the Super Bowl, except for maybe the St. Louis Rams, and they have three ingredients. They have a strong defense, and they beat you with a combination of running and passing. If you get the running game going it takes the pressure off the passing game. It helps to have all three clicking, as well as your special teams.

All three of us thought we should be the starting quarterback. You always feel that way. Chuck had a tough decision. I called a little different game than each of them. I was more ingrained in the running game. You had to possess the football and get the first downs. You wanted to give the defense a rest so they could be even more productive.

I knew all along from Day One that Terry Bradshaw would be the starter. They didn't draft somebody No. 1 and expect him to be a backup. For awhile, we took turns running the offense. Terry would screw up and I'd go in, and then I'd screw up and Terry would go back in. Then Joe got into the mix. He was the starter at the beginning of the 1974 season, but gave way to Terry after we were tied by Denver (35-35) in the second game of the season.

You could see the talent with Terry. It just took him time to get his act together. He struggled at the start. It was a lot like the John Elway situation in Denver. Early in his career, when Terry felt the rush he just wanted to tuck the ball in and run it. That's bad. You lose your offensive line when you do that. You want those guys to bust their butts to keep you safe back there. If you start running too much they won't work as hard to hold their blocks. Our tackles, John Brown, near the end of his career, and Mike Taylor, a No. 1 choice out of USC who never lived up to his college reputation, were our offensive tackles back then. They didn't provide the best protection. You were telling them not to hold because we couldn't afford the 15-yard penalties.

Noll absolutely made the right decision when he went with Terry Bradshaw. Four Super Bowls later, it was obvious he made the right choice. How it would have been under Joe or me is strictly speculative. You can't argue with success.

Sometimes I would like to live in Terry Bradshaw's world. He sees it only his way. He was treated royally here.

He should count his blessings and those four Super Bowls. He should kiss the earth Chuck Noll walks on. Every time I hear Terry Bradshaw saying something bad about Chuck Noll or Pittsburgh or the fans here I want to throw up. Hey, when you're a quarterback and you threw a few interceptions you're going to get booed. When you throw touchdown passes you're going to get cheered. It's that way in Pittsburgh; it's that way in every city. That's how the business works. You have to accept that and move on. Nobody got more cheering in this town than Terry Bradshaw. And that includes Roberto Clemente and Mario Lemieux.

Chuck brought out the best in Terry Bradshaw. Chuck was the quarterback coach in one stretch, and he gave Terry more personal attention than anyone else on the team. They were always having one-on-one meetings. He got more attention than any quarterback who played in this league. He also got a lot of attention from the Rooney family.

Terry was Chuck's boy from the get-go. If anybody had a bitch, it was me. I figured if they wanted to go with Bradshaw or Gilliam, then fine, but why keep me around? Trade me. After my second or third year, I wish Chuck had come to me and said, "Listen, Terry, we're going to give you a shot to play somewhere else." My No. 1 dream was to stay and play in Pittsburgh, but if that wasn't going to happen I would have preferred going elsewhere. There were teams that were interested in me. I could have been a starter in the right situation.

Chuck spent hours and hours with Bradshaw, some for football, and some for his personal life. He was in there with Chuck all the time in his first marriage, and in his second marriage. He was always talking with Chuck about his personal life, seeking advice and understanding. I was there, and I know.

I have no bitterness toward Noll or the Pittsburgh Steelers. That's why I don't understand Terry badmouthing Noll or badmouthing Pittsburgh. Terry has dug a lot of holes for himself back here. He had in his TV contract that he didn't have to go to Pittsburgh to do any games. That's so stupid.

Noll had a wonderful football mind. Chuck ran the whole show. He did it his way. He wasn't out there in front of the public or the cameras, either, and I admired that. He stepped back and gave the players all the credit. He never went on a speaking tour, and he could have commanded so much money after winning four Super Bowls. He was never doing commercials. He could have been an ideal representative, someone with integrity and credibility, like Tom Landry, for a lot of major corporations. He was a strong, good-looking guy with a solid reputation. He saw no need for that. He turned down radio and TV shows in Pittsburgh as well.

I was very fortunate in my football career. I had the best possible coaches at every level, with Art Bernardi at Butler High, Ara Parseghian at Notre Dame, and Chuck Noll with the Pittsburgh Steelers. This was a great team to play quarterback for because the defense was so strong. They won in 1976 with Mike Kruczek as the quarterback after Bradshaw was sidelined. The defense gives you the ball at the 50-yard line. You knew they were going to hold teams under 14 points. You didn't have to go out like Danny Marino and have to put 40 points on the board to win, 42-35. If you put 24 points on the board with the Steelers you knew the defense was going to hold them under that and you'd get the win. If you did your job they would do their job and give you a chance to win.

Sometimes Terry and I would share the quarterbacking duties in a game. When he came to the sideline, I would be there standing next to Chuck. I was there if he needed anything, if he needed my input. I was there for him. When I think about it sometimes, when I was playing and I'd come to the sideline it wasn't that way. Where was Terry Bradshaw? Terry Bradshaw would be sitting on the bench, sulking. I always gave him my input. But he wasn't there for me. That's typical Terry Bradshaw.

I feel great. I used to dread mornings. Now it's wonderful to be up and about. People in the office say, "How come you're always so happy?" I say, "Hey, a lot of people didn't get up this morning." I should be happy about that.

Jim O'Brien

Two Notre Dame grads, Terry Hanratty and Rocky Bleier, recall the glory days at the Golden Dome during locker room meeting at Andy Russell's Celebrity Classic golf outing at The Club at Nevillewood.

Frenchy Fuqua
The Immaculate Deception

"I'll take my secret to my grave."

John "Frenchy" Fuqua was one of the favorites at Andy Russell's 26th Anniversary Celebrity Golf Classic for Children played at The Club at Nevillewood on Friday, May 17, 2002. Fuqua is a funny guy, full of stories, some true, some not so true, and he looks forward to coming back to Pittsburgh to be among former teammates and to make new friends. No one smiled more in the club house.

He was wearing the green blazer he'd been given a few years earlier emblematic of participating in at least ten of Russell's roundups. Always a man who had an eye for fashion, Fuqua wears the green blazer as if he'd gotten it for winning the Masters.

"I'm proud of this green blazer," he said. He is also proud of the two Super Bowl rings he wears for being a member of the Steelers' first two NFL championship teams in 1974 and 1975. He likes to show them to people. Fuqua still holds the record for most yards gained rushing in a game with 218 against the Eagles in Philadelphia on December 20, 1970. He had seven 100-yard-plus games to his credit, and was the team's leading rusher in 1970 and 1971, giving way the next season to a rookie named Franco Harris.

It drizzled during the golf play that afternoon, and temperatures were in the mid-50s. So Fuqua's smiling face was as welcome as a fireplace on an otherwise chilly day.

Fuqua is most famous for being the middle man in "The Immaculate Reception," the play that gained the Steelers the first playoff victory in the team's history back in 1972, and the play that has been celebrated as the best single play in the league's history.

It's a controversial play, disputed even today, and Fuqua claims he's the only one who really knows what happened. The consensus of most insiders is that Fuqua, like most of the fans in the stands that December day at Three Rivers Stadium, has no idea of what really transpired. But Fuqua has had fun with it, no matter what. It occurred on December 23, and it was an early Christmas present for Pittsburgh Steelers' fans everywhere.

Terry Bradshaw threw the ball, of course, and it was headed for Fuqua. He and Oakland Raiders' defensive back Jack "They Call Me The Assassin" Tatum collided at the same time the ball arrived. If Fuqua touched the ball first it should have been ruled illegal. At that time, the ball could not be touched by two teammates simultaneously on the receiving end. Today it can be. The rule was changed.

The ball hit somebody and bounced back. Franco Harris, who was supposed to block on the play, was running downfield and he caught the ball before it hit the turf, and ran down the sideline for the

Pirates' World Series hero Nellie Briles and "Frenchy" Fuqua, the middleman in "The Immaculate Reception," talk about their great days at Three Rivers Stadium. Briles is in corporate ticket sales for the Pirates and is responsible for the Pirates Alumni.

Photos by Jim O'Brien

Former Steelers' teammates Mike Wagner and "Frenchy" Fuqua share some funny stories in The Club at Nevillewood where they participated in Andy Russell's Celebrity Classic. They are regulars at that event.

game-winning touchdown. It's one of the most frequently aired sequences in sports history, with the late Jack Fleming describing the action.

It's a historic play that Steelers' owner Art Rooney missed because he had left his box and headed for the dressing room when he thought a defeat was inevitable. He wanted to console his players.

Referee Fred Swearingen didn't signal a touchdown right away. He checked a sideline monitor to help him make the call. There wasn't any official review of plays at the time. Thus "instant replay" was born.

It was a fourth-and-ten call at the Steelers' 40-yard line with 22 seconds left to play, and the Steelers trailing, 7-6. Bradshaw ducked a strong rush, but was flattened as he let the ball go and he had no idea what happened afterward. Rookie receiver Barry Pearson was supposed to be the primary receiver on the call, but he was covered.

"I could have been the hero."

Here's Fuqua's version of what happened: "If the timing had worked out, and the pass protection hadn't broken down — Otis Sistrunk nearly got Terry — I was wide open. I'd have either gotten to the end zone or to the sideline, and Roy Gerela would've had an easy kick for a field goal to win it. I could have been the hero.

"Bradshaw had to duck under and away from the rush — he ran to the right — and in the meantime Tatum left one of our wide receivers, Barry Pearson, and came up to cover me. The ball came my way. The ball was tipped and Franco caught it and ran away with hundreds of thousands of dollars I'd have made on that play. It took 1.8 seconds for the ball to go from my hands to Franco's hands.

"I've watched that play a hundred times. I have it on tape at home. Tatum wasn't near me, at first, when I went into my hook. I was around their 30-yard line and I'd have taken an angle, and we'd have been in, or at the least in a position where Roy couldn't miss it.

"Franco should have been nowhere around that ball. But some players just have a nose for it. A guy like him is always at the right place at the right time. I'm glad he was."

Chuck Noll has said, "Franco made that play because he never quit on the play. He kept running; he kept hustling. Good things happen to those who hustle."

John Madden, the Raiders' coach, was protesting on the other sideline. Madden claimed that Fuqua, and not Tatum, had touched the ball and the pass should have been ruled incomplete, having bounced from one offensive player to another.

"That play is shown on TV at least three times a year," offered Fuqua, "and my boss always gives me a nod at the office the next day to acknowledge it. But what would have happened if Frenchy Fuqua caught the ball? But I was always a team player, and always thought in the team concept. If I had scored, though, I'd have given the reporters a better story than Franco. The controversy is what made that play. I will carry my secret to my grave."

Then Fuqua did an about face, and continued. He can't help himself. "I always have to tell that story," he went on. "I tell them everything that happened, except who touched the ball and how. Jack Tatum had to hit it for it to have been a legitimate reception by Franco. But let's not beat around the bush. Jack didn't touch it. It's the only secret I have left in my life."

So much for secrets. Frenchy said he was saving the story for a book he was going to write someday. He may have to settle for this book for his long-awaited disclosure.

Fuqua gave me his business card. He works in the circulation department for the *Detroit News* Agency. He recruits news-carriers for Detroit's daily newspapers. He started working there part-time, while he was still playing pro ball, in 1975, and full-time in 1978. So he had been working there 26 years, the same span as Andy Russell's golf outing.

When I asked him his age, Fuqua flashed a bright white smile and said, "We can go with 55, or we can go with 46 or 47."

When I got home, I checked my copy of *Whatever It Takes*, which had a chapter on Fuqua. When I last interviewed him in December of 1991, Frenchy was 47. That would make him 57 or 58 in this book. Time stands still for the great ones.

Frenchy Fuqua:

Chuck Noll loved my stereo system. I had a Bowes 901. We were staying at the Roosevelt Hotel on the eve of a home game during the exhibition season in 1970. This was the Thursday before a Friday night game at Three Rivers (the first Steelers' game at Three Rivers). We were playing the New York Giants, the team that traded me to the Steelers for Dick Shiner. I was courting Doris Moore at the time. I would marry her four years hence.

Noll wanted to see my stereo system and he came up to my hotel room. I heard someone knocking at the door. I told Doris to duck into the bathroom, to get into the bathtub and pull the curtain closed. I went to the door and opened it. I was surprised to see Chuck standing there.

He had brought a classical tape cartridge with him and we played it. He stayed about ten minutes; that's all. But it seemed like an hour. I was starting to sweat. He said some nice things about my system. He wasn't as thrilled with my musical taste. I was into Iron Buttlerfly back then. Then he was walking toward the door, and I was saying to myself, "Frenchman, you just got lucky." Then, Chuck turned and came back and walked in the direction of the bathroom door. As he neared it, Chuck hollered out, "You better get out of here!" Then he left.

I asked him years later at a golf outing like this how he knew she was there. He said, "I could smell her perfume."

You couldn't put anything past that guy. Believe it or not, he trusted me. He lived the life that he preached.

My poor late wife Doris — I lost her three years ago — was so embarrassed she couldn't look Chuck in the eye for years after that. We were married for 28 years.

I just visited with Franco recently; he came to my hotel room. I had some lithographs that were made of the Immaculate Reception. And the idea was for me and Franco and Jack Tatum to sign them, and sell them at some autograph show in New Jersey. Franco took time out on Mother's Day to do this. Jack wrote something on the lithographs, though, that Franco didn't like. Jack called it "The Immaculate Deception." So Franco refused to sign them. He gave them back to me.

I get invited to a lot of those signing shows, about 50 some a year. I give a five-minute spiel about The Immaculate Reception. They all want me to tell them exactly what happened, but I always stop short of that. I tell them I want it to remain truly immaculate. I'm carrying it with me to my grave. You say a lot of people don't think I really know what happened. Well, I can tell you, I know exactly what happened.

Thirty years later, I can still talk about it like it was yesterday. I'm very proud of myself. I have the gift of gab. Some put it another way. I've been approached by many to write a book about it. I've been tempted. I've been offered $5,000 and $10,000 to come clean. But this is a lot bigger than the money.

I take a lot of pride in my participation in the Steelers' first two Super Bowl victories, and in that Immaculate Reception. Franco said the Immaculate Reception would be around long after we're gone. It's always on TV.

John Madden and Al Davis are still upset about it. When Davis sees me, he says, "You know you touched the ball, Frenchy." Al Davis can get really sarcastic. I just smile in return.

I was with Jack Tatum at a signing in Dayton, and he said, "I don't know and I don't care. I was just trying to tear your head off."

I don't hate him like I used to. Time changes those things. I get six weeks vacation a year from *The Detroit News*, and I take it to travel to card shows. Whether he likes it not, Jack Tatum is linked to me and Franco for life.

I love getting together with the guys like this. I started preparing for this two weeks ago. I got my hair darkened. I go on a diet. I want to be slim and trim when I get here.

432

I probably don't go to sleep for two days when I'm here. I hung out last night with Moon Mullins. He came out to where we're staying, the Hilton at the airport.

Franco gets a lot more invitations to shows than I do; so do the Front Four, but they can't always make it. They have schedule conflicts.

"I'm going to do it all."

Getting back to my stereo story, you know I never had a roommate in my seven seasons (1970-1976) with the Steelers.

In our dorm hall at St. Vincent's College, they had the veterans on the first floor, the rookies on the second floor and the media and me on the third floor. I had my own wing. That's because of my Bowes 901. They isolated me. I had two speakers and I kept the sound up pretty good.

Players complained that I woke them up in the morning before they had to get up, and kept them awake late at night after the curfew. You'd hear this boom-boom sound. They'd get on me about it. Noll told me a few times to keep it down.

You've heard the stories about what a flashy dresser I was, and how I had these clear high heels with goldfish in them. Doris would bring those fish to me at the banquet, and I'd insert them. Some people don't know this, but when they died I didn't just toss them out. I swallowed them. Everyone got a kick out of that.

That's the Frenchman for you. Anything for a laugh.

Those special shoes I wore were size 10s. I couldn't get them in 11s, which was my size. My feet would be swollen up the next day. I had to walk around in my bare feet. Tony Parisi would get me Triple Es in football shoes so I didn't have any problems.

My philosophy goes something like this: Chuck Noll told us about how his father-in-law was always talking about what he was going to do when he retired. But he got sick and died before he had a chance to retire. So he never did the things he wanted to do.

I'm going to do it all. I never hurt anyone. I've always been a happy-go-lucky guy. No one cares if you're upset or mad. Life goes on.

I always had a smile. It's not always easy to smile. I've enjoyed life. I'm close to retiring, but it's not so I can do what I wanted to do. To this day I have been there and done that and I had a good time.

I've been with two Super Bowl winners. I've been around some great guys. I've made some lifelong friends.

433

After the Immaculate Reception, they had to change that rule about who the ball was allowed to touch on a reception. It couldn't have happened to a better person than Mr. Rooney. I'm glad he was there, even if he didn't see it. As Catholic as he was, he had to believe in miracles and immaculate stuff. It was a fairy tale. It was unbelievable for something like that to happen.

The referee made the right call. Bradshaw . . . he let the ball go. Then pow! Bradshaw said, "I heard a roar. It was a good roar."

That's the way life should be. Every play should be like that. It was the catalyst for the dynasty. It's still good to go out and talk about it. Everyone has heard of the Immaculate Reception. It has its fringe benefits. It's 30 years old and I still love to talk about it. It's only right that the reception was immaculate. It should remain that way.

Three principals in "The Immaculate Reception" were, left to right, "Frenchy" Fuqua, Terry Bradshaw and Franco Harris.

434

Mark Bruener
A beautiful mind

"He's a true gentleman."
— Jim Sweeney

Mark Bruener was doing his best to be a good host. He and Merril Hoge and Hines Ward had their names on the banner above the entry to the pro shop at the Southpointe Golf Club for the 2002 Celebrity Golf Classic for Children.

The three of them were shaking hands with everyone in sight before the 10 a.m. tee-off. Bruener, Hoge and Ward are three of the most able and pleasant individuals ever to don Black and Gold and their gracious manner helped warm their guests on this brisk Monday of May 20. "It was shaky at the start weather-wise, but I'm glad we had such a great turnout," said a beaming Bruener.

The day before had been the coldest May 19 in Pittsburgh history. The next day would be the coldest May 21 in Pittsburgh history. The day of this golf tournament came within one degree of equaling the coldest May 20 in Pittsburgh history. Temperatures dipped as low as 32 degrees during this stretch and never got above the high 40s. It helped that the sun came out, making it look a lot warmer than it really was.

Bill Hillgrove was dressed the way he would dress to broadcast a Steelers' game in December. "It's not so bad," he said. "It's dry and the sun's out. It'll be OK. I've gone out to play golf with a few buddies on days like this. You gotta love it."

Chuck Noll and Bill Cowher, the honorary co-chairmen of the event, were dressed for a stroll on the sideline during the season. Noll favored the layered look, opening one black jacket to reveal another black jacket beneath it, and a sweater under that. Noll and Cowher had been together for lunch in the midst of Andy Russell's 26th Anniversary Classic for Children only three days earlier at The Club at Nevillewood.

There were many current and former Steelers at the site, including Jerome Bettis, and one of the prize celebrities was Jim Kelly, the pride of East Brady and the quarterback who led the Buffalo Bills to a record four consecutive Super Bowls. Kelly would be joining John Stallworth of the Steelers in the 2002 Class at the Pro Football Hall of Fame in August.

At the lunch break, Bettis was asked whether he wanted a hamburger or a grilled chicken sandwich. "I'll have both," he said with that trademark smile. "They don't call me Bus for nothing!"

I caught Kelly at the clubhouse turn later in the day. He had just picked up a box lunch prepared by Max & Erma's, and he was on his cell phone talking to somebody in Buffalo. "It's snowing in Buffalo," announced Kelly with a laugh. "That figures."

So as bad as it was in Canonsburg — the hometown of the late Perry Como and Bobby Vinton — it was even worse in Buffalo that morning. One of the items up for the live auction at the Celebrity Golf Classic for Children was a signed Buffalo Bills game jersey with Kelly's name and number — 12 — emblazoned on the front and back. Terry Bradshaw was his hero growing up in East Brady and when he was at the University of Miami. I remembered seeing Kelly coming through the Steelers' offices as a wide-eyed collegian, and the thrill he experienced meeting Bradshaw in the clubhouse.

It would have been more appropriate to auction off one of the blue and red parkas Kelly wore on the sideline during those Buffalo winters. Another auction item was the kind of red jersey Mario Lemieux of the Penguins wore while playing for Canada in the Olympic Games in Salt Lake City. I have never seen a sports auction in Pittsburgh, silent or live, that did not include something signed by Mario Lemieux. It says something about Lemieux, and maybe even more about Pittsburgh.

Some of the others listed in the celebrity lineup were assistant coaches Mike Archer, Dick Hoak, Kenny Jackson and Tim Lewis. Other Steelers seen on the premises included Steve Avery, R.J. Bowers, John Fiala, Wayne Gandy, Justin Kurpeikis, Will Blackwell, Mark Malone, Josh Miller, Eric Ravotti, Rick Strom, Kendall Gammon, Dewayne Washington, Craig Wolfley and Rod Woodson. Some were missing because they were participating in Joe Walton's golf outing that day. Walton, the head coach at Robert Morris University, had been Noll's offensive coordinator for two seasons in the 1980s. I enjoyed meeting so many topnotch people, including volunteers like Judd Gordon, Dave Lockett, Lynne Molyneaux, Teresa Varley and Keith Maiden. Joe Gordon, the former public relations director, stopped by to see Chuck Noll and others, and he looked like retirement was agreeing with him.

Since 1994, the Celebrity Golf Classic for Children has raised nearly $1.3 million, including matching funds from Highmark Blue Cross Blue Shield, for the Western Pennsylvania Caring Foundation. These funds have provided hundreds of children with health care coverage, and offered hope and healing to children and families grieving the loss of a loved one. Bruener has been a board member of the Western Pennsylvania Caring Foundation for Children for years, and is a motivational speaker for Blue Cross Blue Shield Highmark. He has also been a spokesman for Multiple Sclerosis and, more recently, Cystic Fibrosis. "Before I got to Pittsburgh, Traci lost a good friend to cystic fibrosis, so that hits close to home," said Bruener.

"Mark's one of the finest individuals I've ever come across in my association with the Steelers. There's no air about him. He's a solid individual whose life is built on a firm foundation of faith."
— Father David Bonnar
in *The Pittsburgh Catholic*

Mark and Traci Bruener met at University of Washington where he was an All-America tight end for the Huskies and she was a cheerleader.

East Brady's Jim Kelly, a 2002 Pro Football Hall of Fame inductee, was marquee player in Celebrity Golf Classic for Children.

Photos by Jim O'Brien

Mark Bruener, left, and his buddies, former Steelers Steve Avery, Rick Strom, Eric Ravotti and Kendall Gammon, enjoy reunion at Southpointe Golf Club.

He was voted the Steelers' 1998 Sprint Man of the Year for his dedication to community service.

"He's a true gentleman," said Jim Sweeney, a teammate for four years. "He can show people that you don't have to be a big tough guy to be a great football player. He's a great family man. He's a good role model for kids. I was fortunate to get to know him. He's respectful and well-mannered and loyal, all the things you seek in a friend."

When I told Bruener he had a real booster in Jim Sweeney, he said, "Mr. Sweeney is special. He's the consummate professional."

Bruener has also been a consummate professional and model citizen ever since he signed with the Steelers when they selected him on the first round of the 1995 draft. He has proven to be a solid tight end as well. The Steelers don't throw much to their tight end, but Bruener has made a reputation as one of the best blockers in the National Football League.

He suffered a torn rotator cuff injury and was sidelined for the last six games of the 2001 schedule, and two playoff games. He was put on the injured reserve list and could not return to the lineup. With Bruener and Bettis out of the lineup, the Steelers' running game wasn't as good as it might have been. The fans get a kick out of seeing Bruener helping Bettis to his feet every time he's tackled. But Bruener is a lot more than Bettis' caddy.

He can catch the ball when it is directed his way, and Kordell Stewart has great confidence in him. When Stewart gets in trouble, he will look to Bruener as an escape.

Mark married Traci Toolen in June of 1996. They have two daughters, Allie, 4; Chloie, 3; and a son, Carson, 1. I've met Mark's father-in-law, Bob Toolen, on several occasions and he remains one of Mark's biggest boosters. That's a good sign.

Mark completed his work on a bachelor's degree in economics at the University of Pittsburgh. Traci earned a master's degree in social work at the University of Pittsburgh in 1998. Mark and Traci met at the University of Washington where he was a record-setting tight end for the Huskies, and she was one of the team's cheerleaders.

"We worked out in the same weight room all through school," he said, "but we didn't start dating until our senior year."

Bruener is hailed in the Steelers' press guide as "the consummate team player and a leader in the locker room." They have no finer representative in the community. He's one of the Steelers who knows when to don a sport coat and tie to speak at a business luncheon. Bruener was a good kid when he came to the Steelers, and he's remained the same confident, hard-working, humble young man that first attracted them. A month earlier, former Steeler Andy Russell gave Bruener the "Unsung Hero" award at the Annual Sports Night at the Thompson Club of West Mifflin. He went out with Father Dave Bonnar, a Catholic priest who conducts mass for the Steelers before home games, on a series of visits to Pittsburgh area Catholic high schools to speak about vocations and career choices. Bruener spoke about the importance of his faith, and Father Bonnar was recruiting for St. Paul's Seminary.

At 6-4, 260 or so pounds, Bruener is a big guy with a big heart.

I had lunch with him on May 9 at Atria's Restaurant & Tavern in Wexford, not far from his home in Franklin Park. He was going to be driving the next day to Indiana, Pennsylvania with broadcaster Bill Hillgrove to participate in — what else? — a charity golf tournament. There seems to be one every day of the week.

At lunch, he ordered an "Arnold Palmer" drink. That's half iced tea and half lemonade. He also ordered a bleu burger, one of the city's best.

So he knows his way around these parts. An autographed photo of Mark Bruener is on the wall with other local sports favorites at Atria's.

I found that he was still as well-mannered as he was when he first reported from Washington. He still peppers his conversation with, "Yes, sir," and "No, sir," and was polite to the waitresses and service staff at the restaurant. He addresses older adults as "Mr." and "Mrs." He's too much. There are times when Mark Bruener is almost too good to be true.

Mark Bruener:

I think I've shown enough by now, with my blocking and pass-catching and attitude, that they know what I'm all about. To me, if my teammates believe in me, that's the utmost respect I can get. If I have their back, I'll be there supporting them and they'll be there supporting me. I work as hard as I can, in a game, in practice, in the off-season conditioning. I'll sleep enough when I die, I guess.

I like being a member of the Pittsburgh Steelers, and I like representing them wherever I can be of help. It's not work for me. I like getting out with our fans and meeting people. I know how I wanted to be treated, and I just try to treat everyone that way.

If I can put a smile on someone's face, from the janitorial staff to Mr. Rooney, I want to do that. The Steelers mean something in this community and I want to be a part of that.

I've signed an extension on my contract that should keep me with the Steelers the rest of my career. I had four years added to my contract and I have five years left now. When I finish this contract, I will have been able to play for the Steelers for 12 years.

I'd be happy if I could stay a Steeler the rest of the way. I'm making more money than I ever dreamed of, I've got a great wife and family, I live in a nice neighborhood, and I'm surrounded by great people. What more could I ask for? Well, I might be happier if I could stay healthy this season and we could win another Super Bowl for Pittsburgh.

I realize we don't throw many passes to the tight end, but I wouldn't trade my position or job with any tight end in the NFL. I'm happy to be with the organization I'm with.

The people in the Pittsburgh community are very friendly. They're very open for communication. They don't seem to be in such a hurry as people I've seen in other cities I've visited. They're very genuine. I've had a chance to meet people in many different kinds of social settings here. The majority of people I've met are good people.

I found that the more things I did for people, and not expect anything in return, the more rewarded I feel. Someone's always calling, "Can you help me out with this charity event?" Or simply, "Can you help me out?" I do my best to do whatever I can. I get more in return, as I said, when I don't expect anything. You might meet somebody and in a month or six months they might call back with something that's your reward. Maybe they'll take you golfing someplace special.

Representing the Steelers is more of a responsibility than some may realize. A lot of our guys treat it as a serious responsibility — on and off the field. A tradition has developed here, from back in the '70s especially, for players to reach out to the community to help get things done. I don't know if any other NFL team does as much in this respect as the Steelers.

On Draft Day, we did signings, some of the present Steelers and some from the past, and some people waited in line at Heinz Field for four hours. That's a good example of how the people in Pittsburgh think about the team and the organization. I think the tradition starts with how Mr. Rooney runs the organization.

I didn't have the privilege to know Art Rooney, the founder of the team, but I understand Dan is carrying the torch the way his dad wanted everyone in the Steelers organization to do it. Coach Cowher has told us at many team meetings how we are to conduct ourselves in public, and how we have to give something back to our fans and the people of Pittsburgh and Western Pennsylvania.

We have a good team of Steelers associated with the Caring Foundation. I like Hines Ward. Hines smiles all the time, even in the middle of a game. He's one of the hardest-working professionals I've been around. Hines is not the fastest guy, not the tallest guy, but he treats being a Steeler like it's the most important thing in the world. I met his mom. She's a very nice lady. I know he credits her a lot for his personal development. He's been a big addition to our team with the Caring Foundation. Merril Hoge has been with this event longer than any of us. He and Carnell Lake used to lead this effort. Merril is one of my favorites. He's been good to my family and me. We get along well. We raised over $80,000 at our outing last year.

This is a boyhood dream of mine come true. Just being an NFL player is great. It requires a lot of time and effort to stay at the top of your game, but you've got to find time for your family and the fans as well.

"You show up early. You do extra things."

I was lucky when I got here to have Jonathan Hayes as a role model. He was a veteran tight end. He was in his 11th year in the league when I first got here, and he had played for the Kansas City Chiefs for nine years before that. His family lived here in South Fayette. They were all special people. He really helped me get grounded, and to stay focused. He had great work habits. We came early and stayed later and worked out together. He taught me so much and not just about football. Now I'm trying to do for some of the younger players what Jonathan did for me.

He had a love for the game and a respect for the game. He was a very, very hard worker and I got caught up with his approach to the business. I still have it today. I still have some of his characteristics and qualities. You show up early. You do extra things that are not required by the coaches.

I think we have a two or three-year window with the current core of this club to win a championship. We've been able to keep our key guys. The Baltimore Ravens had a big year and then they had to have a fire sale and release some of their best players to get under the salary cap.

I thought we had a good chance to go all the way last year and that's why it hurt so much to miss the last eight games of the season. It was not fun to watch. In fact, it was very difficult to watch. I was still there in the locker room, but I was not out there doing my part to help us win. You feel like you let your teammates down.

Any time I'm out there I have the belief that I can make a difference. Jerame (Tuman) and Matt (Cushing) did a great job at tight end in my place, and we continued to win games. Then Jerome (Bettis) went down the next week. So two key components of our running game were missing.

You train yourself to be invincible. You do all that conditioning work. Then you get hurt and can't perform. It's tough to deal with. I'm a hundred percent now. I've been that way quite awhile. I've been sidelined too long for my standards.

441

I'm very excited by the team's ability to keep the core intact. We have good locker room guys. A sound locker room will carry onto the field. If you don't have dissent you can get a lot more accomplished. I'm more optimistic about the upcoming year than I was before my second year when we went to the Super Bowl.

In my first year at Washington we went 12-0 and won the national championship. I'd like to have another year like that one.

We have to bounce back from that disturbing loss to New England. The Patriots' coach Bill Belichick is known for being a defensive genius. They did a great job of showing us a lot we hadn't seen in some time and didn't expect it.

They had a lot of players who were unappreciated and overlooked, and everyone thought Pittsburgh was just going to walk over them and go to the Super Bowl. They used that to motivate themselves.

Our guys were in dismay. Guys were wondering, "Why can't we be successful like we were in the other games?" New England had a great scheme. It caused us not to be able to execute. They really wanted to win that game.

With Coach Cowher and Coach Mularkey and Kordell, I think we can recover from that. I thought we had a good season despite that last outing. In the past, people talked about our defense. Last year, we had an offense that was an integral part of our team. We could score.

Mike Mularkey's ability to motivate our team was remarkable. He motivated the same guys from the year before to play at a higher level. I love working with Coach Mularkey. He's made a big difference in our offense since he became the coordinator. I'd tell Mike when he was my position coach, "I want to make you look good," and he'd say, "No, make yourself look good."

When you have somebody like him on your side you want to work twice as hard. If I drop a pass or miss a block, I feel like I let my teammates down or that I let Mike down.

I've been here seven years and last year was the first time we had a quarterback coach. I think Tommy Clements really helped Kordell. Russ Grimm did a great job motivating the offensive line to play at a high level, and Kenny Jackson improved the situation with our receivers. He is working with talent, and he's getting these guys on the same page as everybody else. That wasn't easy.

We've had some great leaders since I've been here, like Neil O'Donnell, Carnell Lake, Dermonti Dawson, Jerome Bettis, Kordell Stewart and Levon Kirkland. You can try to communicate to young guys what we need to do in order to be

Mark Bruener signs autographs for fans at summer camp at St. Vincent College in Latrobe. The Steelers have trained there for 36 years. **Photos by Jim O'Brien**

Mark talks to his TV cohort Bob Pompeani and his proud father, Pat Pompeani, prior to "Unsung Hero" award presentation at Thompson Run Athletic Association's annual Sports Night dinner in West Mifflin.

successful. You can try to help them. They can either take your suggestions or they can turn tail and say, "Don't tell me what to do!"

There's a right way to go about this and there's a wrong way.

I really admire Kordell. He's a true depiction of a guy who never gave up. A lot of people appeared to give up on him. And the way he was depicted by the city. When things weren't going well he took the brunt of the blame. But he wouldn't give up on himself or his teammates. He overcame it. He rose to the level to get to the Pro Bowl. I really respect that. His attitude and his approach haven't changed through up times and down times.

The only thing that was missing was winning the Super Bowl.

By having the guys we have this could be a dominating football team. Coach Noll had his way of doing things and Coach Cowher has his way of doing things. If we all adopted Coach Cowher's attitude we'd never let down against anybody.

For a team to win four championships in one decade is something unreal. They really set the bar high for those who followed, or for what future teams can achieve. I don't know that you'll ever see a team do what they did, but I hope I'm wrong. The coaches and the players know what the tradition is here. We still have the same owner.

Mr. Rooney expects to win any game we go out and play. It makes a difference when you know the man is going to come in the locker room — win or lose — and shake your hand and he knows your name. To me, that makes a difference. How many teams have the same owner they had from the beginning?

One of the things I'm most proud of is to have my life grow the way it has since I reported to Pittsburgh. Since I've come here I have my wife and my children. And the experiences I've had. And to enjoy what I do for a living. I'm not going to take it for granted.

I've done a TV show for two years with UPN19 with Tunch Ilkin that was called "The Mark Bruener Show." I did some shows for KDKA-TV for the playoffs with Bob Pompeani, and I did a Draft Day special with Bob and John Steigerwald, Paul Alexander, Ed Bouchette and Edmund Nelson. I did a weekly radio show on ESPN with Mark Madden and we're signed to do that again this coming season. I'm enjoying doing that. It's something I'd like to stay with. I enjoy the preparation and the production, and working with the guys. I've seen what Mark Malone and Merril Hoge have done on a national level, and what Tunch Ilkin, Craig Wolfley and Edmund Nelson do here, and I'd like to follow in their footsteps. Maybe I can be the next Myron Cope.

Jerome Bettis
Still a Mama's Boy

"This is my home now."

I was waiting for Jerome Bettis to join me at a corner table in the cafeteria on the Steelers' side of the UPMC Sports Complex on the city's South Side. They share the building, four outside football fields and one indoor field with the University of Pittsburgh football program. It's one of the finest facilities of its kind in the nation.

It had been a hot morning for a voluntary practice session — temperatures would rise to 82 degrees that day — and I knew Bettis would be thirsty. This was Friday, May 31, and the Steelers were in the midst of one of the many mini-camps they conduct throughout the year. There is no longer any off-season in the National Football League. It was voluntary, of course, but everybody was there. It didn't count as a real camp. They held an "official" few days of practice the following week.

Bettis had a bottle of pure spring water in his right hand as he passed the counter in the cafeteria. He stopped to place an order for a sandwich and some fixings, and came over, offering a smile and a warm greeting. Bettis had been pictured on the cover of one of my earlier books, *Keep The Faith*. He was one of my favorites. I liked what he was all about. He knew that. "Thank you for your support," he wrote in a copy I brought with me for him to autograph for my personal library.

As we began to talk, one of the taller rookies I didn't recognize, brought him another bottle of pure spring water. Then Kendrell Bell brought him a tray with his order on it. Bell thought he wouldn't have to do this sort of thing in his second season — he wasn't a rookie anymore — but he obliged Bettis and offered a smirk of sorts. "At your service," he said, quietly. Bettis smiled back. Bettis smiles back at everything. That's part of his makeup, part of his charm.

The Steelers' training facility is such a spectacular upgrade from anything they had at Three Rivers Stadium, the mini-grass field they had nearby on the North Side, and certainly from their primitive days at the Fair Grounds at South Park. Their meals at Three Rivers were catered affairs, where they'd pick up food and take it back to the locker room and sit on their stools and — it was always a balancing act and awkward — eat their meals. Now they can sit at tables like regular people and enjoy each other's company while they eat. Parkhurst, a division of Eat 'n Park Hospitality Inc, provides the food.

Bettis had been getting rave reviews for his running efforts at practice sessions that week, getting "wow" responses from his teammates for one particular move he made to leave linebacker Joey Porter in his wake. It had also been disclosed that week by Ed Bouchette in the *Post-Gazette* that Bettis had reinjured his groin in the AFC title game against the New England Patriots. Bettis had been ineffective in that game, causing some to second-guess Bill Cowher for starting him after Bettis had been sidelined for six games because of a groin injury.

Bettis had gotten off to such a great start in the 2001 schedule. "I'm fine," he said. "I don't have any problems now. My situation has been over-exaggerated by the media. I'm ready to go."

Bettis shared his thoughts on several subjects. I came away from that interview, catching the tail end of the Steelers practice and seeing some old friends, feeling pretty good about everything. My wife Kathie and I went to dinner that evening at Eat'n Park at South Hills Village.

It began to rain hard just as we were ready to go home, about 6:45 p.m. The heavy downpour inconvenienced us, but we had no hint what was happening elsewhere. Finally, I ran to my car when the rain slowed up a little. I picked up Kathie at the door.

When we got home, all three Pittsburgh TV stations were carrying live an extended news coverage of a tragedy at Kennywood Park caused by violent thunderstorms and 105 mph winds. The weather reporters called them macrobursts.

Kennywood Park is a vital part of the Pittsburgh and Western Pennsylvania experience. If you grew up here you had gone to summer school and community and ethnic picnics at Kennywood Park. They are usually great family experiences. Kennywood Park gets better publicity than any entertainment offering in the area. Not this night.

The field reports were as sketchy and frenzied as what was going on with the folks at Kennywood Park. Penn-Trafford and Burgettstown were both having school picnics that day, and there were thousands at Kennywood Park. A storm tore through the park with a vengeance, collapsing the roof of The Whip, a historic 84-year-old ride in the amusement park. One woman was killed and 57 other people were hurt. My daughter, Dr. Sarah O'Brien-Zirwas, told me it was a busy night in the emergency room at Children's Hospital when she reported for duty. The scene was similar at several other hospitals in Pittsburgh, Braddock and McKeesport.

It had been such a beautiful day, like it was on September 11. You just never know what's in store for you on any given day.

The storm uprooted trees at the Pittsburgh Zoo and Aquarium in Highland Park and throughout the city's East End and damaged buildings in Lawrenceville, Bloomfield, Wilkinsburg and Homestead.

It uprooted hundreds of trees in Allegheny Cemetery in Lawrenceville. By coincidence, I had gone to Lawrenceville following my interview with Bettis to view some vintage Pittsburgh sports photos in a former fire hall — Engine House No. 25 — turned into a photo studio and gallery owned by Duane Rieder. It's on Penn Avenue near the Doughboy statue. I was asked to come there by Jack Wolf. Rieder and Wolf are two of the city's finest photographers.

446

Jerome "The Bus" Bettis shifts into high gear.   George Gojkovich

Rieder was doing a shoot that day for *Whirl*, a 6-month old high society magazine. Four of Pittsburgh's TV news anchorwomen were dressed in evening gowns, looking their best and they certainly brightened up the old fire hall. They were Patrice King Brown, Sheila Hyland, Peggy Finnegan and Sally Wiggin. They all are the nicest women you'd want to meet. They were covergirls this day.

Sheila Hyland had bought a copy of my book *Remember Roberto* at Ross Park Mall that past Christmas season. Seeing a display of Clemente photos on the wall had reminded her of that, she told me.

Before the night was over, I'd see them all on TV talking about the tragedy at Kennywood Park. I think Sheila Hyland was wearing the same pink outfit I'd seen her in that afternoon in Lawrenceville.

There were photos on display in the fire hall of some of Pittsburgh's greatest athletes. Among those pictured were Honus Wagner, Paul Waner, Josh Gibson, Roberto Clemente, Willie Stargell, Mario Lemieux and, yes, Jerome Bettis. He belonged in that kind of company.

"We have a great opportunity at Heinz Field."

Jerome Bettis is a great running back, but National Football League Commissioner Paul Tagliabue believes he is far more than that. He made that perfectly clear when he introduced Bettis as the 2001 Walter Payton NFL Man of the Year at Super Bowl XXXVI in New Orleans.

"Jerome reaches out to help others in so many ways," Tagliabue said, "from assisting troubled children, to giving scholarships, to upgrading facilities in the community for young people, and addressing public health issues."

Since 1970, the NFL has honored one player each season with its Man of the Year Award — renamed the Walter Payton Award in 1999 — to recognize a player's off-the-field community activities as well as his on-the-field playing excellence.

Several players with Pittsburgh-area ties have been so honored. They include Len Dawson (1973), George Blanda (1974), Franco Harris (1976), Joe Greene (1979), Lynn Swann (1981), Dan Marino (1998) and Jim Flanigan (2000).

Bettis has had a profound effect on the lives of many children through his "Bus Stops Here Foundation," which he founded in 1997 to help troubled and underprivileged children. Since the foundation's inception, youth participants have been provided with scholarships, computer training, mentoring programs, and athletic training. Jerome's commitment to the success of the program is evidenced in his hands-on involvement. He does one-on-one mentoring with children, acts as the football-camp director, teaches conflict resolution techniques, and attends as many foundation activities as possible.

"Jerome is the type of player we want to have in the NFL for many years," Tagliabue said.

Bettis embraced a Steelers' long-standing tradition for community service from his first days in Pittsburgh. He remains one of the team's most popular players with the fans because of his exuberant and friendly manner. He just has a way with people.

"It's the type of award that you really don't ask for," said Bettis. "You try to do things that are special to you and that mean a lot to you."

In late April of 2002, Bettis visited Frankfurt, Germany as part of a four-day USO/NFL tour of U.S. military bases. He even got to ride in a tank. He rode in an Abrams MIA12. "I've been interested in that tank," he said over the telephone to writers in Pittsburgh, "because my middle name is Abram."

Who knows? If anyone had made that association earlier, Bettis might be known as "The Tank" instead of "the Bus" by his faithful fans. He said it was exciting to ride in a tank that was traveling 55 miles an hour, and to meet the troops. Then again, Bettis gets excited about everything he does. He was looking forward to meeting U.S. soldiers who were recovering from wounds from the fighting in Afghanistan.

"I'm just looking forward to saying thank you," said Bettis. "My goal was just to shake as many hands as I could, say as many thank you's as I could and kinda express the thoughts and minds of all the Americans back home that, hey, we're with you guys, we're living it with you. So many times, you never get the appreciation. I wanted to say thank you, we appreciate you for what you're doing for us."

At the same time, Bettis was eager to get back to Pittsburgh to resume preparations for the 2002 season. He had some ground to make up from the previous season. He had resumed running only a week earlier.

His last game as a Steeler had been a major disappointment for him and his team and for the City of Pittsburgh. He had gained only eight yards in nine carries in the Steelers' 24-17 AFC title game defeat by the New England Patriots at Heinz Field. Bettis, who had gotten off to such a great start early in the season, had missed the six games before the title game because of a disabling groin injury.

He was leading the NFL with 1,072 yards in the 11th game. He moved up to 12th on the all-time list with 10,876 yards. Missing nearly half a season at this point in his pro career had to be a real disappointment. He could have added another 500 to 600 yards to his totals. He still managed to finish eighth in the league in rushing.

He had started the season looking as good as ever. He seemed swifter and was cutting this way and that more adroitly than he had in years. He had dealt with knee problems the previous three years and seemed to be back in top form once again. "I am a better back than I've ever been," pronounced the bubbly Bettis during his strong streak.

"His ability to dip in and out of cuts, the way his feet move, it is awesome for a big guy," said Russ Grimm, the Steelers' offensive-line coach.

"He is our ride, our rock and we feed off his mind-set," said Steelers' offensive coordinator Mike Mularkey.

"The most exciting thing," said center Jeff Hartings, in his first year with the Steelers, "is to see him run over someone in the secondary. By the fourth quarter, you can tell they aren't so anxious to hit him anymore."

Then the groin injury — and the disappointment of the title-game outing.

Bettis was aware that he had his doubters as he spoke on the occasion of his 30th birthday on February 16, 2002.

"It'll be 10 years this year," he said. "I don't think I have to prove anything. I just need to be 100 percent healthy, go out there and duplicate what I did last year. Everybody knows what I'm capable of. I'm not really worried about that at all. I know some doubt I can do it.

"I'm used to that. Going into every season, the questions have always been about me, and I've always proved everybody wrong. I'm not really concerned about it. They just need to check my track record. This is something I've been doing a long time."

One of his biggest fans on the ballclub is Hines Ward. "He's a true professional," said Ward. "When he goes on the field he's all business. The players appreciate that, too."

Steelers' director of operations Kevin Colbert is confident Bettis can be the main man in the Steelers' running game once again. The Steelers signed Bettis to a six-year contract before the 2001 season, virtually assuring him of completing his career in Pittsburgh. "We really feel like he wanted to end his career here," said Colbert, "and we wanted him to do that."

Bettis gained more than 1,000 yards in each of his six seasons with the Steelers, and two of his three years with the Rams in Los Angeles and St. Louis. He had missed only three games in his pro career until the 2001 season.

He went into the 2002 season as the NFL's second-leading active rusher behind Emmitt Smith of the Dallas Cowboys. He could reasonably become the NFL's ninth-leading all-time rusher by the end of the season. He needed only 361 yards to pass O.J. Simpson's totals.

Several of the former Steelers felt that Bettis should not have been used in that AFC title game, and they also believe that the Steelers blew a great opportunity to get to the Super Bowl. Dwight White, who was with the Steelers for their four Super Bowl triumphs, has said that the team he played for has cast a long shadow over Steelers' teams ever since and that they can't get out from under it.

Jerome Bettis:

Whenever you've had success, you're always going to live in the shadow of those successful years. But that shouldn't be something that you resent. It should be something that you embrace because it's part of the tradition of the team. If you have a great tradition, that means your fans are supportive, they're loyal, and they're going to be there in good times and bad times. That's beneficial.

Now, we want to set the same type of marks as those other guys did in Three Rivers Stadium. We want to win. That's the mark you want to set and we want to be the guys to set it. If you think of Three Rivers, some names come out of your mouth like Lambert and Ham, Swann and Stallworth, Bradshaw and Harris and those guys. But they haven't played in this new stadium. Some other names will have an opportunity to be mentioned.

We have a great opportunity at Heinz Field. We're the first group of guys to go into that new stadium. We have a great opportunity to start a legacy. The guys before us came in and created a tradition at Three Rivers Stadium that we had to uphold. Now, we get the opportunity to start a tradition that players years down the road will get an opportunity to uphold. We need to understand that and not take that lightly. Let's make our mark as well.

We'll see what we can accomplish. You want to make sure you leave a legacy that the players that come after you remember, that you laid the groundwork for the new stadium to be successful.

Sometimes you don't have big games. Sometimes you've just got to pound away and earn your pay. You just have to strap it up and get ready to go the next time.

It took me one training camp to become a Pittsburgh Steeler. I knew what this team meant, what it was all about, what the city was all about. I fit in pretty well. I was from a blue-collar town, Detroit. That's where Joe Louis came from, and look how he took the world by storm. I didn't hear about him when I was growing up, but I know about him now. I like sports history. I knew what it took to be successful. All they want here is a person who works hard. That's what they do every day of their lives.

No doubt about it, you get energized from the fans and, hopefully, you can energize the fans in return.

It makes me feel good that the fans here appreciate me. It spurs me on. It's not flashy; it's not the glitter. It's hard-nosed, the blue-collar work I do between the tackles. I prefer mixing it up in there and pounding away.

I learned a lot about football and about life when I played for Lou Holtz at Notre Dame. He was great for me. He helped me as a person and he helped me as a player. Off the field, he nurtured me. He always wanted me to be gracious and humble. He ran a tight ship.

I followed the rules. I never did anything from the start to go outside the rules. Anything you do, you have to respect rules. Rules are a part of life. It was nothing new for me. I had rules to follow as a kid. I learned quickly to follow rules.

We had basic rules in our home: no fighting with my older brother and sister. I was the youngest of three. There was no turning on the stove after dinner. No company in your room. Visitors were to be in the living room, not your room. Your parents had to know where you were when you left the house. No hats on your head in the house. We had to abide by the rules. You learn to make it part of your everyday behavior.

With the way kids are being raised, they don't have discipline or manners. When these values are highlighted and promoted, the child understandably follows the lead. In our home, we knew and understood the rules. Plus, I've suffered with asthma since I was a kid, and I've had to be careful about that, too, and make sure I had an inhaler with me at all times. I've had to be responsible.

My mom was always big on manners. She made sure I opened doors for her and other adults. We always said, "excuse me" and "pardon me" and "may I" and "please" and "thank you," stuff like that. She always said she wanted us to make her proud. And we tried our best to do just that. My dad was real quiet. He was the disciplinarian. When there were problems, my mother related them to my dad, and he'd get after us.

I was lucky. I was blessed. My dad was the father to all the guys in our neighborhood. He'd teach them things, too. He didn't want us standing around on the streets. If they were in our house, he didn't want them standing around, either. He wanted them to sit down, and not to sit on the armrests on chairs or couches. He kept all the guys in line. What they did at their homes might not be acceptable at our home. He was real clear about that. My friends respected my dad. It was always "Mr. Bettis this" and "Mr. Bettis that," and all the guys admired him. Only three families out of the ten or so on our street had two parents at home. I was one of the lucky ones.

One of my mother's rules was that you have to show people you respect your home. If you don't, they won't.

"I knew how to stay out of trouble."

I'm a normal guy, like everybody else. When I first got out to California as a rookie out of college, that was quite an eye-opener for me. Here I was, 21 and in a fast-moving city. Being from the inner city, I knew pitfalls and how to get into trouble. So it was easy to stay away from it. I knew how to stay out of trouble.

As a player, you're going to get approached by a lot of people who want your attention, and some of them are bad people. The wrong people, people I was taught to stay away from at an early age. A ballplayer has to be responsible for his own behavior. The guys who get into trouble allow themselves to be in that situation. They have to live with the decisions they make.

Being a role model is part of the job. That's part of being a professional athlete. Whether you like it or not, you're in the public eye. If you do something wrong, you're going to draw the wrong kind of attention to yourself. Regardless of whether or not I think I'm a role model, I can't help but be a role model.

It comes with the territory. You're a role model because of what you do. Kids look up to you and you have to handle yourself in such a manner that you respect yourself and your family, and you respect the game.

"Family is critical to me."

Pittsburgh is some place special because even the little kids know who I am. It's a good city, definitely a good football town.

It would be nice to have the same football environment in Florida or California. I grew up with weather like this in Detroit, but just because you're from it doesn't mean you have to like it. I know it's a great place to play this game, though. I wouldn't change it for the world.

Last year was the most challenging of my career. I couldn't stand to be on the sideline. I tried to keep my spirits up and be a cheerleader for the rest of the team. I might have looked happy, but I was upset that I couldn't play. As a competitor, I want to be out there playing.

Family is critical to me. In tough times, it's all you have. They're at all my football games, home and away. I get them there because I'm happiest when they're with me. I take the whole crew with me. I'm in constant contact with my family. Sometimes my mom tells me she's going to disown me if I don't call her more often.

453

I bought a nice home just north of Pittsburgh, in Hampton, just so my family could all stay with me when they come to town. I didn't want to keep putting them up in hotels. Now they can stay with me. Of course, my mom is still asking me if I'm eating my peas, and stuff like that. It never changes. But it's nice to give her a kiss before I go off to battle.

If I go to the Pro Bowl, my family goes with me. My running backs all go with me, too. But I'm gonna have them double up in rooms. I'm crazy, but I'm not stupid. That gets expensive.

My home is my prison, too. Sometimes it's hard for me to leave and enjoy myself because of all the attention I draw when I go somewhere. I like the people, and I love my fans, but sometimes I just want to be left alone, to live a more normal life.

When I don't want to talk I don't leave my house. It's my world.

Once I close the door I take a big sigh of relief because I'm home.

It sucks being on the sideline, not being able to be out there mixing it up. I used to be able to play if I was 75 per cent all right, but I have to be better than that to go out there now. The difference is my age and the pounding I have taken through the years. I never felt better than I did at the beginning of this year. I was quick and making good cuts, and felt fluid in my motion. That groin has caused me problems in the past.

It's hard to motivate myself when I am rehabbing. I have to think of the prize. That's the goal.

At some point I will have to call it quits. I wouldn't want to leave this team worse off than it is now. Some people don't like their job, usually because of the boss or job conditions. Mr. Rooney is the best owner in the NFL. Bill Cowher is a coach you want to play for. He's got a lot of bark. He does have some bite, too. But he's a good guy in his heart.

I'm doing a TV show of my own with Bob Pompeani and some of the other players are guests. I want to see what that's all about in case I want to get into that later on. I want to have options when the game is over.

When all is said and done, and when I'm finished playing, I want people to say Jerome was a great person. Not only was he a great football player, but he was a great person.

When I see people wearing my No. 36 jersey, it's like an honor to me. After all, the people have their pick of a lot of jerseys. And they can take mine off. They chose to wear my jersey. So it's important that you do all the things to make sure they keep that jersey on.

Dan Kreider (35), backfield coach Dick Hoak and Jerome Bettis (36) come off practice field at Steelers' South Side training facility.

Kordell is the No. 1 man here, and I'm right behind him. I won the team MVP twice and that puts me in some pretty good company. Bradshaw won four Super Bowls, and I would like to get one of those rings. We're that close to the Super Bowl.

I'm on a championship team that is only a win away from the Super Bowl. And that's where I want to go. And I like our chances. We have a solid defense. When you have a solid defense and your special teams play well, you create the opportunity to win a lot of football games. That's what we've got to do, get everything going good at the same time.

"I have to be skinny through a hole."

Eric Dickerson and Tony Dorsett and O.J. Simpson and Jim Brown, guys like that, had a pedigree when they came into the NFL. They had been star runners probably from the first time they played organized football. They were stars in high school and college, and it was no shock when they continued in the NFL. I didn't even expect me to gain this kind of yardage in the pros. I had to teach myself how to run in this league, really.

I have to be skinny through a hole. I am contorting myself because if I run square through the hole, I am too big. So I turn my shoulder or twist my body, whatever it takes to make myself thinner. It's funny when you see it on tape.

Maybe I am past my prime as far as age goes. But I am a better runner now. In the years I struggled, I became more of a thinker on the field. It took me the down years to learn, and now this is the best I have ever done it. I can't ever remember being as shifty and as quick.

My improvement is shown on my long runs, because on most of those I make people miss. Before, I didn't get myself in position to do that. Didn't know how. But now I do.

"It's an honor."

On the field, my stay with the Steelers has been a dream come true in a sense. Having watched the Steelers over the years, I knew the franchise had a history of running the ball. They liked big backs. It's been incredible; it's been everything I expected and more. The team has stuck to running the ball. They play a style of football that fits my character and me more than most teams.

456

Off the field, no other city has embraced a player as quickly as they embraced me when I got here. It's an honor.

The community has been behind me — win, lose or draw. It's been so good I've decided this is where I want to live when I'm finished playing football.

I've heard about Byron "Whizzer" White — he became a Supreme Court justice, right — and I've heard about John Henry Johnson. He also played for the Detroit Lions. So did "Bullet Bill" Dudley. So did Bobby Layne. The Lions were great in those days, too. Buddy Parker coached there before he came to the Steelers. I like history and I have heard about those guys. No, I didn't know about Sam Francis and Joe Geri, the guys you mentioned. I'll have to check on them.

The Steelers' back I know best, of course, is Franco Harris. I heard about him when I was growing up. I've met him many times; he comes into our clubhouse on occasion, especially when we were at Three Rivers Stadium. I know he lived in that neighborhood. I have the ultimate respect for him. He's the one who paved the way for me. From the big running back perspective, he was one of the first guys to glamorize the big running back. I owe him a lot. I learned from him, too. Look how gracious he has been. That really trickled down to myself. He opened a lot of doors off the field so they could see that we're good people. We're not a bad thing to be a fan of; we're upstanding people. That's the way I want to be. When I see him, I give him the utmost respect.

I try to be at my best behavior at all times. People make bad decisions. I made bad decisions in my day. What I try to do is to use those mistakes and hope not to make those same mistakes again. So you won't repeat it.

My family has been a tremendous support system for me. My family has been the biggest part of my success. Regardless of my situation, they've been there for me.

"The expectations are high."

As far as the Steelers' success in the '70s goes, I see it as a plus and a minus. This organization is geared to winning. If you've never won before, how do you know how to win? We understand what winning is all about, and what's needed to succeed. That's the hardest thing to do — to learn how to win.

The hardest part of the job is living up to those expectations. The expectations are high. There are four Super Bowl trophies upstairs and I see them from time to time. They are reminders of the standards the Steelers are held up to. It's a hard accomplishment to match. The bar is raised high.

That's fine. Our job is to give it our best effort, every time out. The fans expect you to win. Sometimes we disappoint them.

I've been in situations where the bar is raised high. Why do you think I went to Notre Dame? If I were afraid of ghosts of the past, or great players to be compared to, do you think I would have gone to Notre Dame? Hey, that was part of the appeal for me. I wanted to be part of a great tradition, a great football program. That should be one of the reasons you want to go there.

I'm pretty familiar with the history of the game. I like to know about those who had been there before. The game itself needs to be respected. The guys before us laid down the road for us. They broke their backs to give us this great opportunity.

I was sad when I got hurt last year. I was having such a great season. It was heart-breaking. Some things like that happen for a reason.

I'm happy here. Bill Cowher is a good guy. He's always treated me with respect and as a man. That's all you want in a football coach. And for him to be honest with you. I give Coach Cowher a lot of credit. Those are three difficult things to do, and he does a good job of it.

I respect what Kordell Stewart did last season. I saw it as a success story. I probably would have become hardened by the treatment, or lack of communication, that went on with Kordell. I probably would have had resentment. But he hung in there and he worked his butt off. I don't know if I could have had that much diplomacy.

The coaching staff made a big difference in this team last year. Whew! They sure did. Mike Mularkey took a great approach to our offense. He had us go through the playbook and find all the plays that worked and used them, and we threw out the ones that didn't work. He allowed us to contribute as players at what we were good at. He let us evolve, and pick up more plays along the way. It made us a good, fundamentally sound football team.

Russ Grimm really stabilized our offensive line and just kind of breathed some fresh air into our offensive line. He really got the best out of the players.

Tommy Clements did a good job of settling down Kordell, and keeping him within his comfort range. He made him a better fundamental quarterback. He played off his strengths. He gave him a place to start over again.

And Kenny Jackson — he pretty much handled a lot of different personalities among the wide receivers, and got better production from guys who had been underachievers.

We want to get everyone on the same page here. That's the goal of every team in sports. Everybody has to buy into it.

Everyone has to be responsible and reliable. They have to realize they represent the Steelers at all times. I try to explain two things to the young players: what's expected of them, and what they should expect of themselves. That's the name of the game. It's nice that I've gotten some great honors for some of the things I've done off the field. But you don't do it to get recognition or awards. My rewards are the faces of the kids. That brings a lot of gratification. Being a pro football player allows me to get out and do special things in the community, to make a difference. In that regard, I am thankful. You want to help.

I knew that the Steelers like to run the ball when I came here, but I didn't know they wanted their ballplayers to be so involved in the community, to do things that show the Steelers in a positive light. Once I got a chance to meet Mr. Rooney and found out the type of person he was, I knew I wanted to carry the ball in that respect, too. I don't think Mr. Rooney would ever turn down anybody. There's a wisdom here. He can clear things up. There is more of a family atmosphere here than you had at Notre Dame, or the other teams I played for.

It makes going to work easy. The facilities here and at Heinz Field are fantastic. It's so beautiful. It makes everything a lot easier. It allows us to do what we do best. If it's cold or snowing, we can go inside. We're never going to have bad conditions in which to practice.

Life is great. I can't complain. I've been fortunate. All I can say as far as the fans are concerned is "Thank you." I thank them for believing in me, for believing what I stood for and supporting me through good times and bad times.

Jerome Bettis is still a cover boy.

Josh Miller
The Patriot

"I'm a big picture guy."

Every so often, Josh Miller wows the crowd, his teammates and even his coach, Bill Cowher, with a deep punt or one that pins the opposition inside its 20-yard line. Cowher leads the cheers when that happens. Miller has also shanked a few that have had left Cowher's chin quivering and their sideline meetings have been memorable after those miscues.

Apparently, Miller's golf game is similar to his special teams play. In the Hoge-Bruener-Ward Celebrity Golf Classic for Children at Southpointe Golf Club on Monday, May 20, 2002, Miller had a hole-in-one. He aced the No. 14 158-yard hole using a 7-iron.

"Everyone else wins a car for getting a hole-in-one at these kind of events," said Cowher at the clubhouse turn. "Josh is a lefty and he wins a right-handed driver." There was a prize of a new car for a hole-in-one elsewhere on the rolling course that runs through corporate headquarters, condos and townhouses in a spectacular setting.

Miller was happy just to be there. He can afford to smile, no matter the prize. Miller makes just over a million dollars a year for taking the field five or six times a game to handle the Steelers' punting. He's become one of the best in the National Football League.

He's become popular in Pittsburgh. He's become a radio and TV personality. Like most kickers, he's a free spirit and he'll say anything for a laugh. He was looking forward to his seventh season with the Steelers.

He handled all kicking duties at the University of Arizona, and began his pro career with two seasons in the Canadian Football League. He graduated with a degree in communications and an interest in acting.

He's done some radio and TV work in Pittsburgh, and might like to pursue a media career. He's married to Angie and they have a year-old daughter Olivia Ryan. They make their off-season home in Jupiter, Florida and live in Wexford during the season.

Josh Miller:

When I signed as a free agent to perform in the National Football League, I wanted to go somewhere where it would open doors for me off the field.

Pittsburgh has been more than I could ever imagine.

The city takes you in. If you're a Steeler you have so many opportunities off the field. You get media opportunities, appearances, speaking engagements. You get to talk to the school kids any time you'd like. It's the best gig in town.

When I go places in Pittsburgh, I don't have to wear a name tag that says, "Hi, I'm Josh Miller." People know me here now.

Football lasts a small window of your life. I want to have something rewarding to do when I leave football. Pittsburgh offers that possibility. I'm preparing for the 30 years after football. I can just walk into a school around here, unscheduled, and get to speak to the kids. Any time you can pass along a good word or two that's good.

Tunch Ilkin has had me on his show a lot. He told me I should think about doing that. He's given me some great advice in that area.

I could have gone elsewhere and gotten a few hundred thousand dollars more, and played in a dome where you don't have to worry about the weather conditions, and maybe had better stats, but to me, it wasn't worth it.

When I think about the Rooneys and Coach Cowher . . . hey, if they wanted me they didn't have to ask me twice. I can see what's here for me. I'm a big picture guy.

Jim O'Brien

Josh Miller grins like a guy who's had a hole-in-one at Hoge-Bruener-Ward Celebrity Golf Classic for Children at Southpointe Golf Club.

Living in the long shadow
Today's Steelers like the view

"Everything looks different from the water."
— Chad Scott

Steelers' cornerback Chad Scott can see Pittsburgh from some unique vantage points and he likes what he sees. He lives and works and plays along its three rivers. Scott and today's Steelers share the UPMC Sports Medicine and Athletic Training Complex on the city's South Side with the University of Pittsburgh football team. It is located on the shore of the Monongahela River.

Both teams play their home games at Heinz Field on the North Side, near the confluence of the Monongahela and Allegheny Rivers that form the Ohio River. Scott and his family reside at Washington's Landing, a sliver of an island just up the Allegheny River from the H.J. Heinz Co. plant. You get off Route 28 and cross a small bridge to get there.

From the deck of his townhouse on Washington's Landing, Scott can see the city's skyline. The Strip District is on the other side of that Allegheny River. He knows the landscape now, his sixth season with the Steelers, and he knows how to get from here to there.

He even has a boat in a nearby slip, a 32-foot Wellcraft Martinique Cruiser, and he can get from here to there along those rivers. If there was a dock or marina at the UPMC Sports Complex, Chad Scott could commute to work by boat. He hadn't given his boat a name yet, but he was thinking about it.

"I go out and cruise up and down the rivers," said Scott. "I love to be out there when they have fireworks in the city for the holidays or at the baseball games. It's beautiful. The whole city — everything — looks different from the water."

Scott is symbolic of the new Steelers. He is a handsome, rich young man — he turned 28 on September 6, 2002 — and he can afford to do whatever he pleases in Pittsburgh. As a starter on the Steelers' vaunted defensive unit, he is recognized in most places. He is popular.

He plays for the Steelers' basketball team in the winter and spring, so he's been to the suburbs and surrounding cities in the tri-state area. The Steelers' basketball team plays local teams, teachers, firemen, policemen, you name it, and it's usually for a good cause in that community. Scott puts on a good show for the crowd, has some fun, meets the fans and signs autographs. It's a time to smile.

Scott shows up for those basketball games wearing floppy black and gold hats and such, something one might expect to see on a Dr. Seuss storybook character, and it makes him less menacing than he sometimes appears as a hard-hitting defensive back in the National Football League. Sometimes he shows up with his nine-year-old son,

CHAD SCOTT
Blount inspires him

DESHEA TOWNSEND
Tony Dorsett fan

Steelers' traveling basketball team includes, left to right, Joey Porter, Chad Scott, Will Blackwell, Hank Poteat, Chad's 9-year-old son Michael, manager Tom O'Malley Jr., and Deshea Townsend.

Michael. He likes to play dad as well as to play basketball. He has two other sons, Chad Jr., 2, and Sivaun, 7 months.

Scott is listed in the Steelers' media guide as 6-1, 201 pounds. That compares with some of the Steelers' renowned cornerbacks of the '70s. Mel Blount was listed at 6-3, 205 pounds, J.T. Thomas at 6-2, 196. Scott has met Mel Blount and J.T. Thomas, and he knows all about the Steelers of the '70s. He sees the four Lombardi Trophies they helped claim with four championship seasons in the mid- to-late '70s, and he knows his team has a way to go to rate comparisons with those teams.

Scott surprised us by knowing more about the local landscape than we figured he might. He knew that there was a steel mill on the flat grounds where the Steelers and Panthers now practice, each claiming two full football fields. The ones with the light fixtures around them belong to the Panthers. Pitt holds more of its practices in the evening.

He never heard of Herr's Island, but he did volunteer the information that pigs were once slaughtered on Washington's Landing, which is what it's been called since they cleaned up the place and put up some fancy townhouses and condominium apartments. Herr's Island, indeed, was infamous for its slaughterhouses and junkyards and the size of its rats, but that's history. It's now one of the city's more fashionable addresses. It's a great example of transforming property along the river to a more beautiful contemporary setting. Mayor Tom Murphy and Pittsburgh's political leaders are eager to do more with the city's riverfront landscape.

Scott didn't know that the steel mill that stood where there are now football fields was part of the LTV Works, which formerly was the Jones & Laughlin Steel Company complex, or J&L Works, but he had fared well in our oral history test.

Standing on those plush green fields while the Steelers were practicing, while Kordell Stewart was shouting out signals and handing the ball off to Jerome Bettis and the boys, I found my mind wandering. Like the little kid in the movie, "Sixth Sense," I can see what others can't see.

I was fast approaching my 60th birthday in August, and I had simply been around longer than most on the field, except for someone like Frank Sciulli, in his 70s, a familiar figure at Steelers' and Penguins' practices, picking up after the players, making sure everything is just perfect. "I'm just happy to be here," he says. "Every morning is a bonus, the way I see it."

Mark Bruener and Justin Kurpeikis call me "Mr. O'Brien," and so do some of the newcomers on the TV, radio and newspaper beats when they say hello and shake my hand in the hallways. Are they just being respectful? Am I getting old? I suppose it's a little of both. I don't mind.

I was 19 when I first started attending Steelers' practices when they were held at the Fair Grounds at South Park. The facilities were so primitive. But Art Rooooney, the founder of the team, was on the sideline, so it was a special place. The same could be said of Three Rivers Stadium. None of the new venues is quite as classy because "The Chief" isn't there. He's not standing on the sideline, or sitting in his box during the games. His five sons like to believe he is still there in spirit.

The Steelers dressed in the basement of a dilapidated old white stone building in those days at the Fair Grounds. Most of the commodes didn't even have seats; the showerheads were missing in most of the shower stalls. Some of the windows were broken in the locker room. But Bobby Layne, Ernie Stautner and John Henry Johnson dressed there, so it didn't hurt their play. Dick Hoak dressed there, too. Now the Steelers' backfield coach for over 30 seasons, Hoak says, "This is a little better. But I never worried about that sort of stuff." He and Dan Rooney, who slips in and out of the Steelers' activity as he chooses, are the only ones who remain from those days at South Park. They can make honest comparisons.

Bill Cowher, the head coach, comes from Crafton, but he didn't spend much time in the city as a kid. Tommy Clements, the quarterback coach, is from McKees Rocks and Mike Logan, a defensive back, is from McKeesport, but they don't know that landscape or the stories the way I do. When I was 19, I used to drink with Tommy Clements' dad, Dr. Harry Clements, at Dante's Restaurant in Whitehall. Dr. Clements was a real dapper guy, always dressed immaculately. That's where Bobby Layne and Ernie Stautner and Gary Ballman and Tom "The Bomb" Tracy and Lou Cordileone used to drink. That's where Pat Livingston, Myron Cope, Bob Drum, Tom Bender and Funny Sam used to drink. I wasn't old enough to be at the bar, but I wanted to be with those sportswriters and sportscasters even more than the Steelers of those days. I like to share stories about the Clements family with Joe Costanzo, the proprietor of the award-winning Primadonna Retaurant in McKees Rocks. The Clements family has dined there through the years and remain a source of pride to the community. I ran into Tom's two brothers, Dave and Frank, at Atria's Restaurant & Tavern in Mt. Lebanon when I was in the homestretch of writing this book. They are happy over Tom's success. They're glad he turned down some offers to go elsewhere. There is an older brother, Michael, also a gifted schoolboy athlete in his day.

My hometown of Hazelwood is just up the Mon a few miles from the Steelers' practice fields. I knew a lot of men, and even some of my buddies, who worked at the J&L, on both sides of the river. I knew men who worked at the Monongahela Connecting Railroad that brought steel-producing materials back and forth across the river on the Hot Metal Bridge that has been converted into a span for public transportation. Many of the Steelers cross it going to and from work.

Temperatures were in the 80s on this particular day in May, when the Steelers were holding what is called a voluntary workout, but all were there. "It was a hot one out there today," said Clements when he came through the Steelers' side of the complex after the workout.

I had buddies who begged me to come there when they were working at J&L, just to see the conditions under which they worked. They wore what amounted to spacesuits, so the fires they worked around wouldn't bake them as well as the iron and steel they were making. The Steelers' working conditions are a lot better.

Back in the earliest days of those steel mills, when their smokestacks darkened the skyline with soot, Pittsburgh was referred to by a visiting writer as "hell with the lid off."

If I look across the Monongahela River, I can see light standards on a ballpark on the edge of a hill above the Parkway East that is now called Dan Marino Field. It was Frazier Field when I played there for the St. Stephen's Grade School team against the St. Regis Grade School team that Dan would quarterback years later. Dan and his family lived on Parkview Avenue, just across the street from the church and school. His grandmother lived nearby. Willie Stargell once lived next door to her when he was playing for the Pirates when they played at nearby Forbes Field. I know men who used to be cops and groundskeepers and ushers who live on that same street.

Bruno Sammartino and Andy Warhol — whose names are never linked — both grew up in that South Oakland neighborhood. So did Joe Gordon, who would play ball on the neighborhood fields and later at Allderdice and Pitt, and would become involved as a front-office administrator and publicist with the Pittsburgh Rens, Pittsburgh Hornets, Pittsburgh Penguins and Pittsburgh Steelers. You can't really see their homes and streets from the South Side, but I could see them. I could see the "Beware of Dog" sign on the fence at the top of the steps, alongside the garage, in the front of the Marino home. The late Father Sam David, who came out of Bridgeville to star on the basketball team for Doc Carlson at Pitt, had a church up there, right across the bridge from Schenley Park.

I could see on the same hillside above the Parkway, a little closer to downtown, a plot across the street from the boyhood home of Frank Thomas, a slugger as a third baseman and outfielder for the Pirates in the 1950s. Thomas later played with the Cincinnati Reds and New York Mets. The family name was Tumis when his dad was working in the laundry at Magee-Womens Hospital.

My first Steeler

I met my first Steeler in Oakland when I was about eight years old. His name was Fran Rogel. He was from North Braddock and Penn State. He was a fullback for those Steelers of the '50s. I met him at Frankie Gustine's Restaurant near Forbes Field where the Steelers played in those days. My dad had to stand me up on a barstool so I could look Fran Rogel in the eyes.

Rogel had been the Steelers' all-time leading rusher when he retired in 1957. Because of the team's penchant for handing the ball off to Rogel for a smash into the line to start every game, the fans had a derisive cheer that went, "Hey, diddle diddle, Rogel up the middle." He was a part of Steelers' lore.

As I was writing this chapter, coincidentally enough, I received a phone call from my dear friend Bill Priatko telling me that Fran Rogel, had died the day before. Priatko and his pal Rudy Celigoi had gone to St. Barnabas Nursing Home in Richland on many occasions the past year to visit their friend Fran Rogel. He had gone there from his farm in Bakerstown. He was suffering from Alzheimer's Disease and Parkinson's Disease. His pals reported to me a few weeks earlier that he wasn't doing well. I had to go back and rewrite these paragraphs. They were still on the computer screen when I got the call from Priatko. Strange, huh?

They had grown up in North Braddock and been big fans of Rogel's. He was 74 when he died. They were playing football for the junior high team when he was starring at Scott High School.

I went to another Steelers' practice session on Wednesday, June 5, and afterward I traveled to North Braddock to pay my respects at the Ronald V. Lukas Funeral Home. That's located right next door to where the high school once stood, and near the Scott High Stadium where Rogel had performed as a coach and player.

I traveled there through some familiar territory, first through my hometown of Hazelwood, and then West Homestead and Homestead.

In Hazelwood, I passed the Carnegie Library where I first gained a love for books, and St. Stephen's Grade School and Burgwin Elementary School, where I went to school for the first nine years of my education. I passed through my old neighborhood and the memories came flooding back. I crossed the Glenwood Bridge where I was nearly killed in an auto accident at age 3, and then past what remained of the Mesta Machine Company where my father and brother and uncles had all worked.

I crossed the Rankin Bridge and went down Braddock Avenue. The main streets I drove through had too many businesses closed and boarded up. They were bustling main streets when I was a child.

Art Rooney used to say after visiting friends at funeral homes, "No one looks good in the box." Fran Rogel didn't resemble the man I'd gotten to know in recent years. He looked smaller and darker. I had emceed a dinner in his honor at the Churchill Country Club in October of 1998, a testimonial in his honor at the borough building in North Braddock, and had seen him when they dedicated a plaque to mark the site of his old school a few years earlier.

His casket was filled with items that were near and dear to him. There was a three-cornered American flag as he had served in the Armed Forces. His Steelers' No. 33 black and gold jersey was neatly folded. There were jerseys from Penn State that had been sent to him by Joe Paterno when he was honored at that dinner, and a jersey from Scott High. There was a plaque his buddy Bill Priatko had made for him, certifying his contributions on every level as a player, coach and teacher.

There was a basket of flowers from his surviving teammates on the 1948 Penn State Cotton Bowl team. There were flowers from his teammates at Scott High. Art Rooney Jr., one of the Steelers' owners, had been there. He signed in just before Lou "Bimbo" Cecconi, a football player and coach at Pitt, who had come with some of his former teammates from Pitt and Donora, Nick DeRosa and Tony Romantino. Ed Kiely, who was the Steelers' publicist when Rogel was playing, and Jack Butler, one of Rogel's teammates, both attended the funeral service. "Art would have wanted me to be here," said Kiely. Hall of Fame football coach Chuck Klausing, who established WPIAL records at rival Braddock, was there, too.

I spoke to Fran's brother Bernie, the only brother still living, and offered my condolences. I met relatives, and learned that one of Fran's great-nephews was going to Pitt. He'd have been proud of him.

Priatko, who played football at Pitt and briefly with the Steelers, Browns and Packers in the late '50s, had visited Rogel a week before he died. He even helped make the funeral arrangements, even though he was in Kansas when he learned of Rogel's death. "He was my guy," said a saddened Priatko. "He was my friend."

Ernie Stautner had been back in Pittsburgh earlier in the year for an autograph-signing session. He also was suffering from Alzheimer's Disease, but he was still up and about, able to get around with the help of a companion. John Henry Johnson was in California with his loyal wife, Leona, and he, too, had serious memory lapses. Bobby Layne was long gone. Byron "Whizzer" White, Sam Francis and Joe Geri, all terrific running backs for the Black & Gold in the early years, had died during the first half of 2002.

When I left the funeral home after paying my respects to Fran Rogel, I drove to the South Hills by way of West Mifflin. I passed Kennywood Park. It was good to see that the park was open. It had been closed for several days following the tragic night six days earlier when a macroburst, with winds up to 110 mph, swept through the park and killed one woman when the roof over The Whip, an 84-year-old historic ride, collapsed over her head. There were nearly 60 other people injured that night by flying debris. Kennywood Park had just been named the sixth most exciting amusement park in the world for all its thrills, chills and spills. Suddenly, that tribute took on a whole new meaning.

"Everybody is expecting you to win."

During the Steelers' practice that day, the engineers on Conrail trains blew their horns as they rattled along the railway tracks that abut the practice fields on their south side. Above the hills on that side of the river were the boyhood homes of Joe Schmidt on Mt. Oliver and

Photos by Jim O'Brien

TIM LEWIS
Green Bay had its ghosts

DEWAYNE WASHINGTON
Remembers Minnesota days

Former Steelers' fullback Fran Rogel was honored in his hometown of North Braddock in his final year.

Johnny Unitas on Mt. Washington. They say George Washington used to stand on top of that hill, later called Coal Hill before it became Mt. Washington in his honor, and look up and down the rivers to see if the Indians might be approaching Fort Pitt in canoes and rafts.

Down that Ohio River were the shells of steel mills in Aliquippa and Beaver Falls, which produced the likes of Mike Ditka and Joe Namath. Those two, along with Schmidt and Unitas, of course, are now in the Pro Football Hall of Fame.

Football fans in Pittsburgh and Western Pennsylvania like to boast about George Blanda of Youngwood and Joe Montana of Monongahela, and the rest of those native sons. They love to talk about the Steelers of the past, the tough ones who preceded the ones who won all those Super Bowls. They're a tough act to follow.

Dwight White, a stellar defensive end on those four Super Bowl winners and now a big success in the investment business in Pittsburgh, says, "I think there's a very long shadow cast on this team and they can't get out from under it."

Hank Poteat, who played at Pitt before he joined the Steelers, doesn't see it that way. He is from Harrisburg, and he grew up as a fan of the Philadelphia Eagles. "I'm sorry, but I don't know about Dwight White," pointed out Poteat, who returns punts and is a reserve defensive back in his third season with the Steelers. "I went through that same stuff at Pitt. People there were always telling you about Tony Dorsett and Danny Marino. So I'm used to that. We're trying our best to make a name for ourselves with the current Steelers."

Deshea Townsend, a 5-10, 191-pound defensive back, was born in Batesville, Mississippi 27 years ago. He's a nickel back in passing situations and performs on special teams for the Steelers. He went to school at the University of Alabama.

"I think the history is one of the good things about a team like the Steelers," Townsend said. "They know what they want, from the front office to the players. Everybody is expecting you to win the Super Bowl every year. I don't think it's a bad shadow. They're so concerned about winning; that's what you want.

"I grew up in Memphis. That was before you had the Tennessee Titans. My family was a Cowboys family. The Cowboys and Steelers have been a rivalry forever. Tony Dorsett was my man. In the back-yard, I was always Tony Dorsett. I loved Tony Dorsett. I have to keep quiet here about being a Cowboys' fan.

"These two teams were both special. The Cowboys were called America's Team, but the Steelers were, too. Every time I go home to Memphis, I see a lot of Pittsburgh fans. Yeah, I've seen Mel Blount. When Mel Blount comes through the locker room, Chad (Scott) says he gets an interception that game. He gets inspired. That's the way we should all respond to seeing those guys.

"We had a chance to get a crack at a Super Bowl ourselves last season. You have to kick yourself in the ass about that. It was there for us. I think we're a better team than the New England Patriots. But they were the better team that day. They played better."

Townsend was not aware that Dorsett was featured in a Hall of Fame display on the second floor of the James Duratz Athletic Complex right next door to the Steelers' side of the UPMC Sports Performance Complex.

Joey Porter played with the Steelers' basketball team, too, and that's where we first met. I couldn't get over his skinny legs. He looked more powerful in a football uniform.

In early May, Joey Porter signed a six-year contract worth $22.5 million. The Steelers had done a good job of keeping together a defense that ranked No. 1 in the NFL during the 2001 season and helped the team to a 13-3 record and the AFC championship game.

They signed backup inside linebacker John Fiala and outside linebacker Jason Gildon before they became free agents in March. They offered inside Earl Holmes a contract and, when he turned them down, they signed free agent James Farrior to take his place. The four linebacker signings would cost them nearly $14 million in signing bonuses.

Things are different these days. It would have been hard to comprehend Chuck Noll and Dan Rooney having to choose whether to sign Jack Ham or Jack Lambert, or Jack Lambert or Andy Russell. Imagine them having to choose between keeping Franco Harris and Rocky Bleier. Or trying to decide whether to keep Mike Wagner or J.T. Thomas because they couldn't keep both and stay under the salary cap. That blows the mind, yet we take that sort of thing for granted these days.

"I'm happy they're making a commitment and knowing I won't have to worry about where I'll play next year," said Porter, who took time out from cutting a teammate's hair to discuss his feelings about being a Steeler. "I'll be in Pittsburgh and, hopefully, end my career here.

"I wouldn't want to play anywhere else. From Day One, they have treated me in a first-class manner. They took a chance on me and drafted me in the third round, and I've tried to live up to their expectations. I'm proud that I've been able to play on a high level. Hopefully, I have a long future here in Pittsburgh.

"As far as the four Super Bowl trophies, and the tradition is concerned, all you can do is give it all you've got every time you take the field. If you give all your effort on every play, and leave it all out there on every play, that's the best you can do. I like the organization and I want to be a part of it as long as I can."

The Steelers announced Porter's signing on the same day an announcement came from the College Football Hall of Fame in South Bend that Dan Marino would be honored in their next class. Induction into the Pro Football Hall of Fame was only a few years away.

#55

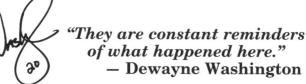

"They are constant reminders of what happened here."
— Dewayne Washington

Chad Scott was the No. 1 draft selection of the Steelers in 1997. He had starred at the University of Maryland and before that at Towson State University. He had played two seasons at each school. He had grown up in Capitol Heights, Maryland and been a football and track & field standout in high school. Injuries slowed him in his early seasons with the Steelers, but he has stayed healthy and become one of the standout cornerbacks in the National Football League. He and Dewayne Washington man the corners for the Steelers.

Washington came to the Steelers from the Minnesota Vikings. That team went to the Super Bowl four times in the '70s, too, but they never won the Lombardi Trophy. Even so, they were on the league's best teams for a long time, and Washington was well aware of that.

"A lot of those Vikings continue to live in the Minneapolis-St. Paul area," said Washington. "But I think there are a lot more former Steelers still living around Pittsburgh. They are constant reminders of what happened here. That's OK with us.

"I get out and do a lot of speaking engagements around Pittsburgh. It's a big city, but it's a small town in so many ways. There are communities within the city, and it has a small town feeling."

Washington is one of the Steelers' best ambassadors. He is always prepared when he appears as a speaker. He is the president of the Dewayne Washington Foundation that establishes links between the local business community and kids in Pittsburgh and his native North Carolina. He serves as a national spokesman for Spina Bifida, and as the Steelers' spokesman for United Way. He has co-hosted a weekly show on ESPN Radio.He and Scott have left their mark in Pittsburgh, on and off the field. They appreciate what they've got going for themselves in Pittsburgh.

"We've got the best facilities in the league now," said Scott. "Everything is nicer than what we had at Three Rivers Stadium. The rest rooms, the locker rooms, the weight rooms, the practice fields, the playing field, everything. It makes you more comfortable. The cafeteria is nice. You can sit at a table now and eat with some of your teammates. Before, when you had your food on your lap you had to worry about dropping it."

Their coach, defensive coordinator Tim Lewis, said it was the same way at Green Bay where he played after he departed Pitt. "You were always compared to the players from the Vince Lombardi era," allowed Lewis. "Those guys would come around, too, so there were constant reminders."

Mel Blount has been a visitor to the Steelers' locker rooms when Scott has been at Three Rivers Stadium and at Heinz Field and the UPMC Sports Performance Complex. So have Lynn Swann and Franco Harris, and guys like that.

Scott likes to see them. There's still some fan in all of today's Steelers. They don't feel pressure because they're often compared to those guys and their accomplishments, and often come up short.

"Back then you could keep your whole team together. You could stay together for years. That's a real benefit. You learn to play with one another. You know what the other guy is going to do," said Scott.

"I thought it was amazing that someone as big as Blount could play corner the way we play it now. He'd be an excellent outside linebacker or defensive end now. You could beat up on people in those days. There are different rules now.

"I've been out to his farm in Washington County. I admire the guy. When he was playing, defensive backs could be more aggressive. He could almost body slam receivers at the line of scrimmage. He could run fast and he was tough to beat. "Mel likes to talk about those days, too. That's all right. It's good. You don't want to play for a team that has a history of losing. I like it here. I have made a lot of friends around here. I'd love to stay a Steeler. But that's up to the Steelers. They have to want to keep me, too."

"It's great to be a part of this tradition."

I returned to the Steelers' practice session on Wednesday, June 5. Temperatures got as high as 88 degrees and it was muggy. Jason Gildon was given a physical following the workout, and stood in a hallway outside the trainers' area, and talked about his role with the Steelers. He was still smiling over his situation. It's no wonder. He has a beautiful home in the North Hills of Pittsburgh. The Steelers' star outside linebacker had signed a five-year $23 million contract when he became a free agent in March. He was given a $6.5 million signing bonus. Nearby on the wall was a photo showing Gildon at the Pro Bowl in Hawaii, posing for a picture with teammates Hines Ward, Alan Faneca and Kordell Stewart. They were flanked by two native hula dancers. Jerome Bettis had been picked for the Pro Bowl, but was unable to participate because of a nagging groin injury.

"It means a lot to me to be a part of the great tradition here," said Gildon. "A lot of great players have been a part of this team. There's been great accomplishment here. I came to a team where the expectations are definitely high. You can approach it in one of two ways. It can intimidate you or you can live up to the expectations. You can live up to the challenge. They've had great success here, and so have we.

"I think I have been a part of real success here, too. We just haven't won that championship yet. We came so close this past year. We have to pick up where we left off, and make the most of our opportunities. You never know when it will happen again. You can't assume you'll get to the same position again the next time.

473

"I want to finish up with the Steelers, With my new contract, I have a chance to do that. That's not easy to do these days. The opportunity is definitely here. I want to be one of those guys they bring back at halftime.

"I love it when they do that. Seeing those guys who were on the great teams of the Steelers is significant to us. You can still see that look in their eyes. You can see what great competitors they were. The guy that sticks out is Mel Blount. He's so impressive. To think this guy was a cornerback. He's built like some of the linebackers of today.

"Franco is impressive. He'd still be a big running back today. I really didn't have a favorite team when I was growing up in Oklahoma. That's Dallas Cowboys' territory, you know. I had favorite players, and Franco Harris was one of my favorite players. Herschel Walker and Tony Dorsett of the Cowboys were two of my favorites. A lot of kids I played with were always Tony Dorsett when we had our games.

"It's great when those guys come in our locker rooms. Everybody has a lot of respect for them still.

"I'm sure they are envious of what we have now in the way of facilities. We have come a long way since Three Rivers Stadium. We actually have windows in our weight room here. At Three Rivers, you didn't know what time of day it was. You didn't know if the sun was out or what. It was like being in a dungeon.

"I'm sure Coach Hoak can appreciate that. He goes back with this team even before Three Rivers Stadium, so I'm sure he has some good stories about what it was like. You can look around and see how nice we have it. Now if we could just get another Lombardi Trophy for upstairs. Those guys should be proud of what they've done.

"We have a chance to make our own history in Heinz Field. I think we got off to a great start in our first year. Now we have to build on that."

"Field of Dreams"

Mike Logan signed as a free agent with the Steelers prior to the 2001 season. He returned to his hometown for his fifth NFL season, and made a contribution as a reserve defensive back and a member of the special teams. He had starred at McKeesport High School and West Virginia University. He grew up in some tough neighborhoods nearby. He knows how fortunate he is that things have worked out for him the way they have.

"I got really emotional when I signed my contract over here," he recalled after a practice session in early June. "My grandfather worked here at the J&L Works. His name was Theodore Harber. He was the first African-American safety manager here.

474

Steelers practice in shadows of abandoned steel mills on city's South Side.

Steelers' linebackers Joey Porter and Jason Gildon like their first-class training facility at UPMC Sports Medicine and Athletic Training Complex.

"He used to wear one of those construction helmets, the safety kind, and it had the same logo on it for the steelworkers that we have on our helmets. I tell people he was the first Steeler in our family. I admired my grandfather because my father admired him so much.

"I first lived here on the South Side, and then in the project at St. Clair Village, and then in the projects in Whitaker. Then we moved to McKeesport where I went to school. So this was a real homecoming for me. I knew all the Steelers by name when I was growing up. I've been surrounded by it all my life. The Steelers mean family, tradition and history to me. They mean everything to me.

"I can get really emotional when I think about all that. I'm fulfilling my dreams on the same soil where my grandfather fulfilled his dreams. He had a gold card and that steelworker's hat. I'm following in his footsteps."

Jim O'Brien

McKeesport's Mike Logan follows in his grandfather's footsteps on South Side fields.

Sports Odyssey
Going back to Green Bay and Appleton

*"People are always asking
us about Rocky Bleier."*
— Donna, Barmaid in Appleton, Wisconsin

A woman was offering a eulogy to her friend at a funeral service at Westminster Presbyterian Church in Upper St. Clair. She was sharing stories about their experiences together, and most of the stories centered on shopping trips they had made to New York and other cities.

My wife Kathie was at work that day, back in 1999, so I went to the memorial service alone. I remember thinking that Kathie never did anything like that, going with her girl friends to faraway places without me. I think I said a prayer thanking God that she didn't. As I have gotten older, I have become a shameless co-dependent. I didn't want to be home alone.

About three weeks later, Kathie asked me a question. "What would you think," she began, somewhat slowly, "if Sharon and I went on a vacation with some other girls? Just the girls . . . on a getaway vacation."

What could I say? Of course, I replied, "I think that would be OK."

She and Sharon Pociask were the best of friends, and so were Sharon's husband, Alex, and I. About a few weeks before the girls were to depart for Scottsdale, Arizona, Alex Pociask and I panicked simultaneously and we decided we didn't want to stay home alone, so we planned a trip to Virginia, North Carolina and South Carolina. We had a great time and we learned that we traveled well together.

He wanted to see some retirement and golf communities and I stopped to see some retired football coaches and baseball players I wanted to interview for my books. Our plans meshed nicely. I had a chance to visit with Dave Hart, a former Pitt football coach and later a big success in college sports administration at Missouri, Louisville and with the Southern Conference. He was living in Asheville, North Carolina, a beautiful community near the western mountains. We visited the famed Biltmore Mansion in Asheville.

We stumbled upon Bristol, Virginia, and I had Alex get off the main road so we could visit a minor league baseball park there. It was in Bristol that Ron Neccai of Monongahela had struck out 27 batters in a Class D ballgame while a member of the Pirates' organization. It was the only time anyone ever did that in pro baseball history. We stopped in Greensboro, North Carolina to see Mace Brown, in his 80s, who had pitched for the Pirates, and had been a witness as a rookie in the summer of 1935 to Babe Ruth's three-home run effort in his finale at Forbes Field. Ruth was playing for the Boston Braves and would retire from baseball a week later. It was a great trip.

I gave Brown a hug before I left his home. It had been my third visit. Brown died while I was working on this book. Alex and I talked about Mace Brown while we were on this summer's getaway vacation.

I encourage everyone to consider taking a trip like this. It's like playing hooky from school.

This time, in late June of 2002, our wives went on their third "girls only" vacation and Alex and I went on our second such trip. We weren't able to do it the previous year because Alex had just taken a new job with USFilter. "You have no idea how good these vacations are," Kathie told me. "For us, it's great not to have to look after you guys for a full week."

Well, Alex and I are fast learners. We now think the "girls only" vacations are a great idea. Now we get to go places and do things that wouldn't particularly appeal to our wives, or their friends.

This year Sharon invited one of her neighbors and friends to tag along, so Karen Saracco went with them to Williamsburg, Virginia. Kathie and Sharon had gone to Palm Springs, California the previous year last year. Sharon's sister, Karen Poppe of Milwaukee, and a friend, Deb Larson of Minneapolis, accompanied them.

Alex planned our trip this time, and I added to it as we went along. He was taking me back to his boyhood farm in Wausaukee, Wisconsin, and his alma mater, Michigan Tech on Michigan's Upper Peninsula. We were going by way of Chicago, where we visited his daughter, Dr. Kara Nance, and her husband Colin, and their two-year-old daughter Karina. Then we went to Milwaukee and visited his in-laws, Jacob and Lori Stearle. They know Milwaukee well and wanted to show it to visitors.

"Pittsburgh is well represented here."
— Bernie Kish

Here are some of the things we did, and you'll see what sports enthusiasts left to their own schedule might do on an eight-day trip while traveling 2,131 miles. For starters, we stopped in South Bend, Indiana, and visited the College Football Hall of Fame.

We received a personal tour of the building. Bernie Kish, the executive director of the College Football Hall of Fame, invited us into his office. Kish, a retired military officer who'd gone to school at Indiana University of Pennsylvania, proudly displayed pictures of Bill Mazeroski and Roberto Clemente on the walls of his office, along with much material from Notre Dame University. He showed me scrap-books that had just been recently been presented to the Hall of Fame by Marshall Goldberg, a member of Pitt's "Dream Backfield" in the late 1930s.

Bernie Kish,
Director of College
Football Hall of Fame
in South Bend, Ind.,
shows off Roberto Clemente
print in his private office.

Photos by Jim O'Brien

There was a "Hog" Rally in South Bend, of all places, and Harley-Davidson riders were everywhere. Some even toured the Notre Dame campus. The new "Four Horsemen of Notre Dame" brought their gals along for the ride during Stadium visit.

"Pittsburgh is well represented here," said Kish. "We want to honor some of the stars of the Pitt-Notre Dame rivalry when Pitt plays here this coming season. We've talked to Ditka and Dorsett about coming in for a special event."

Dorsett, by the way, is the player pictured at the front of the College Football Hall of Fame.

There were plaques of former All-Americans who have been inducted into the College Football Hall of Fame such as Goldberg, Ditka, Joe Schmidt and Lynn Swann.

We checked out the campus at Notre Dame University. We got an up-close look at the refurbished football stadium, Touchdown Jesus and the Golden Dome. We saw statues of Frank Leahy, a former coach, and Moose Krause, a former athlete and athletic director at Notre Dame.

We also saw a lot of bikers as there was a HOG rally going on in South Bend, with the owners and riders of Harley-Davidson motorcycles filling the downtown streets, and even the campus of Notre Dame.

In Chicago, we had dinner on Saturday night at Mike Ditka's Restaurant and Mike stopped by our table and talked to us for awhile. He is so big in Chicago. He sang "Take Me Out to the Ballgame" during the seventh inning stretch two days later at Wrigley Field. Ditka has done that before, but his voice has not improved with practice.

His restaurant is now managed by Pat McDonnell, who grew up in Lincoln Place and now lives in Upper St. Clair. McDonnell owns and operates three Atria's Restaurant and Tavern outlets around Pittsburgh. Two of our daughters' friends from Upper St. Clair, Dr. Jenny Jackson and Kara Spak, joined us for dinner. They are working in Chicago. Mike Ditka's Restaurant is a classy joint. It's two floors with tastefully framed photographs of some of the Bears' greatest sports performers, such as Red Grange and George Halas. Ditka's photos and paintings are displayed everywhere, of course. His No. 89 Pitt football jersey is framed under glass in a hallway on the second floor. Some of his favorites from back home in Western Pennsylvania are everywhere, like his boyhood hero Stan Musial, and Arnold Palmer, Bill Mazeroski and Johnny Unitas. We went back the next day, when there were few customers there on Sunday morning, and took another tour to see the photos better. They had an Iron City beer special for Father's Day.

On Sunday afternoon, we went to the sold-out Cubs-White Sox baseball game at Wrigley Field. Alex was able to get us seats seven rows directly behind home plate. It was like being in the batter's box. It was a 3-D blast. We would duck whenever Cubs' fireballer Kerry Woods would unleash a wild pitch and hit the screen between us. Alex even managed to get us a parking pass right at the main gate of Wrigley Field. We checked out Soldiers Field, where the Bears play, and it was being refurbished. That's another unique venue that needed to be improved and preserved.

We toured Milwaukee and had lunch at Miller Park, which would be the site of the 2002 Baseball All-Star Game. We saw the statue of Henry Aaron and his No. 44 uniform at Miller Park. It's an impressive place.

Later that same day, we visited the bar and restaurant once owned by Rocky Bleier's parents in Appleton, Wisconsin. There are still pictures on the walls of Rocky from his days at Notre Dame and with the Steelers. Bleier now lives in Mt. Lebanon. We visited a memorial park for George Gipp, Notre Dame's first All-American, in Laurium, Michigan.

When I saw Green Bay and Appleton on the map during our travels, I told Alex we had to visit both places.

I took along a copy of a wonderful book I had been reading while I was writing this book. It's called *"When Pride Still Mattered — A Life of Vince Lombardi."* It was written by David Maraniss, a Pulitzer Prize winning writer for *The Washington Post*. The Packers were the pro football team of the 1960s and the Steelers succeeded them as the pro football team of the 1970s. It was interesting for me to compare and contrast the two situations.

I finished reading the book while I was in Wisconsin, which I thought was fitting. It brought the stories to life to see all the places that were mentioned in the book.

Bob Bleier died some time ago, and his wife Eleanor now lives with her daughter near San Francisco. The old Bleier bar-restaurant is now called TrimB's Restaurant & Pub, and is owned by Bob and Tina Packwood. The Bleiers haven't owned the place for nearly 20 years. It's located at the corner of Lawrence & Walnut. A gracious woman who was tending bar identified herself as Donna. In answer to a question, she said, "Lots of people stop by and ask if this was Rocky Bleier's place. His family lived over the bar. Every other day, somebody asks about him."

From where I was standing, I could see through a window and view St. Joseph's Catholic Church on the other corner of the street. That was the church Rocky's family attended. It was a view Rocky Bleier had told me about in our interview. That's what he could see from his bedroom window. It made his story-telling that much more vivid. There was a police station directly across the street from the front door of TrimB's. I felt funny knowing I was standing where Rocky used to hang out, helping his parents take care of the patrons.

Donna directed us to another restaurant in Appleton, Lombardi's, and that was a real treat. It's a large, upscale restaurant and there must be 250 or more photographs, many of them poster-size, of Vince Lombardi and his Green Bay Packers. There was a sports bar next door, and it contained more photos of the Packers, as well as the Milwaukee Bucks, Milwaukee Brewers and Milwaukee Braves.

We stopped in Green Bay and visited Lambeau Field and the Packers Hall of Fame, and restaurants that are shrines to Packers' coach Vince Lombardi. There is a Lombardi Avenue, a Mike Holmgren Way, a Bret Favre Pass, a bridge named after Ray Nitschke that crosses the Fox River, an indoor training facility named after Don Hutson, and a practice field named after Clarke Hinkle. There are bleachers on the sidewalks alongside Hinkle Field where fans can sit and watch the Packers at practice at certain times of the year. The Packers Hall of Fame is nearby. They were building a new indoor facility for concerts and basketball in the same block.

Alex's sister, Mary Alice, and her husband, Gerry Rowley, live on the family's farm in the wilds of Wausaukee. Gerry was kind enough to drive me the hour or so it takes to get to Green Bay, so I could spend a second visit viewing all the Packers' places.

Lombardi and his Packers are honored a great deal more in Green Bay and surrounding communities than Chuck Noll and his Steelers in Pittsburgh and Western Pennsylvania. There is no street in Pittsburgh named after Noll and you would be hard-pressed to find many photos of him on display in Pittsburgh area restaurants. Pro football is the only real game in town in Green Bay, of course, and it's a smaller, even more parochial place — if that's possible — than Pittsburgh. Even so, it seems we have short-changed Noll in Pittsburgh. Lombardi coached in Green Bay for nine seasons and stayed one more as a front-office administrator before going to Washington for one more season as coach of the Redskins. He won five NFL titles during his nine years in Green Bay.

But he became a national sports figure, much more so than Noll. He spoke at important banquets throughout the country, whereas Noll chose not to do that. Lombardi was from Brooklyn, and had coached with the Giants, and had the backing of the powerful New York press behind him. For whatever reasons, Lombardi was lionized more than Noll. Then, too, Lombardi sought the spotlight, and Noll wanted none of that stuff. He avoided attention, preferring his players bask in the spotlight.

After reading the book about Lombardi, though, I am convinced that Chuck Noll is a much better all-around individual, more attentive to his wife and family, and one who has gained the respect of his players even more so today than when the Steelers were winning four Super Bowls. Noll, like fine wine, requires aging to be truly appreciated.

There are streets named after Art Rooney and Bill Mazeroski and — for some strange reason — Tony Dorsett on Pittsburgh's North Side. There should be a street in Oakland named after Dorsett, but not on the North Side. Noll deserves that honor. He's the one who is most responsible for turning the Steelers' fortunes around, and making the franchise what it is today. Dorsett, deservedly, has a stadium named after him in his hometown of Hopewell. Noll deserves some kind of similar honor where he used to do his thing. The Steelers should name their practice fields after him.

There are many signs in Green Bay and Appleton about love for Vince Lombardi and his championship Packers teams. Author Jim O'Brien enjoyed visit to Rocky Bleier's boyhood home, above a bar-restaurant in Appleton. Rocky's remembered with his own Wall of Fame in TrimB's Restaurant.

We toured Alex's alma mater of Michigan Tech in the riverside community of Houghton with three football coaches of the Huskies, including current head coach Bernie Anderson. Two men who preceded him as the head coach, and had worked with Alex, spent time with us as well. They were Bill Lucier and Ted Kearley. We had breakfast with Lucier at the Kaleva Café, famous for its pasties, some concoction of ground meat and potatoes. The place looked like a scene from "Northern Exposure." The natives all sound like Canadians. Kearley took us for a ride on his boat near Lake Superior. We had dinner at the Dreamland Hotel. We stopped to see some of Alex's former teammates. He had been the conference MVP while playing center, quite a feat, and his coaches and teammates all paid tribute to his scholarship, outstanding leadership abilities and work ethic.

Lucier and Kearley recalled how his mother, when they were recruiting him, made them promise that he would some day play for the Green Bay Packers. They must have told her they would do their best. We took four boat rides, one on a canal off Lake Superior and one on Lake St. Clair, up there in size among inland lakes to Lake Champlain. The other two boat trips, on a ferry, took us to and from Mackinac Island, a real tourist treat. We took tours on Mackinac Island on horse-drawn carriages. On the way home, we stopped at Comerica Park and the abandoned Tiger Stadium in Detroit, and saw the stadium the Ford family is building for the Lions. We did that and so much more. We can't wait for the girls-only next vacation trip.

We had stayed with Alex's classmate and teammate at Michigan Tech, Jim Grimes and his wife, Mary Ann. They took us on a ride on their boat and they took us the following morning on a tour of downtown Detroit. We had lunch at Hockey Town, a restaurant just across the street from Comerica Park. There are photos on the walls of the restaurant of all the greats of the Red Wings, like Gordie Howe, Ted Lindsay, Alex DelVecchio and Terry Sawchuck, and the Red Wings' coach Scotty Bowman. There were other familiar faces, like Roger Crozier and Sid Abel, because the Pittsburgh Hornets were a farm team of the Red Wings before the city claimed an NHL franchise and the Penguins came into being in 1967. I received a phone call a week after returning from this trip, from former Pennsylvania Senator Jack McGregor, telling me that Steelers' owner Art Rooney, used his influence to get NHL owners to pick Pittsburgh over Buffalo for an expansion team. I never knew that.

Some of the landscape was familiar to me as well. I had covered baseball, basketball and hockey games in Detroit, and a heavyweight championship fight in which Joe Frazier floored Bob Foster. I had gone there early in 1970 with my wife Kathie and stayed at the old Pontiac Hotel when I was hired to be a sportswriter at *The Detroit News*. I never reported for that job, as I changed my mind and accepted an offer instead at *The New York Post*.

I remembered standing on a street corner in Detroit one night with the legendary Jimmy Cannon and Roy McHugh, two of the nation's finest sportswriters, and commenting on the empty streets.

484

"This town makes Pittsburgh look alive at night," I said. To which, Cannon came back with a roar, "Pittsburgh . . . this town makes Pompeii look alive at night!"

I asked Grimes where the Lindell A.C. was located and he told me, to my surprise and delight, that it was still there, just two blocks down Michigan Avenue from Tiger Stadium. The Lindell A.C. was a legendary bar-restaurant where Bobby Layne used to hold court when he was leading the Lions to championships in the National Football League, prior to his coming to Pittsburgh with Buddy Parker.

There were pictures of Layne and the Lions of his day, and Detroit greats like Joe Louis and Hank Greenberg pictured on the walls of what is now a dingy, dimly-lit bar-restaurant. It was like taking a step back in time to another era.

A few days after returning to Pittsburgh, I attended the Pirates-Expos game at PNC Park. After our road trip, I was more convinced that it might really be the best of the new baseball parks in America. It's not the biggest or the most expensive, and it lacks the legends of Wrigley Field, Fenway Park and Yankee Stadium, but it's the right size and it looks like a baseball park and it shows off the city skyline so well.

I liked Comerica Park in Detroit, and thought Miller Park in Milwaukee was an engineering marvel and prettier on the outside than PNC Park, but not as good a setting when you are in your seats. Wrigley Field still holds its own with any baseball park in America.

Seeing how they have refurbished Notre Dame Stadium, Soldiers Field and Lambeau Field only reinforces my feelings that they should have done the same with Pitt Stadium and Three Rivers Stadium for the Steelers. I think the fans would have been happier. But it's too late now.

Jim O'Brien

Signs of the times point up Packers' pride around Lambeau Stadium in heart of Green Bay, Wisconsin.

A family affair
Reunion of Steelers Hall of Famers

"This was the greatest football team
that was ever put together."
— Dan Rooney

In a perfect world, all the Steelers who are members of the Pro Football Hall of Fame would have been there. The event was billed as SuperCelebration — Hall of Fame Day. It was held at Heinz Field on a sultry Saturday afternoon, July 6.

This was not an official Steelers' promotion, however, nor did the Hall of Fame have anything to do with it. Lynn Swann had summoned the former Steelers in order to film a TV special about the glory days of the Steelers. He teamed up with KDKA's Bob Pompeani to interview some of the Steelers' all-time greatest players for a show scheduled for airing in August. It was Swann's song.

Terry Bradshaw did not come. He has problems about Pittsburgh, Steelers' fans, Chuck Noll, being unappreciated and unloved, which he has detailed in several books. Then, too, Lynn Swann had snubbed him the year before when Swann was inducted into the Pro Football Hall of Fame. When Swann thanked all the people who helped get him to the Hall of Fame, he purposely omitted Bradshaw. In an interview weeks before the induction, Swann took some shots at Bradshaw. Swann had always had great timing, but not this time. Bradshaw was labeled a dumb quarterback during his playing days, before he directed the Steelers to four Super Bowl titles in six seasons, but he is not that dumb. He declined the invitation.

Jack Lambert didn't come, either. Lambert never liked Lynn Swann. They had different agendas, that's all. Swann was never Lambert's kind of guy. His absence had nothing to do with family commitments, the excuse Swann offered.

The Steelers pride themselves on being a family, and that's exactly what they are. Few families are perfect. My wife's family has reunions. Mine doesn't. Everyone doesn't show up for these reunions. Every family has its own feuds, misfits, miscommunications, missing members. Some one said something at a funeral that someone will never forget, stuff like that.

It's no different with the Steelers. Mike Webster, who has suffered through a series of personal problems since his playing days, came to Heinz Field, but he did not appear in the Great Hall with the others for the taping. He stayed behind in a suite somewhere. He did the same thing when all the living members of the Pro Football Hall of Fame were gathered in Canton in the summer of 2000. Webster came, but he stayed inside the building when over 110 others appeared at the induction ceremonies. It's a shame. There wasn't a more well-grounded, more genuine member of the Steelers than Webster during his playing days.

John Henry Johnson, who did appear in Canton in recent years, couldn't come to Swann's party in Pittsburgh. It was reported that he was in a nursing home in California. Johnson just got old, that's all, and he had been suffering from dementia. Ernie Stautner was having memory problems as well, but he was there. Nothing could ever keep Stautner out of the lineup. Stautner was still as tough as they come.

Art Rooney was there, too, in spirit. Rooney would have relished such a gathering. If he had been there, if he had made the call, surely all the Steelers would have shown up. Art Rooney died on August 25, 1988, however, and the Steelers are not the same without him. Bert Bell, Johnny "Blood" McNally, Walt Kiesling and Bobby Layne were there, too. They have died, but they are not forgotten. Fran Rogel wasn't in the Hall of Fame, but he is for those who cared about the Steelers in the '50s. Byron "Whizzer" White, Sam Francis, Joe Geri, Ray Kemp, Tyrone McGriff and Willie McClung had died the previous year. They were there, too. They are Steelers forever.

As for the no-shows, Swann should not take it personally. After all, he picks and chooses what he is willing to do in this respect. He charges big money to make appearances and, even though he is a member of the media, he is not always that cooperative with the media. If they ever name a street after Swann it will be a one-way street. He was a great player, though, and deserving of Hall of Fame status. And he has served Pittsburgh and the community well, on his own terms. We're lucky to have him.

He succeeded in landing most of the big ones. Hall of Fame Day featured Mel Blount, Dan Rooney, Joe Greene, Franco Harris, John Stallworth, Ernie Stautner, Bill Dudley, Jack Ham, Chuck Noll, Dan Rooney and Swann. An estimated 3,500 fans showed up to share in the festivities, and they offered some familiar chants, transforming Heinz Field into Three Rivers Stadium for one Saturday afternoon. It would have drawn a bigger crowd if it had been properly promoted. The sponsors were short-changed.

Most of the attention was centered on the Steelers of the '70s. "This was the greatest football team that was ever put together," related Rooney, the Steelers' owner and president. "There's no other group, no other coach that went to four Super Bowls together and won them all. This is the only group to do that."

Chuck Noll was smiling throughout the day. "When people say it seems like it happened yesterday, I can understand it because it seems that way to me," said Noll. "That was a special time for all of us. It was a special time, and there was a special bond between the fans and the team. I get excited every time I get together with these guys because it brings back so many memories."

Stallworth was a month away from his official induction into the Pro Football Hall of Fame, but he was getting some sense of the specialness of the group he was joining in the pantheon of pro football.

"It really felt good to be a part of this group of Hall of Famers and know that I am now one of them," said Stallworth, a very sweet and very smart man. "To be elected was an affirmation of everything I tried to accomplish during my career. This tells me that the way I went about it was the right way."

Swann pushed for Stallworth's election to the Hall of Fame. He had Stallworth introduce him at ceremonies in Canton in the summer of 2001. "I told him it is a ceremony much like your wedding day," said Swann. "You work so hard and prepare so much for that day. Yet, when it comes, it is over so quickly and you are so mesmerized by it you barely remember most of it. I just told him to make sure he takes it all in and enjoys it."

The same advice can be passed along to fans of the Pittsburgh Steelers. Those of us who grew up loving the Steelers before they won all those Super Bowls can appreciate their achievements even more. We loved the Steelers before they were so super.

It's unlikely we'll ever experience a run like the Steelers had in the '70s, but the memories, as Noll told us, still linger. Hopefully, books like this one help preserve the memories.

Pittsburgh Steelers

Steelers' owner Art Rooney was so proud of Pittsburgh claiming four Lombardi Trophy awards as Super Bowl champions. The late founder of the franchise has been honored as a member of the Pro Football Hall of Fame.

Author's Page

Jim O'Brien was named in January, 2002 to an advisory board at the Heinz History Center to create a sports exhibition paying tribute to the area's greatest athletic figures. He joined a panel that includes the likes of Stan Musial, Arnold Palmer and Franco Harris, an honor in itself.

O'Brien, who turned 60 on August 20, 2002 has been a professional sportswriter since he was 14 years old, and served as the sports editor of his hometown *Hazelwood Envoy*. He has written 17 books, 14 of them in his "Pittsburgh Proud" sports series. He writes a weekly column for *The Almanac* in the South Hills and *The Valley Mirror* in the Homestead-Munhall area.

He has written for the *Philadelphia Evening Bulletin, The Miami News, The New York Post* and *The Pittsburgh Press*. He was the founding editor of *Pittsburgh Weekly Sports* and *Street & Smith's Basketball Yearbook*. He was the editor of *Street & Smith's Basketball Yearbook* for 23 years, and he has been associated as a contributing editor for an additional nine years. He has been associated with Conde Nast Publications in New York the past 32 years. He wrote a column on pro basketball for nine years for *The Sporting News*, and was a contributing writer for *Sport, Newsweek, The Basketball News, The Football News, Basketball Digest, Football Digest, National Football League Properties, The Washington Post* and *The Dallas Morning News*.

He covered the Steelers for four years for *The Pittsburgh Press* from 1979 to 1982. He served as assistant athletic director for sports information at the University of Pittsburgh from 1982 to 1986. He is a graduate of Pitt with a bachelor's degree in English (Writing) and did graduate work there in English Literature. He has taught at Point Park College, Robert Morris and conducted an intern mentoring program at the University of Pittsburgh.

His greatest sports thrills were covering the Ali-Frazier fight billed as "The Fight of the Century" on January 28, 1974, covering the Knicks when they won their first NBA title and the Nets when they won their first ABA title and the Steelers when they won their fourth Super Bowl in 1980.

O'Brien was inducted into the Western Pennsylvania Chapter of the Pennsylvania Sports Hall of Fame. He was presented the Bob Prince Award for his journalistic achievements, the David L. Lawrence Award by the Vectors for promoting Pittsburgh and calling positive attention to the city on a national basis. He was been given special awards by Champions, Inc. and the Pittsburgh chapter of the Italian-American Sports Hall of Fame.

He has been married for 35 years to Kathleen Churchman of White Oak. They have two daughters, Dr. Sarah O'Brien-Zirwas, a pediatrician at Children's Hospital in Pittsburgh, and Rebecca O'Brien, a manager at California Pizza Kitchen in Columbus, Ohio.